A FAREWELL TO WARS

Since World War II, there has been a trend toward fewer wars, the Russian invasion of the Ukraine standing as a major 'aberration'. With decades of experience as an international lawyer, diplomat and head of UN Iraq inspections, Hans Blix examines conflicts and other developments after World War II. He finds that new restraints on uses of force have emerged from fears about nuclear war, economic interdependence and UN Charter rules. With less interest in the conquest of land, states increasingly use economic or cyber means to battle their adversaries. Such a turn is not free from perils but should perhaps be welcomed as an alternative to previous methods of war. By analysing these new restraints, Blix rejects the fatalistic assumption that there will always be war. He submits that today leading powers are saying farewell to previous patterns of war, instead choosing to continue their competition for power and influence on the battlefields of economy and information.

Hans Blix is a Swedish diplomat who has previously served as Foreign Minister of Sweden (1978–1979), Director-General of the International Atomic Energy Agency (1981–1995) and Chairman of the UN Monitoring, Verification and Inspection Commission for Iraq (2000–2003). He has previously published *Disarming Iraq* (2004) and *Why Nuclear Disarmament Matters* (2008).

A Farewell to Wars

THE GROWING RESTRAINTS ON THE INTERSTATE USE OF FORCE

HANS BLIX
Director-General Emeritus, International Atomic Energy Agency

Shaftesbury Road, Cambridge CB2 8EA, United Kingdom

One Liberty Plaza, 20th Floor, New York, NY 10006, USA

477 Williamstown Road, Port Melbourne, VIC 3207, Australia

314–321, 3rd Floor, Plot 3, Splendor Forum, Jasola District Centre, New Delhi – 110025, India

103 Penang Road, #05–06/07, Visioncrest Commercial, Singapore 238467

Cambridge University Press is part of Cambridge University Press & Assessment, a department of the University of Cambridge.

We share the University's mission to contribute to society through the pursuit of education, learning and research at the highest international levels of excellence.

www.cambridge.org
Information on this title: www.cambridge.org/9781009392556

DOI: 10.1017/9781009392532

First published 2023

A catalogue record for this publication is available from the British Library

Library of Congress Cataloging-in-Publication Data
NAMES: Blix, Hans, author.
TITLE: A farewell to wars : the growing restraints on the interstate use of force / Hans Blix, Director-General Emeritus, International Atomic Energy Agency.
DESCRIPTION: Cambridge, United Kingdom ; New York, NY : Cambridge University Press, 2023. | Includes bibliographical references and index.
IDENTIFIERS: LCCN 2023017030 | ISBN 9781009392556 (hardback) | ISBN 9781009392501 (paperback) | ISBN 9781009392532 (ebook)
SUBJECTS: LCSH: Aggression (International law) | War (International law) | Intervention (International law)
CLASSIFICATION: LCC KZ6374 .B55 2023 | DDC 341.5/8–dc23/eng/20230802
LC record available at https://lccn.loc.gov/2023017030

ISBN 978-1-009-39255-6 Hardback
ISBN 978-1-009-39250-1 Paperback

Contents

Foreword

At the end of the World War II, I was a student at the Law Faculty of Uppsala University. Like others, I wondered how the horrors of wars can be avoided in the future. I began to take a special interest in international law and in the ongoing establishment of the United Nations (UN). I felt that an expansion of international law and world organization would be one necessity among many.

Luck had it that in 1950 I won a prize in an essay contest organized by the UN. Writing on the subject of the security system and the Security Council, I had suggested that the veto was in effect a procedural tripwire created in recognition of the great power resistance that could come if the Council should attempt major (i.e., non-procedural) actions without the consent of its five permanent members. Removing the tripwire would not remove possible resistance.

The prize given to me and a dozen others was a journey to New York and a month of study at the UN headquarters and General Assembly. This was during the 1950 session, when the UN armed action countering North Korea's attack on South Korea was still ongoing. The so-called Acheson plan was adopted that traced a way for the Assembly to recommend action in cases where the Security Council had been blocked from decision by a veto. It was an exciting time to be at the UN and I decided to continue with studies in international law.

I was privileged to study under two wonderful professors. Sir Hersch Lauterpacht was one of the world's leading authorities in international law and later Judge of the International Court of Justice. He was an erudite fatherly guide to his students and his encouragement and help during my years at Cambridge led me to my PhD and professional path. At Columbia University in New York, I was privileged to study and work under Philip Jessup, an engaging legal thinker and teacher, later – like Sir Hersch – Judge of the

International Court of Justice. I stand in gratitude to these two inspiring professors and to my professor and friend at Stockholm University, Hilding Eek.

After my studies in the United Kingdom and the United States and a short period of teaching at Stockholm University, I moved from academia and embarked on a life of practical international work. For nearly twenty years, I was active in Sweden's Ministry for Foreign Affairs as advisor on international law, state secretary and minister. I watched the Cold War around us and the risks of it erupting into armed conflicts – notably during the Cuban nuclear missile crisis 1962.

I came also to better understand how the ever-growing fabric of legal commitments by states is fundamental for the operation of the modern world. I felt then and still feel that participating in the creation of conventions and regulations was one of the best ways in which a young lawyer could contribute practically to the development and strengthening of the international society.

I took part in the drafting and adoption of the convention codifying the law of treaties – the law of contract of the world community. Later, as Director-General of the International Atomic Energy Agency (IAEA), I experienced the working out of treaties like the convention on the safe disposal of radioactive waste and the protocol on more effective safeguards inspections of nuclear installations and material. Even international declarations that prepare the ground for or explain existing binding international rules are of importance for the gradual consolidation and evolution of the international community.

I was glad to be an active part in working out the so-called Friendly Relations Declaration that was unanimously adopted in the UN General Assembly in 1970. In that work, I took part in a thorough international examination and useful amplification of the central rules of the Charter prohibiting the threat and use of force and intervention. And at the UN's First Conference on the Human Environment in Stockholm 1972, I played the leading role in the drafting of the Declaration.

The negotiations in the Eighteen Nation Disarmament Committee in Geneva were more frustrating. As legal adviser to Ambassador Alva Myrdal, who headed the Swedish delegation to the Eighteen Nation Disarmament Committee, and later as leader of the Swedish team at the conference updating the laws of war, I often experienced categorical resistance to proposals that would have meant some limitations on military actions.

Even more dismaying has been to witness how generally accepted rules relating to the use of force have been violated. While the grabbing of territory has almost ceased since World War II, Iraq under Saddam Hussein waged a long war against Iran and attacked and occupied Kuwait in 1990. Russia has violated the central UN Charter norms through armed interventions and war in Georgia and Ukraine and through the annexation of territory.

To the shock of much of the world in 2003, the United States and the United Kingdom and some other states that used to champion a rule-based international order occupied Iraq, although they had no support for the action from a majority of the Security Council. The invasion was all the more dismaying in that they ignored the reports of the international inspections (United Nations Monitoring, Verification and Inspection Commission) for which I was responsible; the invading states alleged a continued Iraqi possession of prohibited weapons. Rather than relying on UN observations and reports that they had themselves requested through the Council, they chose to rely on their own erroneous information and ignored the UN machinery. Where did this leave the authority of the Security Council?

On retirement, after seeing our UN inspectors replaced by US troops, I have had time to ponder more generally the different kinds of restraints – legal, military, economic, diplomatic and other – that exist to the interstate use of force. An invitation to give the 2004 Lauterpacht lectures at Cambridge gave me an early opportunity to present thoughts on the subject. Chairing an International Commission on Weapons of Mass Destruction in 2004–06 and participating in the worldwide non-governmental discussion gave further insights and ideas. This book on current restraints to the interstate use of force has slowly emerged.

I am aware that to be treated properly the subject would require a team of specialists in history, philosophy, warfare, nuclear weapons, missiles, cyber techniques, diplomacy, economy, law and psychology. The book I have written does not pretend to be a comprehensive scholarly examination of the subject of restraints to the interstate use of force and intervention. Rather, it presents thoughts and observations based on my studies and work and participation in the worldwide debate. It reflects my active engagement in the work of the General Assembly and under the authority of the Security Council and many years of administration of the IAEA. The text is entirely my own and reflects what I have learnt and experienced and it shows the limitations in that learning and experience.

I must acknowledge three specific limitations. First, my discussion takes into account only events up to mid-December 2022, when the manuscript was submitted. Second, it is centred on Western experience. I apologize for not covering doctrines and practices outside this sphere. Third, I do not deal with civil wars and strife – in which no force is injected from the outside. As a large part of the force used in the world today is in civil wars and in failed or failing states, this is a significant limitation.

My friend Randy Rydell, retired senior officer of the UN Secretariat's Office for Disarmament Affairs with vast knowledge and long experience of international and UN affairs, assisted me in finalizing the whole book manuscript. I stand in greatest gratitude for his extensive and spirited help. I stand in similar debt to The Stockholm International Peace Research Institute for allowing Jakob Faller to assist me. With exceptional skill, he has found and researched relevant material and helped to spot contradictions and overlaps in my texts.

Many other colleagues and friends have read parts of the manuscript and offered helpful advice and suggestions. I thank them all but will only name my lifelong friend Stephen M. Schwebel, former president of the International Court of Justice. He has generously read the whole manuscript and made comments that I have taken to heart.

During my years of writing on this book, my wife and our two sons, Mårten and Göran, have constantly encouraged me and urged me on. Especially after I was hit by tick-borne encephalitis in 2021, Mårten, who lives in Stockholm, has cheered me on and up and given me great and invaluable help and advice. My wife, Eva Kettis, has had the patience to read innumerable drafts of chapters over the years and offered her sound judgement.

The tone and style in this book is – at least is meant to be – dispassionate. I seek to pursue inquiries and provide accounts that are not coloured by emotion. This should not be interpreted as an indifference on my part in regard to different types of governance or government actions. I have been lucky to be born in and grow up in a liberal, tolerant country in which all major groups of opinion are represented in parliament through fair and general elections and where respect for law is high and corruption is rare. This is a kind of governance that I think all would enjoy.

However, political, economic and social history varies greatly between states. While in a super-connected world the winds of thoughts and philosophies reach and influence everywhere, they cannot be imposed by force. States must and will themselves stake out their own future. I take hope in the continued development and influence of what I call the 'public mind'. Over time, laws and the conduct of states and individuals are influenced by the opinions of the public. These may be contradictory within states as between states, but they may also be converging – as they were on the abolition of slavery and now on the need to counter the threat of global warming and loss of biodiversity.

The public mind has also developed and converged – even internationally – on restraints on the use of force and violence. The Islamic State of Iraq and Syria (ISIS) stood for a shocking regional relapse to a mentality of barbarism. I believe the expanding elimination of and resistance to the death penalty is the true reflection of today's public mind. We can also see that while wars of conquest or colonization or interventions by force were often cheered by the public in the past, today's public mind is averse to this use of force. It has been manifested most recently in the worldwide reactions to Russia's armed invasion of Ukraine.

Abbreviations

ABM	Anti-Ballistic Missile
ASEAN	Association of Southeast Asian Nations
AU	African Union
AUKUS	Trilateral Security Agreement between Australia/United Kingdom/United States (2021)
BC	Biological, Chemical (weapons)
BRICS	Brazil, Russia, India, China and South Africa
BW	Biological weapons
CFE	Conventional Armed Forces in Europe (treaty)
DOD	United States Department of Defense
DPRK	Democratic People's Republic of Korea
DR CONGO	Democratic Republic of the Congo
ECOWAS	Economic Community of West African States
ENDC	Eighteen Nation Disarmament Committee
EU	European Union
G7	Group of Seven
G20	Group of Twenty
G77	Group of 77
IAEA	International Atomic Energy Agency
ICC	International Criminal Court
ICJ	International Court of Justice
ICRC	International Committee of the Red Cross
INF	Intermediate Nuclear Forces agreement of 1987
INFCIRC	Information Circular (IAEA)
ISIS	The Islamic State of Iraq and Syria
JCPOA	Joint Comprehensive Plan of Action
LAFTA	The Latin American Free Trade Association
LAWS	Lethal Autonomous Weapons Systems

MAD	Mutual Assured Destruction
MED	Mutual Economic Dependence
NATO	North Atlantic Treaty Organization
NNWS	Non-nuclear-Weapon State(s)
NPT	Treaty on the Non-Proliferation of Nuclear Weapons
NWS	Nuclear-Weapon State(s)
OAS	Organization of American States
OAU	Organization of African Unity
OPCW	Organisation for the Prohibition of Chemical Weapons
OSCE	Organization for Security and Cooperation in Europe
P5	Five Permanent members of UN Security Council
PLA	People's Liberation Army
PLO	Palestine Liberation Organization
QUAD	Quadrilateral Security Dialogue between Australia/India/Japan/United States (since 2007)
R2P	Responsibility to Protect
ROK	Republic of Korea
SALT	Strategic Arms Limitation Talks
SCO	Shanghai Cooperation Organization
SS	Schutzstaffel
START	Strategic Arms Reductions Talks
TPNW	Treaty on the Prohibition of Nuclear Weapons
UN	United Nations
UNCLOS	United Nations Convention on the Law of the Sea
UNMOVIC	United Nations Monitoring, Verification and Inspection Commission
UNSCOM	United Nations Special Commission (Iraq)
WTO	World Trade Organization
WWII	World War II

1

Introduction

WHAT THIS BOOK IS ABOUT

Russia's attack on Ukraine in February 2022 may well prove to be the last-ever war for territorial gain. This book discusses uses of force between states since the end of World War II and suggests – and the title of the book asserts – that 'wars' in the traditional sense comprising the seizing of land and the changing of borders by force are on the way out. It further argues that there is a trend to shroud, downplay or eliminate the element of physical force in interventions that are still undertaken. Hard-ball competition between states is increasingly played through economic and financial pressures rather than through kinetic force.

How can these significant developments be asserted when there are the painful experience of Russian-fomented rebellion in and secession of large areas adjacent to Russia, full-scale armed Russian invasion of Ukraine, and Russian occupation and purported annexation of large parts of Ukraine's territory?

Some, claiming to be realists, may tell us that the Russian actions in Ukraine are world business as usual. Yet there are features in this catastrophe and the reactions to it that set it apart and suggest that it should be seen as breaches of the world order rather than harbingers of a collapse of that order. Russia, the aggressor, has shown awareness of breaching the existing order by claiming to pursue a 'special military operation' – not war. Indeed, it has even forbidden anyone in Russia to use the terms 'war' and 'invasion'. Denial of its instigation of rebellion and secession in Ukraine shows a similar Russian awareness of violating the current order.

Even more striking is that an overwhelming majority of the UN General Assembly, confirming the fundamental norms of the UN Charter, deplored the Russian actions.[1] Many in the world were also amazed and found it hard

---

[1]   UN General Assembly, A/RES/ES-11/1, adopted 2 March 2022. The vote was 141–5 (with 35 abstentions).

1

to comprehend the rationality of the use of force to tie Ukraine to its big neighbour. The actions have seemed out of tune with the twenty-first century. As the prime minister of India, Narendra Modi, was reported to have poignantly told President Putin in front of journalists and cameras at the summit of the Shanghai Cooperation Organization in September 2022 in Samarkand: 'Today's era is not of war.'[2] A G20 leaders' declaration on 16 November 2022 similarly stated that 'Today's era must not be of war.'[3]

The United States and the West have harshly criticized the Russian actions and supported Ukraine with a vast amount of weapons and resources. They have shown a special disapproval of Russia's flaunting of its nuclear capacity and shown determination to restrain their own reactions so as to avoid direct confrontation with Russia and risk of escalation to a nuclear war. Instead, they have resorted to and relied on economic and financial sanctions of an unprecedented breadth and gravity. In a speech at Warsaw on 26 March 2022, US president Biden said that 'together, these economic sanctions are a new kind of economic statecraft with the power to inflict damage that rivals military might'.[4]

The Russian actions have thus been viewed by most – but not all – of the world as shocking, incomprehensible and conscious breaches of fundamental binding international norms – but not as disrupting these norms. As shown by the Nuremberg Tribunal, gross violations of legal rules do not rescind the rules.[5] We can proceed to examine how these rules and restraints against the interstate use of force have evolved and what they now are.

NORMS AND RESTRAINTS ON THE USE OF FORCE BETWEEN STATES

Wars and battles have been glorified throughout the history of mankind and organization for defence and war has often led to the development of states' infrastructure.[6] Although evidence of the horrors of war has been stark since the dawn of mankind, it was only in the nineteenth century that governments – prompted by public opinion – began to make agreements aimed at somewhat alleviating the brutality and suffering linked to war. In the following century, with public revulsion against warfare following the World War I, they created the League of Nations, a major pioneering but unsuccessful

---

[2] Quoted in 'Today's era is not of war'. *New York Times*, 16 September 2022.
[3] G20 Bali Leaders' Declaration, paragraph 4, 16 November 2022. www.whitehouse.gov/ briefing-room/statements-releases/2022/11/16/g20-bali-leaders-declaration/.
[4] President Joseph Biden, speech in Warsaw, 26 March 2022, www.washingtonpost.com/ national-security/2022/03/27/transcript-president-bidens-remarks-warsaw-march-26/. Also see Chapter 18, p. 289.
[5] See Chapter 11, p. 180, regarding arguments at the Nuremberg trials; and see Chapter 11, p. 181.
[6] The point has been made by many historians. See, for instance, Tilly (1992) and Morris (2014).

effort to curtail war through norms, a system of collective security and disarmament. Then, after the end of the World War II, the United Nations was established with greater designed competences for collective action and an expanded global mission.

The very first lines of the Preamble of the UN Charter proclaimed the determination of the members to 'save succeeding generations from the scourge of war'. In the basic principles that follow, the Charter elaborates in detail its primary aim to prevent the interstate use of force. Not only are traditional 'wars' of the kind experienced in World War II to seize land and change borders outlawed. By obliging member states to refrain from 'the threat or use of force against the territorial integrity or political independence of any state', the prohibition also covered many 'measures short of war', measures that are commonly referred to as 'interventions'. What is the record?

THE RECORD OF WAR PREVENTION

Preventing *nuclear war* was placed at the top of the first UN agenda. There it is. The fear that human civilization may be moving toward a slow suicide through global warming is rousing peoples and governments to action, but the risk of nuclear war threatening a quick suicide has remained without any solution. A list at the end of this chapter of cases where conventional arms have been used in the post–World War II period shows that despite some progress the world has a long way to go in effective conflict prevention.

On the positive side, we note that – with two exceptions[7] – the main great powers have not been in direct armed conflict, whether with nuclear or conventional weapons, since the end of World War II. We also note that while the League of Nations lasted only two decades and collapsed with World War II, the United Nations has been in operation four times that long and remains the most important meeting place for all states and an instrument for peace and global cooperation.

We note further that peace research has found trends of some reduction in the number of wars and the number of dead in recent times.[8] It is not, of course, that competition between states has vanished, nor has the risk disappeared of nuclear war by error, mistake or madness. It would be rash, moreover, to conclude that fewer armed conflicts are a result of the entry into operation of the UN and the Charter. Nevertheless, the Charter rules and UN machinery may be important elements among many changed conditions that

---

[7] During the Korean armed conflict that began in 1950 – a Chinese 'volunteer' army and US troops under the UN flag fought a bloody war. See Chapter 3. In 1969, there was an armed clash between China and the Soviet Union on the Ussuri river border. See Chapter 4.

[8] See Pettersson (2021); Lacina and Gleditsch (2005); Leitenberg (2003); and Dower (2017).

restrain the use of armed force. It is a main aim of this book to identify such changes and examine their effects. In a widely discussed book published in 2011, Stephen Pinker presented a conclusion that has seemed provocatively optimistic to many, namely that we may today be 'living in the most peaceable era in our species' existence' and that 'the decline in violence may be the most significant and least appreciated development in the history of our species'.[9]

A REDUCTION OF VIOLENCE OVER TIME

Pinker reinforced his comments about wars by noting that violence more broadly has reduced over time. Even though we are fully aware of the genocides and ethnic cleansings that have taken place in our time, we note that brutalities that were commonly accepted as normal in the past are found barbaric by nearly all in today's world: impaling, crucifixion, torture or enslavement. Also, violence through the caning of children, duels and the death penalty are offensive to an increasing number of people. The **global public mind** – if we dare to speak about this as a nascent part of globalization – is one that has been mostly moving in a humane and more tolerant direction. Democracy has not gained ground in the second decade of the new millennium, but human rights precepts are cited in all corners of the modern world as arguments and as 'global ethics'. The attitude to the use of force between states – except in self-defence – is mostly sceptical, and while ignoring and violating the UN Charter is not infrequent, the supremacy of its rules is universally recognized.

CHANGING WORLD CONDITIONS

With several conflicts going on in the world, it was not surprising that Pinker's judgements were criticized. After the Russian invasion of Ukraine in February 2022, many will brush away any optimism as naïve and be convinced that 'just as there have always been wars, there always will be wars…'.

However, such comments fail to recognize fundamentally important new conditions. Mutual Economic Dependence (MED) – accelerated interdependence of states – is one. In his book *The Great Illusion* that appeared in 1910, Norman Angell pronounced his conviction that the interdependence of states had become so great that the day for progress by war had passed.[10] Sadly,

---

[9] Pinker (2011), pp. xxi, 298 and 692.

[10] Angell (1910). Morris has asked if Angell was the 'worst' or perhaps the 'best' prophet of the future of war, given the growth of interdependence in the twentieth century and the widespread public revulsion to the devastation of the two World Wars. Morris (2014). Also see Pinker, p. 246.

his statement was premature. Yet a hundred years later, the impact of the technological evolution has been momentous and the interdependence of states is one important factor in a new reality. Nuclear weapons, intercontinental missiles and the possible military use of cyber technology, artificial intelligence and outer space are other new realities that face peoples, governments and the commanding generals today. In this new and continuously changing world, the incentives to and restraints against resorting to war and other uses of force are complex. As we shall see in the present study, this presents both new grave risks and some hopeful new signs.

THE MEANING OF KEY TERMS

'Wars' are commonly seen to be armed conflicts between states, mostly but not necessarily of significant scale and duration and combined with the seizure of land and/or change of borders. Despite the Covenant of the League and the Kellogg–Briand Pact, this 'traditional' kind of war was waged by Italy, Japan, Germany and the Soviet Union before and during World War II. A border skirmish – like the Soviet/Chinese hostilities at the Ussuri river in 1969 – is not termed 'war', while engagements that did not aim at acquiring land but were large-scale and long-lasting – like those of the United States in Korea in 1950, Vietnam 1955–73 and Afghanistan from 2001 to 2021, and Iraq in 2003 – are commonly referred to as 'war'.

'Civil wars' now deploy a major part of the armed force used in the world. They are regarded as internal matters in which the outside world is not to meddle. They have other roots than conflicts between states, and preventing and stopping them requires other measures than those needed for international conflicts. They are not taken up in this study except where they are internationalized through participation by foreign states – as in Syria and Libya.

The term 'intervention' is commonly used for coercive – mostly but not necessarily armed – adversarial actions of limited scope with the aim to secure specific objectives, not including the acquisition of land. The term is sometimes even used to describe a verbal attack by one government on another.

Although there is no authoritative definition of 'intervention', the subject is nevertheless dealt with at length in the UN General Assembly 'Declaration on legal principles of friendly relations' from 1970 and the 'Declaration of the inadmissibility of intervention and interference in the internal affairs of states' from 1981.[11]

In a very informative study, Martha Finnemore seeks to distinguish between 'war' and 'intervention' and submits that interventions are 'smaller in scale' and have 'more limited objectives than wars'. In particular, 'they do not include territorial conquest or absorption'.[12]

In the nineteenth century, the 'European Concert' and Holy Alliance intervened with arms – and without intent to acquire land – to prevent revolutionary change in several states. Consistent with this basic principle, armed interventions in this period often had regard to the protection of nationals and their property. In the interwar period, there were many interventions by states, notably in China and in the Civil War in Spain. Since World War II, despite the broad UN Charter prohibition of all interstate use of force, states have undertaken armed interventions for a variety of aims – often to bring about 'regime changes'. The UN, different from member states, is enabled by Charter Art. 2:7 and by the doctrine 'responsibility to protect' (R2P) to intervene – even by force – in states in exceptional cases, for instance to stop genocide.

The term 'measures short of war' comprises interventions but also actions or statements that are unfriendly but may not be inadmissible.

THREE AUTHORITIES EXPLAINING STATES' USE OF FORCE

The present study seeks to identify and assess incentives and restraints both to 'traditional war' and 'interventions'. I begin my discussion by citing three respected voices from the 'realist school' to which I feel affinity and which claim to explain the root causes of states' use of force. Hans Morgenthau is perhaps the foremost representative of realist school of international relations. With great knowledge of diplomatic history and international relations, he identifies a 'quest for power' as the universal driving force in the international relations of states.[13] We may note that the US national security strategy presented by the Trump administration in 2017 read like an essay based on Morgenthau: 'The strategy is guided by principled realism. It is realist because

---

[11] UNGA, A/RES/2625 (XXV) of 24 October 1970 and A/RES/36/103 of 9 December 1981.
[12] Finnemore (2003).
[13] Morgenthau (2006), p. 285.

it acknowledges the central role of power in international politics, affirms that sovereign states are the best hope for a peaceful world...."[14]

Through power, material advantages can be sought, but also other gains like status. Morgenthau does not deny that a major part of the international legal rules function well even without courts and enforcement systems and that states' quests for power may be inhibited by various factors, including ethical and international legal norms. However, like St Augustine (354–430) and Hobbes (1588–1679) before him,[15] he believes that the root cause of the use of armed force is that man is aggressive and evil. He is concerned about the dangerous dimension brought into state relations by nuclear weapons and does not place much faith in the UN as a mechanism for peace. He sees no other plausible remedy to the risk of war and violence than balance of power and skilful diplomacy – by which he means statesmanship.

The distinguished American political scientist, Francis Fukuyama, is like Morgenthau allergic to high-sounding claims that international mechanisms can cope with the interstate use of force. He sympathizes with the realist school and its emphasis on balance of power and military strength but thinks it is not aware enough of the demand for 'recognition' – pride, prestige, wish to dominate – that he sees as the main driving force for war in a world of states competing with each other.[16] Although this stressing of self-assertion highlights a highly relevant psychological dimension, in practical terms Fukuyama's explanation of war may not be very different from the 'quest for power' that Morgenthau identifies as the source of conflict and war.

A third prominent voice is that of Azar Gat, a military historian who examines war and peace through Darwinist lenses and argues that we must go beyond Morgenthau's focus and ask why there are 'quests for power'. If we do so, we find the answers in the world of evolution. Egoistic competition and conflict occur in all human groups – from hunting and food-gathering groups to states – and they are all basically explained by men's striving for survival and ascendancy.[17]

---

[14] *National Security Strategy of the United States* (Washington, DC: White House, December 2017), p. 55, https://trumpwhitehouse.archives.gov/wp-content/uploads/2017/12/NSS-Final-12-18-2017-0905.pdf.

[15] See Chapter 5.

[16] Fukuyama (1992), pp. xxi, 145.

[17] Gat (2006), pp. 667–671.

Darwinist writers tell us that through evolution, modern man became biologically programmed with a readiness to compete and fight for scarce resources to survive. The genetic program was developed many tens of thousands of years ago, and although the world and the resources and conditions surrounding man have changed very much, the genetic program remains. It emerged at a time – long before agriculture – when access to resources for sustenance was insecure and only those survived and multiplied who were able to fight – alone or in a kinship group – successfully for them or defend what they had. However, Darwinists tell us that what is embedded in our genes is a potential to compete and fight – not an automatic reflex. The fittest – meaning not just the strongest but the smartest – will survive. David wins over Goliath.

It may be concluded from the above that neither 'realists' nor 'evolutionists' deny that a variety of factors can have an impact on the will of states to use force against other states. They guard themselves against naïveté and any exaggerated hope that international institutions and norms, like the UN and the Charter, will eliminate the 'scourge of war'.

STARTING POINTS OF THIS STUDY

This study will start by recognizing that force continues to be used in interstate relations and the reality that the volume as well as the character of state relations have changed much over time. The incentives to, restraints against, as well as the means of war have evolved over the years. Quests for power or recognition or for riches and resources may be innate and constant, as assumed by Morgenthau, Fukuyama and Gat. However, while they may help to explain the root causes of uses of force that have occurred, these quests do not constantly translate into incentives to use force.

It is normal for states to be ready to use force, if so needed, to defend their territories and independence, but most states have come to co-exist with their fellow states – most of the time – without incentives to use force against them.

A few simple illustrations: there are no plausible incentives for the interstate use of force in North and South America in the twenty-first century, although there was such use in the nineteenth century. Another example: while the history of Europe is replete with wars, incentives for an interstate use of force within the European Union have been all but excluded since its creation. The African continent, despite many arbitrary borders and arbitrary divisions into states, has so far seen few incentives to the interstate use of force, while there has been much internal use of force in African states. By contrast, it is not difficult to see incentives – and restraints – to the use of force in the Middle East and in the relations between competing major powers.

INCENTIVES AND RESTRAINTS TO STATES' USE OF FORCE

Where interstate force has, in fact, come to be used, there has evidently been an incentive, and it has prevailed over possible restraints. In Chapter 4, I shall survey post–World War II cases of conflicts where interstate force was used to try to discern which traditional incentives may still exist (for instance, aspiration to global or regional hegemony), which may have disappeared or become less frequent (for instance, the spread of religion or faith, dynastic claims or the acquisition of land), and which new incentives may have emerged (for instance, environmental degradation or preventing the emergence of new nuclear weapon capacity).

Where incentives arise for states to use force against other states, the actual use will occur if no restraining factor – such as fear of a nuclear or other forbidding response, concern for the costs of lives and resources, respect for an international or constitutional norm or concern for public condemnation – prevails. I shall discuss a range of possible restraint factors but devote most attention to three:

- What role does military deterrence, including nuclear deterrence, have today?
- What role is played by mediation, judicial institutions, disarmament and diplomacy to prevent the use of force by preventing conflicts?
- How have the norms of the international community developed and what restraining power do the legal norms and institutions have?

President Obama assessed accurately where we were when he pronounced the following hopeful lines in a speech at Hiroshima on 27 May 2016: 'Our early ancestors, having learned to make blades from flint and spears from wood, used these tools not just for hunting but against their own kind. On every continent, the history of civilization is filled with war, whether driven by scarcity of grain or hunger for gold compelled by nationalist fervor or religious zeal.' And: 'We are not bound by genetic code to repeat the mistakes of the past. We can learn. We can choose. We can tell our children a different story – one that describes a human community; one that makes war less likely and cruelty less easily accepted.'[18]

President Obama recognized that while the genetic program that was engrained in humans tens of thousands of years ago remains, it does not condemn us to a blind constant quest for power or recognition or for scarce

---

[18] Obama (2016).

resources through the use of force. Rather than mercilessly and blindly cata-
pulting us to the risk of death and disaster in such quests, our genes are smart
enough to allow us to be deflected by a variety of factors to hold us back from
force, or to use means other than force.

Indeed, this is what has come to pass when human societies have pro-
gressed. At the highest level of development – the territorial state – many
different kinds of restraints hold us back from using physical force, fraud
or many other unacceptable ways of exercising our quest for power, asserting ourselves or acquiring assets. Whether our natures are basically 'evil' as
St Augustine, Hobbes and Morgenthau have held, or merely DNA directed
as Gat may suggest, we evidently can be – and need be – restrained through
social and legal norms. It is not that our quests for survival, opulence or
self-assertion need to be erased. It is rather that our societies – the publicly
organized and the civic communities – through rules and other means and
sanctions, create a framework for acceptable forms of competition between
individuals.

In a similar manner, there is a framework for competition among the states
of the international community. The community tolerates many forms and
means of competition and seeks to steer its members to use those by deflecting
them from forms – notably the use of force – found unacceptable.

In its development of a system of competition for states, the international
community has obvious and well-known handicaps, such as the absence of a
common legislature and the paucity of means of enforcement. On the positive
side, the number of states is less than 200. What they do and how they compete is mostly visible and open to general scrutiny, criticism or reaction. In
state societies of millions, or hundreds of millions, the competing individuals
may hide more easily and escape society's reaction.

Before going into a systematic discussion of forces and factors that may
be relevant as incentives to and restraints on the use and non-use of force
in interstate relations today, I will first present a broad panorama of cases of
post–World War II interstate uses of force and of tensions that might lead to
the use of force. Short surveys might suffice to give us an overview of the real
world and the relevant forces and conditions that we must study to be able to
identify the factors that are at play and to assess their roles.

Accordingly, this and the following two chapters are devoted to surveys of
actions involving the interstate use of force and tensions that we have seen
after World War II. A box containing a long chronological list – that does not
pretend to be complete – of actions includes not only 'wars' but also some
interventions and some other items of relevance. In Chapters 2 and 3, I shall
examine how the cases of conflict and uses of force have been spread over the

world's main geographic regions and over the main phases in great power relations: the long bipolar East–West Cold War, the détente period and unipolar world that followed the break-up of the Soviet Union, and the world that is emerging thereafter.

As many cases of conflicts are examined from different angles in different chapters, the same conflict may figure in several places and contexts. This results in some inevitable overlap but makes each chapter more self-contained.

INTERSTATE USES OF FORCE AND SOME OTHER EVENTS AT AND AFTER THE END OF WORLD WAR II

- In 1944, at the end of World War II, the Baltic states – Estonia, Latvia and Lithuania, were incorporated into the Soviet Union, as a result of annexation in 1940.
- In 1945, the adoption of the United Nations Charter restricted the threat and use of force and created machinery meant to provide disincentives to and stop such state conduct.
- Following World War II and Soviet occupation, Soviet-controlled Communist takeover in Bulgaria, Hungary, Poland and Romania.
- In 1945, following World War II, continued occupation and division of Austria and Germany. (State treaty for the Re-establishment of an Independent and Democratic Austria with Austria 1955 and German reunification 1990.)
- Iranian/Azerbaijan crisis 1945–46, Soviet Communist-aided insurrections.
- Greece 1946–49, Communist insurrection assisted from the outside. (Prompted Truman Doctrine 1947 to counter similar actions.)
- Berlin blockade 1948–49.
- Arab-Israel War 1948 (Officially ended in 1949).
- Indonesian War of Independence 1945–49.
- Czechoslovakia 1948, Prague Communist coup, fomented by the Soviet Union.
- NATO was established in 1949 to create a disincentive to Soviet Communist use of force or subversion.
- Invasion of Tibet by China 1950 (Seventeen Point Agreement signed in May 1951).
- Korean War, 1950–53.

- Iran, in 1953 United States-CIA organized a military coup deposing Prime Minister Mossadegh.
- China-US armed clashes of 1954–55 about the islands of Quemoy and Matsu near the Chinese mainland.
- Viet Nam War of national independence from France (1946–54) and war with the United States (1965–73).
- Anglo-French-Israeli attack on Suez Canal and Sinai 1956.
- Hungarian uprising 1956 crushed by Soviet armed intervention.
- US intervention in Lebanon 1958.
- Tibetan Revolt against China 1959.
- Algerian War of Independence from France 1954–62.
- Congo Crisis following national independence from Belgium and involving foreign intervention 1960–65.
- Angolan War of Independence from Portugal 1961–74.
- Indian occupation and annexation of Portuguese–controlled enclave Goa, 1961.
- Bay of Pigs 1961: the US-organized (failed) invasion of Cuba.
- Cuban Missile Crisis 1962 between the United States and the Soviet Union.
- India-China War 1962 in the Himalayas.
- Algeria-Morocco 'sand' war, 1963.
- British Guyana: CIA actions to topple Cheddi Jagan, 1964.
- India-Pakistan war in 1965.
- Intervention in the Dominican Republic by United States, 1965.
- Israel-Egypt Six Day War, 1967 (with Syria and Jordan involved).
- Namibian War of Independence from South Africa, 1966–88.
- Biafra (failed) civil war of independence from Nigeria, 1967–70.
- Prague 'Spring' was crushed by the Soviet Union in 1968.
- Soviet-China armed border clashes in 1969 at Zhenbao island, Ussuri River.
- US bombing and later armed intervention in Kampuchea, 1969–70.
- India-Pakistan War, 1971.
- Yom Kippur War in 1973 involving Israel and Egypt.
- Military coup of General Pinochet in Chile, 1973.
- Arab Oil Embargo 1973–74 following the Yom Kippur War.
- Coup in Cyprus and Turkish military intervention in response, 1974.
- Syrian intervention in Lebanese civil war (with the tacit approval of United States and Israel), 1976.
- Israeli interventions in Lebanon, 1978 and 1982.

- Helsinki Conference on Security and Cooperation in Europe and Declaration laying down rules of conduct, 1975.
- Indonesian intervention in East Timor, 1975.
- Uganda: Israeli intervention to save hostages at Entebbe, 1976.
- War between Ethiopia and Somalia in Ogaden region, 1977–78.
- Kampuchea: Viet Nam-armed intervention, 1978.
- China invasion in northern Viet Nam, 1979.
- Tanzania intervention in Uganda, 1978–79.
- Central African Republic: French intervention to help depose 'Emperor' Bokassa, 1979.
- Soviet Union-Afghanistan war, 1979–89.
- Iraq-Iran war, 1980–88.
- Israeli attack on Iraqi research reactor Osirak in 1981.
- Falkland (Malvinas) war between Argentina and the United Kingdom, 1982.
- US intervention in Grenada, 1983.
- US intervention in Nicaragua, 1983–84.
- Armenia-Azerbaijan War over Nagorno-Karabakh, 1988–94.
- Panama: US intervention, 1989.
- Iraq: the occupation of Kuwait, 1990.
- UN: Security Council-authorized armed action launched against Iraq, 1991.
  'Ecuador and Peru 1995: an armed clash with roots in a border war in 1941.'
- D.R. Congo: armed conflicts with neighbours 1996–97 and 1998–2002.
- Ethiopia and Eritrea: War over the Badme territory, 1998–2000. (Peace agreement signed in 2000 followed by new tensions and violence in 2016. New peace agreement signed in 2018.)
- Yugoslavia: civil war involving many participants, including the UN, NATO, the United States and Russia. (Ended with NATO intervention in 1999), 1998–99.
- 9/11 2001: Al-Qaeda terrorist attacks in the United States.
- Afghanistan: war engaging the United States and several other states, 2001–21.
- Iraq: war engaging the United States and an alliance of 'friendly states', 2003.
- Lebanon: Israeli intervention vs. Hezbollah, 2006.
- China: demonstrating space war capacity by using a missile to destroy a defunct Chinese weather satellite, January 2007.
- Estonia: many objects subjected to cyber-attack, 27 April 2007.

- Syria in 2007: Israeli attack on alleged nuclear installation at Al Kibar.
- Russia in 2008: intervention in Georgia.
- Sudan (civil) war and conflicts between North and South Sudan, 2011.
- Iran in July 2010: cyber-attack with virus called STUXNET, probably from Israel and United States, on centrifuges for the enrichment of uranium.
- Syria: civil war starting 2011 – engaging many states, including Saudi Arabia, Iran, Turkey, Russia and the United States.
- Libya: civil war starting 2011 – engaging NATO and other states.
- Saudi Arabia 2012: Cyber-attack with virus called Shamoon – destroyed thousands of computers at Saudi Aramco in August 2012.
- Russian annexation of the Crimea and intervention by armed actions in East Ukraine, 2014.
- Islamic State (ISIS/DAESH) against several states and UN-authorized armed action to eliminate ISIS/DAESH, 2014.
- Yemen: civil war with major interventions by Saudi Arabia and the United Arab Emirates, 2015.
- Syria: United States, United Kingdom and France: attacks in Syria as punishment for Syrian use of chemical weapons, 2018.
- Iraq, 3 January 2020: US drone attack at Baghdad airport killing Iranian General Qasem Soleimani.
- Azerbaijan and Armenia war over Nagorno-Karabakh, 2020.
- Ethiopia/Tigray civil war, 2020–2022.
- Russian invasion of Ukraine, 2022.

Sources used: Ciment, James, ed., *Encyclopedia of Conflicts since World War II*. 2nd ed. Vol. 1–4 (Armonk, NY: M.E. Sharpe, 2007). *The Statesman's Yearbook: The Politics, Cultures and Economies of the World 2017* (London: Palgrave Macmillan, 2016). https://doi.org/10.1007/978-1-349-68398-7. 'Uppsala Conflict Data Program.' n.d. *UCDP Conflict Encyclopedia, Uppsala University* (blog). Accessed January 5, 2022. www.ucdp.uu.se. In some instances: *Encyclopedia Britannica*.

2

Interstate Uses of Force, Tensions and Restraints by Regions since World War II

This chapter will provide brief descriptions by geographic region of cases of post–World War II interstate uses of force and interventions. The aim is to get an idea of how common are local or regional conflicts in main areas of the world, as distinguished from conflicts in which great powers play a role. Conflicts that played out in a region but were essentially part of the global struggle between great powers may be noted in this chapter but will be described in Chapter 3 that surveys post–World War II uses of force by main phases in great power struggles. The distribution of cases between the chapters may sometimes appear somewhat arbitrary as local and regional tensions and uses of force may be part of struggles between a few great powers as well. The mapping of conflicts around the world is undertaken by continents and will show that several continents and regions have had few conflicts in the period after World War II.

AFRICA

In the period surveyed armed actions have killed and displaced large numbers of people in Africa, but lethal armed conflicts *between* states in Africa have been uncommon. A few have been triggered by conflicts over state borders and more such conflicts could perhaps arise in the future, as the borders of many African states have remained where colonising states once placed them without much regard to regions of tribes or language.

The so-called 'sand war' between Algeria and Morocco in 1963 concerned an area that had not been demarcated in pre-independence times. Both the OAU and the Arab League played a role in settling the controversy which ended in 1972 through the Treaty of Ifan and the demilitarisation of an area. Morocco ratified the treaty in 1989.

In 1978, border violations by Uganda triggered Tanzania to respond and the response expanded to become a significant armed intervention that led to the ousting of the reckless Ugandan leader, Idi Amin in 1979.[1]

The Democratic Republic of Congo (Kinshasa), which had seen much turmoil at its birth, was involved in internal conflict in 1996 and 1997, when the long-time dictator Mobuto was driven from power by Laurent Kabila. Neighbouring states Rwanda, Uganda and Angola gave armed support to the rebellion. A year later, rebel groups in East Congo started a second Congo War (also called Africa's World War I) and were supported from the outside by Rwanda, Uganda and Burundi. Several other states, including Angola and Zimbabwe, gave both indirect assistance and direct military support to the government. This war ended with a peace settlement only in December 2002. In a case between DR Congo and Uganda, the International Court of Justice decided in December 2005 that the military intervention of Uganda in DR Congo had constituted a grave violation of Art. 2:4 of the UN Charter and the principle of non-intervention.[2]

An armed conflict between 1998 and 2002 between Ethiopia and Eritrea had its origin in earlier border disputes. An international judicial ruling in favour of Eritrea in 2002 was not accepted by Ethiopia but was left smouldering until 2018 when Ethiopia's Prime Minister Abiy Ahmed Ali accepted it. He was awarded the Nobel Peace Prize the following year. After that hopeful moment, civil war erupted in Ethiopia with an uprising in the Tigray region and intervention on the side of the government by Eritrea.

After having endured two previous civil wars (1955–1972 and 1983–2005), Sudan suffered its third from 2013 to 2020, after the secession of the new state of South Sudan in 2011. The conflict, which has been an economic and humanitarian catastrophe (nearly 400,000 killed), formally ended in 2020, though violence continues involving armed factions. Following the military ouster of former President Bashir in 2019, Sudan briefly had a military-civilian government until another coup in October 2021.[3]

Much of the armed violence in Africa has been and continues to be inside states. In newly established states, regional divisions and internal structures

---

[1]   See the description in Chapter 16, p. 242.
[2]   See Ciment, J., ed, *Encyclopedia of Conflicts since World War II* (2nd ed., Routledge 2007) and see *Armed Activities on the Territory of the Congo* (Democratic Republic of the Congo v. Uganda). 2005. International Court of Justice. www.icj-cij.org/en/case/116.
[3]   For a detailed overview of the civil war, see www.cfr.org/global-conflict-tracker/conflict/civil-war-south-sudan. A recent update is found in 'Sudan's fragile transition to democracy at stake as rival camps flex muscles', *France 24*, 21 October 2021, www.france24.com/en/africa/20211021-sudan-s-fragile-transition-to-democracy-at-stake-as-rival-camps-flex-muscles. See Chapter 10, p. 154 for the International Criminal Court case against Bashir.

may not have had time to settle and many internal disturbances and armed conflicts have erupted, often engaging local tribal societies. Examples are found in Zaire/Congo, Rwanda, Burundi, Angola, Nigeria, Côte d'Ivoire, Mali, Sudan and Uganda. In a few of them – notably the Congo and Angola – interventions by outside powers have been significant

Most African states attained their independence without the use of armed force, but in several cases, self-determination was achieved only after a 'war of national liberation' against the former colonial state, for instance in Algeria, Angola and Namibia. Perhaps the struggle for self-rule by a majority in Zimbabwe (formerly Rhodesia) should be placed in this category. No outside colonial power was a party but the United Nations sanctions were adopted supporting the majority side.

Armed conflicts for self-determination are one-time events that should not be encountered again. In some cases, however, demands self-determination have been directed to already existing independent African states and led to armed conflicts, for instance in Biafra, Western Sahara and South Sudan. Little or no great power intervention has been noted in these cases. Future self-determination conflicts may occur based on demands similar to those raised elsewhere in the world, such as in Scotland or Catalonia.

Armed conflicts prompted by internal division – sometimes exacerbated by terrorism – have been common in Africa. Somalia has long been a 'failed state' as a result of a civil war in which great powers have played a minor role and in which the peace- making efforts of the international community (UN and OAU) have not been successful. The causes of the massacres in Rwanda in 1994 have similarly been mainly internal, while the involvements of international institutions (United Nations, Organisation of African Unity) were woefully insufficient to prevent genocide and led to the soul-searching at the United Nations and adoption in 2005 of the doctrine R2P – responsibility to protect – and a mandate for international action in similar cases.[4]

In the case of Libya, the Security Council in March 2011 authorised an international intervention to prevent the Gaddafi regime from attacking its own civilian population.[5] A NATO-led operation was mounted, including a no-fly zone and extensive operations on the ground to assist indigenous forces that fought and eventually toppled the regime and killed Gaddafi. The intervention was urged on humanitarian grounds but might not have materialised and the civil war that followed might not have occurred if it had not been for outside interest in the large Libyan oil resources. It was criticised (especially

---

[4]   See Chapter 13, p. 69.
[5]   S/RES/1973, 17 March 2011.

by Russia) as exceeding the authorisation given by the Security Council and it was clearly deficient to establish a peaceful order. As in Iraq after the unauthorised 2003 invasion by the United States, the United Kingdom and other states, prolonged anarchy rather than democracy following the collapse of the dictatorship. The situation allowed terrorist movements to infiltrate. By 2020, the situation had grown even worse through interventions of several outside states – Turkey, Egypt, Russia and others. An UN-appointed mission has sought to bring about a negotiated national reunification.[6] In retrospect, the international intervention justified as the protection of civilians and leading to 10 years of anarchy stands out as a failure.

In Mali, Central African Republic, Niger, Nigeria, Cameron and several other states, terrorist movements sometimes with links to movements such as Islamic State of Iraq and Syria (ISIS) have been active and caused much death and disruption. Despite considerable agreement within the organised international community about the need to help eradicate such terrorist movements, both common action under UN authority and bilateral assistance by great powers have had limited success (by 2022). While in the past local or regional terrorist groups were often neglected by the outside world as unimportant to it, the links of such groups to larger movements – such as ISIS – have led to increasing international involvement.

The turmoil and uncertain living conditions in Northern Africa have also led to large numbers of people fleeing and trying to emigrate to Europe. European governments and the EU have engaged with African governments in Mali, Libya and elsewhere to establish order. With the authorisation of various African governments, the US has also maintained small military bases that can render some assistance and, if deemed necessary, be rapidly expanded. The United States has even a special military command for Africa (located in Stuttgart, Germany). Great power interest in rapidly developing Africa is shown by the establishment in Djibouti of American, French and Chinese military bases, potentially able to perform military actions in Africa. Russian mercenaries – Wagner forces[7] – have played significant roles in the Libyan civil war since 2020 and are reported to be present and active in several other African states, such as the Central African Republic, Mali and Mozambique.[8]

---

[6] For further information, see United Nations Support Mission in Libya (UNSMIL), https://unsmil.unmissions.org/.

[7] See Chapter 6, p. 110; Chapter 15, p. 219; Chapter 18, p. 287.

[8] See Federica Saini Fasanotti, 'Russia's Wagner Group in Africa: Influence, Commercial Concessions, Rights Violations, and Counterinsurgency Failure'. *Order from Chaos, Brookings Institution* (blog), February 8, 2022, www.brookings.edu/blog/order-from-chaos/2022/02/08/russias-wagner-group-in-africa-influence-commercial-concessions-rights-violations-and-counterinsurgency-failure/.; Ilya Barabanov and Nader Ibrahim, 'Wagner: Scale of Russian

The comments about the inadequacy of the assistance from the organised international community to eliminate terrorist activities in various parts of Africa should not hide the fact that no area in the world has had as much support as Africa from UN peacekeeping force, peace enforcing and peace-building efforts by outside institutions. Since 1960, the United Nations has fielded over 30 peacekeeping missions in Africa, more than any other region, and in 2021 there were over 50,000 UN troops in Africa.[9] Some operations have been undertaken directly by the United Nations. Others – like actions under ECOWAS (Economic Community of West African States) – have been undertaken by regional organisations in Africa with the authorisation of the OAU (later AU) and the UN.[10] African states have pursued determined efforts to reduce the traffic in small calibre weapons to tackle a very real problem of internal peace; and through the Pelindaba treaty (1996), the states of the continent have made Africa a nuclear-weapon-free zone.

EUROPE

At the end of the World War II, the Soviet Union took advantage of its military presence in East Europe to transform many Eastern European states into satellites. This expansion and how it was countered will be described and discussed in the next chapter, which deals with the great power East-West conflict.

The development of a common military defence deterring Soviet Communist expansion was not the ambition driving the initiative of statesmen in France and Germany – Schuman, Adenauer and Monnet – to create the European Coal and Steel Community, an enterprise that gradually evolved to become the European Union. The aim was rather to develop practical, industrial and economic cohesion, in particular between Germany and France. It was to have the epochal function of preventing further war in Europe.

The bonding in Europe was facilitated by the reality that fast modern communication and transportation create a demand for more economic harmonisation and integration. Markets – both production and consumption – benefit from large-scale operations. The aim has also been stimulated by the need of a great many individual states of various sizes to come together to

Mercenary Mission in Libya Exposed'. *BBC News*, August 11, 2021, www.bbc.com/news/world-africa-58009514.; and Marten (2019).

9   Claire Felter and Danielle Renwick, 'The Role of Peacekeeping in Africa'. *Backgrounder* (New York: Council on Foreign Relations), 5 October 2021, www.cfr.org/backgrounder/role-peacekeeping-africa.

10   See Chapter 13, p. 203.

gain greater strength in their economic and other relations with big outside actors, like the US, China and Russia.

The Community became a magnet and a large number of states (in the East, North and South of Europe) have joined and more may wish to do so. The attractiveness of the economic–political–social systems of the states of the EU lies behind the ambition of Georgia, Ukraine and Moldova to be linked to the European Union. Only a few Western European states have deliberately avoided formal membership (Iceland, Norway and Switzerland) while after a referendum the UK has become the first country to exit the EU (Brexit).

It is conspicuous that the European Union which is evolving to defend and promote the interests of its members, is not directly organised for military defence of the union. At various times ideas have surfaced for a European defence capability, but they have not gone very far. The main explanations may lie in the history and military evolution. After World War II the US has been the unquestioned anchor of Western (including European) defence against feared Soviet expansionism. Although France and the UK possess nuclear weapons capacity, only the US has had a capacity sufficient to match that of the Soviet Union as a potential military adversary. The Russian invasion of Ukraine in early 2022 has driven European countries together, but also to a renewed reliance on the United States that holds the main hand of the NATO umbrella (and pays for much of it). Undoubtedly the NATO alliance has also satisfied an interest of the United States to hold an influential – in addition to the protective – hand over European states and to recruit potential allies for US military activities outside the North Atlantic region, for instance, Afghanistan, Iraq and the West Pacific.

While a break-up of the euro currency union has been feared at times and the passport free travel under the Schengen agreement could possibly be disrupted, the unravelling of the Union seems unlikely despite the British withdrawal (Brexit). It has developed a vast body of common laws and institutions that can hardly be dismantled or rolled back. The free movement of people and goods brings great economic advantages and despite criticism of centralism and bureaucracy, many understand that the Union can defend their interests better in globalised competition than separate states can do.

Even though based upon many common European values, the union is not a vaccine against nationalist and authoritarian trends within member states and individual members might break-up. Further, while one cannot feel confident that there could not be tensions between Union members, the close interdependence makes it unlikely that member states would ever engage in armed actions against each other. Such differences as may still exist about one borderline or another or about slices of territory are unlikely to go out of control.

The grim warfare and brutal ethnic cleansing that took place at the end of the 1990s in former Yugoslavia occurred outside the rules and realm of the EU. The use of force followed many years of pent-up tensions that existed under the firm-fisted rule of Tito. The outside intervention comprised both remarkable joint military operations between Russia and the West, and the NATO bombing of Kosovo ignoring the need for UN authorisation.[11] While national interests may have been an incentive for some of the foreign interventions, humanitarian considerations weighed heavily in the efforts to minimise the pain of the break-up. It is a sign of the hopes attached to the EU that the gradual incorporation of states of former Yugoslavia is now seen as a way of eliminating the risk of armed conflicts between them. It seems justified to say that the probably most war-torn region in the world – the area covered by the EU – is developing into a zone in which a future use of force between states is highly improbable. This is a major evolution in the world community.

The large-scale Russian armed intervention in Georgia in 2008 raised much concern in the West and Russia's annexation of Crimea in 2014 and interventions in East Ukraine thereafter caused further alarm. In 2022, Russia went on to launch a brutal invasion of Ukraine. It met heroic and successful Ukrainian resistance and censure by the UN General Assembly. The United States and other Western states imposed far-reaching economic and financial sanctions on Russia and extended large-scale assistance with arms – but avoided direct military intervention on the ground or in the air. The Russian efforts to control Ukraine will be described and discussed in the next chapter, which focusses on the phases of global relations that have resulted from the shifts in great power relations.

THE AMERICAS

In Europe, the development away from centuries of armed conflicts was brought about only after the World War II and with a deliberate union design that joins national economies and comprises supranational features. In the Americas, once states had emancipated to become independent, interstate armed conflicts have gone from relatively few in the nineteenth century to near zero in the twentieth century – without a close union.

The Spanish-American War took place in 1898, the Chaco War between Bolivia and Paraguay raged between 1932 and 1935, and a brief border war took place in 1941 between Ecuador and Peru with a flare-up in 1995.

---

[11] See Perry (2015), p. 148, and on Kosovo, see below Chapter 16, p. 244.

Another matter is that civil wars, revolutions and armed and non-armed interventions to bring about regime changes have been common. While the Monroe Doctrine made it clear as early as 1823 that the United States objected to any European interventions in the Western hemisphere the United States, itself, was not restrained.[12] Post–World War II, inroads made by the Communist ideology and economic system in Latin America, in particular through the Cuban revolution, led to a number of US interventions such as the 1961 failed Bay of Pigs armed invasion in Cuba, the armed intervention in the Dominican Republic 1965, the intervention in Nicaragua in 1981 and Granada 1983.[13]

Nevertheless, in many Latin American states, the role of the military has gradually become weaker and the take-over of governments by military hands has become infrequent. The power exercised and violence related to the drug trade, on the other hand, is staggering within some countries, especially in the Central American countries and Mexico.

The cases of regime changes brought about through armed or other coercive intervention by the United States have gradually become fewer. In a sentence of 1986, the International Court of Justice judged the US paramilitary activities in and against Nicaragua and aiming at toppling the Sandinista regime in Nicaragua to be a violation of the principle of non-intervention.[14] The anti-American postures of the Chavez-Maduro regime in Venezuela triggered open US economic sanctions and less open support to a potential coup but did not (2022) lead the United States to follow earlier patterns of intervening by the use of arms.

The legal, economic and institutional integration in the Americas is growing, but much less advanced than in Europe and no supranational institutions have yet been established. It is likely to increase as modern techniques and trade bring ever more regional trade and communication. The Spanish and Portuguese languages and common Latin roots and culture are likely to facilitate unity projects. Many law-making and institution-building treaties bind states together in the Americas, for example, the Organization of American States (OAS), the Latin American Free Trade Association (LAFTA), and the Tlatelolco Nuclear-Weapon-Free Zone Treaty. An important factor for inter-state peace may well have been that over time state borders for the most part have become settled. There have been some controversies and skirmishes over the border between Ecuador and Peru and Peru and Chile, but differences have subsided. Controversies between Argentina and Chile about the Beagle Channel were solved by arbitration in 1977.

---

[12] See below, Chapter 4, p. 77 and Finnemore (2003, pp. 27 ff.).
[13] They are discussed in Chapter 3, p. 36 as Cold War interventions, see also Chapter 15, p. 213.
[14] See below, Chapter 15, p. 214.

THE MIDDLE EAST

The Middle East is recognised as the world's most conflict-prone region and it has had much to do with its vast oil and gas resources. The expected drastic future reduction of the use of fossil fuels could make the competition between great powers for influence in the region less sharp. Until now the region has suffered armed conflicts and tensions between as well as within states. Immediately on the ending of the British mandate over Palestine the Arab-Israeli War broke out. It finished in 1949 with several armistices and a division of territory. Since then, many armed conflicts have taken place linked either to defence or capture of land or the prevention of incursions and cross-border attacks.

Following Egypt's nationalisation of the Suez Canal (1956) the UK together with France and in cooperation with Israel launched an operation aimed at the Anglo-French seizure of the Suez Canal. It was interrupted and called off after US pressures. The incentives for the dramatic conflict were diverse. For Israel, control of the Sinai meant strategic security and more land. For Great Britain and France, asserting great power prerogatives, ensuring free shipping and preventing the seizing of British and French property more than control of land per se were driving factors.

There were many unique features in the affair. In the United Kingdom, the Labour opposition leader, Gaitskell promised Prime Minister Eden support but only on the condition that the UN Security Council approved the action. The Eisenhower administration in the US despite favouring Israel and being negative to nationalisations demonstrated its anti-colonial attitude and threatened to sell UK government bonds. The Soviet Union, in close relation at the time with Egypt, is reported to have considered military action.[15]

In the Six-Day War (5–10 June 1967), following Egyptian threats and closure of Israel's access to the Red Sea Israel through armed pre-emptive action took the Sinai Peninsula and Gaza from Egypt, the West Bank of the Jordan River from Jordan and the Golan Heights from Syria. In the Yom Kippur War (6–25 October 1973) Egypt and Syria through surprise action sought – but failed – to take back Sinai and the Golan Heights.

In 1977, the President of Egypt Anwar Sadat in a dramatic quest for peace flew to Israel, met with Israeli Prime Minister Begin and addressed the Knesset. Following long negotiation with US assistance at Camp David in the United States in 1978 a peace treaty was reached in 1979 under which the Sinai Peninsula was given back to Egypt, Israel was recognised, passage

---

[15] Fukuyama (June 1980).

for Israeli ships through the Suez Canal guaranteed and stationing of UN personnel was foreseen. Much later, after the first Oslo Accord between Israel and the PLO (Palestine Liberation Organization) a peace treaty was reached between Israel and Jordan in 1994. As the proposed Israel-PLO Oslo accords and numerous other initiatives have failed to settle Israel's conflict with the Palestinians, conflict has remained a dangerous chronic inflammation, leading to Israeli interventions and occupation of territory in Lebanon and impeding thaw in the region.

Nevertheless, a new phase seems underway despite Israel's declared annexation of the Syrian Golan Heights, the continued Israeli occupation of and increased settlements on the West Bank of the Jordan River and no progress on the two-state solution – a Palestinian state living next to Israel. With the active support of the US Trump administration, diplomatic relations have been opened in 2020 between Israel and the United Arab Emirates (UAE), Bahrain and Morocco while relations with Sudan have thawed. Contacts with other states in the region–except Iran–have become less frozen.

In view of Israel's military power – including nuclear weapons – and ironclad US support any major armed attack on Israel from the outside has long seemed out of question. However, since the armed conflict with the Iran-supported Hezbollah movement in Lebanon in 2006, armed violence has continued between Israel and the Hamas movement in Gaza and during and after the long war in Syria Israel has frequently bombed Iran-linked objects in Syria.

From the Cold War to this day the United States and Russia have competed for influence in the region but avoided any direct clashes. They seem to remain on this course. The United States retains its vast military bases in Kuwait, Qatar and Bahrain while reducing its presence in Syria and Iraq. Russia has increased its presence and activities. Western – especially American – dependence on oil from the region has decreased. While the Asian need for oil is growing and especially China is increasing its trade, investment and presence in the region. The great powers are not in confrontation modes in the region and long-term it should lose some of its importance as the world turns to non-hydrocarbon energies and threats to Israel are gone.

SADDAM HUSSEIN'S WAR ON IRAN IN 1980 AND KUWAIT IN 1990: THE 1991 GULF WAR AND THE 2003 IRAQ WAR

Saddam Hussein's attempts to expand the territory of Iraq led to many years of war. His effort to grab land from Iran at a moment in 1980, when after a convulsive revolution the country seemed weak, resulted in nearly a decade of gruesome warfare. His brutal occupation of Kuwait to gain financial resources and regain land that had once been part of Iraq was stopped in 1991 by a collective military intervention that was authorised by the UN Security Council (with Russia supporting, China abstaining and Cuba and Yemen voting against) and led by the United States. Saddam's armed adventurism abroad and reign of terror at home were eventually finished by the armed intervention and occupation that the United States and allied states launched in 2003 without UN authorisation.

Saddam's motives for going to war in 1990 appear to have been in large measure an old-fashioned ambition for the aggrandizement of his country and his own power, a conviction of the historical rights of Iraq and a wish to grab Kuwaiti financial resources. The US initiative under President Bush (the elder) to launch a UN-authorised armed action in 1991 (the 'Gulf War') may have been prompted by several factors but first of all a determination to prevent Saddam from grabbing land in Saudi Arabia.[16]

What motivated the United States, the United Kingdom, and allied states to undertake armed action in 2003 (the 'Iraq War') is less clear. The most often stated aim – undoubtedly expected easiest to find public acceptance – was to eliminate an allegedly existing threat of weapons of mass destruction. Was there an ambition in the US and UK governments to act as good self-appointed world sheriffs to eliminate a second part of an 'axis of evil' (after Afghanistan and before Iran) and help establish democracy? Perhaps the most likely dominant US aim was to finally bring about a regime change that for years had been on Washington's agenda? A regime that long had defied US hegemony in the region?

It is noteworthy that in an interview in the journal *Vanity Fair* on 9 May 2003 – then – US Deputy Secretary of Defence, Paul Wolfowitz, said that 'we settled on the one issue that everyone [in the US government bureaucracy] could agree on, which was weapons of mass destruction as the core reason…' He noted also that one 'unnoticed' but 'huge' point was that the war in Iraq had enabled the United States to 'remove almost all our forces from Saudi Arabia … Their presence there over the last 12 years has been a source of enormous difficulty'.[17] Despite Russian opposition to the war, it cannot be said that the action was in any way part of a power struggle between East and West.

Whatever the deeper motives the almost unanimous assessment has been that the armed action without UN authorisation was a grave and costly mistake

---

[16] No evidence has been found that Saddam had any such intention. See Sjöberg (2006), pp. 274 ff.
[17] A full transcript is available at www.sscnet.ucla.edu/polisci/faculty/trachtenberg/useur/wolfowitztanenhaus.html. Also see Chapter 13, p. 201.

that replaced tyranny by anarchy. The action added doubts about the possibility of building democratic orders through unilateral military intervention in a country without any previous democratic experience.[18]

ISIS (THE ISLAMIC STATE OF IRAQ AND SYRIA)

Significant numbers of Iraqi Sunni military personnel who were disbanded by the US occupation force in 2003 became a part of a new armed force – the extremist Islamic State (ISIS or DAESH).[19] They saw themselves as a religious movement seeking to transform Syria, Iraq and other areas into parts of a Caliphate ruled in accordance with extremist readings of the Koran. It perceived itself as taking revenge for the humiliations that the Muslim world had suffered. They soon became notorious for their fanaticism and total brutality and succeeded in rousing all to action. Condemned by the Security Council, they got not only their host countries Iraq and Syria against themselves but also states that did not otherwise fight side by side. The United States and Western states, Russia and Iran joined in the operations that have defeated their main cadre but led remnants of the movement to continue as terrorists spread in Africa and Afghanistan.

IRAN

After many years of negotiations between Iran and the five permanent members of the Security Council plus Germany and the EU a 'Joint Comprehensive Plan of Action (JCPOA)' was jointly drafted in the summer of 2015. It was designed on the one hand to limit the Iranian nuclear activities to what was strictly needed for a peaceful programme and to remove fears that Iran would make a nuclear weapon and on the other hand to commit states to lift any sanctions that they had on Iran. The action plan became an authoritative instrument when it was unanimously endorsed by the Security Council.[20] Later – in 2018 – the US Trump Administration and the government of Israel, both opposed to the deal, sought to wreck it. Flatly ignoring the Security Council resolution, the United States imposed maximum economic sanctions on Iran and brought pressure on all states to stop all imports of oil from Iran. Using its financial and economic power over corporations around the

---

[18] See also Chapter 13, p. 202.
[19] See https://ucdp.uu.se/actor/234.
[20] S/RES/2231 (2015). On implementation, see Erästö (2021). For more discussion of the JCPOA see also Chapter 10, p. 166 and Chapter 4, p. 73.

world the US managed to stop a major part of Iran's oil export. Further, several Iranian nuclear experts, including senior scientist Dr Mohsen Fakhrizadeh, were assassinated and the possibility of an armed attack on Iran was frequently talked about by Israeli leaders. Large US forces – including aircraft carriers and heavy B-52 bombers – were deployed to the Gulf from time to time. With the Biden administration taking over in the United States in January 2021, the possibility of a US armed attack on Iran seemed to recede and drawn-out talks have taken place about the revival of the joint plan of action. Even by November 2022, these talks, undertaken through the EU had not, however, brought full agreement and it was made clear from the US side that it might resort to force to ensure that Iran could not make nuclear weapons. Although there have been some contacts between Iran and Arab states (end of 2021 and in 2022), Israel has remained highly critical of any conciliation and subversive activities have remained.

THE CIVIL WAR IN SYRIA (2011–2021)

The Syrian civil war will be discussed below in Chapter 12 to illustrate the difficult application of the rule of non-intervention.[21] In the present context, the focus is on the diverse political aims that collided. Like other 'Arab spring' uprisings, the conflict within Syria had its roots in non-violent demands (in 2011) for more democracy. However, in the case of Syria, the international insertion of weapons, money, military advisers, and combatants from the out-side soon transformed the civil war into an armed conflict in which a number of governments were engaged in Syrian and Iraqi territory.

Adherence to the Sunni or Shia branch of Islam, to other religious groups or to the Kurdish nation became important factors. Despite the importance attributed to the religious adherence of different belligerent parties the con-flict in Syria – drawing to an end in 2021 – may have been driven less by reli-gion than by concerns about regional influence. None of the actors – except ISIS (DAESH) and Turkey – appears to have been motivated by a wish to modify borders or to grab territory. However, a wide variety of other motives can be identified:

Saudi Arabia and Gulf states have feared an increasingly dynamic Syria-Iran-Iraq Shia alliance. Iran has feared losing friends in Damascus and land access to its ally the Hezbollah movement in Lebanon. Turkey has feared unity among Kurds across borders. The United States has been motivated

---

[21] For a short and compact overview of the key moments and key international actors, see www
.cfr.org/article/syrias-civil-war.

by a wish to see the dictatorial Syrian regime replaced by a representative inclusive government ready to improve relations with the US and Israel. Russia has feared losing a naval base on the Syrian Mediterranean coast and the Syrian government as a friend and longstanding partner. Israel, which has routinely sent its air force to bomb Iranian and Hezbollah targets anywhere in Syria, has above all wanted to counter Iranian military presence in Syria and the ability to transfer arms to Hezbollah in Lebanon. While Russia and the US in part have competing agendas and interests in the Syrian conflict, they have also had some common interests – in particular defeating ISIS (DAESH) and avoiding any armed clash between themselves.

THE WAR IN YEMEN (2015–PRESENT)

While the gruesome civil war in Syria and the heavy foreign interventions in it have attracted much international attention, another long-lasting civil war has been raging less visibly in the poorest country of the region – Yemen.[22] The recognised government has exiled itself to Saudi Arabia that together with the UAE has intervened notably by large-scale bombing in Yemen. The larger part of the land, including the capital, Sanaa, has been controlled by the Houthi rebels who receive support from Iran. Although the United States, especially under the Trump administration, provided extensive assistance with weapons and intelligence to the Saudi intervention, it may have largely avoided intervention on the ground and gradually come to encourage a settlement. As in Syria, the civil war in Yemen is in essence local but through the large-scale Saudi armed intervention and the Iranian support for the Houthis, it has become part of the regional Saudi-Iran competition. Although the US Trump administration had been an ally of Saudi Arabia against Iran, while Russia is close to Iran, the war in Yemen is hardly part of a larger great power struggle.

AFGHANISTAN

Next door to the armed conflicts in the Middle East, international and civil war has raged in Afghanistan almost continuously since Russia invaded the country in 1979.[23] The modification of borders and the acquisition of land have not

---

[22]   For a broad overview of the general conflict, involved actors, humanitarian costs, see www.cfr
      .org/global-conflict-tracker/conflict/yemen war-.

[23]   For a recent monograph on the subject, see Malkasian (2021).

been the motives of any of the foreign participants in this tragedy. The Soviet intervention in 1979 sought to prop up a pro-Russian government, while other states' later clandestine intervention – including US support for them – by arms and fighters aimed at and succeeded in eliminating the Soviet domination. Competition and conflict among clans and warlords was a constant element eventually giving way to the Taliban movement taking control in 1996.

Following the 9/11 2001 attacks on New York and Washington, the US with a green light from the UN Security Council and with wide approval in the world launched and led an armed attack that toppled the Taliban government that had hosted the terrorist movement responsible for the attack – Al Qaeda. For the US, what began as a punitive campaign turned into an outside intervention in Afghan civil war and the longest-ever US overseas military operation (from 2001 to 2021 compared to the US Vietnam engagement of 8 years, from 1965 to 1973). As time passed additional rationales were perceived for US armed action in Afghanistan, notably that of promoting a modern social order, including the emancipation of women.

For an outside military force to take on the role of pacifying a divided country and engage in 'nation building' proved frustrating and fruitless. For the United States, the armed engagements in Afghanistan (against the Taliban), Iraq (against Saddam Hussein) and Syria (against Assad and DAESH) have meant maintaining troops for combat abroad over long periods and at high costs in lives and resources without any sure final gains. The engagements – certainly the crushing of the Taliban government after the 9/11 attacks on the United States –may have had the support of the US public but keeping boots on the ground in distant places and for long has not on the whole been welcome to the general US public.

For Russia, with a large population of Muslims, a rationale for its remarkable support of the US intervention to topple the Taliban was the risk that an extreme brand of Islam might spread its contagion to Russia.

For Pakistan, the need for good relations with the US has required support for American action. However, at the same time personal and political bonds between groups in Pakistan and the Afghan Taliban have made loyal cooperation with the United States difficult.

At the end of August 2021, all American troops left Afghanistan and the Taliban took over a devastated country, cut off from financial sources that came with a US presence. Moreover, unless it softens the rigid Muslim policies it displayed before being ousted by the US, it will have a sizeable part of the Afghan population against itself and difficulties in obtaining economic assistance from abroad. It may have a grave problem pacifying the country and defeating groups of ISIS that have infiltrated.

ASIA AND THE PACIFIC REGION

In the Asian and Pacific regions, huge areas have experienced little or no interstate armed conflicts in the period under review, but some of the most intractable tensions and large-scale and persistent armed conflicts are also found within this region of the world. It is, of course, of the greatest importance that two of the biggest states in the region – China and Russia – with long borders that were once in dispute, have been able to live side by side peacefully and almost without incidents since World War II, regardless of what governments have been in control.[24]

The borders between China and India, on the other hand, have seen several armed conflicts – war in the 1960s and limited confrontations in 2020.[25] The borders run at high altitudes in sparsely populated land in the Himalayas. Both parties are conscious of their great power status and their nuclear capacities (China since 1964, India since 1974). They are anxious to avoid drifting into a major armed confrontation. Yet, there are clear risks that their overall competition in Southeast Asia may increase and it is obvious that for quite some time the United States has sought to add India to its side in its 'pivot' against growing China. What has appeared like minor traditional controversies between India and China about border lines in 2020 has the potential – if not wisely handled – to develop into something dangerous.

Sharp frictions also arose in 2020 between the US and China flowing from Beijing's claim to and US relations with Taiwan and from Beijing's claim to islands in the South China Sea and US asserting the right to free navigation in the area.[26] Coming on top of a US-China trade war and a naval arms race in the Pacific area these frictions have an ominous potential for conflict.

In response to China's growing economic and military presence in the region, the United States in 2007 created the 'Quadrilateral Security Dialogue' (QUAD) for military, diplomatic and economic cooperation among the United States, Japan, Australia and India. More recently (2021), the AUKUS (Australia/United Kingdom/United States) deal has been reached in which the United States and the United Kingdom agreed to assist Australia in acquiring nuclear-powered submarines among other advanced military technologies. China has strongly opposed both initiatives.[27]

---

[24] On the clashes at the Ussuri border river in 1969, see below, Chapter 4, p. 61.
[25] A short overview can be found, for example, in Davis (2021a).
[26] See below, Chapter 3, p. 51 and Chapter 4, p. 58.
[27] See 'The Quad in the Indo-Pacific: What to Know', Council on Foreign Relations 'In Brief', 27 May 2021, www.cfr.org/in-brief/quad-indo-pacific-what-know?amp; and 'Australia's

Cooperation in international frameworks, such as the BRICS group (Brazil, Russia, India, China and South Africa), the Shanghai Cooperation Organization and the Russian-initiated Eurasian Economic Union, while hardly making the Asian parties close allies, may develop a certain sense of solidarity within the group and against the Western industrialised nations with which they seek to catch up.

INDIA AND PAKISTAN

Several wars have been fought between India and Pakistan over the border between them in Kashmir (1965 and 1971 and 1999).[28]

India also intervened with arms when Bangladesh separated from Pakistan. The countries are engaged in a nuclear arms race. It is a classic case of controversy about borders and territory but also about the standing of the two big countries in Asia. The potential risks of a bilateral conflict between the two nuclear-armed states are compounded by the support given to the two by outside powers, given to Pakistan by China and the closer relations between India and the United States. The potential conflict is thus not only between India and Pakistan about land and a border but also one between China linked with Pakistan and US linked with India. The awareness of all parties of the risk that any live conflict could escalate to nuclear war may be assumed to have a restraining effect.

CENTRAL ASIA, SOUTH ASIA AND SOUTH OF ASIA

In central Asia, several of the states that became independent when the Soviet Union broke apart lack stability, but apart from the conflict between Armenia and Azerbaijan, armed actions have not occurred between them.[29] The area of Nagorno-Karabakh with the Armenian population located as an enclave within Azerbaijan has caused several armed conflicts. The latest of these ended in 2020 through Russian mediation with some losses of land for Armenia and with Russia providing some peacekeeping units to supervise the full implementation of the agreement. While Turkey actively helped Azerbaijan great powers did not engage in the conflict.

Aukus Nuclear Submarines Could Cost as much as $17 bn, Report Finds'. *The Guardian*, 13 December 2021, https://amp.theguardian.com/world/2021/dec/14/australias-aukus-nuclear-submarines-estimated-to-cost-at-least-70bn.

[28] See Davis (2021a), pp. 95–109.

[29] See Davis (2021b), pp. 127–132.

Under the surface, rivalries about influence in central Asia exist between Russia, the United States, the EU, China, Iran and Turkey. From time to time, they come to the fore not in armed confrontations but in controversies, for instance about the location of pipelines for oil and gas or concerns about the huge Chinese Belt and Road project.[30] Remarkably, relations have remained fairly smooth between Iran and Turkey despite big internal changes in both countries and divergent interests in the Syrian conflict.

Regional cooperation increased in 2006 when the five Central Asian states signed a treaty creating a nuclear-weapon-free zone, the first such zone established north of the Equator.[31]

To the south of the Asian continent, the region including Australia and New Zealand has remained free from interstate armed conflicts, with some exceptions – for instance Indonesia's invasion of East Timor in 1975. Serious non-international armed conflicts have taken place inside many states – Cambodia, Indonesia, Malaysia and Pakistan (with Indian intervention at the emergence of Bangladesh), Sri Lanka and the Philippines.

EAST ASIA

The Korean War of 1950 and the Vietnam War of 1965 were perceived and pursued by the United States and the West as part of the struggle with an expanding Communist world during the Cold War. They will therefore be discussed in the next chapter. The post–Cold War questions relating to Korea, Taiwan and the islands in the Pacific, are all affected by the new phase of tensions arising from the increased power of China and growing tension with the United States. They are therefore also discussed in the next chapter.

---

[30] A short overview can be found at www.cfr.org/backgrounder/chinas-massive-belt-and-road-initiative.
[31] Further information is available at https://treaties.unoda.org/t/canwfz.

3

Interstate Uses of Force, Tensions and Restraints during Major Phases of International Relations since World War II

Chapter 2 provided a survey of post–World War II interstate uses of force and tensions by continents and regions. It noted the presence and impact of great powers in many conflicts and also that these powers avoided being drawn into direct armed conflicts between themselves. This chapter will survey the direct and indirect struggles that have been waged between them and that have shaped the main successive phases of global political relations after World War II – the bipolar US-Soviet Cold War, the détente period, the US unipolar world, and now (2022) a world of tensions that have emerged.

World War II was the first truly global war, but in several respects, it was of a traditional kind. Germany's incentive – its aim and driving force – was to acquire land (Lebensraum) and to rule ('*Deutschland über alles*'). Armies fought each other on the ground. Land was conquered and occupation regimes and vassal rulers were installed. There was further an exceptionalist credo that the German people (the '*Herrenvolk*') should rule and a racist programme that led to the extermination of millions of Jews and other people. Major air wars and missiles were new ingredients. With the Cold War that began right after the end of WWII, the spread of the Communist ideology and state models became a global driving factor, and with nuclear weapons and missiles in the hands of a few powers the risks of conflicts and the character of warfare changed.

THE COLD WAR (1945–1990)

With Germany defeated, the Soviet Union used its power as a victor and occupying state to annex territory in some regions, notably the Baltic states, and seizing large areas of Poland, but mostly expanded its control through the creation of puppet governments in states that became satellites. The aim was to expand the power and military control of Russia and extend globally the reach of the Soviet Communist ideology and social, economic and political system. Where this was not possible to achieve through normal political competition, and where the Soviet Union could not act under its own umbrella as occupation power, such an extension was sought through subversion and with the help of Communist parties and sympathisers while open and direct armed Soviet action was avoided.

As the United States and the West woke up to resist Soviet expansionism the Cold War began – and lasted until the break-up of the Soviet Union some 45 years later. Throughout this long period of East-West bipolarity, there was strong ideological and military tension between market economy countries led by the United States and a Communist world that comprised the Soviet Union and its European satellites, North Korea and China.

Resistance to the Soviet aim for global expansion was led by the United States and eschewed direct armed actions. The first response came in 1947 in the so-called Truman doctrine that was developed to help Greece defeat a Communist insurgency but was given the wider bearing to help any state threatened by Communist expansion. Another response came in the shape of the Marshall Plan (1948), which strengthened the economic health of war-ravaged European states. Yet another response came after the 1948 Communist coup in Czechoslovakia: In 1949, NATO (North Atlantic Treaty Organization), was established as a military alliance for collective self-defence to create a disincentive to any attempt by the Soviet Union to expand the Communist-ruled world by direct aggression in Europe.

The Berlin blockade took place in 1948–49. The Soviet Union closed land access to the Western zones of occupied West Berlin and sought to force the United States, the United Kingdom and France to abandon the city. As both sides wanted to avoid the active use of force a Western airlift to the city was possible and led the Soviet side to end the blockade.

The strategy of defence developed in the West against the Communist expansion was termed the 'policy of containment'. As the term suggests, it did not seek a push-back by arms or other means but aimed rather at everywhere firmly holding the Communist world, notably the Soviet Union, back and waiting for it to change internally. In the period 1989–91, when the Soviet Union and the Communist Party dissolved, the calculation behind the policy of containment proved right: a 'rolling back' of Communist rule by armed force was unnecessary. The Communist rule and creed eroded from the inside

THE KOREAN WAR 1950

Early during the Cold War and with blessings – but not help –from Stalin, North Korea led by President Kim Il Sung launched a war on South Korea in 1950. The aim was not just to remove a border or to conquer territory. It was also to unite the whole peninsula under a Communist political and social order. The attack was reported by official UN observers on site and triggered a massive armed international response led by the United States that was determined to stop what it saw as an attempt by the Communist world to expand. A recommendation adopted by the Security Council in the absence of the Soviet Union placed the action under the UN flag and brought participation from many member states.[1]

As the UN forces successfully moved North closer to the Yalu River that forms the border with China, an army of Chinese 'volunteers' became a new factor. The use of nuclear weapons was considered repeatedly and supported by many in the US military leadership. However, it was concluded that use would be inappropriate except under the most compelling military circumstances.[2] While the hostilities were very costly in lives, the state of war between the United States and China was somewhat blurred through the official status given to the forces: those under US command were formally UN troops and the army under China's command was – improbably – described as 'volunteers'. Nevertheless, China's action was condemned by the UN General Assembly.[3] In 1953, after some five million casualties, the war ended with an armistice that divided the peninsula along the 38th parallel. The Korean War served as a sharp signal that the United States and the 'free world' would resist Communist armed attempts at expansion anywhere.

Defeated during the Cold War in the 1950s North Korea came back as a potential threat some fifty years later – now with nuclear weapons capacity. While it had been plausible to view the war in the 1950s as a push by world communism, North Korea now was more like a troublesome stepchild to China and Russia. The new situation will be described below.[4]

THE VIETNAM WAR 1965–1973

The decades–long-armed struggle in Vietnam started in 1946 by the Communist leader Ho Chi Min as a war of 'national liberation' from French colonial rule. It went on until 1954, when France was defeated at Dien Bien Phu and the country was divided at the 17th parallel. In the 1950s, dominant United States and Western Cold War thinking held that a united Communist world aimed at expansion wherever it could – the Korean War in 1950 being seen as one instance – and had to be contained at all fronts. In a speech in 1954, President Eisenhower articulated the 'domino theory', suggesting that a defeat for France

[1] See Chapter 13, p. 201.
[2] See Tannenwald, *The Nuclear Taboo* (2007), pp. 117–122.
[3] A/RES/498 (V) on 1 February 1951.
[4] See, this Chapter, p. 35.

would be like one falling brick in the wall of a domino play, leading to the fall one by one of the nearest bricks – Thailand, Burma, etc. The US pursuit of the war in Vietnam from 1965 led to defeat in 1973 and to a collapse of the domino theory. While the United States aim was never to acquire territory, its incentive for the long-armed action had been based on a misinterpretation of the motive of the North, which was national self-determination for a unified Vietnam rather than an expansion of international Communism.

INTERVENTIONS DURING THE COLD WAR

Moscow used its armed presence in Eastern Europe not only to establish Communist rule in satellite states but also to uphold this rule through armed interventions. It was done in the case of the 1956 Hungarian uprising and the case of the suppression of the 'Prague spring' in Czechoslovakia in 1968. It evolved into the 'Brezhnev doctrine' that Socialist states will not allow 'encroachments' on the border of 'the socialist commonwealth' – it was a duty to assist Socialist states to defend their system, if need be by armed force.[5]

As the nuclear-armed Soviet Union and the United States were anxious not to meet in open armed conflicts their competition for influence and control often took place through actions and activities that involved subversion and a limited use of weapons but with no aim to acquire territory.

In the era of the Cold War, several armed interventions were launched by the United States to prevent states in the Caribbean and in Central America to become led by regimes believed to be pro-Communist. It may suffice in this context to name only a few. The Bay of Pigs operation in Cuba in 1961 was an attempted direct armed invasion aimed at toppling Fidel Castro's Communist rule. While supported by the United States through the CIA, the invading group consisted of Cuban exiles and could formally – but again not very convincingly – be denied to be a US force attacking an ally of the Soviet Union. Other Cold War US interventions took place, for instance, in the Dominican Republic in 1965 and Nicaragua in the 1980s. How they were justified by the United States and judged by the UN will be described in the chapters below.

The United States and other Western interventions during the Cold War were not about conquering land or re-establishing colonial rule. Using many different means – military force, economics, propaganda, clandestine operations – the ambition was rather to help restore public order, to maintain influence and to prevent inroads by Communist groups.

---

[5] See Ouimet, M., *The Rise and Fall of the Brezhnev Doctrine in Soviet Foreign Policy* and see Chapter 4, p. 76.

CUBAN MISSILE CRISIS 1962

While the United States and the Soviet Union consistently avoided direct armed confrontations during the Cold War, they came perilously close to armed conflict during the 1962 Cuban missile crisis.

Realising during that crisis that any firing of weapons could escalate to an uncontrollable nuclear duel with catastrophic global consequences, President Kennedy and Chairman Khrushchev shied away from the actual use of any weapons. Using the diplomatic channel, they developed a solution comprising a Soviet withdrawal of missiles and nuclear weapons from Cuba and a US commitment not to attack Cuba and to withdraw missiles from Turkey.[6]

The Cuban crisis was a scary experience of how close the world could come to a nuclear Armageddon. This shock and understanding helped to bring about the conclusion in 1963 of the Partial Test Ban Treaty and of the Nuclear Non-Proliferation Treaty (NPT) in 1968.[7] Neither treaty prevented the nuclear-weapon states from continuing their development of nuclear weapons but the treaty banning tests in the atmosphere was important to prevent further radioactive pollution. While under the NPT all parties committed themselves to efforts at nuclear (and general) disarmament, it is questionable whether there was much sincerity behind the nuclear-weapon states' promise to seek to reduce their nuclear armaments.

What is clear is that the states possessing nuclear weapons – notably the United States and the Soviet Union that had faced each other eye to eye in the Cuban conflict – shared a concern that the world would become even more dangerous and volatile if more states were to acquire nuclear weapons. The political lesson of the Cuban crisis was later (1985) captured in the famous phrase agreed by President Reagan and President Gorbachev that 'a nuclear war cannot be won and must never be fought'.[8] It was reported that the US Trump administration opposed confirmation of this statement in conclusions proposed for the NPT Review conference that was scheduled for 2020. However, it was reaffirmed by US President Biden and Russian President Putin at their meeting in Geneva in 2021.[9] And on 3 January 2022, the five nuclear-weapon states parties to the NPT (the United States, the United Kingdom, France, China and Russia) meeting to prepare joint

---

[6]   See Chapters 4, p. 67 and 10, p. 165.

[7]   See Chapter 9, p. 147.

[8]   Geneva summit joint statement, 21 November 1985, www.reaganlibrary.gov/archives/speech/joint-soviet-united-states-statement-summit-meeting-geneva.

[9]   US-Russia Presidential Joint Statement on Strategic Stability, 16 June 2021, www.whitehouse.gov/briefing-room/statements-releases/20.

positions at the forthcoming NPT Review conference issued a statement jointly affirming this conclusion.[10]

DECLARATIONS OF NORMS GOVERNING RELATIONS DURING THE COLD WAR

The tense East-West relations during the Cold War stimulated efforts to develop some kind of 'code of conduct' to make it possible for states of different economic and political systems to live side by side without conflict. An early list of principles was adopted in 1955 in the so-called Bandung declaration by many Asian and African states that did not want to 'align' themselves with either side in the Cold War.[11] While the Communist bloc gladly saw the anti-colonial group distance itself from the Western industrial states, the latter looked with suspicion at proposals to codify rules of 'peaceful co-existence'. Arguing that such rules existed in the Charter, the West agreed only to examine a number of central rules that were embedded in the UN Charter and governed all state relations.

Under a title that borrowed terms from the Charter's Art. 1:2 – 'Principles of International Law concerning Friendly Relations and Cooperation among States in accordance with the Charter of the United Nation' – these rules were examined in the light of how they had been understood and applied by the UN. After years of work by a Commission of government representatives, the legal analysis and discussion resulted in the so-called 'Friendly Relations Declaration' that the General Assembly adopted in 1970.[12] The author of this book represented Sweden at all sessions of the Commission and served as the 'rapporteur' of its first session. As the declaration was adopted by unanimity, its clarifications and amplifications of central UN Charter rules – notably those concerning the use of force and intervention – have been seen as authoritative.

If Western states had been somewhat reluctant to engage in the 'Friendly Relations' project, it was more positive to work out a similar catalogue of 'principles guiding relations between states in Europe' in 1975. The Declaration adopted by the Helsinki Conference on Security and Cooperation in Europe echoed rather closely both the UN Charter and the Friendly Relations text. However, through a selection of principles amplified and their formulation, it

---

[10] 'Joint Statement of the Leaders of the Five Nuclear-Weapon States on Preventing Nuclear War and Avoiding Arms Races' (Washington, DC: The White House, 3 January 2022), www.whitehouse.gov/briefing-room/statements-releases/2022/01/03/p5-statement-on-preventing-nuclear-war-and-avoiding-arms-races/.

[11] Final Communiqué of the Asian-African conference of Bandung (24 April 1955).

[12] A/RES/2625 (XXV), 24 October 1970.

was designed to confirm – to the satisfaction of the Soviet Union – that existing borders (especially in Europe) were inviolable and – to the satisfaction of the West – that all states' respect for human rights was a legitimate concern.[13]

THE DÉTENTE OF THE 1990s: THE UNITED STATES AS SOLE MILITARY SUPERPOWER

With the break-up of the Soviet Union, the collapse of Soviet Communism, and the dissolution of the Soviet bloc, there was no longer an ambition in Moscow to spread the Communist economic and political system to others. The military power to back up such policy also rapidly eroded. This ended the Cold War and its potential to erupt into armed conflicts. Perhaps the most remarkable feature was the absence of any attempt forcibly to prevent the liberation of the states that had been under Soviet control, including the let-go of Eastern Germany. A new phase began characterised by détente, disarmament – and the overwhelming global military superiority of the United States.

Very visible evidence of the changed political climate were the agreements achieved in 1990 and 1991 in the Security Council to authorise armed collective action led by the United States to reverse the Iraqi occupation of Kuwait.[14] The new cooperative relations between the permanent members of the Security Council made it possible for the Council to authorise action with the force that the authors of the UN Charter had originally intended. Although the Security Council had little control except authorising the action that did not even fly a UN flag but was practically 'delegated' to the United States, President Bush the elder, spoke of it as a 'new international order'.[15]

With the détente, many of the Cold War tensions and low-intensity proxy wars and conflicts that had simmered in various parts of the world (for instance in Angola and Central America) dissipated and cooperation became possible. A reduction began in the huge arsenals of nuclear arms in Russia and the United States. The numbers shrank rapidly from the Cold War peak of around 70,000 warheads in 1986 to an estimated 13,000 in 2021.[16] Conventional arms, too, were much reduced in NATO-Europe and Warsaw Pact-Europe and mutual openness was increased. For several European states, the mission of their military forces was no longer territorial defence but rather availability for international peacekeeping or peace enforcing missions.

---

[13] See Blix, article in the *Egyptian Journal of International Law*, vol. 31 (1975) and see Chapter 12, p. 190.

[14] See Chapter 2, p. 24 and Chapter 13, p. 201.

[15] Sjöberg (2006), p. 306.

[16] Federation of American Scientists, 'Status of World Nuclear Forces', 2021. https://fas.org/issues/nuclear-weapons/status-world-nuclear-forces/.

The new climate yielded a rich crop of important agreements in the fields of arms control and disarmament. Examples are the European Treaty on conventional armed forces in Europe (the CFE convention) in 1992, the Chemical Weapons Convention in 1993, the decision in 1995 to give the Non-Proliferation Treaty unlimited duration, and the adoption in 1996 of the Comprehensive Nuclear-Test-Ban Treaty.[17]

THE PHASE OF DÉTENTE IN REVERSE FROM 1996

Despite continued cooperation between the permanent members of the Security Council in the 1990s allowing the launching of many UN peacekeeping operations, the world political climate deteriorated. The US military superiority was accentuated by the erosion of the Russian military power. As of the middle of the 1990s, the Conference of Disarmament (CD), the central global negotiating body for arms control and disarmament, became unable to agree even on a work programme, contributing to and demonstrating the new immobility in the field of disarmament. Even in 2022, the CD remained in a coma.

In 1998 civil war broke out in – and broke up – former Yugoslavia. It has been described above[18] how it came to involve United Nations, the United States and NATO-led operations, action by the OSCE (Organization for Security and Cooperation in Europe) and how Russian participation with armed forces on the ground was a high-water mark in Russian engagement in UN multi-national forces. Later, as the bombing was undertaken in Kosovo by NATO without Security Council endorsement, Russia complained that it had been ignored by the United States and the Western states.

In 1999 and 2004 NATO expanded. Former East European members of the Warsaw Pact as well as the Baltic states became members. Perhaps the driving force behind the expansion was fear among the new members for a Russian resurgence more than an ambition in the West to strengthen its camp. In any case, the new NATO members' change of sides led to bitterness in Moscow, where it was felt that the Soviet withdrawal from Eastern Europe had taken place with a concomitant Western (unwritten) commitment not to expand NATO.[19] How firm that commitment was has become hotly discussed.[20]

---

[17] See also below, Chapter 10, p. 157.
[18] See Chapter 2, p. 21.
[19] The matter has been extensively discussed. See, for instance, Trachtenberg (2020/2021), pp. 162–203.
[20] For a discussion of both sides of this debate, see Mike Eckel, 'Did the West Promise Moscow That NATO Would Not Expand? Well, It's Complicated', RadioFreeEurope/RadioLiberty, 19 May 2021, www.rferl.org/a/nato-expansion-russia-mislead/31263602.html.

Talks between the United States and Russia about further bilateral disarmament (START II) took place in Helsinki as late as 1999, but in the deteriorating climate, there were no results. In the same year, the US Senate voted to reject the US ratification of the Comprehensive Nuclear-Test-Ban Treaty – an action that has contributed to the treaty not coming into force even 20 years after it was signed.

The strong sense of US abundant military power was reflected in a document that was published by the US Department of Defence in May 2000 and that proclaimed the need for 'full spectrum dominance' on the battlefield.[21]

9/11 2001 AND THE ERA OF TERRORISM[22]

On 9/11 2001, civilian airplanes hijacked by members of the terrorist group Al Qaeda flew into the World Trade Centre in New York and the Pentagon in Washington killing thousands of people and evoking worldwide solidarity with the United States. In retaliation, and with a green light from the UN Security Council, the United States launched an armed intervention in Afghanistan leading to the toppling of the Taliban government that had hosted the Al Qaeda leadership. After some 20 years of war in which the United States was joined by NATO, foreign forces were withdrawn from engagement in Afghanistan in 2021. The victorious Taliban took over a country free from foreign forces but still torn by indigenous forces and groups belonging to the terrorist movement ISIS.

The 9/11 attack led to the US-declared 'war on terrorism' and a new assertiveness by the lone superpower. In language that suggested a new US readiness to act as a good world sheriff, 'the *US National Security Strategy* of 2002 declared that: 'The US national security strategy will be based on distinctly American internationalism that reflects the union of our values and our national interests. The aim of this strategy is to help make the world not just safer but better...'[23]

The subject of terrorism has remained high on the US agenda after the attack of Libya under Gaddafi on American targets in the 1980s and the attack by Al Qaeda on the US embassies in Nairobi and Dar Es Salaam in 1998.[24] This

---

[21] *Joint Vision 2020* (Washington, DC: US Department of Defense, June 2020), https://web .archive.org/web/20011130011718/http://www.dtic.mil/jv2020/jvpub2.htm.

[22] Cf. Chapter 1, p. 13 and extensively in Chapter 15, p. 224 ff.

[23] *The National Security Strategy of the United States of America* (Washington, DC: White House, September 2002), https://history.defense.gov/Portals/70/Documents/nss/nss2002.pdf?ver=oyVN99a EnrAWijAc_O5eiQ%3d%3d.

[24] See Chapter 15, p. 227.

has had great consequences in terms of the employment of new war methods, for instance, increased surveillance and the use of remote-controlled weapons (drones). Moreover, as terrorist organisations and their members can go anywhere to pursue or prepare armed actions, the United States as the state most targeted has felt a need to extend its responses to any area where the adversary may be found. Thus, US special forces have been inserted in several states in Africa and elsewhere. Such a deployment will normally take place with the consent of or at the request of host countries, but questions may arise about how widely a state – mostly the United States – subjected to or threatened by terrorist attacks can cast its net and who is considered a lawful target.[25]

In the years that have followed 9/11, a great many other terrorist attacks have taken place, most of them in the Middle East and Africa, but many also in major cities, such as London, Madrid, Paris and Istanbul. While we tend to lump together as 'terrorism' all armed violence that uses methods which ignore both the international laws of war and national law, the incentives driving 'terrorist' groups to use armed force are diverse. Thus, the rejection of demands for self-determination or for autonomy may sometimes trigger terrorism (as in the Basque region), but terrorism can also be in response to brutal oppression, or revenge for injustices. Terrorism may also be simply a method used to grab power, goods or other resources without any restraint flowing from respect for national or international law.

As terrorist groups usually direct their actions against established state orders, it is not surprising that governments – regardless of differences they may have – often show understanding for each other's anti-terrorist actions and agree ad hoc on cooperation as well as on conventions regarding common lines to take. The most conspicuous example of such joint action is the war that a large number of states – including the United States, Russia, Iran, Turkey and Arab states – waged against the Islamic State (ISIS or Daesh) on Syrian and Iraqi territory and in Africa.[26]

IRAQ WAR 2003

The attack on Iraq in March 2003 by the United States and a 'friendly alliance' of states and the incentives to it has been discussed above.[27] In this section, it need only be stressed that while the action was not caused or linked to

---

[25] The US action in 2011 to kill the Al Qaeda leader Osama Bin Laden on Pakistani territory raised questions of this kind. See below, Chapter 15, p. 232.

[26] 'The Global Coalition to Defeat ISIS', *Fact Sheet* (Washington, DC: US Department of State, 28 June 2021), www.state.gov/the-global-coalition-to-defeat-isis/.

[27] See Chapter 2, p. 18.

competition between major powers it was resented in particular by Russia as a case of US superpower arrogant unilateralism. It ignored the need for consent by the Security Council, including the need for consent by Russia.

Although the US superpower engagements in Afghanistan and occupied Iraq were not encouraging, President George W Bush in his second term (2004–2008) continued to place emphasis on the combatting of terrorism and on countering the risk of nuclear proliferation (with a focus on North Korea and Iran). Global US military presence and supremacy in all types of weapons, including those for space and cyber warfare, was maintained.

GEORGIA 2008

In 2008, immediately following a low-level attack by Georgia on the capital of the separate enclave of South Ossetia, Russia launched a large-scale armed invasion of Georgia. It came after years of tension during which Georgia modernised its armed forces with US assistance and sought NATO membership. Although the first shots were fired from the Georgian side the massive Russian armed intervention was clearly disproportionate and a breach of international law.[28]

After wide international criticism of its attack and appeals from the EU, Russia withdrew militarily from Georgia while engineering declarations of independence in the provinces of South Ossetia and Abkhazia. In practice, the provinces are under the control of Moscow. They have been recognised by very few states and remain 'frozen conflicts'.

The six months long Russian intervention in Georgia may have had the limited aim of demonstrating that Russia remained a great power to be treated with respect rather than an aim to re-establish control over a former part of the Soviet Union. Be that as it may, the armed action must be seen as a part of a larger competition between the Western transatlantic community (EU and NATO) and Russia. It raised some concern in the West about possible Russian revanchist intentions. At the same time, the NATO membership for Georgia, which was urged by the United States under President Bush and anathema to Russia, was put on ice.

THE OBAMA – MEDVEDEV INTERLUDE 2009

The US presidential election campaign in 2008 showed important differences in domestic US attitudes on foreign affairs. The Republican side was still

---

[28] See Berner (2029), pp. 237–263 and see Bildt (2022), pp. 286 ff. A detailed discussion of the case and the legal aspects is found below in Chapter 15, p. 219

eager to shoulder the role of world sheriff. In the view of Senator McCain all states that wanted to join NATO should be admitted provided they were democratic and willing to fulfil the conditions for membership. The attitude of the Democrats was far more cautious. After the end of the Bush era and the failure that the United States was widely perceived to have suffered in Iraq, many wanted to stay away from military adventures expensive in lives and budgets. Senator Obama (as he then was), who had voted in US Congress against authorising the Iraq War was, of course, well placed to meet the mood of the country. It was remarkable, however, that the Republican Presidential candidate, Senator McCain joined Senator Obama in favouring far-reaching disarmament.

In 2009 President Obama met in London with the President of Russia, Mr. Medvedev, and together they issued a declaration that was remarkably positive to détente/disarmament: the Cold War was declared definitively over and the two countries were now to embark on a joint course of disarmament – leading eventually even to a complete elimination of nuclear weapons. They immediately set in motion negotiations for a mutual reduction of nuclear weapons.[29]

A year later a new US-Russia START agreement (Strategic Arms Reduction Treaty) was signed that limited the number of deployed strategic nuclear weapons on each side to 1550. Other limitations had regard to delivery vehicles and a machinery of mutual verification was retained.

The negotiation had been remarkably swift, but the result met considerable resistance both in Moscow and Washington. In order to achieve approval of the START treaty by the US Senate President Obama had to go very far in committing to a costly modernisation of the US nuclear weapons sector.[30] In 2020, the Trump administration vacillated on a prolongation of the treaty and it would have expired in February 2021 had not President Biden who took office in January 2021 agreed with Russia on a prolongation.

OBAMA SHOWING MILITARY RESTRAINT

President Obama pursued several policy lines aiming at renewed détente and lowered military threat. In particular, the US nuclear posture review (2010)

---

[29] Joint Statement by Presidents Obama and Medvedev, 1 April 2009, https://obamawhitehouse
.archives.gov/the-press-office/joint-statement-president-dmitriy-medvedev-russian-federation-
and-president-barack-.

[30] See Tom Z. Collina, 'Senate Approves New START', *Arms Control Association* (blog), n.d.,
www.armscontrol.org/act/2011-01/senate-approves-new-start.; Brian P. McKeon, 'Recalling
the Senate Review of New START', *Arms Control Association* (blog), October 2019, www
.armscontrol.org/act/2019-10/features/recalling-senate-review-new-start.

was adjusted to stress that the use of nuclear weapons could only be contemplated in an extreme situation. (A similar line was subsequently taken in the corresponding Russian document.)

Other important steps were large withdrawals of US troops from Iraq beginning in 2007 and some from Afghanistan beginning in 2011.[31]

During the 'Arab spring' in Tunisia and Egypt in 2011, there was no foreign armed participation, and in the case of Libya, the United States limited its support for the 2011 NATO-led armed intervention in Libya to intelligence and logistics. Despite considerable domestic political pressure, the Obama administration refrained from armed attacks on Syria after chemical weapons had been used near Damascus in 2013.[32] It spent much effort and political capital to achieve a nuclear agreement with Iran and avoided being pressed to attack Iran on the basis of contentions that Iran was developing a nuclear weapon. While these policies showed restraint and a wish to avoid armed interventions, US action to deploy an anti-missile shield in Romania in 2016 and in Poland with the stated purpose of countering missiles from non-European bases – notably Iran and DPRK – led to tension with Russia.

THE WORLD IN THE SECOND DECADE
OF THE NEW MILLENNIUM

After the dissolution of the Soviet Union, the United States had become the lone superpower. Even though Russia had a Balancing nuclear weapons capacity the United States with an overwhelming military and economic power had felt freer to ignore Russian objections, notably in the cases of Kosovo (1999) and the invasion of Iraq (2003).

The US economic and military power remained formidable as the world entered the second decade of the new millennium, but as the economic power of many other countries, particularly China, had increased very fast the US power diminished – in relative terms. With the rise of China, the Republic of Korea, Indonesia, India, Iran, Turkey, Brazil and others a 'multipolar' world seemed to emerge.

Realising the increasing difficulty of maintaining predominant US influence in this changing world, President Obama had a further reason (beyond the wish to promote détente) to exercise military restraint and to give priority

---

[31] Iraq: 'Timeline: Invasion, surge, withdrawal; US forces in Iraq', *Reuters*, 16 December 2011, www.reuters.com/article/us-iraq-usa-pullout-idUSTRE7BH08E20111218; Afghanistan: www .cfr.org/timeline/us-war-afghanistan.

[32] Further comments are found in Chapter 16, p. 251 and Chapter 17, p. 263.

to areas and issues deemed to be of increasing importance to the United States. Thus, on the one hand, he continued the process that began under his predecessor to carefully watch China's growing strength and to strengthen the US influence and position in the fast developing Asian and Pacific regions (the pivot). On the other hand, he showed some restraint in US engagement in conflicts in the Middle East. He avoided intervening with boots on the ground to fight the Assad regime in Syria and lowered tension with Iran by allowing the United States to play a leading role in reaching a multilateral deal about Iran's nuclear programme.[33] These policies of restraint were pursued despite domestic political pressures for the United States to use its 'exceptionalism' and power to secure the success of regimes desirable from a US perspective.

THE UKRAINE CONFLICT (2014–PRESENT)[34]

The concern aroused in the West by the Russian intervention in Georgia in 2008 reappeared and was intensified following the Russian actions that began in 2014 in Ukraine. First, as briefly noted in the previous chapter, a barely veiled military occupation of the Crimean peninsula was followed by annexation, including notably the historical Russian naval base, Sevastopol. Second, an armed rebellion in several areas of East Ukraine was fomented by and actively assisted by Russia. The actions, which were evident violations of the rules of the UN Charter, the Helsinki Declaration and the Budapest Memorandum of 1994, were in no way provoked by any territorial move by Ukraine but rather by the ousting of a pro-Russian President and by the decision of the new government to proceed with the conclusion of an association agreement with EU.

Looked at in one way the conflict was the result of a collision between the efforts to link Ukraine (and several other states) economically and politically to the EU through the EU Eastern Partnership and the ambition of Russia to link the same countries to itself and the Eurasian Economic Union. However, beyond the failure to reconcile the two economic ties, there was a clash between a strong aspiration within Ukraine to transform the country into an independent Western-type democratic market economy and a Russian wish to see it remain militarily non-aligned (outside NATO) and to remain culturally, politically and economically closely tied to Russia. The Association Agreement with the EU comprises a provision that Ukraine will seek a gradual convergence of its foreign and security policies with those of EU (Art. 4). The

---

[33] On the JCPOA, see Chapter 2, p. 26 and Chapter 10, p. 166
[34] Cf. Chapter 7, p. 117.

commitment shows that the agreement is not simply about trade but also a part of a competition for influence between Russia and the transatlantic West.[35]

Diplomatic efforts were made to reduce the level of hostilities in the rebellious regions and observers from the Organization of Security and Cooperation in Europe (OSCE) played a role, but the conflict continued with thousands of casualties and significant areas and parts of the border with Russia remaining beyond the control of the Ukrainian government. Efforts made by Germany and France to find a peaceful solution, notably through the so-called Minsk Agreement, failed. Then, as noted in the preceding chapter, in 2021 sizeable Russian military forces that had for a long time been deployed on the border to Ukraine led to an acute fear of armed conflict. Russia denied having any intention to go to war and explained that every country has the right to deploy its military forces as it wishes within its own territory. It must be concluded, however, that the deployment and the campaign conducted amounted to a 'threat of force' prohibited under 2:4 of the UN Charter.

On 17 December 2021, Russia presented to the US and NATO allies a package of two draft agreements designed, in the view of Russia, to guarantee security in Europe. They provided commitments *inter alia* on the non-deployment of warships and aircraft to areas from where they could strike each other's territory, restrictions on Western military activity in Europe and a halt on the expansion of NATO in Europe. As could be expected, NATO dismissed the sweeping proposals for restraints on existing activities and the future scope of NATO but declared readiness to discuss less dramatic changes. In the public discussion in the West, the rejected proposals were often branded as a Russian abandonment of the 'rule-based international order'. Such language may be understood as a part of rejections of the general Russian posture. However, the Russian demands for limitations on the size of the NATO alliance and its deployment of forces looked more like a fanciful political wish list than the renunciation of a globally agreed order. Their presentation could not and did not affect the order valid within NATO.

In the face of the dramatically increased Russian threat in the months before the invasion in 2022, EU states and the United States warned Russia that going from threats to military action on Ukraine would be met by unparalleled economic sanctions. Ukraine, the Baltic states as well as Eastern European nations received increased military assistance and support from NATO and the United States. NATO naval exercises took place in the Baltic and the

---

[35] Text of Association Agreement: https://trade.ec.europa.eu/doclib/docs/2016/november/tradoc_155103.pdf; also see Jakob Tolstrup, *Russia vs. The EU: The Competition for Influence in Post-Soviet States* (Boulder, CO: Lynne Rienner, 2013) and Bildt (2022), pp. 394 ff.

Black Sea – even touching the territorial waters of Russian annexed Crimea.[36] While such military action and prodding occurred – with some risk of incidents – US President Biden stated explicitly that the United Sates would not intervene with American armed units in any active conflict, as a direct armed confrontation between the United States and Russia would mean a world war.

On 24 February 2022, Russia surprised the whole world with its armed invasion of Ukraine. The General Assembly of the United Nations condemned the action and demanded that Russia should immediately withdraw all its military forces.[37] While this did not happen, Ukraine vigorously and successfully defended itself. Western states supplied Ukraine with much military equipment and weapons but – to reduce the risk of a spread and an escalation of the war – followed the policy laid down by President Biden not to assist with forces on the ground or in the air.

Due to courageous and skilful Ukrainian defence, massive assistance from abroad, and poor Russian military performance, Russia was forced to reduce its ambitions. In September 2022 'denazification' and 'demilitarisation' of the whole of Ukraine seemed no longer to be the primary ambition. The aim appeared rather a consolidated control and an expansion of Ukrainian regions occupied by Russia. Sham referenda were arranged in the regions of Luhansk, Donetsk, Kherson and Zaporizhzhia – as once had been done in the Crimea – to demonstrate a popular will for adherence to Russia. Not surprisingly, President Putin declared Russia's readiness to accommodate this allegedly popular will, and the four regions signed treaties of accession to the Russian Federation.

At the same juncture, Russia declared a partial military mobilisation to allow the expansion of the occupation forces in Ukraine. It was also made clear that once the four territories were annexed any attack on them would – in the Russian view – constitute a violation of Russia's territorial integrity. Soldiers could be told that their fighting in the occupied territory would now be defence of Mother Russia. Moreover, as Russia's nuclear doctrine stipulates that nuclear weapons may be used 'when the very existence of the state is threatened',[38] any future attacks on newly annexed Russian land could be argued by Moscow to justify the use of nuclear weapons if it chose to determine that such attacks 'threatened the state'.

---

[36] See Trenin, Dmitri, 'Sailing into troubled waters. Russia counters Britain in the Black Sea' in Carnegie Moscow Center, 25 June 2021; and see 'HMS Defender: Russian jets and ships shadow British warship', BBC, 23 June 2021, www.bbc.com/news/world-europe-57583363.

[37] See A/RES/ES-11/1, 18 March 2022. See also the description of the intervention, below in Chapter 15, p. 224.

[38] See Chapter 8, p. 9.

The dramatic developments and declarations described increased the tensions between a humiliated and apparently shaken leadership of a nuclear-armed Russia and the West led by the US denouncing the annexations and not allowing itself to be intimidated by Russian talk about the possible use of nuclear weapons.[39] In a speech on 6 October, President Biden described the situation as the most dangerous since the Cuban missile crisis in 1962 and said that the world could face Armageddon if Russia were to use tactical nuclear weapons in order to win the war in Ukraine.[40] In December 2022 talk about nuclear use subsided somewhat and speculations about some cease-fires appeared in various Western states. However, it was clear that Moscow would contemplate a cease-fire only if the territory occupied by it would remain in its hands. Kiev, for its part, would think of a cease-fire only upon Russian retreat from all territory occupied by it – including the Crimea. Hence, there was no basis for cease-fire talks.

An end to the armed conflict fully respecting the 'rule based international order' – that is the rules of the UN Charter – can be reached only if all occupied territory is evacuated. Should an end to the armed actions be agreed even though some territory remains occupied, recognition will in all likelihood be denied any annexation or secession of such territory. Whatever the end will be of the Russian War against Ukraine, the judgement will remain that the action was an aberration in what the Indian Prime Minister Modi called an 'era not of war'.[41] The war was countered by Ukraine's self-defence supported by massive material and moral assistance and economic sanctions of a great many members of the world community – especially the United States.

Some have claimed that the Russian aggression in Ukraine has been a sign of an ambition to re-establish influence in the whole former Soviet sphere and that failing to stop it would encourage Russia to proceed. For instance, in a video appearance before the UN Security Council on 5 April 2022 Ukrainian President Zelensky said that 'Russia's leadership feels like colonisers – as in ancient times'. However, others may see behind the Russian conduct a view that Ukraine as an outlying part of the old Russian empire

---

[39] On 3 October 2022, the lower house of the Russian Duma endorsed the annexation of the four partially occupied regions of Ukraine. www.euronews.com/2022/10/03/russian-duma-confirms-annexation-of-four-ukrainian-regions.

[40] President Joseph Biden, Remarks at Democratic Senatorial Campaign Committee Reception, New York, 6 October 2022, www.whitehouse.gov/briefing-room/speeches-remarks/2022/10/06/remarks-by-president-biden-at-democratic-senatorial-campaign-committee-reception/. Also see Chapter 8, p. 137.

[41] See earlier discussion of the Modi statement in Chapter 1, p. 2.

must be stopped from drifting away from the Russian cultural, economic and political sphere – however unlikely war, killing and devastation are to achieve this. Whichever speculation is right we can be sure that the first down-to-earth strategic Russian aim has been to prevent Ukrainian NATO membership and the alliance's integrated military system to stretch up to Russia's borders.[42]

NORTH KOREA WITH NUCLEAR WEAPONS

After the Korean War in the 1950s, the two Korean states continued to develop radically different political, economic and social systems South Korea maintained its market economy, moved from dictatorship to democracy, and developed at an admirable pace. China came to combine political Communist state control with a fair degree of market economy and expanded economically at a phenomenal pace, North Korea continued to pursue a special brand of 'self-reliance' – '*juche*' – and stagnated under an apparent hereditary dictatorship. Nevertheless, it maintained its large military power and by the early 1990s, it was clearly working to create a nuclear weapon capacity. The United States sought to prevent this through diplomacy and détente but the efforts failed and in 2006 North Korea set off its first nuclear explosion initiating a new period of tension. The currently (2022) growing nuclear and missile capacity of the DPRK raises dangers for peace and complex security issues in the great power relations in East Asia. The North Korean weapon and missile capacity is perceived as a potential direct threat by South Korea and Japan and a more hypothetical threat by the United States. To China and Russia North Korea is rather like a troublesome stepchild but also a buffer to US-allied South Korea. The efforts to denuclearise North Korea are hampered by tensions between the great powers and their competition for influence and domination in the North-East corner of Asia.

After the failed personal Korean diplomacy of President Trump, a lull arose in the active US-DPRK relations. With further North Korean testing of missiles in 2022 and possible preparation of renewed nuclear tests tension has increased. However, while the United States, China and Russia all want a non-nuclear North Korea, serious differences between them prevent joint action. United States, Japan and South Korea see the North Korean regime as erratic and are nervous about nuclear-tipped missiles. The United States is deterred from taking unilateral preventive armed action, as this would raise the prospect of retaliation. China and Russia would both want North Korea

---

[42] See Gottemoeller (2022).

denuclearised but not through a collapse of the country. One risk arising from the continued nuclear and missile development that appears to be pursued in North Korea in 2022 is that Japan and South Korea might wish to develop nuclear weapons of their own. Were this to happen the situation would become drastically more tense. Defusing the risk of conflict calls for renewed diplomacy. Barring a collapse of the regime in North Korea the country is unlikely to abandon its nuclear capacity but for ironclad assurances – perhaps a regional security order – and much economic assistance. The regime is undoubtedly aware of the fate of the dictators of Libya and Iraq who were without nuclear weapons and it may ponder whether Ukraine would have been attacked by Russia had it not surrendered the nuclear weapons on its territory to Russia in the 1990s.

TAIWAN

Spurred by the conviction of historic rights and by national pride China demands that Taiwan should be reunited with the mainland. Its separation is seen as a result only of Chiang Kai-shek's retreat to the island after having lost the civil war on the mainland of China in 1949. For a long time, the US saw the Beijing claim as part of the Communist world expansion. In 1958, the US government under President Eisenhower was ready to go to war with China, and even the use of nuclear weapons was discussed to prevent Beijing from seizing Quemoy and Matsu, two minor islands that were – and remain – under Nationalist control very close to the Chinese coast.

Over time pragmatism has prevailed. Governments around the world have adopted a formal position that there is only one state of China – governed by Beijing. At the same time, the island remains a uniquely successful, self-governing, democratic unit firmly guarded by the United States. Verbal out-breaks occur at times. The practical cooperation between mainland China and Taiwan has given big economic dividends to both sides, leading to very high levels of trade, much Taiwanese investment in mainland China, and direct travel to and tourism in mainland China.[43]

Yet the underlying tension remains. China has increased its military presence near the island and in 2022, a visit to Taiwan by the Speaker of the US House of Representatives triggered Beijing to intense naval and air activities around Taiwan. The US government continues to express commitment to protect the island and its navy guards the Taiwan Strait.

[43] www.taiwan.gov.tw/content_6.php; and 'China Imports from Taiwan', *Trading Economics*, 2021, https://tradingeconomics.com/china/imports-from-taiwan.

With a few exceptions, Beijing blocks Taiwan from becoming a member of intergovernmental organisations or establishing normal diplomatic relations with other countries. The status of Taiwan has not – so far – caused any use of armed force but it constitutes a major item in the new era of tensions engaging the United States and China. It has been kept from boiling over as all are aware of the advantages of the restraint exercised and of the catastrophic consequences that would follow if any armed force were to be used between them. The government in Beijing is likely to watch how the Russian invasion of a big chunk of land claimed to be a part of its heritage is met and ends.

ISLANDS AND SHOALS

In the new era of tensions many smaller islands, some just shoals, are the subjects of claims by different states in the East and South China Sea. Mention was made of Quemoy and Matsu close to China's coast and nearly triggering war with the United States in 1958. The Kurile Islands that had belonged to Japan were occupied by the Soviet Union at the end of WWII. Although Japan has continued to press for their return on the basis of historic rights no threat or use of force has come to play. The result in the case of these significant islands is a 'frozen controversy'. The same is true for many other less well-known Northern islands claimed by Japan or South Korea or China.

The most serious controversies have regard to islands located in the East China Sea (The Senkaku island) and the South China Sea – such as the Spratlys – and engaging China, Japan, the United States, Vietnam, the Philippines and other states. Strong nationalist emotions to control territory – and sea – to which historical rights are perceived come into play and raise the level of controversy.

The Chinese statesman Deng Xiaoping, who led his country to its phenomenal economic progress, urged a focus on domestic development – 'peaceful rise' – and a low international profile. On the question of a number of islands, however, the profile has tended to be rather sharp. While agreeing that all controversies should be solved by peaceful means and pointing to negotiations being the proper method to use China has insisted that its rights to the islands in question are beyond questioning.

The US Obama administration urged that potential future frictions and controversies regarding islands and waterways should be referred to judicial arbitration. This method has a long history of success as regards disputed islands and does not cause loss of anybody's face. However, the first case brought by and won by the Philippines against China was brushed aside as irrelevant by China.[44] The assertiveness coupled with the use of physical means – naval patrolling, construction of artificial islands and preparation of air landing strips to cement its presence on various islands and shoals – have raised concern in the region about future neighbourly relations and an interest in balancing China's growing weight with a strong US naval presence.

The current situation contains risks of conflict and the use of force. It is not hard to see that the US 'pivot to Asia' – a shifting of priority strategic attention from the European and Russian spheres to Asia and the Pacific – takes place to meet China as a new fast developing potentially powerful competitor. As a policy of precaution, the United States is building up its Pacific fleet and seeking strategic partnerships with India and deeper ties with Australia through initiatives such as the QUAD and AUKUS, discussed in the preceding chapter. The political wish to create strong ties with democratic India prevailed over the long-standing US policy to withhold nuclear cooperation from all states that remained outside the Nuclear Non-Proliferation Treaty. The United States is also stationing troops at Darwin in Northern Australia, and maintaining close military links with Japan, Taiwan and South Korea. Future controversies may be nasty and could engage the United States and China and their allies in a wrestling match about domination.

---

[44] 'The South China Sea Arbitration', Permanent Court of Arbitration, 2016, https://pca-cpa.org/en/cases/7/.

4

Incentives to the Interstate Uses
of Force and Restraints

The preceding two chapters have described cases of interstate uses of force and interventions but also of tensions and détente in the post-World War II world. With the 'reality panorama' presented as background, this chapter will seek to identify different kinds of incentives for the use of force and some responses.

TWO GENERAL COMMENTS

A first comment is that not just one but several different incentives may have triggered an armed action and that explanations and justifications presented may not reveal what was the dominant incentive. For instance, in the case of the 2003 Iraq War, it is hard to say which – if any – of the explanations presented truly moved the United States and the United Kingdom to action. Interventions presented as 'humanitarian' may also have had mainly other real incentives than that of protecting groups of people.[1] In addition, various bureaucratic, political and economic factors – including for example an influential military-industrial complex – can generate additional domestic incentives to engage in armed conflict.

A second general observation is that not surprisingly it is easier to identify incentives than disincentives to the use of armed force. The actual use of armed force is visible and there must have been some incentive(s) that one can look for. Where there is no use of armed force it may be hard to pin down the reasons. Were there disincentives that prevailed or simply an absence of incentives? In some cases – like the Cuban crisis in 1962 or the occasion in 2013 when the US refrained from attacking Syrian targets to punish the use of chemical weapons – we know that the use of armed force was considered and how the relevant actors were influenced by specific disincentives that

---

[1] Menon (2016), p. 66 ff.

prevailed. In many other cases, it may not even come to our knowledge that a resort to armed force was considered.

WHAT INCENTIVES TO THE USE OF FORCE CAN WE IDENTIFY AFTER WORLD WAR II?

The incentives to the use of force that we can identify in the post-World War II period are of great variety. To facilitate a perspective, we shall first examine if some kinds of incentives that were common in the past are still common:

- to acquire more land,
- *to* enforce inherited rights to land
- to spread a religion or faith
- to offer humanitarian protection.

Thereafter, we shall discuss the emergence of possible new kinds of incentives:

- to acquire specific scarce resources
- to make use of space and cyberspace
- to eradicate threatening terrorist groups
- to prevent the development of nuclear weapons

A final section will be devoted to incentives to use force that may continue to flow from ambitions to establish regional or global hegemony/domination or from pride and honour.

THE AIM TO ACQUIRE LAND AS AN INCENTIVE TO USE FORCE

From time immemorial a wish to add wealth and power has been an incentive for tribal leaders, kings and rulers of all kinds to seek to acquire land – sometimes through marriage, often through force and war.[2] Through a remarkable but uneven process in the twentieth century, this incentive has largely been neutralized or mutated into an incentive to attain influence and benefits through other means – including interventions.

A number of cases must nevertheless be noted of the use of force with the aim of the acquisition of territory post WWII: North Korea attempted to occupy South Korea in 1950. After the Six-Day War in 1967, Israel occupied the Syrian Golan Heights (and in 1981 annexed them) and the West Bank of the Jordan River. A wish for more land, perceived historical rights and

---

[2]   On territory and borders, see Goldstein (2011), pp. 278 and 279.

strategic considerations have been incentives. Concern about international reactions has been a disincentive to formal annexation in the case of the West Bank. Claiming title to the UK-ruled Falkland/Malvinas islands, Argentina attempted but failed to occupy the islands in 1982.[3] Iraq attacked Iran in 1980 with the aim of acquiring territory and in 1990 it occupied and attempted to annex Kuwait to gain land, oil and financial resources and to demonstrate power. Russia seized and annexed Crimea in 2014 and launched a full-scale war in 2022 to control more Ukrainian territory.[4] One might add the forced incorporation of Goa into India (1961), Turkey's seizing part of Cyprus and declaring it independent (1974) and the Turkish occupation in 2019 of a slice of land in the North of Syria, and Azerbaijan's reconquest from Armenia in 2020 of some land in Nagorno-Karabakh. Lastly, Morocco continues its armed actions to acquire the large territory of Western Sahara that seeks independence and China claims Taiwan on the basis of perceived historical rights.

The cases noted above are significant but do not disprove the assessment that the acquisition of land in general and particularly for economic reasons has ceased to be the common incentive for the use of armed force that it once was. How did this fundamental change come about?

THE END OF COLONIES

An early expression of a negative attitude to the conquering of land and a concomitant positive view of the right to self-determination of people on the land is found in the stands of President Wilson and in the peace settlement after the First World War. Historically, the wish to acquire colonies had been a common and accepted incentive for the use of armed force. Over time, new thinking – for instance on the slave trade – changed the attitudes and this became visible in the views on the possession of colonial territories. Under the Peace Treaty of 1919, the German colonies and Ottoman-controlled areas in the Levant were not simply given to victors in WWI as land 'booty' but were treated as 'mandates' under the League of Nations. Some 30 years later they were transformed into 'trusteeships' under the United Nations and all eventually achieved self-governance.

---

[3] The Security Council firmly rejected the Argentine claim, see Franck (2002, p. 130).
[4] A Security Council resolution on the action on the Crimea was vetoed by Russia but the General Assembly adopted several resolutions concerning the Russian actions, notably A/RES/68/262 of 27 March 2014, calling on members not to recognize the Russian annexation of the Crimea. In resolution A/RES/ES-11/1, adopted 2 March 2022 after Russia's invasion of Ukraine, the Assembly reaffirmed that no territorial acquisitions resulting from the threat or use of force shall be recognized as legal.

The selective and limited rejection of colonial control of land in 1919 did not signify an end to the use of force to attain control of other foreign lands for partly similar reasons. In the 1930s the old idea of gaining wealth, colonies and grandeur through the occupation of land still provided an incentive to Italy to attack Ethiopia and Japan to wage war in Korea and China. Germany had been deprived of control of its colonies, but Hitler's determination to acquire more land – 'Lebensraum' – for the people of Nazi Germany became an incentive to use armed force and a major cause of the Second World War. A similar bent for old-fashioned land acquisition and incentive to use armed force to achieve it was shown by Stalin, when in 1940 the Soviet Union annexed the Baltic states and Eastern Carelia and when at the end of World War II in 1945 it occupied four Kurile islands that belonged to Japan.

While China holds that its invasion of Tibet in 1950 was merely an act upholding historical Chinese sovereignty over the area, resolutions passed in the UN General Assembly in 1961 and 1965 recognized the right of self-determination of Tibet and many see the Chinese incentives as similar to those behind colonization and ambitions for regional hegemony.

THE POST WWII DECOLONIZATION

By the end of World War II, the public mind had come to see the colonial possession of land as an unjust enslavement of states and the demand for liberation as a legitimate claim by peoples for self-determination and a reclaiming of their own land. The military cost of suppressing growing liberation movements may also have led countries administering colonies to agree to their emancipation. With some important exceptions, the huge decolonization process was accomplished without the use of armed force. Where there was resistance to decolonization, for instance in Algeria and Angola, it created incentives to the use of armed force for liberation movements to reclaim the land and allow their peoples to exercise their right of self-determination.

Colonialism and the incentive to use armed force connected with colonialism are now things of the past.[5]

Through recognition of the right to self-determination and the emancipation of a large number of states, the international community attained a new

---

[5] It may be noted, however, that the Ukrainian President stated in a video speech to the UN Security Council on 5 April 2022 that the Russians were acting 'like colonizers' in their invasion of Ukraine. www.president.gov.ua/en/news/vistup-prezidenta-ukrayini-na-zasidanni-radi-bezpeki-oon-74121. And cf. Chapter 3, p. 46 ff.

size, a new level of complexity and maturity, and a greater recognition of sovereign independence. It must be noted, however, that demands for self-determination and incentives to use force in non-colonial situations though rare are not things of the past: Bangladesh liberated itself by arms from the young state of Pakistan. Armed force was used – without success – by Biafra to secede from Nigeria and by the Eta movement in the Basque region of Spain. Western Sahara still (2022) seeks independence in a conflict with Morocco, which claims sovereignty over the territory. Thus, rejected claims for self-determination by ethnic or other groups may remain an incentive to the use of force. However, the outside world is often stand-offish to such claims, as it mostly wants to remain on good terms with the governments with which it already has relations.

The process of decolonization has been supplemented by the agreed handover of a few exclaves remaining from colonial times – Hong Kong in 1997 and Macao in 1999. The annexation of Goa in 1961 occurred through the Indian army simply marching in. The incentive was not so much an Indian wish to acquire more land as one to terminate an anachronistic relic of colonialism. A few exclaves remain without apparently creating incentives to use force to acquire the territories through annexation: British Gibraltar (in Spain), and Spanish Ceuta and Melilla (in Morocco).

PERCEIVED HISTORICAL RIGHTS TO LAND
MAY BE INCENTIVES TO USE FORCE

In several cases, perceived historical rights to land have created incentives to use force. Argentina's attempt to occupy the British-ruled Falkland (Malvinas) islands in 1982 was rooted partly in a claimed historical right, partly perhaps in the feeling that the 150-year-old ruling of the islands by a distant European state was humiliating and a remnant from the colonial era. Whatever the world thought of the Argentine motives and arguments, it did not provide much support for the use of armed force.[6]

The island of Taiwan is the most significant case in which claimed historical rights create an incentive to use force to acquire land. The case was described above[7] and it only needs to be underlined in the present context that the status of the island remains highly politically and emotionally charged. Indeed, it is one of the world's flashpoints. A third case in which claimed historical rights lie behind incentives to use force is that of Kashmir where several armed clashes

---

[6] Watkins (1983).
[7] Cf. above, Chapter 2, p. 30 and Chapter 3, p. 51.

have occurred between India and Pakistan.[8] Yet another case to mention is the Israeli-Palestinian conflict in which conflicting historical claims are pressed.

THE DESIRED ACQUISITION OF ISLANDS, CONTINENTAL SHELVES AND AREAS OF THE SEA FOR EXPLOITATION ARE RARELY INCENTIVES TO USE FORCE

There was a time when not all land on the earth had been sliced up and included in some states national territory. By the Treaty of Tordesillas in 1494 all newly discovered land West of longitude 46–30 was attributed to Spain and land East thereof to Portugal – largely in conformity with a bull by Pope Alexander VI.[9] Since that time, long-ago distant territories and islands, territorial seas, continental shelves, economic zones and space have been claimed by many individual states apart from Portugal and Spain and – after innumerable controversies and negotiations – become recognized as national. There is no more *terra nullius*.

It is noteworthy that this long process seems to have taken place mostly without the use of force. Remarkably often, international arbitration and judicial settlement have succeeded where negotiations have not led to solutions. As discussed further in Chapter 10, the world court at the Hague settled the question of sovereignty both regarding the Eastern part of the world's biggest island, Greenland (Denmark winning against Norway in 1933) and regarding some of the world's smallest islands, Minquiers and Ecrehous in the English Channel (the United Kingdom winning against France in 1953).[10] In recent years, the ICJ had settled many cases regarding maritime borders.

Areas outside national control – the high seas and space– termed 'commons' are regulated by the Conventions on the Law of the Sea and the Outer Space Treaty. While activities in these areas have given rise to incidents and controversies – for instance, regarding fisheries – these have not so far escalated to significant use of armed force. It should be mentioned that a special international judicial tribunal has been set up (in Hamburg) to adjudicate disputes that are submitted to it by state parties to disputes related to the law of the sea.[11]

Despite the Cold War a number of states active in the Antarctic region – including the United States and the Soviet Union – succeeded in concluding

---

[8] For a chronology, see Abby Pakraka, 'History of Conflict in India and Pakistan' (Washington, DC: Center for Arms Control and Non-Proliferation, 26 November 2019), https://armscontrolcenter.org/history-of-conflict-in-india-and-pakistan/.

[9] 'Treaty of Tordesillas', 7 June 1494. https://doctrineofdiscovery.org/treaty-of-tordesillas/.

[10] Judgment of 5 April 1933. PCIJ Series A/B and Judgment of 17 Nov 1953. *ICJ Reports* 1953, p. 47

[11] ITLOS (2018). See below, Chapter 10, p. 155. www.auswaertiges-amt.de/en/aussenpolitik/themen/internatrecht/einzelfragen/seerecht/-/231640.

the Antarctic Treaty (1959).[12] It contains remarkably detailed arrangements for a peaceful order for the continent and mechanisms for dealing with differences that arise regarding the territory. The many national claims made to sectors of the Antarctic, although not withdrawn were frozen (sic) and agreement was reached that no arms could be introduced in the area. Countries like China, India, or South Korea are increasing their research presence in the Antarctic and their involvement in scientific and technical bodies. While increasing future tensions is possible, the arrangements have so far worked to minimize friction.

For the Arctic region, the joint international arrangements have been less ambitious, but an interstate mechanism – the Arctic Council – exists for the handling of questions of common interest and the Conventions on the Law of the Sea provide important guidance in a number of matters. In addition to states like Norway and Canada, major powers – the United States, Russia and also China – show a growing engagement in the region due to its increasing strategic and economic importance. Until now, frictions have been manageable, but strategic interests and potential competition about natural resources like oil, gas, minerals and fisheries have led to tensions, the flaunting of military power in the region and risks of great power conflicts.[13] It is ironic – or worse – that global warming partly caused by the excessive burning of oil and gas has now led to so much melting of ice in the arctic areas that new oil and gas resources in these areas may become exploitable. A more welcome effect is the possible opening of the Northwest Passage connecting East Asia with Europe, a development that may have huge economic and strategic consequences.

'Failed states' might be thought of as something akin to *terra nullius*, but while the power vacuum they present might tempt outside states to seek influence it does not seem to provide them incentives to grab and annex land. Somalia has for long periods been without effective government – 'a failed state'. Yet, no outsiders seem tempted to go in and rip off some piece of land. The cost of administering anarchy may be a disincentive.

POST WWII, DIFFERENCES ABOUT BORDERS HAVE RARELY PROVIDED INCENTIVES FOR THE USE OF ARMED FORCE

Over centuries differences over land borders have been settled by various means – negotiations, war and sometimes by judicial means. With globalization

---

[12] The treaty's history is described in 'The Antarctic Treaty Explained', British Antarctic Survey, www.bas.ac.uk/about/antarctica/the-antarctic-treaty/the-antarctic-treaty-explained/. See also Lehmköster (2019).

[13] Anthony, Lliendo, and Su (2021).

and freer trade, many borders may have become somewhat less practically important. Conflicts over borders are, of course, merely a special kind of controversy regarding the sovereignty over the territory. However, borders have often been and still remain lines about which people have strong emotions and for which they may be ready to fight and risk their lives. Perhaps it is a sign of the globalization and maturing of neighbourly relations in the international community that by the arrival of the third millennium some land borders have become almost irrelevant (as within the European Union) and most have ceased to be a potential source of conflict.[14]

In Europe, where throughout history innumerable armed conflicts have taken place over borders, the Oder-Neisse rivers formed a tense and grim but generally respected border between the East and West during the Cold War. Today, it is an internal waterway within the European Union.

An important part of the objective of the 1975 Helsinki Conference on Security and Cooperation in Europe was to confirm that the post-World War II borders could not be changed by force by any participant. Art. II of the declaration of general principles of the Conference provided that the participants

> …regard as inviolable all one another's frontiers as well as the frontiers of all States in Europe and therefore will refrain now and in the future from assaulting these frontiers.
>
> Accordingly, they will also refrain from any demand for, or act of, seizure, and usurpation of part or all of the territory of any participating State.

It is ironic that this principle – which the Soviet Union saw as a guarantee against any assault on the borders of the satellite states it controlled – is one that the West invokes today (2022) against Russia's armed intervention across the Russo-Ukraine border.

There is a fortunate absence of differences about borders between several of the big powers in the world and hence no incentive on this ground for the use of force between them. The United States and Russia have no common land border at which the two nuclear superpowers are pitted against each other.[15] Between Russia and China borders that were once forced on China along the Amur and Ussuri rivers seem solid, although an armed clash occurred in 1969

---

[14] For a brief discussion of the evolution of borders in human history, see 'Simply … The History of Borders', *New Internationalist*, 5 September 1991, https://newint.org/features/1991/09/05/simply. See also Chapter 6, p. 108.

[15] Cf. Pinker (p. 256), borders are frozen; Goldstein (p. 279); see also on the norm of territorial integrity Goertz et al. (2016), p. 100.

at the Zhenbo island in the Ussuri.[16] It is also of importance that in a politically volatile part of the world the border between Iran and Turkey –one of the oldest in the world – is stable.

Nevertheless, despite innumerable unproblematic borders in the world today, there are a few that provide incentives to the use of force and even lead to armed conflict. The most significant involves India. One is the long border between India and China, including the so-called McMahon line in the Himalayas that was drawn up in March 1914 in the Simla Convention. It is not recognized by China and has caused wars. The disputed border between China and India, a legacy of the colonial area, has caused tensions and armed incidents on several occasions – for example, in 1959, during the 1962 Indo-Sino War, in 1967, 2017, and 2020. In 1987 and 2013, armed incidents were close to happening but tensions could be de-escalated. It will take pragmatic attitudes in the two Asian giants to make sure that this remote and so-far unsettled border does not present significant danger lines in the future.[17]

The second conflict-prone Indian border is with Pakistan, notably in the disputed area of Kashmir where wars have taken place in 1947/48, 1965, and 1999. Here tension still reigns and the risk of use of force is rarely far away although the awareness of mutual nuclear weapons capacity may be assumed to constitute disincentives to armed actions.

The regional survey in Chapter 2 noted a few border conflicts in which armed force has been used. One might have expected many claims for border changes in Africa, where borders were often drawn suiting colonial powers rather peoples. Yet, the many new African states seem to have generated but a few border disputes. In recent times, we have witnessed the war that began in 1998 between Ethiopia and Eritrea over border and land and that ended in 2000, though a final peace was agreed only in 2018.[18] In November 2020, a civil war began in Ethiopia's Tigray region, an ongoing conflict that has produced a humanitarian catastrophe with multiple claims of war crimes.[19] We have also noted the armed border conflict between the new state of South Sudan and the Sudan from which it seceded.

---

[16] Sergey Radchenko, 'The Island that Changed History', *New York Times*, 2 March 2019, www.nytimes.com/2019/03/02/opinion/soviet-russia-china-war.html. See also Maxwell, N., 'How the Sino-Russian boundary conflict was finally settled: From Nerchinsk 1689 to Vladivostok 2005 via Zhenbao Island 1969', *Critical Asian Studies*, vol. 39, no. 2 (June 2007).

[17] Russell Goldman, 'India-China Border Dispute: A Conflict Explained'. *The New York Times*, 17 June 2020, www.nytimes.com/2020/06/17/world/asia/india-china-border-clashes.html.

[18] Tesfalem Araia, 'Remembering Eritrea-Ethiopia border war: Africa's unfinished conflict', BBC, 6 May 2018, www.bbc.com/news/world-africa-44004212. Also see above, Chapter 2, p. 16.

[19] Declan Walsh and Abdi Latif Dahir, 'Why Is Ethiopia at War with Itself?'. *New York Times*, 12 January 2022, www.nytimes.com/article/ethiopia-tigray-conflict-explained.html.

It is remarkable and possibly thanks to the comprehensive law of the sea conventions that in the post-World War II period many economically important borders of continental shelves, territorial sea and economic zones have been settled without serious controversy. Examples are an agreement reached in 1988 between Sweden and the Soviet Union about the border between their economic zones in the Baltic[20] and the agreement of 2010 between Russia and Norway on their important border in the Barents Sea[21] A severe controversy arose, however, in 2020 between Turkey and Greece about the border between them in the Eastern Mediterranean, where the interest in newly discovered gas resources is high and provide incentives to advance claims and show claws. However, the risk of incidents between naval units circulating in the area seems to have been averted through third states.[22]

RELIGION, CULTURES AND HEREDITY CREATING INCENTIVES TO INTERSTATE USES OF FORCE

The spread and promotion of religious creeds have been the major – but not exclusive – incentive for crusades and for many wars between states and peoples. Muslim armies invaded Spain in the eighth century and Catholic crusaders ransacked Orthodox Constantinople in 1204 and invaded the Holy Land. In Europe, the Protestant North was pitted against a Catholic South in the 30-year war in which a large part of the population perished by diseases or battles.[23]

In many cases, religion (often combined with ethnicity) still stirs internal strife (as in Nigeria) but it is today hardly a source of conflict between states (for instance between Israel and Arab states). With one recent exception, religion has nowhere been an incentive to international armed conflicts between states in the period after World War II. The exception is ISIS (Islamic State of Iraq and Syria), the extremist Islamic movement that sought to re-establish a Muslim caliphate in Iraq and Syria.[24] While it hardly qualified as a state and was not recognized by any governments as such, ISIS did for some time succeed to establish civilian and military control over large areas in Syria and

---

[20] 'Sweden-Union of Soviet Socialist Republics: Agreement on Principles for the Delimitation of Sea Area in the Baltic Sea', Stockholm, 13 January 1988, http://extwprlegs1.fao.org/docs/pdf/bi-5121.pdf. And see *Sveriges Överenskommelser med Främmande Makter* 1988, 38–40.

[21] See Thilo Neumann, 'Norway and Russia Agree on Maritime Boundary in the Barents Sea and the Arctic Ocean'. American Society of International Law. *Insights*. 10 December 2010.

[22] Dalay (2021).

[23] See Pinker, p. 556.

[24] See above, Chapter 2, p. 18.

Iraq. The movement was universally condemned and lost most of its territorial power as it was attacked by multinational armed force. Religious faith could continue to be an incentive for remnant groups of ISIS or some similar movements to pursue *jihad*, but it seems unlikely that significant armed conflicts could be triggered by them.

Hereditary claims to territories have historically been a reason for large and long-lasting armed conflicts,[25] but with the disappearance or reduced importance of monarchies, this ground has altogether disappeared as an incentive for armed conflicts.

A 'clash' of civilizations was predicted in a book that appeared in 1996 and was much discussed for some time.[26] The speculation has mostly been rejected. While Islamophobia has certainly been on the rise in the Western world in the last decade, predictions about wars between Muslim-dominated and Christian-dominated states are not plausible. Some states, including China and Russia, are wary of sizeable Muslim minorities within their territories, but none of the governments of big Muslim-dominated powers stands for a belligerent Islam. All big Christian-dominated powers are firmly wedded to the freedom of religion and do not want to see religious strife in their societies. There could be somewhat better reasons to ask whether the two main branches of the Muslim faith – Sunni and Shia – might push states they dominate to conflicts, as the Orthodox and the Catholic branches of Christianity once did. However, if the tensions between Israel plus Sunni-dominated states – notably Saudi Arabia and the Gulf states – and Shia-dominated Iran were to translate into armed action, geopolitical competition rather than religion would be the main incentive.

COMMUNIST IDEOLOGY CREATING INCENTIVES FOR INTERNATIONAL EXPANSION

While the use of the sword to expand the realms of religions is receding in our memory, the faith in and ambition to spread the Communist ideology and economic/political system was the most serious incentive to the interstate use of force for several decades at and after the end of World War II. For several reasons, the main adversaries sought to limit themselves to Cold War and avoid direct and open conflicts.[27] They succeeded in this – with

---

[25] Mention may be made of the wars of Alexander's Successors (ca 322 to ca 282 BC) after the death of King Alexander the Great of Macedon; or of the War of the Spanish Succession (1701–1714) after the death of King Charles II of Spain.

[26] Huntington (1996).

[27] See above Chapter 3, p. 34 and below, p. 36.

the exceptions of the big wars in Korea and Vietnam and near wars at the Berlin blockade and the Cuba crisis.

As noted above, the Soviet Union under Stalin had used armed force to expand the Union by seizing and annexing the neighbouring Baltic states and Finland's East Carelia in 1939–40. At the end of the Second World War the Soviet Union as the principal carrier of the Marxist-Leninist flag was ready to use its armed forces or to lend a 'helping hand' – even one supplying weapons – to realize the 'inevitability' of the Communist revolution and world-wide introduction of its own socio-economic system. In Eastern Europe, it used its war victory and military occupation to install Communist regimes. The incentive was not just to grab and exploit land to acquire wealth but to expand the Communist world and to create buffer zones around the Communist heartland. Blurring the image of occupation of land the Soviet Union created the model of satellite states, which was grudgingly recognized by the world.

In non-occupied Iranian Azerbaijan, the Soviet government sought to promote Communist control by using supporters and by helping to foment rebellion rather than by entering and using force openly. The same was true in Africa and Latin America including the Caribbean. In Greece, a Communist rebellion was supported by East European Soviet proxies in 1946–49. As the conflict triggered US assistance (Truman doctrine) to the Greek government it marked the beginning of the Cold War. In settled democratic states, as in Western Europe, 'indirect aggression' was eschewed and the incentive to promote the expansion of Communism led to active support for political movements and parties sympathetic to Moscow. This will be discussed in the next section covering Western responses.

The incentive to expand the sway of the Communist ideology was not confined to the Soviet government. As described above,[28] North Korea under Kim Il Sung attacked South Korea in 1950 to extend Communist rule to the whole of Korea. It was seen in the Western world as a new dimension of the struggle of the world Communist camp to expand its area of control. The attack triggered the successful defence of South Korea by a US-led armed action under the UN flag. The expansion of Communist rule through force was thus firmly stopped – but there was no 'roll back'.

That a rigid pattern of 'containment' was to be followed in Asia was amply demonstrated in 1954–1955 and 1958 when the Government in Beijing made some attempts to use force to take the small Taiwanese-controlled islands Quemoy and Matsu. As described above, the US showed immediate readiness

---

[28] Chapter 3, p. 35.

to join Taiwan in military defence and even the use of nuclear weapons was discussed on the US side.[29]

In the same period, the US government – and many others – saw the impending victory of Ho Chi Min over the French colonial rule in Vietnam as a new phase in a global Communist conspiracy for a step-by-step march to world domination. It provided an incentive for the long US armed intervention – the Vietnam War – that began in 1965 and ended – in defeat – only in 1973.[30]

Subsequent analyses have concluded that although North Vietnam had the support and sympathy of the Communist world, including Russia and China, the incentive to the struggle was essentially an anticolonial and nationalist demand for independence. The Communist world was not monolithic and was not pursuing a joint conspiracy.

THE ATTEMPTED EXPANSION OF COMMUNISM WAS AN INCENTIVE FOR THE WEST TO TAKE DEFENSIVE ACTIONS – BUT NOT TO ATTEMPT A ROLL-BACK

The incentive of the Soviet Union to expand the sway of Communist ideology and power after WWII was not mirrored by a Western missionary zeal to transform Communist-ruled countries into market economies. The Western policy led by the United States accepted the subjection of the Eastern European countries to Communist rule as Soviet satellites as a fait accompli through the World War. However, it was geared to defend the world of a free market economy, to deter Communist military action but, if possible, avoid direct military confrontations.

The reasons for the overall defensive – and successful – policy were obvious. The Russian military power – including its nuclear weapons – was sufficient to deter any Western attempt to topple a Communist regime by the use of force. As the Soviet Union was equally anxious to avoid direct armed confrontations and chose open political means or proxies and subversive means ('indirect aggression') to pursue Communist expansion, the collision between the two main contenders never resulted in full-fledged armed conflict. Even when cracks occurred in Communist-controlled countries – as during the Hungarian uprising in 1956 or the Prague Spring in 1968 – the Western side refrained from extending any armed assistance to the anti-communist side.

---

[29] See above, Chapter 3, p. 51.

[30] See above, Chapter 3, p. 35 A good overview of the Viet Nam conflict is provided by James S. Olson and Randy W. Roberts, *Where the Domino Fell: America and Vietnam 1945–2010*, 6th ed. (2013).

The main response of the West led by the United States was to use economic policies and measures (Marshall Plan) to European states practicing the market economy system and to strengthen the capacity for a military defence through the creation of the NATO alliance. Open and large-scale military engagements occurred only in Asia in the Korean and Vietnam Wars, as described above. An exception on a small scale might be seen in the attempt in 1961 to roll back Communism in Cuba by the invasion of the Bay of Pigs.

In the Cuban missile crisis (1962) between the United States and the Soviet Union, their confrontation became naked and direct and it confirmed the views of both sides that they could not allow the Cold War to lead to direct active warfare between them.[31] A solution came through diplomacy including the insight that humiliation must be avoided.

The struggle to expand Communism and the response to resist that expansion continued after the Cuban crisis in forms that eschewed, minimized or blurred the use of force or concealed the direct responsibility for such use, for instance, subversion or the use of proxies. Several examples from the competition in the Caribbean and Nicaragua are offered below.[32]

While the imposition of Communism was once a major aspiration and a potential incentive to use force, today the spreading of ideology hardly remains an incentive to use force between states. Russia's invasion of Ukraine in 2022 may have had several causes. One was surely anger at a possible military integration of Ukraine into the West and NATO military installations along the Russian border. If anger at Ukraine's choice to emulate a Western state model was another cause, the reaction of Ukraine's people has shown that armed force and occupation are not ways to make liaison with Russia attractive. Western market economies and state models demonstrate some great attractions: economic systems that give reasonably stable growth, and political systems that give people freedom and influence. Free and honest elections that allow orderly and violence-free changes of power.

HUMANITARIAN CONCERNS AS INCENTIVES TO THE USE OF FORCE[33]

In the not-very-distant past, humanitarian concerns have sometimes been an incentive for a few states to use force for 'humanitarian interventions' to rescue citizens in jeopardy in foreign lands. On many occasions the motive

---

[31] See below Chapter 6, p. 124 and above, Chapter 3, p. 36 Also see Kennedy (1969).
[32] See below, Chapter 15, p. 213 ff.
[33] On humanitarian intervention, see Kaldor (2008), p. 27; Goldstein (2011), p. 324 and Menon (2016).

was genuine, but the label was also used for interventions that were in fact undertaken mainly for other reasons. In the post-World War II world cases in which the saving of endangered citizens was the genuine chief incentive for interventions by force have become rare – possibly because there is generally greater respect for other states' territorial integrity. A modern case in which the humanitarian concern seemed to have been the real incentive was Israel's armed operation at the Entebbe airport in Uganda in 1976 to liberate passengers of an Israeli passenger plane that had been hijacked and forced to land.[34] More often scrutiny of cases in which 'humanitarian' motives have been invoked shows that the main incentives were other – such as achieving or preventing *regime change*.[35]

A highly controversial case in which the incentive to use force was claimed to be humanitarian was NATO's bombing of Kosovo in 1999. While it was asserted to have been necessary to prevent massacres on the ground, it clearly was a part of the military campaign against Serbia, was not authorized by the Security Council and cost many lives. It will be discussed below in the context of interventions.[36]

In the case of the 2003 war on Iraq, one incentive (among several) referred to was the wish to eliminate an odious dictator – Saddam Hussein. To the British Prime Minister, this humanitarian motive may have been of great significance. In a speech in Chicago in 1999, Mr Blair spoke about 'intervention to bring down a despotic dictatorial regime'. He was careful to hedge a permissive doctrine with limitations, but rhetorically posed the question of where intervention is 'practical' and where change will not come by evolution 'should those who have the military power to intervene contemplate doing so'[37]

President Bush's reference to Iraq as part of an 'axis of evil' – that presumably was deemed collectively responsible for the 9/11 attack on the United States – points to his sharing Blair's line of thinking.

An odd reference to a right of humanitarian intervention was made in the Security Council by the UK seeking to justify the bombing by the United States, the United Kingdom and France of targets in Syria in 2018 to punish Syria for the use of chemical weapons.[38]

---

[34] For further discussion see Chapter 16, p. 244.
[35] For the legal aspects, see below, Chapter 16, p. 240 ff.
[36] See below, Chapter 16, p. 245 and see Goldstein (2011), p. 324.
[37] See below in Chapter 16, p. 246; comments on Blair's speech in Friedman (2017); and Goldstein (2011), p. 324.
[38] See Chapter 16, p. 251.

The elimination of blood-stained dictators is not likely often to be an incentive for individual states to intervene with force. Instead, one might think, the international community should have an incentive collectively to act for humanitarian reasons in national situations of horror, especially if it worries that individual states might otherwise claim a role as world sheriffs. The painful failure of the world and the United Nations to prevent the genocide in Rwanda in 1994 did indeed lead the General Assembly in 2005 to adopt the so-called R2P resolution – Responsibility to Protect. It declared that where states gravely fail to protect human rights there is a responsibility for the UN to intervene – in extreme cases even with armed force – to prevent or stop extreme violations of human rights, like genocides. While well justified, the doctrine has yet to prove successful.[39]

NEW CATEGORIES OF INCENTIVES TO THE USE OR THREAT OR USE OF FORCE

The extent to which familiar types of incentives to the interstate use of force continue to exist has been surveyed above. Below is a discussion of various new factors that may create such incentives. They relate to the need for key natural resources, risks from the uses of space and cyberspace, risks for attacks by foreign-based terrorists, and risks of further nuclear proliferation, arms races and prodding.[40]

INCENTIVES RELATED TO SCARCE NATURAL RESOURCES

There has been speculation that environmental changes like desertification and higher sea levels will have security implications potentially creating incentives for the use of force.[41] While the fear may be justified that environmental changes might come to create many refugees in the future, we should note that the major part of the exodus of people from the Middle East and Africa to Western Europe after 2010 was of refugees from armed conflicts. Only a smaller part was 'environmental refugees' from areas where sustenance has become difficult due to climate change. However, current streams might grow to floods in the future.

---

[39] For a history and evaluation of R2P, see Thakur (2016). Also see Menon (2016), pp. 84 ff.

[40] A systematic survey of future risks of conflicts is found in a publication of the UK Ministry of Defence: *Global Strategic Trends: The Future Starts Today (2018)*.

[41] Report: 'Climate Change, Intelligence, and Global Security', Harvard Belfer Center, May 2021, www.belfercenter.org/publication/report-climate-change-intelligence-and-global-security.

Incentives to – and actual use of – force has clearly been triggered by competition about a few key natural resources, above all oil and gas. The 1990 military occupation of Kuwait by Iraq is deemed to have been caused primarily by the wish of the Iraqi leader, Saddam Hussein, to grab Kuwait's financial and oil resources. There was also a fear that Saddam Hussein, after occupying Kuwait, could aim to grab oil wells in Saudi Arabia and other Gulf states and this is likely to have been part of the incentive for the United States to lead the UN-authorized operation to reverse the occupation.[42]

Nearly thirty years later, Turkish claims to areas of sea bed possibly covering gas resources in the Mediterranean have led to serious controversy involving a number of states and a risk for naval confrontations, as they have clashed with claims by Greece and Cyprus.[43] Similarly, the controversies about islands in the Pacific and the belief that there may be deposits of oil or gas under the sea-beds surrounding islands in the South China Sea exacerbates the conflict that is mainly caused by strategic and hegemonic interests.

As fresh water has become a scarce resource in many parts of the world the sharing of river water between states upstream and downstream is increasingly often an issue that has led to strains and risk of conflict. Most recently it has led to a serious controversy regarding the River Nile between Sudan and Egypt (downstream) and Ethiopia (upstream). Controversies about the Jordan River contributed to the outbreak of the Six-Day War and continue. In Asia, the building of hydroelectric dams, especially by China in the upper part of the Mekong River raises grave problems for millions of people who live downstream in Indochina and depend on the river for their livelihood.

It is clear that in not a few cases the sharing by several states of international river resources creates strains and potential incentives to conflict. It should also be noted, however, that such frictions alone have only rarely led to the use of force between states.[44]

---

[42] See above, Chapter 2, p. 25.

[43] See earlier discussion, Chapter 4, p. 63. See 'Turkey-Greece: From Maritime Brinkmanship to Dialogue', Europe Report No 263 (Brussels: International Crisis Group, May 31, 2021), www.crisisgroup.org/europe-central-asia/western-europemediterranean/263-turkey-greece-maritime-brinkmanship-dialogue.

[44] Mandel (1992). Mandel studied 14 river disputes and found that 'only 4 reached what he called a high severity of conflict' (Euphrates, Jordan River, Rio Grande, and Shatt al-Arab), and not all of these involved armed conflict. Also see Wolf (2007).

SPACE AND CYBER ACTIVITIES COULD CREATE
INCENTIVES TO THE USE OF FORCE

Although surveillance and verification of military activities currently constitute a large part of states' activities in space, they do not by themselves create incentives to interstate uses of force. By their contribution to openness and transparency they do, in fact, contribute to confidence about the absence of threats; however, would an armed conflict appear imminent, there would immediately be incentives to damage or destroy satellites useful to an enemy's military effort and escalation could lead to chaotic and incalculable conditions in navigation and global communications.[45]

Cyberspace, like space, is used intensely to the benefit of all. It also raises opportunities for criminal use by individuals and opportunities for state actions ranging from the dissemination of propaganda and misleading information to disturbing elections, espionage and the damaging of important activities and functions in other states. Many instances of adversarial use have been registered. The US has made it clear that it may consider cyber-attacks of sufficient gravity 'acts of war' – even justifying nuclear response.[46]

INCENTIVES TO USE FORCE TO ERADICATE
AND PUNISH TERRORISM

Terrorism has usually played out in the national sphere and it is the task of national authorities to pursue and suppress terrorist acts under criminal law. This remains true but a new feature has been that a terrorist movement based in one or several states (notably Al Qaeda) has directed action against other states. For the United States that has been a chief target, terrorism – notably in the 9/11 2001 attack – created an incentive to go beyond criminal law cooperation with countries from which terrorists have operated to claim a right to attack terrorists and their bases directly by arms at any time and even without the consent of host countries. The legal aspects of the international community's countering terrorism are discussed extensively below.[47]

---

[45] See below, Chapter 8, p. 131.
[46] See below in Chapter 8, p. 129. The Centre for Strategic and International Studies has a list (that is constantly updated) with 'significant' cyber incidents since 2006. You find the list here: 'www .csis.org/programs/strategic-technologies-program/significant-cyber-incidentshe. US 'Nuclear Posture Review' for 2018 stated that US nuclear weapons were intended to deter both nuclear attacks and 'non-nuclear aggression'. The *Wall Street Journal* reported on 31 May 2011 that the Pentagon regarded cyberattacks as 'acts of war', www.wsj.com/articles/SB100014240527023045 63104576355623135782718.
[47] See Chapter 15, p. 224.

INCENTIVES TO USE FORCE TO PREVENT THE
DEVELOPMENT OF NUCLEAR WEAPONS

The development or acquisition of nuclear weapons by a state may have such a dramatic impact on strategic situations that it creates incentives to use force in attempts to seek to prevent it from happening.

In 2003, the US declared a 'Proliferation Security Initiative', a policy that could allow it to use armed actions for the purpose of 'counterproliferation'.[48] To prevent Iraq from developing weapons of mass destruction was often cited as one of the stated objectives of the 2003 war. However, the war was never termed a 'counterproliferation' operation.

The incentive of using force to prevent nuclear proliferation is not a novelty. A case of counterproliferation long before the term was coined occurred in 1943, when during WWII a sabotage expedition took place in German-occupied Norway to destroy a facility for the production of heavy water. The incentive for the action was to prevent the occupying power, Germany, to get hold of material – heavy water – for use in the development of a nuclear bomb. The story is thrilling and the expedition was successful.[49]

After World War II the US government, it is reported, contemplated but decided against armed actions In China in 1958 to destroy facilities engaged in developing a nuclear weapon.[50] One reason for the negative US conclusion must have been concern about what such an attack might have set in motion. Another might have been the awareness that If Chinese scientists and engineers had the knowledge to make nuclear weapons, the bombing of facilities could only delay but not prevent it from happening. China had its first nuclear weapon test at Lop Nor in 1964.

The attempt of the Soviet Union to place nuclear weapons on US doorsteps in Cuba in 1962 created strong incentives for the United States to take preventive armed action. As described above the understanding of the adversaries that they could be on the way to a nuclear war led them to a diplomatic solution and insights that impact fundamentally on strategic thinking even today.[51]

---

[48] For a discussion on the legal aspects of the distinction between non-proliferation and counterproliferation, see Joyner (2005). The author cites specific counterproliferation actions, including the Spanish Navy's interdiction of an unflagged North Korean ship transporting missile parts destined for Yemen.

[49] Bascomb (2016).

[50] 'Risk of Nuclear War Over Taiwan in 1958 Said to Be Greater than Publicly Known', *New York Times*, 22 May 2021, www.nytimes.com/2021/05/22/us/politics/nuclear-war-risk-1958-us-china.html. The report was based on a classified 1966 report by Morton Halperin, then of the RAND Corporation, that was leaked by former US Defence official Daniel Ellsberg. The full text appears as a link in this article. See also Tannenwald (2007).

[51] See above, Chapter 3, p. 37 and below in Chapter 8, p. 132 ff.

In 1981, Iraq was about to fill fuel in the newly built research reactor Osirak. To Israel, the suspicion that the reactor was meant to produce fissionable material for nuclear weapons created an incentive to the preventive action by which it bombed and destroyed the reactor.[52] The same incentive may be presumed to have led to two other armed actions that are widely believed to have been taken by the Israeli intelligence agency Mossad. One was the assassination in Paris in 1980 of the Egyptian scientist who headed the nuclear project at Osirak. The other was the destruction in a warehouse in Marseille of the nuclear core intended for the reactor.[53]

Less facts are available about Israel's destruction in Syria in 2007 of a facility at al-Kibar claimed to be a North Korean-designed research reactor. There is no doubt that the incentive was the concern that the facility could in time contribute to the development of nuclear weapons.[54]

As described in Chapter 2, Iran's nuclear energy programme was the subject of a deal (the Joint Comprehensive Plan of Action (JCPOA)) that was endorsed by the Security Council in 2015. The deal was designed to ensure that the programme remained peaceful, but the Israeli government continued to suspect that Iran intended to develop a nuclear weapon and strong voices in Israel and in the United States urged the bombing of facilities in Iran. No such bombing has ever occurred but some Iranian uranium enrichment plants have been made inoperative through cyber-action (Stuxnet) believed to have been a joint and US-Israeli project.[55] The Biden administration has continued to threaten the use of force but has not so far (December 2022) acted upon the threat.

PRIDE AND ASPIRATIONS FOR HEGEMONY/DOMINANCE MAY PROVIDE INCENTIVES FOR THE INTERSTATE USE OF FORCE

As described above, many specific traditional factors that have created incentives to the interstate use or force – expansion of realms, the spread of religion or faith, etc. – have disappeared or become less relevant, while a few distinctly new ones – like malevolent use of cyberspace–can be identified. To conclude

---

[52] Cf. below, Chapter 8, p. 132 and Chapter 17, p. 262.

[53] In the voluminous literature on the Osirak event, see the recent work by Braut-Hegghammer. See also Vargo (2015).

[54] See below, Chapter 15, p. 237.

[55] See Chapter 15, p. 238. Israel was widely believed to be behind the assassination of a prominent Iranian nuclear scientist in Iran. The action reportedly involved the use of a remote-controlled machine gun. ('The Scientist and the A.I. Assisted, Remote-Control Killing Machine', *New York Times*, 18 September 2021, www.nytimes.com/2021/09/18/world/middleeast/iran-nuclear-fakhrizadeh-assassination-israel.html).

this chapter focus will turn to two age-old factors that have low specificity and that have often generated incentives to use force – the ambition to attain or maintain regional or global hegemony/domination/ influence and the defence of pride. They are akin to Morgenthau's and Fukuyama's general explanations for the use of force – the quest for power and the quest for recognition.[56]

HURT PRIDE AS AN INCENTIVE TO USE FORCE

Fukuyama speaks of the quest for 'recognition' as a cause of war. It sounds like a subtle explanation, but it may be understood by anyone who has seen Chaplin's film 'The Great Dictator' and the scene where Hitler and Mussolini sit side by side in a barber's shop and both seek to raise their adjustable chairs in order to look down on the other. Humans, peoples, rulers and governments have a strong demand to be respected – recognized – and conversely anger at denials of recognition and humiliation. Not so far back in time, proud men who felt insulted could challenge each other to lethal duels to 'defend their honour' and proud rulers could order armed actions to exact respect for their person and flag. Today, we shake our heads at various past reactions to injured pride and find them vain and petty but we should be aware that the feelings still create fury and incentives to use force. Below are some examples.

The 9/11 2001 attack on the US killing thousands was not only a brutal crime. It was also an act perceived as a humiliation for which immediate ret-ribution through the smashing of Al Qaeda bases was not deemed sufficient. 'War' was declared on all terrorism and 'Axis of Evil' states that were named.[57] The war in Afghanistan after having focused on Al Qaeda turned to defeating the Taliban movement. From Afghanistan, Al Qaeda and the Taliban the war against evil extended to the invasion of Iraq – where in fact Al Qaeda was absent – and the ousting of Saddam Hussein. A potential next extension of the armed response to 9/11 to Iran, the third party of the 'axis of evil', has had advocates in the United States but has not occurred (September 2022).

Another case in which hurt pride may be sensed as a part of the incen-tive for using force was the – failed – invasion of the Falkland Islands.[58] The military government of Argentina may well have seen a distant former great power's control of the 'Malvinas' islands as an insult to an adjacent country and a conquest as a proud self-assertion.

---

[56] See above, Chapter 1, p. 6, 7.
[57] See below, Chapter 10, p. 158.
[58] See above, Chapter 4, p. 56.

Some further cases may be cited where pride may play a part: China's claim of Taiwan and islands in the West Pacific may have roots not only in perceived historical rights but also in the feeling that its absence of control is a result of insults that were inflicted on China and that continue. A second case was Russia's annexation of Crimea. One reason might have been fears that if Ukraine were to join NATO Russia would likely come to suffer the humiliation of seeing Sevastopol – a proud place in Russian history – become a NATO naval Black Sea base.[59] Among the possible incentives to Russia's invasion of Ukraine in 2022 might also have been a resentment – a feeling of insult – that Ukraine distanced itself from Mother Russia.

What is the conclusion from these speculations? One may argue about the rationality of the actions as interpreted but there is no point in sneering at reactions of hurt pride. Rather, there should be a greater awareness in international relations that nations, governments and peoples, as Fukuyama suggested, need 'recognition'. Hurt pride and feelings of humiliation – the obverse to 'recognition' – may generate resentment and incentives to use force. Morgenthau, in his pessimistic look at the future of international relations, did not claim that diplomacy was a panacea for peace, but he clearly suggested that diplomacy (that seeks whenever possible to avoid hurting pride and causing humiliation), may help the world to reduce incentives for the use of force.

ASPIRATIONS FOR HEGEMONY/DOMINATION MAY CREATE INCENTIVES TO USE FORCE

Great powers are said to have aspired for 'hegemony' and memories of the Roman Empire, Napoleon and the British Empire are evoked. In this book, the terms 'dominance' and 'domination' are often used to describe the extensive influence that the United States, Russia and China are seeking and – in some areas – competing about.[60] While investments, trade and finances offer states some leverages for influence and domination and while success in productivity and innovation as well as political and social organization may earn respect, the deployment of and readiness to use military force are a direct means to attain domination. Hence, aspirations to attain dominating influence are likely to create incentives to build up, deploy and be ready to use military capacities. Below is a discussion of aspirations shown since WW II by three major world powers – the United States, China and Soviet Union/Russia – to exert extensive influence and the role that military strength and potential use of force plays among the means they use.

[59] See above, Chapter 3, p. 46.
[60] For further discussion of 'dominance' in the case of the war in Vietnam, see Porter (2006).

THE SOVIET UNION/RUSSIA

The Soviet Union emerging victorious from WWII aspired to graft its Communist ideological, social, economic and political system onto states worldwide and, in the process, to seek domination for itself.

It had incentives to use both force and ideological persuasion.[61] Immediately after the war, it began the mission of spreading the Communist system to the world by imposing it by force on Eastern Europe. Henry Kissinger is said to have succinctly remarked that Russian expansion 'was not achieved by referendum'. However, outside the areas of the enlarged Soviet Union and the puppet states in Eastern Europe, the Soviet Union used a variety of methods. In Western Europe and many other parts of the world, the main approach was to promote political parties and movements accepting or leaning to the Communist ideology. In large Communist parties in France and Italy the ideology had much appeal and in many developing countries there were hopes that leaps forward could be taken through an adoption of the Soviet model of state-controlled economies. However, in many areas of the world, traditional political means of influence were supplemented during the Cold War by support for rebel movements and subversion using force.

Communist claims of the superiority of the Socialist system made it logical to hold – under the so-called Brezhnev doctrine – that the introduction by a state of this system was irreversible. Similarly, sustaining Soviet control was the incentive for the long and large-scale armed intervention in Afghanistan between 1979 and 1989[62]

After the dissolution of the Soviet Union and the collapsed belief in its economic and political model, global ideology-motivated interventionist activities appear generally to have been abandoned. The creation in 1991 under the Russian leadership of the Commonwealth of Independent States was part of a Russian ambition to salvage its regional domination without the use of force in areas that had been part of the Soviet Union. In the case of the two states that balked at such continued Russian domination – Georgia and Ukraine[63] – their emancipation and their possibility of joining NATO led Russia to intervene by armed force. It was demonstrated to the two countries and to the world that Russia considered areas termed 'near abroad' as falling within its 'sphere of influence' and required them

---

[61] See also Chapter 3, p. 36, which includes discussion of the Brezhnev doctrine.
[62] The US support – in the same period – of the Taliban resistance was part of its struggle to defeat Soviet Communist aspirations for control of Afghanistan. See also Chapter 2, p. 28.
[63] Cf. Chapter 3, p. 46.

to heed at least vital Russian defence interests. How the lethal wrestling match between Russia and Ukraine will end is not known when this is written (Dec 2022).

Russia's interests in preserving and asserting regional power and influence in the Middle East have led it to intervene on a large scale in the Syrian civil war at the request of the Assad government.[64] Arms and fighter planes have come from Russian military bases in Syria and helped the government to prevail in the civil war. Russia appears also to have deployed mercenaries ('Wagner' units) in conflicts in Syria, Ukraine, Libya and some other countries in Africa, curiously denying direct state responsibility but certainly suggesting aspirations for influence.

An overall conclusion is that Russia has been ready to use open or shrouded armed forces to pursue interests in its immediate neighbourhood, in Syria, the Mediterranean and Africa (Wagner units). Both in its vicinity and in its distant deployments Russia has been anxious to avoid that its aspirations for influence lead to military clashes with other great powers. At the same time, Russia has restored its military capacity from the low levels at which they were at the end of the period of détente. It seems to have retained top competence and capacity in nuclear and other modern weaponry and missiles, as well as in the ability to pursue both first and second strikes in cyber- and space warfare. In the economic, political and social, spheres Russia will for a long time have little attraction as a leader for its neighbours, and the declared (2022) ambition of President Putin to spearhead a global coalition and battle against an oppressive and exploitative Anglo-Saxon world does not look promising.[65] China may well want to break the Western dominance but it has so far seemed lukewarm to President Putin's battle calls.

THE UNITED STATES

The United States is seen today by many as a state with aspirations for worldwide domination. It took some time for the country to move from isolationism to claim the status of a lone superpower with a mission to uphold a 'liberal world order'. As noted, the Monroe Doctrine of 1823 claimed a kind of regional hegemony: it declared that European states should refrain from interventions in the Western hemisphere just as it was US policy not to intervene in Europe. While the United States did not assert a US right of domination

---

[64] See above, Chapter 2, p. 24, and below p. 194.
[65] 'Putin Building Anti-West Global Alliance as He Tries to Reshape World Order'. *Newsweek*, 20 July 2022, www.newsweek.com/putin-iran-turkey-alliance-syria-north-korea-china-1726295.

in the Western hemisphere it committed to no restraint.[66] In fact, although the United States had a strong influence in the area through investments and finances, it also used force in many armed interventions. Even after World War II, when the states in the region had a greater capacity to defend their independence, the US continued to have a strong hand in the region and used force many times – perhaps mostly to prevent feared Communist expansion. The following are some examples:

- US attempts to topple the Castro government in Cuba.
- US armed intervention in the Dominican Republic in 1965.
- US subversion in Chile in 1970 to help topple left-leaning President Allende.
- US invasion and occupation of Grenada in 1983 to oust a Marxist government.
- US armed intervention in Nicaragua in 1983–1984.
- US intervention in 1989 in Panama to topple and seize General Noriega.

Outside Latin America, the US engaged during the Cold War in major wars in Korea and Vietnam and in many lower-level conflicts. The motivation of the United States was less to have predominant influence than to contain activities believed to aim at global Communist domination. With the aim of stopping economic policies of nationalization (as of the Anglo-Iranian Oil Company) perceived adverse to the West, the US intervened in Iran in 1953 to help topple the first democratically elected prime minister, Mossadegh.[67]

When the Soviet Union disintegrated through inner decay and the bipolar world ended the US was left as the only state with the economic, political and military capacity to seek world primacy. It was often urged by other states to use its power and many leaders in the United States were keen to accept the challenge. Former Secretary of State, Madeleine Albright, said famously that *'if we have to use force it is because we are America, we are the indispensable nation'.*[68]

Even though the military sector in the United States – as in other states – decreased in size with the end of the Cold War, 'the unilateral moment' allowed US aspirations to increase. Its global power and reach expanded through its economic/financial strength. Its military superiority increased through a policy of 'full spectrum dominance', a multitude of military bases

---

[66] Cf. Chapter 2, p. 22.
[67] See Chapter 16, p. 241 and Chapter 18, p. 286.
[68] Madeleine Albright, Interview on NBC, 19 February 1998, https://1997-2001.state.gov/statements/1998/980219a.html.

around the world and a manifested readiness to use force. With the unprecedented power came a sense of right and a responsibility to lead and uphold the liberal world order.[69]

Being the leading member of NATO has enabled the United States to take stands and action with its strength cumulated by the considerable power of the alliance. While the organization had originally (1949) 12 members and was designed to meet the risk of Soviet attacks, its powers and influence -and indirectly those of the United States – have grown by its membership increasing to 30, including several states that were once under Soviet domination. In 2022 the Russian invasion of Ukraine triggered Finland and Sweden to apply for membership. The alliance's scope of geographic action has been widened through acceptance of roles in Afghanistan Iraq and Libya and its power and influence have widened through programmes of 'Partnership for Peace' and similar agreements with non-members – including Georgia, Ukraine, and, indeed, Russia. Moreover, the mission of the alliance is no longer confined to the defence of the North Atlantic and states around it, but extends to the Black Sea, its riparian states and to specific missions accepted (Afghanistan, Libya, Iraq). The memento must be added, however, that US proposals for actions by NATO require unanimity, which is not automatic. One might recall the comment ascribed to Napoleon that he would rather fight an alliance than lead one.

The QUAD (discussed earlier) is a group of four states comprising the United States, Japan, India and Australia. By 2021, it is held together by common security interests to face a more assertive China. A -virtual – summit was held in March 2021 at which the mantra was the advancement of a free and open Indo-Pacific rules-based order rooted in international law. After the armed Himalayan border clashes with China in 2020, India has been more committed to the group. Joint naval drills have taken place and an expansion of the group, though not on the current agenda, is not excluded. While China asserts that it will support a UN-based multilateralism, QUAD is now clearly a US-led collective effort to thwart Chinese efforts to use its rapidly growing economic power to equal or replace the United States as the dominant force in the Indo-Pacific area. China has branded the group as an 'Indo-Pacific NATO'.[70]

---

[69] See: Pentagon report 'Joint Vision 2020' (issued in 2000), which introduced FSD: www.hsdl .org/?view&did=446826.

[70] See article by Kevin Rudd 'Why the QUAD alarms China' in *Foreign Affairs* 6 August 2021. The 2021 AUKUS deal – in which the US and UK agreed to assist Australia to build nuclear-powered submarines – was also widely seen as a response to a growing Chinese presence in the region. ('Aukus: the United Kingdom, the United States and Australia Launch Pact to Counter China', BBC, 15 September 2021, www.bbc.com/news/world-58564837).

The US reach and power are enhanced by a little-noticed but frequently used form of international cooperation – direct agreements between the armed forces of the United States and those of other states. The cooperation under which the US provides training to foreign military and security personnel might appear to be merely assistance among professionals. However, it also means a US military influence in many states that are not linked to NATO and is presumably designed to facilitate joint armed operations, if such were to be agreed at the government levels.[71]

The US federal budget is evidence of the cost of the effort to be the superior global force. For the budgetary year of 2021 and a few preceding years, it has been around 700 billion dollars – higher than the sum of the budgets of the ten next biggest military state budgets in the world.[72]

The United States also maintains a large number of military bases around the world – from Greenland in the North to Darwin in Australia. They project power and enhance the ability of the United States to take quick military regional action.[73] Moreover, separate military commands are established in seven geographic regions (including Space Command) for US forces and operations within the regions.[74] Only the command for Africa is located outside the region.[75]

While it is obvious that the United States today continues to use its economic and financial power – for instance a rich array of sanctions – and the subversive activities of the CIA to exercise influence all over the world, it

---

[71] According to an article by Nick Turse in LobeLog 15 August 2017 the United States has since 9/11 2001 spent more than 250 billion dollars training foreign military and police. In 2015 almost 80,000 soldiers and security officers from 154 countries were said to have received 'foreign military training' (FMT). See also Center for International Policy, *Security Assistance Monitor*, 2020. Accessed at https://securityassistance.org/.

[72] US Department of Defence, 'DOD Releases Fiscal Year 2021 Budget Proposal', News Release, Washington DC, 10 February 2020, which proposed $705 billion, www.defense.gov/Spotlights/ FY2021-Defense-Budget/ Later that year, Congress expanded the request to over $777 billion. 'Biden signs enormous US military budget into law', *Aljazeera*, 27 December 2021, www .aljazeera.com/news/2021/12/27/biden-signs-enormous-us-military-budget-into-law. For a table of military expenditures of a number of states, see below, Chapter 7, p. 123 On 8 December 2022, the US House of Representatives agreed to a 2023 defence budget of $858 billion, $45 billion more than proposed by President Biden. Reuters, 8 December 2022, www.reuters.com/ world/us/us-house-backs-sweeping-defense-bill-voting-continues-2022-12-08/.

[73] 'Infographic: History of US interventions in the past 70 years', *Aljazeera*, 10 September 2021, which claims the United States has 'about 750 bases in at least 80 countries', www.aljazeera .com/news/2021/9/10/infographic-us-military-presence-around-the-world-interactive.

[74] For a list of US military commands: www.defense.gov/About/combatant-commands/.

[75] See an interesting letter to the editor of the *International Herald Tribune*, 15 October 2004: 'An American Proconsul for Africa'. From Richard Wilcox, Director of UN affairs on the US National Security Council from 2000 to 2001.

seems that with the end of Cold War and of the fear of Communist expansion the United States has had less incentive to make sharp use of its formidable military power. Nevertheless, we must note that the United States has undertaken several significant armed actions in recent time:

- in Afghanistan and several other states after 9/11 2001 – to crush the Taliban movement and terrorist groups like Al Qaeda.
- in Iraq in 2003 together with the UK and others to bring about regime change – allegedly to force Iraq to fulfil its obligation to disarm.
- in Yemen since 2015 to support its preferred regional order.
- in Somalia and other African states to help defeat terrorist groups.[76]

Iran has been subjected to pressures and threats by the United States through a strong US military presence in the Persian Gulf, through subversive activities to undermine the theocratic government and – since 2018 – through US-induced crippling economic sanctions. The incentive is often declared to be a concern about Iranian nuclear ambitions and 'misbehaviour' in the region. Whether or not these concerns are well founded, the aim of the pressures has been to shape the US (and Israeli)-preferred regional order. With the US Biden administration has engaged the EU as an intermediary in lengthy negotiations with Iran about a normalization of the situation through the revival of the Joint Comprehensive Program of Action, but these had not – even by December 2022 – brought agreement.

In conclusion, during the Cold War, the United States often had an incentive to prevent other actors – notably the Soviet Union – to realize Communist aspirations for national, regional or global power. When these threats disappeared, the US aspirations for global and regional influence may have provided incentives for open-armed interventions only in relatively few cases. The United States has refrained from using force to help oust some governments that it may well have wanted to see toppled, such as Bolivia and Venezuela. In the Middle East, the risk of an uncontrollable spread of conflict has led it to refrain from direct military actions against Iran. Conscious of the dangers of a direct and open conflict, the United States has so far (2022) met China's forays into the US-dominated Pacific not by active force but by naval and air movements that demonstratively ignore Chinese claims of sovereignty. Finally, as has been described in Chapter 3, the United States has made it clear that while it supports Ukraine in a major

---

[76] A news analysis by Eric Schmitt in the *International New York Times*, 17–18 October 2020 reported that there were about 700 American troops in Somalia, most of them Special Operations forces scattered at bases across the country.

way with weapons and resources for defence against the Russian armed invasion (2022) and mounts unprecedented economic sanctions to weaken Russia it will avoid direct armed confrontation with Russia.

CHINA

Historically, it has been customary for China to aspire for and to exercise domination in the Eastern part of the Asian continent. However, for a long period before the Communist government gained control over the country China's power was limited due to internal division, weakness and humiliating foreign domination. Even until recent years, China has engaged in struggles for territorial control mainly to defend or recover areas to which it claimed to have historic rights. This confirms what seems very likely, namely, that perceptions – valid or not – that a right to land, border, sea, or whatever has been wrongfully taken away often create incentives for recovery even by force.

As noted earlier, during the Korean War in 1950 China deployed an army of 'volunteers' – not to help North Korea occupy South Korea but – to defend China's border at the Yalu River, when US forces were advancing toward it.[77] In 1950, China also incorporated the territory of Tibet, an action that it saw as no more than extending its administration to land to which it claimed historical rights. Asserting historical rights China has consistently claimed sovereignty over Taiwan but refrained from military action that could trigger armed conflict and intervention by the United States. Even attempts in the second half of the 1950s to seize the small islands Quemoy and Matsu very close to China's coast but under Taiwan's control were abandoned, when they risked triggering US military action.[78] The visit to Taiwan in 2022 by the Speaker of the US House of Representatives, Ms Pelosi, triggered Beijing to extensive military demonstrations but not the use of force. However, on several occasions, China has engaged actively in armed border conflicts with India (wars in 1962 and 1967 and lesser confrontations in 2020) over land to which it claimed to have a title.

Even when the economic expansion was under way under Deng Xiaoping, China's international profile was not associated with aspirations for greater geopolitical control but with a 'policy of peaceful rise'. China successfully obtained the return of Hong Kong and Macao through peaceful means. Perhaps it was thought at the time that the stated goal of 'one country, two systems' would help to attract Taiwan. If so, it was a miscalculation.

---

[77] See above Chapter 3, p. 35.
[78] See above, Chapter 3, p. 51 and Chapter 4, p. 58.

The 'belt and road initiative' launched in 2013 is a spectacular and dynamic geopolitical infrastructure project designed to open fast links between China and the Middle East and Africa as well as Europe. It may be expected to increase China's economic and political influence and has evoked praise as an international development project but also concern that it may make poor parties very dependent on China. The same is true of China's vastly increased world trade and the large economic investments made in many parts of the world. Within the UN system, China has become an active supporter of multilateralism, not least to maintain free trade to keep world markets open for Chinese exports. Some features in China's economic expansion have triggered much criticism and a near trade war with the United States (2020). There have been charges that 'private' Chinese investments are under the ultimate control of the government and may be used by China to intervene in the operation of strategic foreign infrastructure.

With its phenomenal rise in recent years, with a population of 1.4 billion and with an economy, which rivals that of the United States in size, China may have entered a new phase with incentives to play a greater economic and political role in the world and to exercise a greater influence particularly in the Asian-Pacific region.

China's new economic strength and aspirations have been paralleled by expanded resources for modern warfare, including nuclear weapons, new missiles, naval, space and cyber capacity. It has expanded its contacts with some island states in the South Pacific and established a naval base in Djibouti at the entrance of the Red Sea.

The new economic and military strength is accompanied by some significant ambitions on the ground. On the most sensitive issue, Taiwan, the consistent claims have remained combined with restraint. As noted above,[79] it may be assumed that China attentively watches what degree of determination the United States and NATO countries show in helping Ukrainians prevent Russia from taking over their country. With growing power, including naval power, China, long sealed off from influence in the Pacific, is developing a greater presence in the West Pacific and the East and South China seas and is claiming sovereignty over many islands and air and sea space around them.[80] Japan's control of some islands (the Senkakus) is disputed and incidents have occurred. Even more serious is China's occupation of islands to which the Philippines claim sovereignty in the South China Sea. As noted above, attempts to find a solution through arbitration have failed.[81]

[79] Chapter 3, p. 46.
[80] See above, Chapter 3, p. 52.
[81] See above, Chapter 3, p. 52 As the islands are located in areas that – although thousands of miles away from the American continent – have been under US domination since World War

COLLIDING ASPIRATIONS FOR DOMINATION RISK
CREATING INCENTIVES FOR THE USE OF FORCE:
UKRAINE, MIDDLE EAST AND WEST PACIFIC

Aspirations for domination risk leading to the threat or use of force, when states targeted for domination resist pressures. Where two or more great powers compete for influence/domination in the same area there is a similar risk and, in this case, any belligerent confrontation could be like the collision of tectonic shelves. Fortunately, the great powers though vast are neither tectonic shelves, nor are they moving on autopilot but led by leaders in whose power it is to apply brakes and use diplomacy.

Competition about global domination is what we saw in the Cold War between the Soviet Communist bloc and the Western bloc led by the United States. However, we could also see that both sides were anxious to avoid armed confrontations and concealed or blurred their authorship of force to avoid the risk of confronting each other directly. In this, they were fortunately successful although the Cuba crisis in 1962 was a close call.

When the aspirations of the Moscow-led Communist bloc disappeared with the break-up of the Soviet Union, the aspirations of the United States for world leadership were left unchallenged – even stimulated. The competitive 'bipolar' world became for a short period a 'unipolar' world under a 'Pax Americana'. However, slowly, the economic and military power and aspirations of other states, notably China, have grown and a world may be in the making in which not only the biggest powers – the United States, China, European Union, Russia and India – but many states, such as Japan, Indonesia, Iran, Turkey, Israel, Egypt, Nigeria, South Africa, Brazil, Mexico aspire and compete for a share of influence. The result could be a truly multipolar world but also a new bipolar world in which the US aligned with the large NATO group and many individual states (Morocco? Brazil? ...) would form one side and China with the support of Russia and individual states (Iran? Afghanistan?...) would form the other side. This development contains risks of frictions, conflict and the use of force.

One region where great power aspirations for influence/domination collide is a zone that engages the interest of Russia and the European Union, the Union States and NATO – Ukraine. After the Russian seizure and annexation of Crimea in 2014, there was a long-lasting low-intensity conflict within

II, the United States is being challenged. An excellent analysis of these challenges and possible ways for the United States to meet them constructively and without force was presented 30 July 2021 by Rachel Esplin Odell in Brief No. 15 of the US Quincy Institute: 'Promoting Peace and Stability in the Maritime Order Amid China's Rise'.

Ukraine between Russian-assisted insurgents and forces of the Ukrainian government (partly armed by the West). In February 2022 Russian pressure and threat were followed by a large-scale armed invasion of Ukraine. While President Putin curiously stated the aim to be to 'demilitarize and denazify' Ukraine, another aim, probably seen as realistic, was to halt Ukraine's drift away from Russia economically and politically.

In this Russian fight to maintain hegemony by force the United States, its NATO allies and other friends, have been determined not to engage directly on the ground in ways that could risk escalating to a big war. Instead, they have adopted unprecedentedly strong sanctions against Russia and supplied Ukraine with huge quantities of arms. They are convinced that Ukraine's (and Georgia's) drift to a market economy-society modelled on and linked with Western liberal democracies will continue and that Russian armed actions have only led to stronger strivings for independence in the two countries.[82]

A second region of colliding interests is the Middle East, where for a long time, the United States aspired to be the strongest external influence. With diminishing strategic importance for the United States and the West of oil from the region, the cost/benefit of such influence has been falling and the United States has for some time signalled a pivot to its interest in and competition with China. Nevertheless, the aspiration to influence the politics in the Middle East and care for the remaining economic interest in oil is still demonstrated by the United States through troops in Kuwait, a huge naval base in Bahrain and a huge air base in Qatar. It is nourished by the determination to protect and assist Israel and by the animosity against Iran that has prevailed since 1980 when the Shah was toppled and Ayatollah Khomeini took power. As Russia and China support Iran there are risks of clashes of interest with the United States.

However, as in the war in Syria, where the United States and Russia engaged in different armed missions, they were anxious not to confront each other by mistake. They reached understandings of how to avoid clashes between their airplanes and set up procedures for implementation. The same attitude seems likely to prevent other confrontations between them in the region.

The third region where the aspirations for influence/domination of great powers collide is the Western Pacific and the Indian Ocean. Since the end of World War II, this region has been dominated by the United States. As described above, an economically and militarily increasingly powerful China

---

[82] See footnote 65.

is now showing aspirations to exercise more power and influence. Attention is currently focused on the controversies over the Spratly Islands.[83] Chinese fortification of natural islands and construction of artificial islands has led the United States to send naval units and airplanes through the area to demonstrate rejection of the Chinese claims. So far, the stand-off between the United States and China has not led to live confrontations but the risk is not zero that armed force could come to be used by miscalculation or misunderstanding. The Spratlys are currently possibly the world's most serious flashpoint.

---

[83] See above, Chapter 3, p. 52.

5

Historical Evolution of Norms and Other Means to Restrain the Use of Force

EVOLUTION OF SOCIAL NORMS AGAINST THE USE OF FORCE

This book seeks to identify restraints that currently exist on the use of force **between** states. Before focusing on this task, it may be helpful for perspective briefly to look also at the roots and development of restraints on the use of force generally.

We may assume that calculations that a potential adversary is more powerful are a factor of restraint (deterrence) on the use of force between individuals within a society as well as between societies. We may further be sure that even in the earliest human societies some reactions and customary norms against the use of force **within** the societies arose and worked as restraints. On the other hand, as this chapter will show, norms against the use of force **between** societies have emerged only in recent history. We shall begin by discussing the evolution within societies.

RESTRAINTS ON USE OF FORCE *WITHIN* SOCIETIES

Some authorities have been of the view that men[1] are born 'evil' and must be restrained.[2] Others disagreeing have argued that all kinds of evil behaviour – the use of force, theft, oppression – flow from the social organization that evolves, notably the concept of private ownership. In line with this thinking, some have thought, for instance, that hunter-gatherer societies were peaceful and egalitarian. No piece of land is claimed to be privately owned and members are thought to share their kills and catches. However, the evidence

---

[1]   I am using this term in its universal sense to mean all human beings.
[2]   St Augustine; Hobbes; and Morgenthau.

seems to speak against this idealistic picture and it is reasonable to believe that force was sometimes used both between and within hunting bands.[3] It is also reasonable to assume that generally the proximity of people – whether in simple hunter-gatherer groups or in large settlements – results both in cooperation and differences. As some solutions to frictions and conflicts are found, repeated and enforced – whether by payment of damages or penalties – they grow to usage and mature to become customary norms perceived as binding. Thus, norms applied may arise and constitute restraints against the use of force even by members of early human groupings.[4]

THE EARLY AGRARIAN SOCIETY

The transition from hunter-gatherer societies to the agrarian society that began some 10.000 years ago in the Middle East brought fundamental changes in humanity's condition. While large areas of land were required to sustain hunter-gather groups, limited areas of concentrated cultivation could sustain large agrarian societies. The proximity of individuals increased dramatically and led to trade and urbanization. Differences in levels of wealth, specialization and stratification arose. Population density, land ownership and trade prompted social organization for cooperation and defence. Rules and mechanisms emerged to solve differences and conflicts between members of communities and to ensure enforcement of norms against the use of force. In societies headed by governing rulers, edicts by the ruler offered a route to binding norms. A famous ancient body of written norms is the code promulgated by King Hammurabi in 1776 BC, a time when the agrarian societies in Mesopotamia formed the Babylonian Empire.[5] The Code offers generous insights into the society of that time and introduced heavy penalties for various acts of violence in order to stop citizens from taking individual revenge.

In ancient Rome, a sophisticated legal system developed including penal law provisions designed to deter the use of force. Many centuries later states, like England, France and Sweden emerged. Historians have analysed how in Europe this complex process comprised legal orders and a much-increased power of Kings.[6]

In the context of this inquiry, it may suffice to note that the primary tasks of kings were to use their power to defend their realms against external enemies

---

3   Gómez et al. (2016).
4   On the formation of customary law, see also below, Chapter 11, p. 174.
5   The full text is available at: https://avalon.law.yale.edu/ancient/hamcode.asp. Also see Mack (1979).
6   For instance: Tilly (1992) and Moberg (2014).

and, by upholding systems of law, to maintain internal peace and order. The key role of a powerful central government was stressed by Hobbes (1588–1679).[7] He had witnessed the misery and disasters that were brought by civil war and anarchy when people were not subjected to laws and enforcement that keep them from plundering and revenge. His central tenet was that peace and order could only be maintained within a nation if all military power and power of legislation, judicial settlement and enforcement were entrusted to or otherwise assumed by a ruling authority (Leviathan), whether a monarch or a parliament. The ruler would have a monopoly on the possession and use of arms and would settle people's disputes and thereby prevent acts of revenge. Without such an almighty and lofty authority people would be endlessly feuding with each other.[8]

Although Hobbes asserted that a fundamental law of nature obliged man to strive for peace, he claimed at the same time that where there was no supreme power there could be no law. Contracts become binding, he said, only when there is a power that can force people to respect them. Without the power of the sword, contracts are empty words.[9] His categorical message ignored the many other ways through which individuals are induced to respect the social order and refrain from the use of force but he did make a point that remains valid. Even today anarchy may be worse than dictatorship and oppression.

RESTRAINTS ON THE USE OF FORCE BETWEEN INDEPENDENT SOCIETIES

Turning from the question of the use of force **within** societies to the force used **between** independent societies, we find a very different evolution. To be sure, restraints to use force between societies have always been prompted by a great defensive capacity (deterrent) in a potential adversary. Increasing contacts and proximity have also over time generated many customary and treaty-based rules regulating relations **between** societies (international law). However, as we shall see, rules prescribing restraints specifically on the interstate (intersociety) use of force emerged only a hundred years ago through the Covenant of the League of Nations and Charter of the United Nations – and they still remain fragile ...[10]

---

[7] Hobbes (1968, English edition).

[8] Pinker, pp. 35, 56, 61, 680. Also see Hobbes (1968, edition) and Ertman (1997).

[9] Hobbes (from original *Leviathan* in 1651), Chapter XVII. His specific quote: 'And Covenants, without the Sword, are but Words, and of no strength to secure a man at all', www.gutenberg .org/files/3207/3207-h/3207-h.htm.

[10] Neff (2005) traces the general history and development of the conceptions of war from the most distant retrievable past to the present day. He rightly notes (pp. 279–280) that it was in the League of Nations period that for the first time the resort to war was legally restricted.

THE BIBLE REFLECTS NO RESTRAINTS ON THE
USE OF FORCE BETWEEN SOCIETIES

In the narratives that the Bible provides us about war, there is no trace of normative restraints on the resort to arms between independent societies or on the conduct of war. There are, on the other hand, many descriptions of hostilities pursued with unlimited brutality between societies. Two verses may be cited:

> Now go, attack the Amalekites and totally destroy all that belongs to them. Do not spare them; put to death men and women, children and infants, cattle and sheep, camels and donkeys.[11]
> This day the LORD will deliver you into my hands, and I'll strike you down and cut off your head. This very day I will give the carcasses of the Philistine army to the birds and the wild animals, and the whole world will know that there is a God in Israel.[12]

These quotes call to mind the modern term 'massive retaliation'. The world of the Old Testament was obviously very far from the idealistic guidance given by Jesus that 'if someone strikes you on one cheek, turn to him the other also' or the prophecy of Isaiah that after the advent of Messiah: 'they shall beat their swords into plowshares... nation shall not lift up sword against nation...' (Isaiah, Ch 2:4)

THE GREEK AND ROMAN AND CHRISTIAN CIVILIZATIONS

Swords were not beaten to plowshares by the Greek, Persian, or Roman civilizations when they blossomed in the period of thousand years that bridged BC and AC. Kings and other leaders engaged in wars for power, glory, riches, or revenge. However, Greek writings reflect the view that various conditions had to be fulfilled for a war to be considered justified, such as initiation by a proper authority (if not, the action would be banditry), and the existence of a just cause, such as self-defence or response to some wrong-doing.[13]

In Rome, similar notions – partly inherited from Greece – were articulated. During the time of the Roman Republic, criteria for just war, *bellum justum*, were discussed by Cicero and others. In the Christian Church that arose in the Roman Empire, the waging of any war met moral objections and its members

---

[11] 1 Samuel 15:3, New International Version (NIV). www.biblegateway.com/passage/?search=1+Samuel+15%3A3&version=NIV.

[12] 1 Samuel 17:46, NIV. http://topverses.com/Bible/1%20Samuel/17/46.

[13] See O'Driscoll (2015). Neff (2014), pp. 42–48 sees the roots pf international law in Greece and Rome.

were prohibited to be soldiers.[14] However, In 312, Emperor Constantine was converted to Christianity and the Christian Church now influenced rulers to protect and spread the Christian faith. In this period the Church abandoned its absolute pacifism.

Building on the earlier Greek and on Roman concepts, St Augustine (354–430) elaborated a doctrine on what constituted just wars (*bellum justum*). While resting on the past thinking it was an important doctrinal judgement[15] and it was to reverberate for many centuries in European theology and jurisprudence.[16] An immediate practical result was that since war could be just, Christians could serve in the Roman armed forces. Further, as in Greek thinking, wars to be justified had to be initiated by 'proper authority'. Minor rulers and warlords were not accorded any right to wage war. Consequently, their resort to the use of armed force stood condemned and punishable as simple banditry.

Other parts of the doctrine stipulated that while just wars could not be waged for the purpose of conquest or for simple revenge, they could legally be waged for *justa causa* – in response to a prior injury that was not followed by a willingness to repair. Presumably, the Church was best placed to judge whether a war was just.[17] The military crusades to retake the Holy Land – the first in 1096, the sixth in 1239 – presumably fell in this category even though they were sometimes supported by groups with secular interests.

Some eight hundred years after St Augustine, the great Catholic authority Thomas Aquinas (1225–74) confirmed the doctrine of just war without, however, bringing much more precision. It continued to hold that to be just wars had to be authorized by a proper authority and

- there had to be *justa causa*; and it was required that
- the belligerent had the intention to promote good or to avoid evil.[18]

Although the Church had remained a strong and coherent force in Europe after the breakdown of the Roman Empire, its doctrine of just war had little practical impact in the secular world. Nor could the Church prevent Europe from sliding into a long era of power fragmentation and endless turf battles among innumerable feudal lords. Toward the end of the Middle Ages, however, several sizeable states – monarchies – were formed when through war and other means rulers gained power and maintained order over larger areas of land and cities.

---

[14] See Bailey (1972), p. 2.
[15] See O'Driscoll (2015) and Nussbaum (1954), p. 35.
[16] See Nussbaum, p. 10.
[17] See Bailey, p. 6.
[18] Nussbaum, p. 36, Brownlie, p. 6.

THE USE OF FORCE AND THE DOCTRINE
UP TO THE PEACE OF WESTPHALIA

Kings saw defence – if need be by armed force – of their realms and their subjects as a primary task. But which factors – if any – made the rulers themselves desist from using their armed force against neighbours and other countries? Various realities, such as cost, insufficient domestic support, and the risk of defeat might – as always – have discouraged kings from embarking on war, but no rules of treaties or customary international law stood in the way. Doctrine was a different matter.

Throughout the fourteenth, fifteenth and sixteenth centuries, doctrine continued – as at the time of St Augustine – to permit just and ban unjust war. An evolution occurred, however, regarding the foundation invoked for the distinction – from a purely religious one to a secular one. While de Vitoria (1483–1546) and Suarez (1548–1617) followed the theological tradition other writers – like Hugo Grotius (1583–1645) – found a basis in 'natural law',[19] often reflecting their own humane and reasonable moral views.[20]

The most remarkable departure from the just war school was Machiavelli (1469–1527). He was a bitter enemy of the Church and papacy and scholastic teachings that purported to subordinate the relations among rulers to the demands of moral theology. In order to achieve the unity of Italy he was ready to apply any ruthless method. As cited by Brownlie, he stated simply: 'that war is just which is necessary' and every sovereign entity may decide on the occasion for war.[21]

HOBBES'S LEVIATHAN ABSENT ON
THE INTERNATIONAL SCENE

Hobbes (1588–1679) discussed primarily how the use of force could be eliminated within societies. As described above, he held that social peace could be achieved only through the rule of a strong central authority – Leviathan – who would enact, administer and enforce law. Thinking in this way, Hobbes could hardly have given many pennies for rules – whether forbidding the pursuit of unjust wars or anything else – claimed to govern relations between states without an International Leviathan enforcing them. Had Hobbes been asked whether there was any rule of law that limited the freedom of rulers to wage

---

[19] See Nussbaum, pp. 17, 107.
[20] Brownlie, p. 10.
[21] Brownlie, p. 11, citing *Il Principe*, Chapters 3 and 26.

war he would probably – like Machiavelli – have said no: there is no Leviathan enforcing a ban, hence no ban.

Hobbes was of the view that natural law required that rulers should strive for peace but he denied the legally binding effect of any norm that was not upheld by sanctions. He could certainly have seen nothing but a free warring in the international sphere. In his own era, he could see that while many states consolidated under strong kings, wars continued to rage between European states, triggered by many of the same causes as in the past, such as dynastic claims and religious conflicts.

There is something refreshingly simple and robust about Hobbes' view. He was essentially right in explaining to the world the reality that to maintain reliable peace in a social order you need an authority that has a monopoly on the possession and use of arms. This notion remains basically true but is too categorical for the international society of today. As will be discussed later most rules of international law – including those laid down in thousands of treaties – are routinely respected today despite the absence of Leviathan.

THE PEACE OF WESTPHALIA 1648

The Westphalian Peace was concluded in 1648 after 30 years of grim war in Europe and almost four years of negotiations. The settlement has been seen by many as a water divide leaving the Holy Roman Empire with insufficient strength and hegemony to maintain peace and order and replaced by a modern European order of territorial and sovereign states, which recognizes an emerging law of nations (international law) as relevant for their mutual relations, and that seeks to preserve the peace through a balance of power. The view is not unchallenged. Another view has been advanced that the order confirmed and perfected a system of autonomous states and strengthened legal systems that penalized the use of force.[22]

Whichever view one takes, the formal parties to the two treaties were the monarchic rulers of the Roman Empire, France and Sweden. The treaty was a settlement between them, not between a great number of territorial European units. The concept of balance of power is nowhere referred to in the treaty texts but it may well have been seen as a way to preserve peace among the many

---

[22] See Kissinger (2016), p. 6: the Westphalian principles are today 'the sole generally recognized basis of what exists of world order'. An alternative view holds that 'The Peace of Westphalia did not establish the "Westphalia system" based on the sovereign state. Instead, it confirmed and perfected something else: a system of mutual relations among autonomous political units that was precisely not based on the concept of sovereignty'. Sander (2001), p. 270.

constituent parts of Europe when the cohesive force of the Roman Empire eroded.[23] It has remained a valid tool for governments to forestall conflict.

Despite the different evaluations of the Westphalian peace settlement, it can certainly be seen as a new point of departure. It resulted in greater autonomy for many territorial units, the beginning of the practice of European powers meeting at large multilateral conferences to solve common problems, and the use of permanent diplomatic missions for continued contact. The treaties had no formal mechanisms for supervision or even provisions about further meetings, but their enduring nature was stressed, consultations were foreseen, and France and Sweden were to guarantee the respective treaties and even, if need be, intervene against breaches.

From the perspective of this inquiry, it should be noted that although 'unjust wars' had been condemned for hundreds of years in doctrinal teaching, law as a barrier to future wars between states, was an instrument left unused by the Peace of Westphalia. However, it did contain an embryo of what later would be called collective security. The treaty of Münster included a norm of multilateral solidarity for the maintenance of peace (Article 1), an obligation to solve existing disputes by peaceful means (Article 123) and an obligation to help a victim of aggression through joint action (Article 124). These provisions were, in a sense, forerunners to corresponding articles of the Covenant of the League of Nations and the United Nations Charter.[24] Despite the good intentions behind the provisions and efforts to stabilize relations between states through balance-of-power policies more wars were pursued.

FROM WESTPHALIA 1648 TO VIENNA 1814–1815

The Enlightenment and the French Revolution exerted a tremendous influence on the thinking and attitudes in Europe. What prominent writers and philosophers wrote about war during the Enlightenment must have blown like winds of rationality and humanism into the minds of many – including rulers. In his famous novel *Candide* (1759) Voltaire had a character defining war as 'a million assassins in uniform, roaming from one end of Europe to the other, murder and pillage with discipline in order to earn their daily bread.'[25]

During the Enlightenment, several ambitious schemes were presented for lasting peace. Although they seem to have had as little impact on rulers as the doctrines of just war, they are of interest as parts of the historical and mental

[23] Bring (2000); pp. 62 ff. discusses different meanings given to the concept.
[24] See Bring (2000), pp. 61–62.
[25] Cit. from Pinker, p. 165.

evolution. The peace schemes went beyond the approach of simply condemning wars that were not just and they showed an understanding that maintaining peace between countries would require organization and institutions and even collective action in the face of violations.

One famous scheme was presented by Abbé de St Pierre in 1713.[26] He proposed that a federation of Christian states should be formed to prevent both international and civil wars. It would have a permanent assembly, called the Senate, which would decide in cases of disputes. States not complying with such decisions would be forced by war to submit. Only the bigger states would have full voting power. Smaller states would have to vote in groups with each group having a vote. It is interesting that no notion of equality of states was allowed to stand in the way of action where the bigger states agreed.

An even better-known scheme was prepared by the German philosopher Kant. In his essay 'Toward a Perpetual Peace' (1795) he foresaw that standing armies should be abolished and he, too, envisaged a federation of free countries to be created. They should be under republican rule, as in a republic the citizens are aware of the costs of war and of the fact that these will be borne by themselves as taxpayers. Kant believed that trade and more communication would bring peoples closer to forming a single community.[27]

Despite the Enlightenment's and the French Revolution's generally critical attitude to war,[28] and despite schemes such as those by Abbé de St Pierre and Kant, the Enlightenment did not primarily focus on elimination of war but rather on doing away with cruelty and suffering that were not seen as inevitable for the pursuit of victory.

Rousseau, in his *Social Contract* (1762) insisted that wars take place between states and not between individuals. From this premise several rational conclusions were drawn: War gives no right to inflict any more destruction than is necessary for victory. Individuals are enemies not as human beings but only as soldiers and those not taking part in hostilities – the civilian population and those who have laid down their arms and become prisoners of war – should be spared and respected.[29] These rational and humanitarian views came to be reflected in intergovernmental conventions that were adopted in the nineteenth century.

---

[26] See Nussbaum, p. 142; Gihl, p. 80; and Hinsley (1962).

[27] See Pinker, p. 166, Kissinger, p. 40 and Nussbaum, p. 143. Kant would have been delighted to see the development of the European Union of democratic states knit ever closer through trade and close communication.

[28] A constitution adopted in 1791 during the French Revolution contained a prohibition of 'aggressive' war. See Brownlie, p. 18.

[29] Rousseau (1968), p. 57. See Rosas, A., 'J.J. Rousseau and the law of armed force' in Bring (2008), p. 224; and see also Rousseau's treatise on *Perpetual Peace* (1756). See also Nussbaum., p. 139.

Sadly, but unsurprisingly, neither the scholarly teachings about permissible 'just' wars and prohibited 'unjust' wars, whether based on theology or natural law, nor the pursuit of a balance of power, nor the Enlightenment stressing rationality stopped rulers of independent European powers from fighting wars for a great variety of reasons.[30] The doctrines may have been seen as providing moral teaching rather than legal rules.

SIGNIFICANT EUROPEAN WARS BETWEEN THE PEACE OF WESTPHALIA AND THE VIENNA CONFERENCE[31]

- Anglo-Dutch War 1652–1674
- Austro-Turkish War 1663–1664
- Franco-Dutch War 1672–1678
- The Nine Years' War of Louis XIV vs League of Augsburg 1688–1697
- Spanish succession war 1701–1713
- Russo-Swedish War 1741–43
- Frederick the Great's invasion of Silesia 1740
- Louis XIV Seven Years War, of the Spanish succession 1756–63
- Seven years' war between France and Great Britain 1756–63
- Russo-Swedish War 1788–1790
- French revolutionary wars 1792–1802
- Napoleonic Wars 1803–1815

THE CONGRESS OF VIENNA IN 1814–1815. 'THE EUROPEAN CONCERT'

The Enlightenment and the French Revolution did not inaugurate a period of peace but of revolutionary wars that evolved into the era of Napoleonic Wars. When Napoleon's attempts to create French hegemony were defeated, a strong ambition emerged among the rulers of the great powers that had opposed Napoleon – Austria, Russia, Prussia and Great Britain – to recreate a balance of power and fortify the monarchic order of states as the basis for stability in order to maintain peace. This was achieved through the 1814–1815

---

[30] Before invading Silesia in 1740 and after the invasion of Saxony, Frederick the Great presented explanations as to the legitimacy of the action. See Brownlie, p. 17.

[31] There are many sources listing wars in this period. For a lengthy compilation, see www .britannica.com/topic/list-of-wars-2031197. And see Tilly, C. (1992), pp. 165 ff.

Congress of Vienna and treaties and alliances that preceded and followed it, including the so-called Holy Alliance and the Concert of Europe.

Among the authoritarian rulers looking for a new European peace order, there was, of course, no sympathy for a liberal peace project like that presented by Kant. As in Westphalia in 1648, there was also no ambition to pursue the institutional and normative approach taken by scholars to preserve peace or by specifying and outlawing what would be unjust wars. However, while in 1648 France and Sweden committed themselves in a general way to ensure respect for the Westphalian treaties, the great powers at Vienna committed themselves to actively intervene to uphold the peace and political order that they brought about. A proclamation issued at Vienna on 13 March 1815 set the tone by declaring that they would use all means to preserve the general peace against measures that threatened to drive peoples to revolutionary upheavals.

Members of the European Concert – a term originally coined in the 1814 Treaty of Chaumont referring to a *'parfait concert'* – did in fact intervene in a great many controversies. Ad hoc conferences[32] became an important mechanism for decisions on joint actions. However, the attitude to intervention differed greatly between Great Britain on the one hand and authoritarian-ruled Austria, Russia and Prussia on the other. Great Britain was ready to take ad hoc decisions on intervention but unwilling to give any carte blanche. Mr. Castlereagh, the British Foreign Secretary, stated that the Alliance 'was never intended as a union for the government of the world, or for the superintendence of the internal affairs of other states'.[33]

One issue of great significance in this era of European colonialism was the question of support for the King of Spain against rebellious colonies in South America. The idea of European intervention in Latin America was opposed by Great Britain and triggered the so-called Monroe Doctrine, under which in 1823 the United States declared a policy of non-intervention in European conflicts and its view that any intervention by the allied European states in the Western hemisphere would be an unfriendly act.[34]

The 'era of congresses' was a short but remarkable effort by a few European great powers to meddle and intervene – by armed force if need be – in major and minor matters on the European continent to preserve a peaceful order and autocratic regimes. No international norms or institutions stood in the way.

---

[32]   See Bridge (2014), ch. 2. See also Gihl, p. 95.
[33]   Viscount Castlereagh, 'Confidential Minute of Viscount Castlereagh on the Affairs of Spain. Communicated to the Courts of Austria, France, Prussia and Russia in May, 1820', *Hansard* (UK), 21 April 1823, https://hansard.parliament.uk/Commons/1823-04-21/debates/834b4163-8414-46bc-a5c2-75895c321314/AdditionalPapers—Spain—France—Portugal.
[34]   Nussbaum, p. 189.

To the twenty-first century, many of the legacies of the 1814–1815 Congress of Vienna and of the European Concert look reactionary, but others presaged a more modern world. Most important was perhaps the further development and confirmation of the practice of calling multilateral conferences to tackle common regional questions, big and small. There was, further, an acceptance and development of international rules to cover and regulate common interests. The Final Act of Vienna concerned itself with rules on the free navigation of European rivers traversing or separating several states and on the rank of diplomatic agents. It also agreed to the suppression of the slave trade and in a separate convention, the neutrality of Switzerland (which had been infringed during the Napoleonic Wars) was guaranteed.

While the legal scholars of the period identified a fairly large body of common international rules, for instance on the law of the sea and the law of treaties one might wonder whether these were perceived by the rulers as mandatory norms or merely as common practices. When it came to state conduct relevant to peace between European nations, it would seem clear that the rulers subscribed to fervently held but ill-defined principles rather than any defined norms. An example is the Protocol signed at the 1818 Congress of Aix la Chapelle declaring that

> The Sovereigns, in forming this august Union, have regarded as its fundamental basis their invariable resolution never to depart, either among themselves, or in their Relations with other States, from the strictest observation of the principles of the Right of Nations; principles which, in their application to a state of permanent Peace, can alone effectually guarantee the Independence of each Government, and the stability of the general association.[35]

In other places, the Aix- la-Chapelle documents refer variously – and without definitions – to 'a system', 'the order of things established in Europe', and 'the principle of intimate Union'... The approach to peace was transactional. It might be seen even as a forerunner of modern peacekeeping, when in 1848–50 it brought about the deployment of a military contingent from the Union of Sweden and Norway to reinforce the armistice after the first Schleswig War.[36] By contrast, it showed no interest in pronouncing norms restraining the right to resort to war or other use of armed force, whether in Europe or outside the continent, where European colonialism was in full blossom. Despite its ambitions to maintain order and balance of power, new wars took place and significant change occurred in Europe through the unification of Germany.

[35] Annex C, 'Peace of Europe, Union of the Five Powers', of the Protocol signed at the Aix La-Chappelle conference on 15 November 1818. https://en.wikisource.org/wiki/Congress_of_Aix-la-Chapelle_(1818).

[36] Bring, pp. 20–21.

SOME NINETEENTH CENTURY EUROPEAN WARS

- 1848–51: The first Schleswig War.
- 1848–49: The first Italian War of independence.
- 1853–1856: The Crimean War.
- 1859:The second Italian War of independence
- 1864: The second Schleswig War (Prussia – Denmark)
- 1866: The Austria-Prussia War.
- 1870–71: The Franco-Prussian War.
- 1877–1878: Russo-Turkish War
- 1897: Greco-Turkish War.

Sources: Items picked from Wikipedia 'List of conflicts in Europe'. Cf. Tilly, C.(1992), p. 169.

PEACE STRIVINGS 1820 TO 1907
(SECOND HAGUE PEACE CONFERENCE)

In the nineteenth century, the proximity of states and peoples increased through more communication, transportation and trade. Continuous multilateral cooperation far beyond the Vienna 1815 agreements on international rivers and other matters developed to cover functional needs common to all states in fields like post, telegraph, rail and health. The seeds of public international administration were planted.[37] Moreover, public opinion began to actively engage in questions of conduct of war, maintenance of peace and disarmament.[38] Civic society – often religious groups like the Quakers – raised its voice, and national and international movements arose as a new 'public mind' for peace, supporting arbitration of disputes, disarmament and action to limit the sufferings caused by war.[39]

Governments showed aversion to restrictions on their armaments and on their freedom of action in the international field, but they joined the wish to mitigate the cruelties of warfare and the new humanitarian thinking led to several conventions.

---

[37] See Bowett (1963), pp. 5–8.
[38] See Bring (2000), pp. 72 ff.
[39] Victor Hugo was a prominent participant at many of the European Peace Congresses in this period. (For excerpts of his statements at the congresses in 1849, 1851, 1869, and 1871, see Lucia Ames Mead, *A Primer of the Peace Movement [n.d.]*, www.gavroche.org/vhugo/peacecongress .shtml.) For excerpts from Hugo's speeches to international Peace Conferences, see www .gavroche.org/vhugo/peacecongress.shtml.

In 1863, the Red Cross was created by Henri Dunant in Geneva. A number of international peace conferences – the first in Paris in 1889 – were held at the non-governmental level. At the intergovernmental level, the new efforts culminated in the 1899 and 1907 Hague Peace Conferences.

At the Lateran Councils in the Middle Ages, the Church appealed to humanitarian feelings to urge limitations in the pursuit of war.[40] The nineteenth-century conventions sought inspiration also from the argument of the Enlightenment that there was no rational reason to tolerate cruelties and sufferings that were not dictated by the necessities of war. The preamble of the 1868 St Petersburg declaration prohibiting the use of certain explosive projectiles clearly explained the rationale:

> Considering that the progress of civilization should have the effect of alleviating as much as possible, the calamities of war: That the only legitimate object which states should endeavour to accomplish during war is to weaken the military forces of the enemy,
>
> That for this purpose, it is sufficient to disable the greatest possible number of men;
>
> That this object would be exceeded by the employment of arms which uselessly aggravate the sufferings of disabled men, or render their death inevitable;
>
> That the employment of such arms would, therefore, be contrary to the laws of humanity;[41]

As the pursuit of war should be directed against the 'military forces', the civilian population and soldiers incapacitated or taken prisoners should be spared. Warfare should not be indiscriminate and should not go beyond the measures needed to 'disable' the enemy.

These thoughts were the central philosophy behind conventions concluded in the latter part of the nineteenth century.[42] The first was the 1864 Convention for the Amelioration of the Condition of the Wounded in Armies in the Field. Conventions concerning the protection of prisoners of war were adopted in 1899 at the Hague Peace Conference and were succeeded by modernized conventions in 1928 and 1949.[43]

Perhaps the most important instrument adopted by the first Hague Peace Conference in 1899 was the comprehensive convention (with regulations) on the Law and Customs of War on Land. The conference also adopted a

---

[40] See Nussbaum, p. 17. Thurer (2011), p. 62.
[41] St Petersburg Declaration, signed 11 December 1868, https://ihl-databases.icrc.org/applic/ihl/ihl.nsf/Article.xsp?action=openDocument&documentId=568842C2B90F4A29C12563CD0051547C.
[42] Schindler and Toman (1981). See Bailey (1972); Nussbaum, p. 225.
[43] Nussbaum, p. 266 and 1949. See Detter (1987), p. 282.

declaration against the use of the so-called dum dum bullet, which had a soft nose and expanded when it hit a human body and therefore caused greater injury than was needed for the legitimate aim of disabling a soldier. Another declaration prohibited the launching of projectiles and explosives from balloons, a method of warfare that was seen as inherently incapable of discriminating between civilians and combatants.

The Second Hague Peace Conference[44] of 1907 adopted no less than thirteen conventions. This included an updated version of the convention of 1899 regarding the laws and customs of war on land.[45]

One ambition pursued at the first Hague conference at the instance of the initiator Tsar Nicolas II, and fervently pushed by the peace movements, was disarmament. As on many later occasions it ran into solid, even scornful resistance. It was able only to adopt an anaemic resolution on the matter reading:

> The Conference is of the opinion that the restriction of military charges, which are at present a heavy burden on the world, is extremely desirable for the increase of the material and moral welfare of mankind. [and]
>
> The Conference expresses the wish that the Governments, taking into consideration the proposals made at the Conference, may examine the possibility of an agreement as to the limitation of armed forces by land and sea, and of war budgets[46]

While there was no readiness for disarmament at The Hague in 1899, the world had slowly become ready during the nineteenth century for a greater use of mediation, arbitration and judicial means to settle disputes and, thereby, avoiding the resort to armed actions.[47] The First Hague Peace Conference established the Permanent Court of Arbitration. It was essentially a set procedure and a list of available arbitrators. Thus, it was not much of a court but it is still operative[48] and it became a forerunner to the Permanent Court of International Justice and the UN-linked International Court of Justice.

It remains to note from the Second Hague Conference a little-noticed convention that is of some interest in terms of legal development. The so-called Porter convention prohibited the use of armed force by one state against

---

[44] 'Final Act of the International Peace Conference', The Hague, 29 July 1899, https://ihl-databases.icrc.org/applic/ihl/ihl.nsf/385eco82b509e76c41256739003e636d/ffdea4cf83d0789fc1256 41e0034a70f?OpenDocument. Also see Schindler and Toman, pp. 50, 53; and Nussbaum, p. 229.

[45] At the Nuremberg trials and later at the United Nations the rules of the convention were held to be declaratory of customary international law. See Schindler and Toman, p. 57.

[46] 'Final Act' (1899), op. cit. note 44.

[47] See Nussbaum, pp. 215 ff.

[48] It was engaged in the dispute about islands in the South China Sea in 2016, when it ruled against Chinese claims, see Chapter 3, p. 52.

another in the collection of contract debts unless the debtor state should refuse acceptance of arbitration or failed to abide by an award.[49] The case that will be referred to in somewhat greater detail below in Chapters 6 and 12 is remarkable as it seems to be the first occasion that a normative approach – a multilateral convention – was taken to restrict the interstate use of force.[50]

There had been plans for a third Hague Peace Conference to establish periodic conferences as a means addressing the increasing number of international problems that came with an increasingly connected world. However, World War I came in the way and the war was followed by a much more ambitious project: a permanent world organization.

THE LEAGUE OF NATIONS 1920–1946

If during the nineteenth century peace movements had been an important factor both before and at the Hague Peace Conferences, after the horrors of the World War I public opinion provided even stronger pressure on governments to create a peace order. Thanks to President Wilson of the United States there was this time a powerful political response. He provided a blueprint for a permanent world organization and pressed it vigorously and successfully on the other victor states. He designed the Covenant to be an integral part of the Versailles Treaty with the hope of providing a mechanism to resolve many matters raised or left open by the treaty.[51] The Covenant and the League represented enormous innovation and new experience: After over a hundred years of ad hoc multilateral conferences, there was now a permanent global intergovernmental institution with a constitution and with organs meeting at regular intervals, a permanent seat and a permanent Secretariat of civil servants.

The many functional intergovernmental organizations that had come into being in response to the practical needs of a growing and integrating community of states – for post, telegraph, health controls, labour relations, rail traffic, river traffic, etc. – now formally ranged themselves as subsidiaries of the League. They continued to develop with little intervention by the League and relatively little disturbed by political tensions.

As the great powers victors in 1815 had done at the Congress of Vienna, the great powers victors in World War I ensured a dominating role for themselves in the League (and did the same in the United Nations after World War II). It was only under pressure that the Covenant had come to stipulate that a number

---

[49] See Nussbaum, p. 217. The convention has its name from the US general and diplomat Horace Porter.
[50] See Chapter 6, p. 112 and Chapter 12, p. 188.
[51] On the creation of the League, see Mazower, pp. 116 ff.

of seats in the Council were to be reserved to be filled on a rotating basis by smaller member states. All members – big and small – were able to participate in the Assembly and make their voices heard in the world and different from the order in the United Nations states that stood accused of wrong-doing could not participate in the League in votes regarding conflicts in which they were parties. International law was declared in the Preamble of the Covenant as the norm for government conduct and arbitration and judicial settlement were given a central role. Art. 10 of the Covenant specifically committed members to 'respect the territorial integrity and political independence' of other members and to join in protecting them against external aggression. However, what 'respect' required members to refrain from was not specified, except 'external aggression' and 'war or threat of war' (Art. 11). Nor was any explicit mention made of the right to self-defence and how extensive it was.

By the adoption of the Statute of the Permanent Court of International Justice, the League furthermore defined where the norms of international law were to be found, namely (abbreviated): international conventions, international custom, general principles of law, and as subsidiary means, judicial decisions and teachings of qualified publicists.

The principle of collective security was established whereby each member was obliged to take action (economic sanctions) automatically against a state that it judged had gone to war in violation of its obligations under the Covenant. Lastly, Members recognized (Art. 8) the requirement of reduction of national armaments to the lowest point consistent with national safety and the enforcement by common action of international obligations. Moreover, the Council was charged with the task of formulating plans for such reductions.

The Covenant and the League marked a leap forward in the organization of the states of the world and in the efforts to prevent war. Yet, as will be noted in the chapters below, on major matters the experience proved disappointing: the disarmament efforts failed, the rule requiring respect for the territorial integrity and political independence of other members was violated and the collective security system did not work.[52]

THE BRIAND KELLOGG PACT OF 1928

The 'pact' was signed and ratified by 63 states which 'renounced' war as an instrument of national policy and condemned recourse to war for the solution of international controversies. As noted below,[53] it has been seen by some as

---

[52] See Chapter 11, p. 179.
[53] Chapter 11, p. 179.

mainly hortatory. However, more often it has been understood as a legally binding norm covering 'war' as well as acts 'short of war' and even effecting rules governing neutrality. For instance, in 1941 a memorandum by Hersch Lauterpacht argued that while the Pact did not impose on neutrals a duty of qualified neutrality discriminating against aggressor states it gave them a right to do so. The reasoning was used by the – still neutral – US government to justify its aid to the Allies short of war.[54]

The Pact was incorporated in the Charters of the Nuremberg and Tokyo tribunals and invoked on many occasions as the legal basis for condemning various actions, for instance, Italy's aggression against Ethiopia (1935) and the Soviet Union's attack on Finland (1939).[55] One authority concludes that the Pact and the League Covenant should be credited for reversing the presumption in favour of the right of war.[56]

CHARTER OF THE NUREMBERG TRIBUNAL 1945

After the end of World War II France, the Soviet Union, the United Kingdom and the United States reached an agreement on the prosecution and punishment of the major war criminals of the European Axis.[57] The trials took place in Nuremberg in 1945–46. After the League Covenant (1919) and the Kellogg Briand Pact (1928) the agreement, the trials and the UN's subsequent confirmation must be seen as further steps by the international community to create disincentives to crimes against peace, such as wars of aggression. A description of the Nuremberg agreement and its relevance as a precedent for the outlawing of the use of force is provided below in Chapter 11, which deals with law as a means to restrain the use of force between states. The 'Tokyo Tribunal' had the same function for trials of crimes of the peace, war crimes, and crimes against humanity.[58]

The United Nations 1945

It is said that generals always plan for the last war, seeking to preserve the strengths and remedy the weaknesses that they had experienced and failing to see many new conditions which they will meet. It could also be said about

---

[54] See Schwebel (2005), p. 728. And see Brownlie (1963), p. 87.

[55] Brownlie, pp. 77, 79–80.

[56] Brownlie, p. 92.

[57] For further discussion of the London Agreement of 8 August 1945, see www.roberthjackson .org/article/london-agreement-charter-august-8-1945/.

[58] See Cohen and Totani (2018).

the authors of the UN Charter who gave the organization an architecture very similar to that of the Covenant of the League but sought to learn from and remedy weaknesses it had shown. Like the generals, they could also not foresee new important conditions to which the United Nations would need to respond – cold war, nuclear threats, terrorism and climate change.

Below, I shall point to some major features in the UN structure and how it marks a second leap forward in the twentieth-century evolution of normative and institutional restraints on the use of force between states.

The first point to note is the universality of the UN. It is significant for the authority of the United Nations that (practically) all the world's states, including all great powers, are members (193). The League of Nations remained a European-dominated club missing several great powers, including the United States.

A second point is that in San Francisco in 1945 – as at Westphalia in 1648, Vienna in 1814–1815 and Paris in 1919 – the great powers that had won the preceding war took the reins. The participation of some small powers in the Security Council was never questioned in the composition of the UN in the way it was when the Council of the League was constructed. On balance, however, they were given less power in the UN, where decisions both in the Security Council and the General Assembly are taken by the majority but where each of the five permanent members in the Council – but no other member – has veto power and is in a position to prevent any decisions.

A third improvement over the Covenant is that the Charter places upon the Security Council – and does not leave to individual members – the task of determining who in any particular instance is responsible for a breach of the peace and how collective security is to be exercised. If – and it is a big if – the five permanent members support a particular action the outlook for implementing collective security should be good. The power of the Council is further strengthened by Charter Art. 25, which obliges all members to accept and carry out decisions taken in accordance with the Charter.

That a muscular collective security system under great power leadership was envisaged emerges from many accounts of discussions between the wartime allies. It is also shown by a group of articles – arts. 43–48 – concerning the conclusion of agreements under which members are to make armed forces available to the Council and concerning a Military Staff Committee consisting of the chiefs of staff of the permanent members.

In Article 109 of the Charter, it is further somewhat cryptically stipulated that the P5 are to consult on 'joint action' that might be necessary for the maintenance of peace and security 'pending' the conclusion of the agreements with members on making armed forces at the disposal of the Council.

While this provision might have been intended as a basis for talks between the P5 about a stronger system of collective security no agreements have been made with states on supplying armed forces, nor have – as far as we know – such consultations taken place and the Military Staff Committee has played no role.[59]

A fourth point relates to the role of international law. In both the Covenant and the Charter respect for and development of norms are central tasks that include the codification of customary law and the creation of new law, for instance, conventions on human rights, or arms control. This role will be discussed below in Chapter 11, which deals with law as a means to restrain the interstate use of force.

A fifth point that deserves to be mentioned is that the architects of the Charter preserved and strengthened the role of the Secretary-General and the civil service nature of the Secretariat. In an organization of nearly 200 states pushing for their own preferred conclusions and actions, it is of great importance that the Secretariat remains factual and impartial and loyally performs the tasks that are laid upon it by the competent organs.

A last point: The League of Nations lasted some 20 years – between the First and the World War II. The United Nations has now (2022) lasted more than 75 years and no one of the 193 member states has exiled itself from the organization. It is the central forum for the states of the world to meet, to try to solve differences and to tackle common challenges. Over time and especially after the end of the Cold War the United Nations has helped to solve or contain many conflicts and it has often been innovative in its actions. Nevertheless, its system for collective security, like that of the League of Nations, has so far proved defective. The latest evidence of its weakness to prevent or stop the use of force in violation of the Charter is its inability to act against Russia's aggression in Ukraine.

---

[59] On the convergence of the great powers' views regarding UN forces, see Mazower, pp. 204–206.

6

Overview of Disincentives to and Restraints on the Interstate Use of Force

In the first three chapters of this book, I have tried to present a broad picture of the role that the use of force between states has played in the world after the World War II, and in the fourth chapter I sought to identify specific incentives that may exist to use force today. In the fifth chapter, I looked back at the efforts from early history up to the United Nations to create restraints on the use of force. In this and the following chapters, I shall discuss developments and factors that today may create disincentives to and restraint in the use of force between states.

While readiness to use force – for gain or defence – may be genetically engrained in human beings, this readiness does not mean blindness to obstacles and risks or to gains that can be had without the use of force. Indeed, we find that in the modern world, states live cooperating with their neighbours and other states most of the time without using force. The spectrum of disincentives and restraining influences is wide and states' cost/benefit calculations – if made – on the use of force evidently mostly comes out against such use.

In this and the next four chapters, I focus on the possible role of a number of developments and factors as disincentives and restraints, including military deterrence and diplomacy. In chapters thereafter, I examine what restraints legal norms and institutions, notably the Charter and the operation of the United Nations system may have created.[1]

SOME FACTORS POSSIBLY BEHIND RESTRAINTS OBSERVED

In the post-World War II world, the most conspicuous restraint exercised in the use of force is that the great powers, despite tensions and many crises, have consciously and successfully avoided direct armed confrontations with one

---

[1]   Cf. Henkin (1968), p. 135.

another. The risk of nuclear war and catastrophic injury – in the extreme case 'mutual assured destruction' (MAD) – is commonly given as the main reason for this restraint and it will be discussed below in Chapter 8. However, many more factors have contributed to reduce or eliminate incentives to the use of force between states.

One modern development to note is a reduced interest among states to acquire more territory. In the nineteen-thirties, the seizing of land was still the ambition of Germany, Italy and Japan, but the decolonization process after World War II marked a reduced economic, political and prestige interest in the acquisition of territory. It is telling that none of the big post-World War II armed conflicts in which the United States has been the leading party – Korea, Vietnam, Afghanistan and Iraq – was about gaining territory. As noted, there are some important exceptions to the trend[2]: Israel, Argentina, Iraq and Russia (in Ukraine). Yet, we may conclude that today generally pain and little gain seem to be seen in the use of force to acquire territory and – again, with some important exceptions – there may today be a reduced penchant for the use of force to change borders.[3] Could it be that after centuries of slicing and re-slicing the global territorial cake, drawing and redrawing national borders, most issues regarding territories and borders have been settled?

We should also discuss what perhaps looks more like an absence of incentive than an active disincentive. Many rulers of states were in the past evidently more triggered to use force than today's governments of the same states. In the territory of my own country, Sweden, wars waged by internal warlords and by Danish kings were frequent up to the early sixteenth century, when the country was unified under one king. Many Nordic wars and several hundred years later relations and borders between all the Nordic states were so stabilized as to exclude any resort to the use of force among them. It is tempting to think that over the centuries possible gains by the use of force dwindled and such solid patterns of mutually rewarding cooperation and handling of differences emerged that incentives to use force disappeared and restraints against any armed actions were solid.

Somewhat similarly, on the North American continent, where there were once armed actions involving Great Britain, France and Spain and Mexico, a tradition of good neighbourliness developed that today forms a reliable restraint against all use of force between the United States, Mexico and Canada. While in South America internal strife and upheavals have been common even in

---

[2]   Cf. Chapter 4, p. 58.
[3]   See Goldstein, Joshua S, *Winning the war on war. The decline of armed conflict worldwide* (2017). For the exceptions India vs China and India vs Pakistan, see above, Chapter 4, p. 62.

modern times, habits of cooperation and restraints against interstate use of force have developed giving a continent almost without interstate use of force.

The European region is an even more instructive case. History tells us that Charlemagne (*742–814*) needed to spend a large part of every year on campaigns to defend his vast European realm and feuding remained endemic in the multitude of units that came to exist with the erosion of the 'Holy Roman Empire'.[4] Over centuries, wars and peace agreements, royal marriages, and not least the unification of Germany and of Italy in the nineteenth century caused the number of independent territorial actors that could start armed conflicts to diminish.[5] The latest legs of that journey were the creation of the Coal and Steel Community in 1951 and the development of the European Union. Today's cohesion, strength and institutional bonds make any use of force between members highly improbable – even though the individual members continue to control independent armed forces.[6]

We may conclude that while the Middle East shows that competition about land in a region may, indeed, generate incentives to the use of armed force, cooperation in a region may create mutual bonds and benefits that remove such incentives. It could – and seems to – happen even in the Middle East.

OTHER FACTORS THAT MAY CAUSE RESTRAINTS
IN THE USE OF FORCE: LOSSES IN LIVES

One would expect that foreseeable losses in lives through armed conflicts should be a significant restraint on states to use force. The strong US domestic opposition to the war in Vietnam clearly had much to do with the loss of lives for a purpose that to many did not appear related to the defence of the United States. A general reluctance to put soldiers 'in harm's reach' may also be sensed, when there is talk in the United States about sending 'boots on the ground' in areas of armed conflict. When the United States was still engaged both in Afghanistan and Iraq and the question was discussed of a deeper engagement in Syria, the then US Secretary of Defence, Robert Gates is reported in the *New York Times* to have said that '*anyone who suggests that the US should engage in a third armed conflict in the Middle East should have his head examined*'.[7]

---

4   See Chapter 5, p. 93.
5   See above, Chapter 4, p. 61.
6   Cf. above, Chapter 2, p. 20.
7   www.nytimes.com/2011/02/26/world/26gates.html.

We must note, however, that there are ways in which governments may still pursue armed conflicts and take enemy lives without much upsetting a war-sceptical domestic public opinion. One is an extensive reliance on bombing (both the United States and Russia in Syria in 2016), or the launching of drones or autonomous weapons. Another way is the extensive use of professional soldiers. In many countries the armed forces consist of enlisted volunteers and no longer of conscripts. A consequence is that the broad civilian society from which soldiers are drafted no longer is there to critically ask whether the war is one of 'necessity'.

Part of the public engagement for or against war may in this way become more a question of the tax burden than a question of the risk of the death of relatives and friends.[8] This and a tendency to increasingly use mercenaries and to outsource armed action to privately run security organizations may weaken domestic opposition to armed action.[9]

ECONOMIC COSTS AS A POSSIBLE RESTRAINT ON THE USE OF FORCE

One might have expected that the soaring cost of modern arms and war should have been an important restraint for governments to prepare for and engage in the use of armed force. However, while undoubtedly always of relevance the costs of armaments and pursuit of armed conflicts do not seem to have decisive importance as a restraint to the launching of or participation in armed conflict.

There is generally a readiness to accept costs for the defence of whatever land, islands or sea one considers one's own – regardless of economic or other value. This provides governments with a rather wide allowance to resort to armed forces. A factor not to be overlooked is also that growing

---

[8] In a statement quoted in the International New York Times on 4 September 2018, Karl Eikenberry, former commander of the American forces in Afghanistan and later US ambassador to Kabul, said: 'Our soldiers are volunteers, permitting the American people and their elected representatives to be indifferent about the war in Afghanistan ... We continue to fight simply because we are there'.

[9] See, for instance in International *New York Times,* 31 December 2018 about Saudi Arabia's hiring of soldiers from Sudan for the pursuit of the armed intervention in Yemen. For the same armed conflict, Abu Dhabi has recruited guerrilla soldiers from Latin America. 'Wagner' soldiers have been deployed to pursue Russian aims in Syria, Libya, and Sahelian states. On 4 December 1989, the UN General Assembly adopted the United Nations Mercenary Convention, which defined and prohibited the use of mercenaries, though none of the Security Council's permanent members is a party. It was discussed in a UN Security Council meeting on 4 February 2019 dealing with mercenaries in Africa. A convention on the elimination of mercenaries in Africa was adopted as early as 1977. See also Chapter 18, p. 287.

economies have reduced resistance to growing military spending. Currently, military budgets are increasing almost everywhere, including in many developing countries.

HAVE ANY RESTRAINTS EMERGED ON MEASURES 'SHORT OF WAR'?

The preceding discussion has dealt with developments of restraints on governments' readiness to use force. However, 'force' comes in different forms and at different levels – not only as full-scale wars. We might ask whether restraints have developed specifically regarding what has been termed 'measures short of war'.[10] As noted in Chapter 1, the term covers interstate adversarial actions that have limited scope and duration and aim to secure specific objectives that do not include the acquisition of land. They are, as we noted, often lumped together under the term 'intervention' and may range from the open use of armed force to other forms of injury or pressure and verbal attacks.

As we shall see in following chapters, many such actions that comprise coercive elements of lesser gravity have come to be regarded as unlawful. It is as if a domestic scale of actions from punishable 'murder and robbery', 'assault and battery' and 'defamation', to non-punishable 'insult' had international parallels in unlawful international acts from 'war and land grabbing', 'injurious physical actions of limited scope and objectives' and 'subversion and fomenting of strife' to adversarial but not illegal means, such as economic or political pressures or verbal attacks. Former President Obama seems to have had in mind such a scale of gravity of actions when he compared the 2014 Russian armed actions + annexation of Crimea and the US 2003 invasion of Iraq and said, 'We did not claim or annex Iraq's territory. We did not grab its resources for our own gain ...'[11]

The question of interest here is not how grave an intervention may be but whether states are developing any restraints against launching themselves into interventions of varying gravity. We can certainly note that the public and governmental attitudes to interventions, like the attitudes to traditional war, have changed in the last hundred years. At the beginning of the twentieth century, when legal objections were not raised even to war, measures 'short of war' – interventions –were obviously also regarded as legally unobjectionable. A legendary story about US President Theodore Roosevelt comes

---

[10] See Wright, T. (2017).
[11] Speech in Brussels 26 March 2014.

to mind: Before the United States intervened with arms in 1903 to secure the secession of Panama from Colombia, the President is said to have asked the US Attorney General whether a legal argument could be made to justify the action. It is reported that the high legal official replied 'Why let such a beautiful operation be marred by any petty legal considerations...'[12]

However, as described in Chapter 5, discussions not long thereafter – at the second Hague Peace Conference in 1907 – show that time was beginning to run out for a cavalier attitude. At the proposal of the United States, a convention – the so-called Porter convention – was adopted that had as its main purpose to restrict the practice of powerful states sending gun-ships to poor debtor states to force them to pay their contract debts.[13] A hundred years later an idea to send a gunship to Athens or Buenos Aires to force the payment of debts would sound exotic! A rescue boat from the International Monetary Fund would be more likely. During these hundred years, **the 'public mind'** and government attitudes have obviously evolved. In the view of Brownlie, the adoption of the Briand-Kellogg Pact in 1928 marked the time when not only traditional wars but also intervention by 'any substantial use of armed force' became unlawful.[14] With the UN Charter broadly outlawing 'the threat or use of force' there is now no doubt that current law requires states to refrain from armed interventions. Where uncertainty in law remains – as will be discussed below in the chapter on legal norms – is on what is regarded as 'force' or equivalent to 'force' and where the border is between illegal intervention and adversarial but permissible conduct.

The evolution in public and legal attitudes, we must note, is not reflected in evidently new restraints in the state's conduct. In the period between the two world wars, there seems to have been little qualm about numerous armed interventions, notably in China. After World War II, different official tones may be registered. In 1958, US Secretary of State, Dulles, stated in connection with civil strife possibly threatening American lives and property in Lebanon that *'we do not introduce American forces into foreign countries except on the invitation of the lawful government of the state concerned'*.[15] We do not know in how many situations this attitude may have worked as an actual restraint on sending US forces. Cases that have come before the United Nations do show subsequent US interventions by US armed forces – to remove presumed left-leaning regimes.[16]

---

[12]   From *American Journal of International Law*, July 2004, p. 519.
[13]   See Lesaffer (2017), p. 21. See also Chapter 5, p. 101 and Chapter 12, p. 188.
[14]   Brownlie, p. 87.
[15]   Brownlie p. 294.
[16]   See below, Chapter 15, p. 217.

INTERDEPENDENCE AS A POSSIBLE RESTRAINT ON THE USE OF FORCE AND AS OPENING A POSSIBLE WAY TO EXERT PRESSURE WITHOUT THE USE OF FORCE

Accelerating globalization makes modern states increasingly dependent upon each other in trade, economics and finance (MED – Mutual Economic Dependence).[17] One might expect that governments should be aware of the risks of ruptures or other serious damage to their own economies if they allow controversies with other state(s) to escalate to a threat or use of force. This may well be true but it may be hard to show that accelerating interdependence generally leads to political restraint. Foreseeable negative economic consequences did not stop Russia from attacking Ukraine in February 2022.

Looked at from another angle, growing interdependence might enable states to exert strong pressures on other states – notably in the economic sphere – as an alternative to resorting to various uses of force. This may be of significance for the United States, which frequently leverages its economic and financial power in bilateral relations – sometimes perhaps more to satisfy domestic groups than to have a real impact on a foreign state. The 'maximum economic pressure' that was brought by the US Trump administration for several years on Iran may well have served as an alternative to the use of force that was urged by important groups in the United States. The economic measures taken by the same administration against the Maduro government in Venezuela may also have been a non-force option opened by interdependence.

It is not suggested that unilateral economic sanctions could be a panacea to achieve restraint in the use of force, but a trend to replace shooting war with hard economic measures and other non-kinetic or non-subversive measures should perhaps not be regretted. It is obvious that when it comes to the United Nations, collective economic sanctions have priority over military action. Art. 42 of the UN Charter provides that the Security Council may take action by air, sea or land forces, but only if it considers that measures not involving the use of armed force 'would be inadequate'.

While cyber techniques are now a means available to states to exert pressure without resorting to the use of force, they differ from economic or financial measures in their potential to lead to direct horrendous physical damage. They will be discussed below in the context of the deterrent effect of different weapons.[18]

---

[17] Cf Pinker, p. 286.
[18] See below, Chapter 8, p. 129.

FUTURE INTERVENTIONS MIGHT BE
DISCOURAGED BY FAILURES OF PAST ONES

Failures of achieving aims of the use of armed interventions have not brought an end to such belligerent endeavours. Nevertheless, it is striking that a number of major unilateral armed interventions by the United States and Russia have turned out to be costly and unsuccessful and have caused some soul-searching at home. While in 2022 this did not restrain Russia under President Putin from embarking on a major armed intervention to oust the government of Ukraine perhaps the result of this and earlier experiences will lead to greater restraint by the two states in the future:

- Vietnam by the United States 1955–1973
- Afghanistan by the Soviet Union 1979–1989
- Afghanistan by the United States from 2001 to 2021
- Iraq by the United States and a 'friendly alliance' from 2003
- Georgia by Russia 2008
- Libya by a number of states from 2011
- Syria by several states from 2011
- Ukraine by Russia 2022

THE PUBLIC MIND HAS OVER TIME BEEN INFLUENTIAL
IN INCREASING RESTRAINTS ON THE USE OF FORCE

Public opinion may influence states' use of force in two different contexts. There is, first, public opinion that arises in relation to particular government actions. Examples are the campaign in the United States against the Vietnam War and the opposition in the Soviet Union to the war in Afghanistan. How much such public opinions have restrained governments is harder to know. In 2003 there were protests in the streets of New York, London and other places against the invasion of Iraq. They undoubtedly constituted a political obstacle in the UK, but in this and many other cases, the public opposition did not prevent the governments from proceeding to use force. However, we may also note that the UK Parliament declined to support the government's wish for Britain to join the United States in armed action to punish the Syrian use of chemical weapons in 2013. It is certain that opposition in Russia to the 2022 intervention and war in Ukraine worries the Russian government, but it is hard to know strong influence it may have.

International public opinion is sometimes reflected in resolutions adopted by intergovernmental bodies like the UN General Assembly. They may urge conflicting parties to stop using armed force or condemn specific armed actions. The impact of such resolutions on the states addressed is uncertain. They may at any rate serve to legitimize economic pressures by member governments.

There is another stream of public opinion that opposes policies and means of warfare rather than acute actions. Peace movements that started in the nineteenth century expressed revulsion against war and pressed for disarmament and for the settling of disputes by arbitration. While they proved insignificant as an obstacle to World War I, their negative attitudes to war found articulation in US President Wilson's successful drive to create the League of Nations. There is no doubt that the use of nuclear weapons, genocides, concentration camps and wars in Vietnam and other places have had strong impacts on the general public the world over and led to many spontaneous movements – especially opposing nuclear weapons.

I have ventured to refer to these diverse movements as the '**public mind**'.[19] While often appearing deaf, governments are not immune to their messages and may be influenced to show restraint – or at least pay lip service to the need for restraints – on arms races and the use of armed force. We can hardly disagree with Pinker's observation that over time peoples' and states' attitudes have changed both to international violence and violence in the national sphere.[20]

Indeed, so influential is the sceptical attitude of the 'public mind' to war and the use of armed force that today's official and administrative language everywhere refers to all military expenses and activities as 'defence'. In the past, there was no compunction about having 'ministries of war'. Today, they are 'ministries of defence' and budgets are always for defence – never for war. Even Hitler's army was a 'Wehrmacht' and his political armed units were called 'Schutzstaffel' (SS). We may sneer at the double speak, but perhaps we should not, as it reflects official acceptance – whether genuine or not – of a public view that armed force is legitimate only for defence.

[19]   See Chapter 1, p. 4.
[20]   For the comments by Pinker, see above, Chapter 1, p. 4.

7

Military Strength to Deter Others from Using Force

DETERRENT IN ROMAN TIMES AND TODAY

It remains a broadly accepted view that military strength is a principal way to deter potential adversaries from using force. The famous Roman line: *Si vis pacem para bellum – if you want peace prepare for war –* is still revered as gold standard advice on how to restrain potential adversaries.

The adage was coined in the fifth century, a time during which the rulers of the Western Roman Empire had to keep a constant vigil and pursue constant armed struggle to protect its borders and territory. The basic assumption behind the advice is simple and still valid: a potential adversary is unlikely to resort to armed force if defence can be expected to make the risk of failure likely or cost in own lives and resources look forbidding.

However, the advice is limited. It does not mention that there can be other ways than military strength to avert the threats of armed attacks. Even for states with much military power diplomacy may often be a less costly path to avoid armed conflict. The Roman advice further understandably does not say anything about what strength is needed to deter attacks and preserve peace. In the United States, for example, the question has been debated whether it could be enough to have two methods to deliver nuclear weapons on the enemy – through missiles from submarines and through bombers – or whether there must be a 'triad', including land-based missiles.[1]

How well advised it is for a state to build up military strength to deter the use of force must be evaluated against the background of place and time. Today's realities are in fundamental ways different from those that existed up to the end of World War II and conditions differ in different parts of the

---

[1] For a recent example, see Daniel Ellsberg and Norman Solomon, 'To Avoid Armageddon, Don't Modernize Missiles – Eliminate Them', *The Nation*, 19 October 2021, www.thenation.com/article/world/eliminate-nuclear-missiles/.

world. One post-World War II new reality is, for all states, the establishment of the United Nations. Did it make national military strength to deter the use of force less relevant? The answer is no. It could perhaps have been argued that the system of collective security of the UN should have limited the relevance of national defence to deter hostile uses of force. Under Art. 39 of the Charter, the Security Council is to determine if there have been breaches of the peace and decide on measures to restore peace.

However, despite this security architecture, Art. 51 of the Charter assumes that Members might need to cater for their own defence – at least until the Council has taken the necessary action.[2] The UN Charter thus proceeds from and recognizes the reality that most Member states will have armed forces for self-defence and that the Security Council may not come immediately – or perhaps at all – to the rescue of a state attacked. National military forces and arrangements for 'collective self-defence' through membership in alliances like NATO are in reality seen as the principal means to deter potential adversaries from the use of force. Action by the Security Council is seen as uncertain. This was very much the view during the military bipolarity of the Cold War and, after a period of great power cooperation in the Security Council during the détente in the 1990s, a new polarization is on the way – with China as a main new participant.

Another post-World War II reality, noted above[3] is that the acquisition of more land has lost attraction and that sovereignty over most land and most national borders on land and at sea is settled and undisputed. Invasions of the kind that Germany, Italy, and Japan pursued in and before World War II to acquire territory have become unlikely events in the twenty-first century.

Nevertheless, a number of states consider that they have strong reasons to maintain ready military forces to meet possible attacks on their territory. The cases are serious and include Iran to deter possible military intervention by Israel or the United States and some Arab states. They include India and Pakistan, which deter each other over claims regarding Kashmir, and they include the two Korean states that have stationed massive military forces on each side of the 38th parallel, the armistice line that divides them. In addition, we must note that not only Taiwan but also ASEAN states and India (which has had serious armed clashes with China at their disputed border in the Himalayas) have concerns about the future attitudes of increasingly powerful China. We should also note that Ukraine and Georgia have not only been fighting Russian interventions. As immediate neighbours of Russia these

---

[2]   For an analysis of Article 51, see below Chapter 14, p. 205.
[3]   Chapter 6, p. 112.

states – and Moldova – may have concerns about potential Russian designs on parts of their territories that Russia sees as 'near abroad' and where there are many Russian-speaking people.

A third – game-changing – post-World War II reality are the nuclear weapons and other sophisticated means of warfare, such as long-range missiles, cyber techniques, means to fight space wars, and artificial intelligence. They raise fundamental questions about deterrence and defence: can they deter potential adversaries from using force[4] and the more pressing question: what restraints, if any, can there be on the owners of such weapons and means?

HOW DO STATES ASSESS THE NEED
FOR MILITARY DETERRENCE?

States calculate whether and how much military power and what military alliances they may need to deter the use of force against them. Many factors influence the calculation. Military-industrial and political interests often have roles in the *process*. A famous warning was that of President Eisenhower in his farewell address on 17 January 1961: '*In the councils of government, we must guard against the acquisition of unwarranted influence, whether sought or unsought, by the military-industrial complex*'. **Nevertheless**, the main factors are geographic location, the political climate and the size, military strength (including nuclear capacity) and aspirations of possible adversaries. After Russia's attack on Ukraine in February 2022, public opinion in Finland and Sweden favouring joining NATO rose sharply as many came to worry that Russia might have the aspiration to attack more states in its neighbourhood. States will also consider the existence of options besides the military to reduce the risk of attacks – such as diplomacy and political assurances – that can be used to induce potential adversaries to observe restraint. The amount of money and the share of GDP that individual states devote to build military strength may tell us something about the degree of importance they attribute to deterrence.

Underestimating the strength needed to deter potential adversaries or having naïve views of their intentions or of the broader risk of war may prove fatal. On the other hand, developing military strength that is not needed or is excessive to neutralize potential risks, may lead to temptations to resort to the use of force. US Secretary of State, Madeleine Albright appears to have been tempted. In her memoirs, she relates asking (then) General Colin Powell: '*What's the point of you saving this superb military*

---

4   Gat (2006), pp. 641 ff.

for, Colin, if we can't use it?'[5] Efforts to develop a superior military capacity may also lead to arms races that result in military balances at higher levels. Another aspect of arms races is that public money is devoted to cannons instead of butter. President Eisenhower may be cited again offering the famous sad reflection in a 1953 speech that *'Every gun that is made, every warship launched, every rocket that is fired signifies, in the final sense, a theft from those who hunger and are not fed...'.*[6]

PERCEIVED NEED FOR DETERRENT IS MOSTLY LINKED TO LEVELS OF RISK ASSESSED

The key factor in a state's assessment of the need for deterrent military strength is the risk of armed force it deems itself to be exposed to. Some states may judge the risk to be at the lowest end of the spectrum. Costa Rica, which is located far from likely theatres of great power competition and has no hostile neighbours, may have made such a judgment and decided not to have any military force. A good number of other states with a low risk of external attacks nevertheless maintain national armed forces perhaps to deter and cope with possible internal disorder. It is less understandable that states with negligible external threats equip their armed forces with the most modern fighter planes or nuclear-propelled submarines.

Some states see various degrees of risk of external attacks due to troubled neighbour relations: Greece/Turkey, Armenia/Azerbaijan, Iran/Saudi Arabia and India/Pakistan. Others see risks to themselves spilling over from the tensions between the major military powers. Many join cooperative arrangements for the military defence to augment the deterrent force of their own military power with the expected support of allies. Depending on how alliance commitments are constructed, such arrangements may also raise problems. A clause of 'all for one and one for all' might oblige a party to rally to the armed support of another party that perhaps through reckless measures has triggered a war against itself.

A case that comes to mind is that of Georgia, which under President Saakashvili attacked some targets in South Ossetia releasing the 2008 large-scale armed Russian intervention. That intervention was preceded by many years of troubles, agreements, and peacekeeping arrangements. The Georgian attacks came before the Russian invasion and reportedly killed some Russian

---

[5] Quoted in 'Reluctant Warrior', *The Guardian*, 29 September 2001, www.theguardian.com/world/2001/sep/30/usa.afghanistan.

[6] President Dwight D. Eisenhower, 'The Chance for Peace', speech delivered 16 April 1953, Washington, DC, www.presidency.ucsb.edu/documents/address-the-chance-for-peace-delivered-before-the-american-society-newspaper-editors.

peacekeepers.[7] Russia may have even welcomed the Georgian action as a ground for its intervention. Had Georgia been a member of NATO – which it was not but wanted to become – the solidarity clause of the alliance might have obliged other members to engage in direct conflict with Russia.

Examples of cooperative arrangements in the field of defence include:

- NATO (the North Atlantic Treaty Organization) now (May 2023) comprises thirty-one states and is expected – with the adherence of Sweden – to become thirty-two. The Alliance stretches from the United States and Canada in the North-West to states riparian to the Black Sea in the East.
- Bilateral defence arrangements between the United States on the one hand and many other states, for instance, Japan, South Korea, Australia, and New Zealand.
- The QUAD (the quadrilateral security dialogue) comprising the United States, India, Australia and Japan is not a defence alliance but conducts joint military exercises.[8]
- AUKUS, the arrangement between Australia, the United Kingdom and the United States to provide Australia with nuclear-propelled submarines and other modern military equipment
- The Collective Security Treaty Organization (since 1992) for mutual defence between members of the Commonwealth of Independent States (of the former Soviet Union).
- The Shanghai Cooperation Organization comprises China, Russia and a number of Asian states. While not committing members to collective security, it organizes joint military exercises.
- The Organization of American States (since 1948) consists of 35 states in Latin America, North America and the Caribbean. Its Charter has specific provisions for collective security.

There remain many states – especially many developing countries – that are not formally aligned with any of the major powers and that maintain military forces of various strengths not linked in arrangements with others committing to deter possible military threats through collective self-defence. In Western Europe, Austria, Finland, Ireland, Sweden, and Switzerland have belonged to this category. Even though dedicated to their independent military defence none of them would be able to deter an improbable isolated attack by Russia. Nor, however, would their national forces, in reality, be left alone to deter

---

[7] 'Over 10 Russian peacekeepers killed in South Ossetia: agencies', Reuters, 8 August 2008, www.reuters.com/article/us-georgia-ossetia-losses/over-10-russian-peacekeepers-killed-in-south-ossetia-agencies-idUSL818726020080808.

[8] Cf. above, Chapter 4, p. 79.

and resist such an attack, as even without formal alliances it would most likely trigger EU and NATO intervention. In a similar way, hypothetical attacks on non-aligned India or Indonesia by China are in all likelihood subject to the deterrence that they would trigger a wider war. It is also probable that the deterrent effect of North Korea's own considerable military power – including nuclear weapons and missiles – against a US attack is backstopped by a Chinese readiness to intervene (as China did during the Korean War in 1950).

MILITARY STRENGTH AS DETERRENCE
BETWEEN THE THREE MAJOR POWERS

All three major military powers – the United States, Russia and China – seem convinced that military force remains the most important means to deter each other from the use of force. While a thin diplomatic dialogue continues between them (2022), and hostile economics and cyber actions play an increasing role in their competition, the three major powers have been in a military build-up phase for some time. In the face of a new Chinese assertiveness and rapidly increasing military power, the United States has been performing a 'pivot' in shifting some of its political and military attention from Europe and the Middle East to Asia. US military expenditures remain incomparably high and the long-declared policy to maintain 'full spectrum dominance' seems to remain. Russia has restored its military capacity from the erosion it underwent in the 1990s and has reported new means of delivering nuclear weapons. China has considerably augmented its military strength and its naval presence in the West Pacific.

All this has meant a strengthened mutual deterrence against the use of force – and increased tensions. Some actions and policies have suggested more dynamic intentions than mere deterrence. NATO has extended its activities well beyond the perimeter of its membership – to Afghanistan, Iraq and Libya – and conducted joint military drills near Russia in Georgia and the Black Sea. As noted in Chapter 4, Russia has increased its presence and operations in the Mediterranean area and Africa (through Wagner mercenaries) and China its activities and operations in the South and West Pacific.

RED LINES AND PRODDING

Military deterrence builds on the reasoning that states' individual or collective possession and display of sufficient armed force and determination and ability to handle it will signal to potential adversaries that they had better refrain from using their arms to attack. States further often strengthen the signal by indicating red lines – mostly national borders on land, at sea or in air space – that they declare cannot be crossed without triggering resistance. The aim is to minimize the risk of armed confrontations by maximizing clarity where transgression or trespassing would likely ignite a clash. Common space open to all, at sea or in space beyond national jurisdiction or buffer or neutral zones are viewed with some concern as vulnerable to possible grabs or domination by an adversary.[9] Hence, the freedom of military movement in or above, for instance, the Baltic, the North Sea, the Black Sea and the South China Sea, is firmly asserted.

The notion is not accepted by all, however, that ignition of violence is more easily avoided by adversaries standing on each side of a red line than if they are removed by a mile or hundreds of miles and have agreed on no launches on warning. The notion is also not consistently followed. We find that to avoid increasing tensions, governments may unilaterally commit themselves not to deploy weapons or missiles or to permanently station troops in specific areas.[10] At the end of the year 2021 filled with diplomatic conflict between Russia and NATO members Russia demanded that there should be no NATO arms in Ukraine, presumably wishing Ukraine to be a buffer between itself and NATO countries.

Where a red line notion is relied on it becomes particularly important to avoid provocation. The strategy needs to be combined with openness, easy communication and demeanour that cannot be misinterpreted. Strangely, a military practice that seems to be global leads military forces of great powers often to mark their presence in common space and to sail or fly near red lines to test their freedom of movement and to demonstrate their capacities. The almost ritualistic practice of prodding is not without risk of incidents, as air units scramble or naval units show up to demonstrate that they are alert and ready to defend a red line and to prevent any intrusion.[11] It is curious that there appears to be no debate whether the deterrent value of this military practice justifies the risks that it raises.

SUPPORT FOR POLICIES OF MILITARY DETERRENCE

Depending somewhat upon the temperature of states' foreign relations, the doctrine of military deterrence to prevent armed conflict has general support

---

[9] Cf. below Chapter 10, p. 152 on diplomacy's favouring areas of reduced armed presence.

[10] See Ahlström (2004). Several treaties have designated specific uninhabited (or partially inhabited) areas as demilitarized zones, including Antarctica (1959) and the Moon (1979). The Outer Space Treaty (1967) prohibits the stationing of weapons of mass destruction in outer space and bans military activities on celestial bodies. For texts of these treaties, see https://treaties.unoda .org and for further discussion of demilitarized zones *per se*, see ICRC, 'Demilitarized Zones', https://casebook.icrc.org/glossary/demilitarized-zones.

[11] See Trenin, Dmitri, 'Sailing into troubled waters. Russia counters Britain in Black Sea', paper published by Carnegie Moscow Center, 25 June 2021 and Galen Carpenter, Ted. 'Why Russia Likes to Play Aerial "Chicken"' with America' in *The National Interest*, 8 August, 2020.

in the world and in particular national constituencies: those in the armed forces of a country will mostly urge that their own strength should be equal or superior to that of potential adversaries. Another support group is formed by those in a state's political establishment (including the legislature and bureaucracy) which is convinced of – and/or hopes to gain votes by pleading for – a need for a strong defence. A third supporting and resourceful constituency may in some countries be found in weapons and other war materiel industries that stand to gain economically from a stronger demand. Lastly, in the general public, there may be many who support strong armed forces out of concern for an uncertain international political climate or out of national pride.

The faith in the deterrent effect of weapons and armed forces is reflected in the budgetary resources that states devote to military aims. Vast sums are consumed by newer and more technically advanced weapons and other equipment, such as drones, missiles, antimissiles, artificial intelligence and means for cyber war. The following table shows figures of military budgets in dollars and as a share of GDP of 20 countries for the years 2010, 2015 and 2020.

Military expenditure of (in constant 2019 US$ billion)

Country	2010	2010 (% of GDP)	2015	2015 (% of GDP)	2020	2020 (% of GDP)
USA	865.3	4.9	683.7	3.5	766.6	3.7
China	129.4	1.7	192.8	1.8	244.9	1.7
India	54.0	2.9	56.8	2.5	73.0	2.9
Russia	49.8	3.6	74.6	4.9	66.8	4.3
UK	63.2	2.6	54.0	2.0	58.5	2.2
Saudi Arabia	53.6	8.6	88.5	13.3	55.5	8.4
France	48.4	2.0	48.0	1.9	51.6	2.1
Germany	41.0	1.3	40.6	1.1	51.6	1.4
Japan	46.4	1.0	47.6	1.0	48.2	1.0
Korea, South	32.2	2.5	37.2	2.5	46.1	2.8
Australia	21.1	1.9	23.8	2.0	27.6	2.1
Brazil	25.4	1.5	25.1	1.4	25.1	1.4
Israel	15.7	5.9	18.3	5.5	21.1	5.6
Turkey	10.9	2.3	12.0	1.8	19.6	2.8
Iran	18.2	2.8	14.0	2.8	12.2	2.2
Taiwan	10.2	2.0	10.6	1.9	11.6	1.9
Pakistan	6.2	3.4	8.1	3.6	10.1	4.0
Algeria	5.3	3.5	10.5	6.3	10.0	6.7
Sweden	5.0	1.2	5.1	1.1	6.2	1.2
South Africa	3.4	1.1	3.8	1.1	3.5	1.1

Source: SIPRI, Military Expenditure Database, 2021

How far will the three major world powers go in increasing their military capacities? On 27 February 2022, German Chancellor Olaf Scholz announced that Germany would immediately increase its defence budget by 100 billion euros ($118 billion) and would raise its defence budget in years to come to over 2 per cent of GDP.[12] If it had followed the 2 per cent NATO target in 2020 Germany alone would have had a much higher military budget than Russia.

China is announcing an aim to vastly strengthen its military power and both China and Russia aim at having the most technically advanced weapons. Whether or not they aim at parity with the United States in all military assets – nuclear warheads, missiles, aircraft carriers, etc. – we may be sure that, as discussed in the next chapter, they strive for equality in the ability to bring pain calculated to be unacceptable for adversaries – their cities, population, and infrastructure.

DIPLOMACY TO OBVIATE THE USE OF FORCE

Diplomacy is a major alternative to military deterrence to prevent the use of interstate force. Its role is discussed below in Chapter 10 and examples of successes and failures are given. The display of military force to deter potential adversaries has much greater visibility and often generates more appreciation than the sight of diplomats with briefcases suspected of containing drafts of concessions and compromises, perceived as painful or undignified. The diplomats are likely to be suspected of retreats even before started. Yet, it needs to be said that, but for situations of acute military attacks, good reasons speak for opportunity or even priority to be given to diplomacy to prevent the use of force. Deterrence may help restrain fingers from pulling the triggers but it does not remove or reduce differences. Diplomacy is geared to do that – sometimes with the background leverage that failure could mean resorting to force. It is saddening to hear, when deterrence has failed and years of gruesome conflicts have raged, the conclusion that 'the conflict had no military solution'.

An important and sometimes ridiculed feature in diplomacy is the attention to pride and courtesy discussed below[13] – the factor that Francis Fukuyama sees as central and calls 'recognition'. States like individuals mostly find it less difficult to accept concessions than humiliation. The Cuban Missile Crisis

---

[12] Melissa Eddy, 'In Foreign Policy U-Turn, Germany Ups Military Spending and Arms Ukraine', *New York Times*, 27 February 2022, www.nytimes.com/2022/02/27/world/europe/germany-ukraine-russia.html.

[13] Chapter 1, p. 7.

of 1962, described earlier,[14] illustrates some of the points made above. There was a fundamental joint immediate interest in avoiding a possible nuclear show-down with potentially tens of millions of casualties. It was President Kennedy's own conscience, skill, and diplomatic sense that in a few dramatic and stressful days led him and the Russians to a way out and it is striking that a key aspect of the solution was that of avoiding losses of face.

Will states – notably the great military powers – in the brave new world of instantly available destruction and instantly available opportunities for communication continue in an incessant race for more and innovative arms and for deterrent or deterrent plus? Or, will they recognize that they have by now attained such a capability of mutual mega-destruction that they find any weapons use too risky and conclude that they must use diplomacy to edge away from positions that may trigger confrontations between themselves and think of longer-term security? Even in the early days of the nuclear age, when the US nuclear program was clearly superior to its nascent Soviet counterpart and China still had no nuclear weapons, US presidents on some occasions considered and refused to approve nuclear attacks proposed to them and during the Cuban Missile Crisis in 1962, the United States and the Soviet Union were held back by awareness of a risk of nuclear war. With a many times stronger destructive capacity at their disposal including cyber and space weapons and artificial intelligence – and no ability to foresee the consequences of the use of any of it – will the leadership of today's major powers, turn to diplomacy?

---

[14] Chapter 3, p. 37.

8

Nuclear and Other Non-conventional Weapons
and Means as Deterrents and Threats

Chapter 7 discussed in a general way how military defence remains central for many states to help deter the use of armed force by potential adversaries. This chapter will turn specifically to the role of 'unconventional' weapons. The 'long-timers' are ABC – atomic, biological and chemical. The newcomers are currently ASC – lethal autonomous weapon systems (LAWS), and means for space (S) and cyber (C) wars. The existential questions of how the threat of these weapons and means of warfare, in particular nuclear, can be eliminated or reduced will be discussed below and in the following chapter on disarmament. At this point, the focus will be on the question of whether – apart from posing horrendous risks and threats – the different unconventional weapons and means of warfare can deter threats and uses of force, including those from other weapons of mass destruction.

BIOLOGICAL AND CHEMICAL WEAPONS[1]

Some of the legal bans on the use of specific weapons have been prompted by a common human revulsion against what is perceived as treacherous ways of killing in war. Art. 23 of Convention II from the 1899 Hague Peace Conference on rules regarding land warfare generally prohibits such killing but enacts a specific ban only on 'poison or poisoned weapons'. The Geneva Protocol of 1925, adopted after the massive use of gas during World War I, amplified the Hague rules by prohibiting the use of gases and analogous material and extended the rules to cover 'bacteriological methods of warfare'.

Military authorities seem generally to have shared the aversion against biological and chemical weapons and also to have seen them as not very useful.

---

[1] The literature on both subjects is extensive. For an overview, see Spiers (2021).

They may have been judged 'indiscriminate' (including risks to the user side) or causing 'unnecessary suffering', that is suffering not 'justified' by military advantage. In any case, military authorities around the world appear to have endorsed all the bans that have been introduced.

The pre-World War II rules on BC weapons were confined to bans on use and did not call for standing inspection and verification mechanisms. However, the parties to the modern conventions on biological weapons (1972) and chemical weapons (1993) went beyond bans on use. They assumed the more ambitious obligation not to produce, acquire or possess the banned weapons. Evidently, this commitment gave a stronger guarantee of non-use: Without weapons – no use! However, to create confidence that no prohibited secret production and stockpiling takes place a new need arises for monitoring and verification. For chemical weapons, this has been achieved through a separate control and inspection system under the Organization for the Prohibition of Chemical Weapons (OPCW). For biological weapons, the parties to the BW convention have so far failed to agree on commitments to accept monitoring and inspection.

Although generally deemed not to be militarily very useful, chemical weapons were a horrible part of Iraq's war against Iran in the 1980s and for the massacres of Iraqi Kurds (Halabja). Since then, chemical weapons have played a sporadic and much-publicized role as a terror weapon in the war in Syria (2011–). Biological weapons are generally difficult to handle and disseminate and have not been part of any modern armed conflicts. Iraq under Saddam Hussein had a large BW program and weaponized anthrax but never made use of it. The program was mapped through the inspections carried out by the United Nations Special Commission (UNSCOM) and the United Nations Monitoring, Verification and Inspection Commission (UNMOVIC) under mandates from the Security Council.[2] It has been claimed that North Korea has stocks of B-weapons, including anthrax, but no evidence has been presented.[3] There is also a detailed record of the BW activities of Japan's notorious 'Unit 731' in China during World War II, reportedly responsible for the deaths of hundreds of thousands.[4]

---

[2]   See 'Disarming Iraq: The Legacy of UNSCOM', Special Issue, *Bulletin of the Atomic Scientists, July 2021*, https://thebulletin.org/magazine/2021-07/. A history and documents relating to the work of UNMOVIC can be found at 'United Nations Monitoring and Verification Commission', www.un.org/depts/unmovic/.

[3]   *See Stimson Center, 'North Korea and Biological Weapons: Assessing the Evidence', 6 November* 2020, www.stimson.org/2020/north-korea-and-biological-weapons-assessing-the-evidence/.

[4]   Williams and Wallace (1989).

B and C weapons are generally seen as terror weapons.[5] Simple C-weapons, made for instance of chlorine, might yet come to be used by terrorist movements and events show that some states' intelligence organizations have been ready to use both poison and radioactive substances for assassinations.[6] Yet, there is nothing to suggest that possession of biological or chemical weapons by a state (or terrorists) would have any importance to deter the use of force against it. If there were suspicions of the unlawful existence or production of chemical weapons somewhere, the most likely outside reaction today would be to maintain a capacity for protection against C-weapons in the field and for medical care.

LETHAL AUTONOMOUS WEAPON SYSTEMS (LAWS)[7]

LAWS are weapons that once launched are able to target and strike objects without human intervention. They are currently the subject of much international discussion.[8] The European Parliament has adopted a resolution (2018) calling for an international ban, but states members of the European Union do not have any agreed position and no common international conclusions have yet emerged. LAWS may make it possible for technologically advanced belligerents to perform attacks while not risking the lives of their own soldiers. However, the belligerent's obligation to discriminate between lawful and unlawful targets is not fully exercised when weapons are released without the control of a human that remains responsible. It is understandable that autonomous weapons have been objected to on ethical and legal grounds. There is scant reason to think that these weapons would have any deterrent effect on potential adversaries.[9]

---

[5] See Weapons of Mass Destruction Commission (2006).

[6] On the Skripal novichok poisoning see: www.theguardian.com/news/2018/dec/26/skripal-poisonings-bungled-assassination-kremlin-putin-salisbury; and Litvinenko polonium poisoning: www.npr.org/2021/09/21/1039224996/russia-alexander-litvinenko-european-court-human-rights-putin.

[7] See 'Background on LAWS in the CCW', UN Office for Disarmament Affairs, www.un.org/disarmament/the-convention-on-certain-conventional-weapons/background-on-laws-in-the-ccw/.

[8] They were the focus, for example, of the November 2018 meeting in Geneva of the parties to the Convention on Certain Conventional Weapons. For general background on CCW and LAWS, see www.un.org/disarmament/the-convention-on-certain-conventional-weapons/background-on-laws-in-the-ccw/. The 2018 meeting was discussed in: https://reachingcriticalwill.org/images/documents/Disarmament-fora/ccw/2018/hcp-meeting/CCWR6.12.pdf.

[9] For a recent update, see Congressional Research Service, 'International Discussions Concerning Lethal Autonomous Weapon Systems', 21 December 2021, https://sgp.fas.org/crs/weapons/IF11294.pdf.

CYBER WAR[10]

Cyber actions long identified as means of mischief and industrial espionage, have come to be seen as an ominous branch of adversary interstate action – both in peace and war. Cyber techniques can be used by states not only to spread information and traditional propaganda but also to disseminate false information, to cause disturbances in national elections and to damage civilian and military controls in society. Through the ever-growing dependence on digital means vital functions in society, including defence, air surveillance, generation and distribution of electric power, supply of water, communications and financial and banking systems, have become subject to new vulnerabilities. Cyber-actions have been used to immobilize banks, paralyze government authorities and destroy centrifuges for the enrichment of uranium and to place large numbers of computers out of action.[11]

Cyber is everywhere and can be used by all who have developed sufficient technical know-how. In early March 2021 alone two news items in the International NY Times reflected the existing concerns. One referred to a major blackout that had occurred in Mumbai in 2020. It reported speculations that malware from China might have been placed in Indian electric grids and critical infrastructure as a warning to India of what China could do in a controversy. In the other item the Russian Presidential spokesman, Dmitry Peskov, on 9 March 2021 expressed concern caused by a report in the New York Times that US cyber attacks were 'not ruled out' in response to alleged Russian hacks in the United States.[12]

Governments, industries, and businesses seek to immunize their digital systems against accidents and attacks. Several governments have concluded that they also need the ability to deter attacks by a capacity and readiness to counterattack. Hence, the risk of cyberwar has arrived. Can states' development of capacity for cyber action serve as a general deterrence against the threat or use of armed force?

All great powers may be assumed to possess advanced cyber capability and the mutual capacity for a second strike should be a restraining factor – as it is with nuclear weapons. However, the risk of cyber war might be greater than the risk of nuclear war: the use of even a low-yield nuclear weapon would require stepping over a threshold and mark the breach of a taboo. Cyber 'operations' could begin low-key and risk escalating seamlessly to the most

---

[10] For a discussion of legal aspects of cyber war, see Nils Melzer, 'Cyberwarfare and International Law' (Geneva: UN Institute for Disarmament Research, 11 February 2011), https://unidir.org/publication/cyberwarfare-and-international-law.

[11] For the Stuxnet case, see above, Chapter 4, p. 73.

[12] For the Indian case, see article by D. Sanger in *International New York Times*, 2 March 2021; for the Russian case, see article by D. Sanger in *International New York Times*, 9 March 2021.

devastating attacks on vital infrastructure. Viewed from another angle, the flexibility could be an advantage: without dramatically overstepping a threshold, unacknowledged cyber-attacks could be launched as a warning.

Even small states – and terrorists – may wield digital weapons and have some capacity to launch injurious cyber actions. Possible adversaries must take this into account. Both North Korea and Iran have been named as probable authors of successful hostile cyber actions. However, the deterrent power that small states are able to mobilize by cyber means may be modest.

No international convention or even code of conduct has until now (2022) been reached on any specific restrictions on cyber operations. Discussion has been lively but without agreement at the UN. Some hopeful progress was reported in March 2021 in the open-ended UN working group.[13] There seems to be a broad understanding that the laws of war apply to cyber conflicts, but the precise implications of this are not clear. It has been claimed with the reason that a cyber-attack to inflict injury would – like an armed attack with conventional weapons – trigger the same right of self-defence.[14]

SPACE WAR[15]

Outer space is today often identified as a possible new theatre of war. What adversarial action could be taken in the sky and what restraints could there be? The General Assembly of the United Nations has adopted resolutions on preventing an outer space arms race.[16] Despite proposals for multilateral talks no agreements or even understandings have been reached on these matters. We have to go back to the 1967 Outer Space Treaty to find relevant basic rules. It stipulates, for instance, that exploration and use of outer space shall be carried out for the benefit of and in the interest of all countries (Art. I), that nuclear weapons and other weapons of mass destruction must not be stationed in space or on celestial bodies (Art. IV) and that testing, the establishment of a military base or military maneuvers shall be forbidden. (Art. IV).

[13] See Taylor (2021). Also, in May a government group of experts adopted a consensus report. See Tim Johnson 'As U.S. issues warning to Iran, Persian Gulf cyberwar takes on new meaning'. *Miami Herald*, 1 February 2017. www.miamiherald.com/news/nation-world/world/article130131929.html.

[14] Thus, the 2014 NATO summit declared that the North Atlantic Council would decide on a case-by-case basis whether a cyber attack would trigger invocation of Art. 5 of the Treaty. The summit thus envisaged the possibility that a cyber attack could be equivalent to an 'armed attack' and justify armed self-defence under Art 51 of the UN Charter. It would also seem reasonable to hold that the general principle of proportionality should apply to cyber-attacks.

[15] For a recent survey, see UNIDIR, 'Conference Report: 2021 Outer Space Security Conference' (Geneva: UNIDIR, 2021), https://unidir.org/publication/2021-outer-space-security-conference-report.

[16] For 2019, see resolutions 74/32, 74/33, 74/34, 74/67, and 74/82.

While satellites today play a vital role in communications, navigation and weather forecasting, a great number of satellites serve military aims. They are used for surveillance and the transparency they provide is of importance to give warning, to help verify respect for commitments and to maintain mutual confidence. They are also used in war for the identification of targets and for the aiming of smart weapons. Hence, adversaries in a conflict could have reasons to attack and destroy satellites. A deterrent would exist in possible retaliatory strikes. In the United States, the risk of adversarial actions in space and the need to protect US dominance in the space domain were deemed so serious in 2018 that a space corps was established as a new separate military branch.[17] China, Russia and the United States have demonstrated a capacity that undoubtedly some other space powers have as well, to destroy satellites by missile or other action from the ground.[18] The great amount of debris that results in space from such actions can be a grave hazard and the United States has proposed that an agreement be concluded to curb such actions.

Space warfare might be open to relatively few states so far, but it seems capable of bringing societies to paralysis and collapse. As with cyber warfare, there is great uncertainty about its possible scope and effects.

NUCLEAR WEAPONS[19]

Nuclear weapons global stocks are reported to have stood at some 70.000 during the Cold War.[20] Some 13.000 weapons still remain, enough to wipe out human civilization in a quick suicide. Most of the weapons are in the United States and Russia but their presence in nine states has a fundamental impact on the geopolitical situation and raises many questions including what deterrent effect they may have.

THE DETERRENT EFFECTS OF NUCLEAR WEAPONS

It is obvious that a state's possession of and capacity to launch nuclear weapons is likely to induce caution in potential adversaries. In the short period after World War II, when the United States alone had a significant nuclear weapons capacity, this arsenal was a deterrent to all other states, including in

---

[17] See *American Journal of International Law*, vol. 114 (2020), pp. 323–326.
[18] See *International New York Times*, 27 January 2021.
[19] For general information, see the nuclear-weapons chapter in the latest *SIPRI Yearbook*, https://sipri.org/sites/default/files/2021-06/yb21_10_wnf_210613.pdf.
[20] Federation of American Scientists, 'Status of World Nuclear Forces', 2021. https://fas.org/issues/nuclear-weapons/status-world-nuclear-forces/.

particular the expansive Soviet Union, to undertake armed or other actions unacceptable to the United States. The US nuclear weapons had been developed to counter the risk of a possible German nuclear capacity and their use against Japan was explained to have been to shorten the end of the war. It has been suggested that the bombing in Japan served also to send a signal to the Soviet Union to exercise restraint – to be aware that the United States would have the capacity to stop any Soviet moves it might find unacceptable.[21]

There can be no doubt that Israel is convinced of the deterrent effect of nuclear weapons. Although it does not confirm its possession of an arsenal – 'the world's worst kept secret'[22] – Israel counts upon all states in its region to be deterred from any attacks by awareness of these weapons. Israel has further repeatedly taken drastic measures to prevent the deterrent power of its nuclear arsenal be reduced or neutralized by any other state in the region acquiring nuclear weapons capacity. This has been the aim notably of the bombing of the Iraqi research reactor Osirak in 1981 and of an installation at al-Kibar in Syria in 2007[23] as well as of actions in Iran.

The destructive capacity of nuclear weapons is so great that even a small arsenal may induce restraint in powerful potential adversaries, provided there is a credible risk that it can be delivered on chosen targets. Thus, the weapons may not only deter but to some extent also equalize. The case of North Korea in 2019 is telling: the country has shown in tests that it has nuclear weapons and the capacity to launch them not only in its own region but possibly also – by intercontinental missiles – to reach the United States. For its part, North Korea would most likely be deterred from using its nuclear capacity to attempt a first strike against the United States, knowing that the US has a vast nuclear and non-nuclear capacity with which it could deliver devastating retaliatory blows. Nevertheless, the US government would hardly risk launching a preventive attack on North Korea. Even the limited nuclear and missile capacity and hypothetical second-strike capacity of North Korea would probably impose restraint on the United States. The case of North Korea also illustrates the danger of proliferation: a strong increase in regional tensions.

Where a potential adversary of a nuclear weapon state develops or otherwise acquires nuclear weapons and the ability to deliver a retaliatory second strike, the first nuclear weapon state loses its nuclear trump card. This was

---

[21]   A leading proponent of this position is Gar Alperovitz, whose several publications are identified at https://garalperovitz.org. See also Tannenwald (2007), p. 75.

[22]   A recent competent estimate puts Israel's nuclear arsenal at around 90. See https://thebulletin .org/premium/2022-01/nuclear-notebook-israeli-nuclear-weapons-2022/.

[23]   See Chapter 4, p. 73.

the case when the Soviet Union, China, India, and Pakistan acquired their nuclear weapons. Had the Soviet ships that in 1962 were on their way to Cuba delivered their cargoes of missiles and nuclear weapons and had these been installed, Cuba would have been largely protected against US attack.[24]

The even more important aspect was, of course, that the weapons would have become an – unacceptable – threat to the United States. Realizing how close they were to a possible nuclear show-down the United States and USSR found a diplomatic solution. It deprived Cuba of the nuclear arms designed to deter the United States from attacking it (and of the means to threaten the United States). In return, it committed the United States to not attack Cuba and to withdraw missiles from Turkey. The most important lesson from the Cuba crisis was, of course, that two nuclear weapon states in an acute controversy have to be aware that a possible first nuclear strike can be expected to be met by a retaliatory second strike and that an ensuing nuclear war might lead to mutual assured destruction (MAD).

It was understood after the Cuban crisis that mutual deterrent and restraint might fail if either nuclear side were to believe that the other side was, in fact, unable to retaliate by a nuclear second strike. With the wish to ensure continued mutual deterrent and restraint through mutual vulnerability the United States and Russia concluded the Anti-Ballistic Missile Treaty (ABM) in 1972. It limited them to establish missile shields against nuclear attacks at only two sites (of which respective capitals were one), thus mutually placing vast territories and big cities before a risk of a retaliatory nuclear strike. The treaty-based vulnerability was supplemented by more confidence-building measures, like 'hot lines' and arrangements for mutual transparency to reduce the risks of mistakes and to allow crisis management.

The strategic nuclear stability attained through mutual deterrence between the superpowers was supplemented by commitments providing protection against nuclear threats – 'nuclear umbrellas' or 'extended deterrence' – to many other states, including Japan and the members of NATO. Through such arrangements states can be assured of protection against nuclear attack and the protecting nuclear weapon state can demand that the protected state does not develop an independent nuclear weapon capacity. With some reason – but also with some contradiction – it has been claimed that the nuclear weapons of the superpowers have deterred not only nuclear threats between themselves but have also helped to uphold stability more broadly.[25]

---

[24] Chapter 3, p. 37, Chapter 4, p. 67.
[25] See, for instance Henkin (1968), p. 10.

TERRORIST GROUPS CANNOT BE DETERRED

It is sometimes suggested that if terrorist groups were to acquire nuclear weapons, there would be no way of deterring them from use or threatening use. They may not reside in sites that can be hit and may be insensitive to retaliation anyway. The warning cannot be just waved away but must lead to special efforts to prevent nuclear proliferation by terrorist groups. The risk that a terrorist movement would be able to acquire both nuclear weapons and the capacity to deliver them to targets while not zero is small. While terrorists could perhaps make so-called 'dirty bombs' containing radioactive material that could contaminate, even a crude explosive nuclear device would likely be beyond their capacity. As we have seen in the cases of Iraq and DPRK, the development of nuclear weapons are big undertakings even for states.

THE CONCEPT OF NO FIRST USE

States that possess nuclear weapons invariably stress that their primary rationale for having the weapons is to deter nuclear attacks by other states. China has gone further and declared as official policy that it will not be the first to use nuclear weapons in a conflict. India has done the same but with an exception made in case of an attack with BC weapons. If all states possessing nuclear weapons committed to a no-first-nuclear use policy the weapons would – logically – never be launched. Only conventional weapons would remain to deter armed attacks. However, no agreement on such commitments has been made so far and there is a question of how much reliance would be placed on them-

NUCLEAR WEAPON STATES' READINESS
TO USE THEIR WEAPONS

Neither the United States nor Russia has committed to using nuclear weapons only in retaliation for nuclear weapons use against themselves. In their respective nuclear posture reviews[26] both the United States and Russia point to

---

[26] On 27 October 2022, the US released a declassified text of its 2022 Nuclear Posture Review, which was included (along with a Missile Defense Review) in a larger document called the 2022 National Security Strategy. The texts are available at https://media.defense.gov/2022/Oct/27/2003103845/-1/-1/1/2022-NATIONAL-DEFENSE-STRATEGY-NPR-MDR.PDF. Russia's nuclear doctrine is discussed in: Congressional Research Service report R45861 of 22 March 2022, 'Russia's Nuclear Weapons. its Doctrine, Forces, and Modernization' by Amy F. Woolff. http://crsreports.congress.gov, and in www.sipri.org/commentary/blog/2020/russias-nuclear-doctrine-moves-focus-non-western-threats. See also Woolf (2022).

possible nuclear use in 'extreme circumstances'.[27] The United States indicates also a possible use in retaliation for an adversary's use of prohibited weapons of mass destruction or a cyber attack of comparable severity.[28]

Nuclear weapon states seem torn between a wish to use their nuclear weapons capacity for broad deterrence and another wish to assure the world about the great restraint they will observe. Thus, in a documentary released on 7 March 2018, President Putin explicitly stressed that Russia would not use nuclear weapons preemptively and would only respond with a second strike when there was a certainty that Russian territory had been struck. He is reported to have said:

> 'The decision to use nuclear weapons can only be made if our early warning system not only detects a missile launch but clearly forecasts its flight path and the time when warheads reach the Russian territory, '... 'If someone makes a decision to destroy Russia, then we have a legitimate right to respond'.[29]

In a statement before the Senate Armed Services Committee on 20 March 2018, General John Hyten, in charge of the US nuclear arsenal, said in similarly cautious tones that if Russia launched two nuclear-tipped ballistic missiles at the United States, the United States should not retaliate until the incoming missiles had reached their targets or were destroyed in-flight by defence systems. He added: 'If we do have to respond, we want to respond in kind and not further escalate the conflict out of control'.[30]

Statements such as these suggest restraint but as with commitments to no first use, how reliable are they? While nuclear posture statements signal – and perhaps genuinely reflect – attitudes of great restraint of possible uses, those in nuclear weapons states who want to obtain a maximum deterrent effect from the weapons oppose issuing any assurances that the weapons are retained exclusively for the purpose of deterring other states from attacking with nuclear weapons. They are keen to read elasticity in formulations to warn potential adversaries that the weapons might be used in a variety of situations. A similar warning may be attained by the pattern of deployment of stocks and

---

[27] This is in line with but gives a greater latitude for use than what the International Court of Justice indicated as a possibly legal use of nuclear weapons in 'an extreme circumstance of self-defence in which its very survival would be at stake'. See ICJ, Advisory Opinion of 8 July 1996, para. 97.

[28] Klare (2019).

[29] 'Putin Praised Trump, Assails Sanctions, Vows to Defend "Great Power" Russia', RadioFreeEurope/RadioLiberty, 7 March 2018, www.rferl.org/a/putin-social-media-interview-praises-trump-assails-sanctions/29085457.html. Also see his remarks at 'Meeting of the Valdai International Discussion Club', plenary session, 18 October 2018, http://en.kremlin.ru/events/president/news/58848.

[30] CNBC, 21 March 2018, www.cnbc.com/2018/03/21/heres-what-us-should-do-if-russia-launched-nuclear-attack-gen-hyten.html.

by the stocking of low-yield nuclear weapons that may have a low threshold of use. We may note that Russia has a large stock of tactical nuclear weapons and in the United States, the Trump administration added and the Biden administration retained a program for the production of lower-yield nuclear weapons.

We may also note that at the time – end of February 2022 – when Russia was condemned by a strong majority of governments for its invasion of Ukraine and during its war with Ukraine in 2022, Russia several times caused concern by pointedly reminding the world of its nuclear weapons capacity. Possibly in order to reduce these concerns, a cooling statement was made by the Russian foreign ministry at a briefing on 18 August 2022 that 'Russian military doctrine allows a nuclear response only in response to the threat of mass destruction, or when the very existence of the state is threatened.' It was added in the explanation: 'That is, the use of a nuclear arsenal is possible only as part of a response to an attack in self-defence and only in emergencies'.[31]

Nevertheless, only a month later, in connection with the partial Russian mobilization on 21 September, President Putin warned about possible Russian use of nuclear weapons.[32]

Further, when after arranged referenda in and annexation of occupied territories in Ukraine, it was made clear that Russian defence of annexed territory against Ukrainian attacks would be regarded as self-defence of Russian state territory. Any attack affecting Russian territory could – it was implied – under the Russian doctrine allow the use of nuclear weapons. We must conclude that the language of restraint in the Russian nuclear doctrine is not taken at face value. However, restraints will remain on Russian use even of tactical nuclear weapons but they may be caused by the nuclear taboo and the public mind and by fear of catastrophic consequences promised by the United States,

SHIELDS AGAINST NUCLEAR WEAPONS
COULD IMPAIR STRATEGIC STABILITY

On the US side, the notion of mutual deterrent and vulnerability as protection against nuclear war was never attractive. Costly work has continued for many decades on what has been called 'star wars' – an anti-missile shield designed to protect against incoming nuclear-charged missiles including second strikes. In 2002 the United States withdrew from the ABM treaty that was meant to solidify the mutual vulnerability. Work on a US missile shield remains ongoing in the 2020s. It is often explained to aim at effectiveness only against

---

[31] Reported by Reuters on 18 August 2022. Cf. Chapter 3, p. 48.
[32] See above Chapter 3, p. 45.

states like Iran and North Korea that have or might acquire a limited nuclear weapons capacity. Russia and China may continue to doubt that it will prove technically feasible for the United States to develop effective shields against nuclear strikes. They are nevertheless concerned about the US deployment of anti-missile units in Romania and South Korea for fear that these may reduce the deterrent effect of their own nuclear weapons. This fear has contributed (2021–) to drive an arms race in which Russia and China seek to develop new means by which they can continue to be sure of their second-strike ability that is to deter a US nuclear first strike.

THE TREATY ON THE PROHIBITION OF NUCLEAR WEAPONS AND DETERRENCE

It does not seem clear whether the US Biden administration will continue the categorical denunciation that the preceding US administration together with the governments of other nuclear weapon states has voiced regarding the Treaty on the Prohibition of Nuclear Weapons (2017). One might have thought that nuclear weapon states should have welcomed that by adhering to the Treaty on the Prohibition of Nuclear Weapons (TPNW) a great many non-nuclear weapons states parties to the NPT assume a second commitment to non-proliferation (beyond the one they have made under the NPT.) However, the five major powers seem to think that the credibility and deterrent effect of their nuclear weapons may somehow be damaged by the new treaty that clearly envisages a world without nuclear weapons. The treaty will be further discussed below in the context of disarmament.[33]

It is perhaps understandable that those who claim that deterrent is the main function of their nuclear weapons seek to make maximum use of such effect by opening for possible use, for instance in response to attacks by B or C weapons or cyber means or being ambiguous about possible circumstances that may trigger use. Others object that any such deterrent effects are vastly outweighed by the risk of death and destruction that would be caused by any actual use of nuclear weapons and possible escalation to nuclear war. They note also that possession of nuclear weapons has not deterred India and Pakistan from armed conflicts and that Israeli nuclear weapons have not deterred adversaries from attacks. They make the irrefutable point that so long as nuclear weapons exist there remains the risk that they may come to be used.[34] In a number of

---

[33] See below, Chapter 9, p. 148.

[34] At their review conferences in 2000 and 2010, the NPT States parties agreed by consensus that: (a) 'The Conference reaffirms and recognizes that the total elimination of nuclear

cases, decisions to use nuclear weapons have been close and in other cases, only luck prevented misunderstandings to cause disaster.[35] Accordingly, they urge the elimination of all nuclear weapons.[36]

While there have been no meaningful negotiations about nuclear disarmament and we do not know how seriously nuclear posture statements will govern the actions of nuclear weapons states, restraints other than the deterrent of a second strike do exist and will be discussed below.

EVIDENCE OF RESTRAINTS ON THE
USE OF NUCLEAR WEAPONS

The fear of a retaliatory nuclear strike (between the biggest NW states fear of 'MAD' or 'mutually assured destruction') is often regarded as the foremost factor inducing restraint. So long as no credible shield or other means develop to stop retaliatory second strikes, they may, indeed, continue to deter from any use of nuclear weapons between powers that have them and on states under nuclear 'umbrellas'.

However, MAD is not the only restraint. In the period before 1970, the United States and Soviet governments considered the use of nuclear weapons on a number of occasions, and even though they faced no risk of a retaliatory nuclear strike they refrained from the awesome decision of a first use.[37] The Soviet Union reportedly considered using nuclear weapons in the conflict with China at the Ussuri River in 1969.[38] Indeed, while the United States and Soviet nuclear arsenals grew to preposterous size during the Cold War with big cities as potential targets, no cases of contemplated use are reported from around 1970.

It is noteworthy that the 1972 ABM treaty through which the United States and the Soviet Union mutually renounced protecting their territories and cities against nuclear ballistic missile attacks, made an exception regarding their

---

weapons is the only absolute guarantee against the use or threat of use of nuclear weapons...' (2010 NPT RevCon Final Document). www.un.org/ga/search/view_doc.asp?symbol=NPT/ CONF.2010/50%20(VOL.I).

[35] See, in particular, Perry (2015) and Leitenberg (2018).

[36] The demand is voiced by many organizations, including the International Campaign to Abolish Nuclear Weapons (ICAN) and Global Zero.

[37] Use of nuclear weapons was considered at high military levels in the United States during the Korean War 1950, in the conflict over the small islands of Quemoy and Matsu in 1958 and in the Vietnam War in 1968. See Tannenwald (2007), p. 182. Also see Ellsberg (2019).

[38] William Burr, 'The Sino-Soviet Conflict, 1969: US Reactions and Diplomatic Maneuvers' (Washington DC: National Security Archive, 12 June 2001). https://nsarchive2.gwu.edu/NSAEBB/NSAEBB49/.

capitals plus one more site. Allowing these four sites to have a defence against ballistic missiles suggested a mutual understanding that there must be some restraints even on second strikes.

But were the parties really prepared to act without restraint when it came to other huge cities like Leningrad or New York? Probably not – and if a restraint could be assumed in these cases, could we not assume that the thought of using strategic nuclear weapons for 'assured destruction' of any one of the world's fast-growing number of big cities must have become more and more alien? The strong engagement of the – more recent – organization 'Mayors for peace' for disarmament issues is evidence of a massive public opinion in the world's big cities for restraint and against any repetition of Hiroshima and Nagasaki, but also of Tokyo, Hamburg, Dresden, Coventry, et al.[39]

Further, the longer the time that no government has taken a decision to use one of the many thousands of existing strategic nuclear weapons against a population centre, the stronger a restraint against such action is likely to grow.[40]

The testing in the 1970s of neutron bombs reflected the idea of making military use of the atom while showing some restraint in physical destruction. However, weapons that killed people by radiation but spared hardware like houses and tanks, struck the public mind as satanic and the ideas were abandoned. Perhaps there will be broad condemnations also of the nuclear weapons of low yield that may be deployed. The 'public mind' once drove the ban on gas warfare and later contributed to the complete prohibition of biological and chemical weapons. The current public anti-nuclear wave – including the Treaty on the Prohibition of Nuclear Weapons – suggests that a strong public opinion exists that rejects all nuclear weapons.

Some restraints have been shown in the geographical deployment of military force, notably nuclear weapons. The interrupted Soviet nuclear deployment in Cuba in 1962 demonstrated what crisis could follow if no restraint was shown. The proximity to the United States and the brief reaction time this would have given in case of use was clearly provocative. Less dramatically, the removal of US missiles from Turkey reduced the threat against the Soviet Union. It should also be noted that decades later NATO declared it would not deploy nuclear weapons in the Eastern European states that joined the alliance.

---

[39] As of September 2022, Mayors for Peace has 8,206 member cities. www.mayorsforpeace.org/english/.

[40] Tannenwald (2007).

STIGMA AND TABOO

The horrors of Hiroshima and Nagasaki attached a stigma to any use of nuclear weapons and continue to sustain a massive worldwide public opinion. Undoubtedly, this background was part of the reason why the leaderships in the United States and the Soviet Union sought and came out of the Cuban missile crisis with only deep shock. Taken together, the experiences of use and threats and of nuclear tests have resulted in a kind of taboo around touching the 'nuclear button'.[41]

It is true that taboos can be broken, but there remains an element of unreality about a deliberate first use of a nuclear weapon. In a famous article in 2007 the distinguished quartet of four US statesmen – George Shultz, Sam Nunn, William J. Perry and Henry Kissinger – wrote that 'the end of the Cold War made the doctrine of mutual Soviet-American deterrence obsolete'.[42] After 2007, a severe chill and a mutual arms race returned between the United States and Russia and extended beyond them. Indeed, after its invasion of Ukraine in 2022 Russia has even allowed itself 'nuclear rattling' in response to the strong assistance of weapons to Ukraine from outside states.

Nevertheless, the element of unreality of risk that the four seasoned statesmen spotted in the bilateral US-Soviet relation, may still be there and have regard to other major powers as well. Military leaders in these states calculate how they may use their human and weapons assets in any armed conflict. This may include advance planning of retaliating nuclear second strikes. However, decisions on the actual use of any nuclear weapons most likely are a matter reserved for political decisions by government leaders. Over time restraints against decisions on the first use of nuclear weapons may have become so strong that while the physical existence of the weapons remains only too real, an actual governmental decision on the first use of them has become implausible, if not inconceivable.

COLD WAR IS GONE. NEW COMPETITION
AND NEW MEANS OF STRUGGLE

If question marks have developed for first strikes by nuclear weapons, we must also ask if the latest array of means and techniques of warfare – cyber, space, artificial intelligence – add further question marks and restraints.

---

[41] See Tannenwald (2007) and Solingen (2007); and see articles in *Foreign Affairs*, November/December 2018, notably Muelle, J., 'Nuclear Weapons Don't Matter'; and Tannenwald, N,. 'The Vanishing Nuclear Taboo'.

[42] *Wall Street Journal*, 4 January 2007.

During the Cold War, a pervasive conflict raged between governments that aspired to attain a Socialist economic order in every corner of the world and governments determined to preserve a free market economic order everywhere. The stakes were high. In 1958, the US considered – but rejected – nuclear action to prevent the Beijing Government from taking the two small Taiwan-controlled islands Quemoy and Matsu very close to the Chinese mainland. With today's eyes, such action would appear wildly disproportionate.

Today, major powers continue to wrestle, but what is the wrestling match now about? Amazingly, it is hard to say! The ideological conflict of the Cold War is no more. Nor – despite Russia in Ukraine – is the match about land and borders, as often in past history. Nor about access to raw materials. Greater diversity has developed in oil resources and there is less dependence on the Middle East. Is the arms race and wrestling match today one between the aspirations of the liberal democratic states led by the United States and claiming primacy as productive, tolerant and providing ways of peaceful and relatively orderly government change through honest elections and, on the other side, authoritarian China claiming recognition as equal with an ability to mobilize all its power for action without erosion through internal squabbling? Or, are we simply witnessing a wrestling match rooted in DNA, as explained by the Darwinian Azar Gat or by a 'quest for power', as concluded by Hans Morgenthau or a 'quest for recognition', as suggested by Francis Fukuyama? Or all of these?

Whatever the answer, we note with both relief and continued anxiety that the great powers have – so far – exercised restraint in their struggle in order to avoid clashing in direct armed conflicts. While demonstrating their abilities to use innovative techniques to inflict disarray and pain on adversaries, they increasingly and aggressively use their non-military – notably economic – power and flag the excellence of their respective cultures, scientific prowess, including even their ability to fast produce a vaccine and the ambition to be first on Mars.

Are we witnessing a shift of aspirations in the major powers and in the means they use to pursue them?

The main editorial of the International New York Times on 19 March 2021 ended as follows: 'Of all the threats that China poses, the greatest might just be its example to the rest of the world of a successful alternative to American democracy, which has been marred by economic inequality, racial unrest and insurrection. To effectively counter China, Americans must get their house in order and remind the world – and themselves – that democracy can still deliver for ordinary people.'

It is nice but hard to think that a 'beauty contest' should be the central feature in the competition between major states. We can hardly doubt that while the appeal of state models may influence the support for the competitors, restraints actually exercised in the threat and use of force, whether in the Middle East and the South China Sea still flow in large part from mutual deterrence. A permanent show of military ankles reminds the parties that they could lose live military fights about local or regional domination or risk celebrating victories in ruins. At the same time, there is an awareness in the major powers that the use of the military means that have become available – cyber, space, artificial intelligence (AI) – would make the course and possible escalation of military measures today intolerably unpredictable. Hence, for very good reasons the great powers continue to avoid coming into direct military confrontation.

While the military-technical evolution has thus made possible contests on this field ever more unpredictable and scarier, accelerated globalization and economic interdependence have increased the vulnerability of all states and opened a new field in which contests may play out. Great powers (and others as well) can – and appear increasingly do – rely on economic measures and cyber means to pursue their interests and to try to undermine the strength of competitors.

We note that under President Trump the United States made unprecedented use of economic sanctions and pressures, above all but not only against China, Iran and Russia.[43] The construction of the gas pipeline Nord Stream 2 from Russia to Germany through the Baltic Sea was put in doubt in 2020 and 2021 when the United States, objecting to European import of gas from Russia, applied economic sanctions against private enterprises that involved themselves in the project. While at that time the pressure did not work, the Russian invasion of Ukraine in February 2022 led the German government to measures that suspended any operation of the pipeline. Russia was thus deprived of an expected big income from gas export, but Germany also placed itself in danger of not having enough gas for industry and housewarming. When Russia in the fall of 2022 increasingly cut gas deliveries to Europe, including those through North Stream 1, which had been operative since 2011, it further hurt its own economy but it contributed as intended to a severe energy crisis in Western Europe.[44] Thus, economic warfare became a highly important part of the overall contest between Russia and the West.

China may expect to gain great economic leverage through the planned 'Belt and a Road' and Russia is repeatedly accused of using cyber means to

---

[43] Cf, above, Chapter 6, p. 113.
[44] See Sarah Marsh and Madeline Chambers, 'Germany Freezes Nord Stream 2 Gas Project as Ukraine Crisis Deepens', *Reuters*, February 22, 2022, www.reuters.com/business/energy/germanys-scholz-halts-nord-stream-2-certification-2022-02-22/; 'Nord Stream 2: How Does the Pipeline Fit into the Ukraine-Russia Crisis?,' *BBC News*, February 22, 2022, www.bbc.com/news/world-europe-60131520.

influence the United States and other states' elections. Contests by other means than weapons are thus available and already in use. We have rightly begun to worry about their effects. If replacing and not merely supplementing the threat of kinetic warfare, perhaps we should welcome the evolution.

AVOIDING NUCLEAR WAR BY AVOIDING CONFLICT

A final important point to make in this section on restraints to the use of armed force is that paradoxically the risk of confrontation with nuclear and other unconventional weapons may be assumed to act as a constant warning to the great powers states not to stumble into or allow themselves to be drawn into controversies that directly or indirectly might escalate to a conflict.[45] In recent years, the P 5 NWS has pursued 'strategic risk reduction' to prevent possible miscalculation, misperception or misunderstanding that may lead to escalation, including the use of nuclear weapons. That in the nuclear age governments need to show prudence to avoid serious frictions that may escalate is shown by a 1973 US-Soviet agreement on the prevention of nuclear war.[46] The agreement called on the two states 'to remove the danger of nuclear war and of the use of nuclear weapons' and *'to prevent the development of situations capable of causing a dangerous exacerbation of their relations'*.[47] This, evidently, is a plea to use diplomacy and create détente to avoid reaching a stage where weapons are brandished.

---

[45] See the history of NATO's 'Able Archer' exercise: https://slate.com/news-and-politics/2017/06/able-archer-almost-started-a-nuclear-war-with-russia-in-1983.html.

[46] US Department of State, 'Agreement Between the United States of America and the Union of Soviet Socialist Republics on the Prevention of Nuclear War', signed and entered into force on 22 June 1973. For the full text, see https://2009-2017.state.gov/t/isn/5186.htm.

[47] In an article of 14 March 2018 in the *Bulletin of the Atomic Scientists*, Adam Scheinman suggests a revisiting or updating of the agreement.

9

Disarmament as Restraint on the Use of Force

The preceding discussion has examined the generally supported view that arms can be an important means to deter a potential adversary from using armed force. Demands for disarmament rest on the diametrically opposed logic: if states sincerely wish to stop the use of armed force, eliminate the arms! Why has it proved – and continues to prove – so difficult to act successfully on that logic?

In the nineteenth century, European and American peace movements campaigned vigorously against war and brutality. Some humanitarian mitigation was attained through conventions and through institutions like the International Committee of the Red Cross (ICRC), but government resistance to disarmament was rigid. It was only after World War I that the governments that formed the League of Nations saw disarmament as a central path to peace. They also encountered difficulties. At the time of the League's great conference in 1932, Salvador de Madariaga, the famous and witty Spanish Liberal, said:

> When the animals met to discuss disarmament, the Lion looked the Eagle in the eye and said, "We must abolish talons" The Eagle looked squarely back into the Lion's eyes and said, "We must abolish claws". Then the bear said, "Let's abolish everything except universal embraces".[1]

Tragically, the great effort made by the League failed and was followed by rearmament and World War II. In structuring the approach of the UN Charter to disarmament, the victor states appeared somewhat less ambitious than the authors of Art. 8:1 of the League Covenant, which recognized that *'the maintenance of peace requires the reduction of national armaments to the lowest point consistent with national safety and the enforcement by common action*

---

[1] Cited in 'Eagle, Lion, Bear', *Time*, 7 March 1932, http://content.time.com/time/subscriber/article/0,33009,743253,00.html. For Winston Churchill's 1929 rendition of this fable, see https://winstonchurchill.org/resources/speeches/1915-1929-nadir-and-recovery/a-disarmament-fable/.

of international obligations'. Unlike the League Covenant, the UN Charter expressly affirms the 'inherent' right of armed self-defence and starts from the assumption that member states are armed. Nevertheless, in Art. 11 the General Assembly is directed to consider *'the principles governing disarmament and the regulation of armaments and may make recommendations with regard to such principles'*. Art. 26 reflects the view that the promotion of peace and security should take place with *'the least diversion for armaments'* of the world's resources. The Security Council is charged with the task of formulating *'plans... for the establishment of a system for the regulation of armaments'* and is to be advised and assisted by a Military Staff Committee on all questions relating to *'the regulation of armaments and possible disarmament.'* (Arts. 26 and 47).

The permanent five members of the Security Council never gave active life to the Military Staff Committee, where the Chiefs of Staff of their armed forces were to meet and consider how they could assist the Council in formulating plans for *'possible'* disarmament. Contacts military-to-military have since come to be regarded as a useful feature of international life. Perhaps a valuable opportunity was missed when the five key military leaders of the permanent members of the Security Council were not made to meet and confer about disarmament in the Military Staff Committee.

Proposals for disarmament were advanced without the benefit of meetings of the Military Staff Committee in the second half of the 1950s – after the end of the Korean War, the death of Stalin and the conclusion of the Austrian State Treaty in 1955. They had regard *inter alia* to the use of atomic energy (Atoms for Peace) and for general and complete disarmament and look amazingly optimistic to a reader in the 2000 twenties.[2] Thus, a UK proposal in 1959 offered a staged program of comprehensive disarmament, including the abolition of all nuclear weapons and the reduction of all other weapons. A Soviet proposal would eliminate all armed forces and armaments within the span of four years. Moreover, a set of principles were agreed by the United States and the Soviet Union (the so-called McCloy-Zorin statement of 1961) on 'balanced', 'staged' and 'verified' elimination of all armed forces and armaments.

However, although the memory of Hiroshima and Nagasaki did not fail to remind all of the risks of the growing stockpiles of nuclear weapons, the Cold War convinced Western states of a need to contain a strongly armed and expansionist Soviet Union and not lightly do away with arms (nuclear or other). Negotiations on the far-reaching proposals failed. Proposals tabled by the United States made clear that they were made for a 'peaceful world' – first peace, then disarmament. The Soviet proposals, by contrast, presumed that

---

[2]   For an excellent survey, see Goldblat (2002).

peace would follow from disarmament. Attention turned to more limited projects called 'partial measures', like nuclear test bans and the non-proliferation of nuclear weapons. Reference was made later in some arms control agreements, notably in Art. VI of the NPT, to general and complete disarmament but the goal has come to be seen as intractable and hardly even earnest.

US-SOVIET BILATERAL 'ARMS CONTROL'

While during the Cold War, the United States and the Soviet Union were unable to agree on nuclear or – with rare exceptions noted below – any other 'disarmament' in the sense of eliminating weapons, they nevertheless concluded valuable bilateral agreements of 'arms control' that regulated use of their nuclear capacities. For instance, after the shock of the Cuban missile crisis, they reached an agreement on hot lines for contacts in emergencies (1963) and an agreement on a partial nuclear test ban (1963) stopped nuclear tests in the atmosphere, outer space and under water. Many other important agreements on specific issues could be cited.

In 1972, they concluded their 'Strategic Arms Limitation Talks' (SALT), which produced the Anti-Ballistic Missile treaty (ABM) (terminated by the United States in 2002) and an 'interim agreement' limiting certain strategic nuclear arms. While these treaties did not provide for the dismantling of any weapons, they were vital to maintaining mutual vulnerability and thereby nuclear deterrence.[3] The Intermediate Nuclear Forces Treaty (INF) of 1987 (terminated in 2019 by the US claiming Russian non-compliance) helped to reduce tensions in Europe by the United States and the Soviet Union agreeing not to make and deploy missiles of intermediate (500–5,500 km range). After the Cold War commitments to some real cuts became possible. Under the treaty of 1990 on Conventional Armed Forces in Europe (CFE), NATO and Warsaw Pact states agreed on very substantial cuts and transparency measures. Through the so-called 'presidential nuclear initiatives' President H.W. Bush and President Gorbachev made reciprocal unilateral commitments[4] that led to the withdrawal from service of some 17.000 tactical nuclear weapons of various categories. The START agreement of 2010 (prolonged in 2021 for five years) placed important ceilings on the number of deployed strategic nuclear warheads and launchers and included inspection.

---

[3]   Arms Control Association, 'Strategic Arms Limitation Talks (SALT)', www.armscontrol.org/treaties/strategic-arms-limitation-talks.

[4]   On unilateral commitments, see Rydell, R., 'Disarmament without Agreements?' in *International Negotiations* 10 (2005). pp. 363–380.

THE NON-PROLIFERATION TREATY (NPT)

The NPT, which was concluded in 1968, sought the commitment of all states that did not have nuclear weapons to stay away from them and the commitment of states parties that had nuclear weapons to move away from them through negotiations about disarmament (Art. VI of the treaty). Thus, the treaty's aim could be said to be a total elimination of nuclear weapons. A disarmament approach was seen as safer than an approach of only prohibitions of use. The same 'disarmament approach' was followed later in the conventions banning biological and chemical weapons.

Although the NPT contains a clause permitting parties to withdraw in extreme circumstances (Art. X) only North Korea has purported to do so and the treaty is deemed to create very valuable legal commitments for non-nuclear weapon states. Their firm adherence has been deemed all the more important as it is well known that the acquisition of nuclear weapons technology for many years has been possible through proliferators like the head of the Pakistani weapons program, the late A.Q. Khan. A Review and Extension Conference in 1995 decided that the NPT would continue in force 'indefinitely'.[5]

Differently from the conventions on biological and chemical weapons that prohibited these weapons to all parties (*erga omnes*), the NPT contained in Art. VI the crucial understanding that the five nuclear-weapon states parties to the treaty were allowed to keep their nuclear weapons while negotiating nuclear disarmament. Art VI reads as follows: 'Each of the Parties to the Treaty undertakes to pursue negotiations in good faith on effective measures relating to the cessation of the nuclear arms race at an early date and to nuclear disarmament, and on general and complete disarmament under strict and international control.'

In its advisory opinion of 8 July 1996 on the Legality of the Threat or Use of Nuclear Weapons, the International Court of Justice (ICJ) stated that the obligation expressed in Article VI '*includes its fulfillment in accordance with the basic principle of good faith.*'[6] Accordingly, the Court decided unanimously that '*There exists an obligation to pursue in good faith and bring to a conclusion negotiations leading to nuclear disarmament in all its aspects under strict and effective international control*'.[7]

However, for over fifty years, the five great powers have failed to negotiate the 'nuclear disarmament' they have committed to as parties. Frustration has

[5]   Discussed further by Dhanapala (2005).
[6]   ICJ (1996), paragraph 102.
[7]   ICJ (1996), paragraph 105.

grown among other parties that the five have relied on Art. VI as a kind of permanent nuclear weapons license.

Although the NPT has not led to the disarmament that it foreshadowed, it remains of great importance as, together with a number of treaties establishing nuclear-weapon-free zones, it prevents some global and regional risks and tensions that could arise.[8]

Since 1975, NPT States parties have agreed to meet every five years for a 'review conference' to examine past compliance and future challenges, with the goal of reaching a consensus Final Document. While the last such consensus document was adopted in 2010, the 2015 and 2020 conferences (the latter held in 2022 due to the Covid pandemic) failed to reach any such consensus; the 2022 conference was characterized by Russian opposition to language addressing the war in Ukraine and objections among the non-nuclear-weapon states over the lack of progress on disarmament.[9] The next conference will be held in 2026.

THE TREATY ON THE PROHIBITION OF NUCLEAR WEAPONS (TPNW, 2017)

In 2017, after a lengthy period during which a campaign was pursued by some states and non-governmental organizations to remind the world of the humanitarian consequences of the use of nuclear weapons, a number of non-nuclear weapon states took the initiative to negotiate and adopt a treaty that prohibits all its parties from possessing and using nuclear weapons.[10] The frustration mentioned above that the NPT has failed to generate any agreements on nuclear disarmament undoubtedly contributed to the conclusion of a treaty (TPNW) that has no clause licensing exemptions.

As noted above, nuclear-weapon states have been strongly opposed to the new treaty. Some of them have even objected that the TPNW undermines the existence of weapons that are indispensable to world peace. However, no one can force any nuclear-weapon states to adhere to the TPNW and do away with their nuclear weapons and, as they clearly will not adhere, there is no prospect that the treaty will bring nuclear disarmament within a foreseeable time. What the treaty does, is to enable states to commit to the aspiration for a nuclear-weapon-free world without in the same breath pronouncing an

---

[8] These zones exist in Latin America and the Caribbean, Africa, Central Asia, Southeast Asia, and South Pacific. For details, see www.un.org/disarmament/wmd/nuclear/nwfz/.

[9] Arms Control Association (2022).

[10] Above, Chapter 8, p. 137.

express unlimited license for five great powers to possess such weapons. The parties to the new treaty might hope thereby to help to delegitimize nuclear weapons and strengthen a nascent general norm against use.[11]

LACK OF DISARMAMENT, MILITARY BALANCE, FUTURE COMPETITION

We must conclude that the risk of deliberate use of nuclear weapons while low is not eliminated and that the weapons continue to hang like a sword of Damocles over humanity. The risk may even increase, if weapons of low yield were deployed or if any nuclear weapon state were to succeed in creating an effective missile shield that made it lose the restraint arising from fear of a retaliatory second nuclear strike.

We must further conclude that while arms control agreements have been and are of very high value, there has been little success to reach agreements on disarmament in the sense of elimination of arms. In 2020 global annual military expenditures stood at nearly 2 trillion dollars rising and the global number of nuclear weapons at over 13,000 (down from reportedly 70,000 during the Cold War).[12]

What causes the inability or unwillingness of nuclear weapon states to reach agreements on smaller deterrent capacities and on restraint in the build-up of military capacity?

It is evident that the United States, Russia and China feel that they will not subject whatever parity or preeminence they deem they have to any risk by letting their military capacity fall to a level that they think might not deter a potential adversary from attempting a challenge of some kind. They believe that they might take unacceptable risks if they were not able to inflict pain and injury of gravity that they deem any potential adversary would find unbearable.[13]

---

[11] In June 2022, the first Meeting of States Parties to the TPNW adopted a Vienna Declaration and a 50-point Action Plan in which they declared that 'We will not rest until the last state has joined the Treaty, the last warhead has been dismantled and destroyed and nuclear weapons have been totally eliminated from the Earth'. www.icanw.org/vienna_declaration_action_plan_overview.

[12] Federation of American Scientists, 'Status of World Nuclear Forces', 2021. https://fas.org/issues/nuclear-weapons/status-world-nuclear-forces/

[13] It may be noted that while undoubtedly holding this view the US Department of Defense also pursues a project aimed at conducting war in ways that reduce civilian casualties. See article by Samuel Moyn on the completion announced by the Secretary of Defense Lloyd Austin of a 'Civilian Harm Mitigation and Response Action Plan' promising institutional changes so that American war-making kills fewer innocent people. The article was published in Responsible Statecraft, 31 August 2022. By the same author: 'Humane: How the United States Abandoned Peace and Reinvented War', (2021). See also the extensive review 'The Case against Humane War' by Daniel Bessner in *The New Republic*, September 8, 2022.

What is a sufficient level of military deterrence could at earlier times have been determined by so-called 'bean counting'. Reducing arms could theoretically be possible by comparing and cutting corresponding military assets category by category – soldiers, ships, airplanes, tanks, cannons, etc. In the current world, where the biggest military powers take into account the risks of several adversaries and threats of conflict and the possible use of several unconventional means of warfare calculations become almost impossible.

If underestimating foreign military threats may be risky, we must recognize that overestimating foreign threats and acquiring excessive military resources may also have negative consequences. A state convinced of its own military superiority – the US term is 'full spectrum dominance' – may run the risk of becoming overconfident.

Former US Secretary of State, Madeleine Albright, is reported to have stressed the exceptional status and strength of the United States, saying that *'if we have to use force, it is because we are America; we are the indispensable nation. We stand tall and we see further than other countries into the future, and we see the danger here to all of us'*.[14] However, Colin Powell, another Secretary of State and experienced general is said to have warned: *'If you break it [Iraq] you own it'*.[15] Starting armed actions may be easier than ending them and they may prove costly in lives and eventually end in failures.

Military superiority may for a shorter or longer time prevent any challenges and give political advantages – as it did for the United States in the 1990s. In the rapidly expanding world economy, the US economic and financial power will diminish in relative terms and military 'full spectrum dominance' – even now no guarantee against other states' second-strike capacity – may be challenged. Dominance and a world police role may also be an evolution that the United States, itself, tired of 'forever wars' is unlikely to wish to pursue.

A more likely – and benign – evolution would be that all the major players continue to compete for influence and control while avoiding direct confrontations – as they have done since 1945 – and simultaneously seek possible mutual accommodation. Today, as noted above, there are some signs that the competition between states can play out in other areas than military power – in the fields of science and economy, cyber activities, culture and social organization. Yet, nuclear weapons still remain on hair-trigger alert and could be set off by accident or misunderstanding and ignite a war that could end human civilization. Accordingly, rules of conduct, hot lines, and mechanisms for conciliation and dispute resolution remain practical means

---

[14]   https://1997-2001.state.gov/statements/1998/980219a.html.

[15]   www.pbs.org/wgbh/frontline/article/colin-powell-u-n-speech-was-a-great-intelligence-failure/.

needed to reduce the risks of conflicts and confrontations. So does diplomacy, arms control, and disarmament.

Experience shows how difficult the search for arms control and disarmament is, where states lack confidence in each other and where transparency is limited. It is sometimes asserted that times of distrust and tension only increase the urgency of disarmament talks. True, but the obstacles also increase. Success is more likely in a climate of political détente where a modicum of confidence has been attained. This requires efforts to understand each other's needs and a will to reconcile. To begin the march, different kinds of confidence-building measures are needed, such as arrangements for transparency, hotlines, space between armed forces, or for the avoidance of military incidents in the air or at sea. If and when the current (2022) cold war climate between major powers subsides, confidence-building measures will need to be first on the agenda. Indeed, even during war hot lines and other means of communication need be open.[16]

[16] On the mission of the UN to permanently and persistently strive not only to reduce the risk of use of nuclear weapons but to eliminate nuclear war through eradication of the weapons, see Duarte (2008).

10

Preventing the Interstate Use of Force by Preventing or Solving Conflicts

Mediation, Arbitration, Fact-finding, Diplomacy

The preceding three chapters discussed military strength as a means of deterring the use of force and disarmament as means of preventing the use of force through the elimination of weapons. This chapter will discuss means through which conflicts and differences may be avoided or solved and the risk of uses of force eliminated. Many important such means are listed in Art. 33 of the UN Charter: diplomacy (negotiation), fact-finding (enquiry), or reliance on a third party (mediator, arbitration tribunal or a court) or resort to regional agencies or arrangements.

Below are some comments on such methods.

MEDIATION

Mediation by a third party to avoid the use of force between states has deep roots in history.[1] A famous case was President T. Roosevelt's bringing the Russo-Japanese War to an end 1904–1905. While UN member states are sometimes assisted informally to solve controversies through the good offices of the UN Secretary-General or his office, mediation seems in modern times to have been relied on mostly in controversies within an area rather than between two states. Examples include the UN-mandated mediation in Palestine in 1948, which tragically ended in the assassination of Count Bernadotte, the Swedish mediator. Fifty years later, mediation was successful in the conflict in Northern Ireland, where US Senator George Mitchell played a central role and helped bring about the so-called Good Friday agreement in 1998.[2]

---

[1] Descriptions of mediation in modern but limited contexts are found in Rifkind and Picco (2014) and in Ohlsson (2022).

[2] www.usip.org/public-education/educators/george-mitchell-building-peace-northern-ireland.

Another recent case was when in 2005, the UN-appointed Martti Ahtisaari successfully mediated a conflict between the Government of Indonesia and the Free Aceh Movement.[3] In the 2012 Syrian civil war, on the other hand, three successive mediators appointed by the UN Security Council – former Secretary-General Kofi Annan, Ambassador Lakhdar Brahimi, and the international official Staffan de Mistura – failed to find solutions. One reason was the mediators' lack of leverage resulting from divisions between the Security Council members United States and Russia. The grim civil war with a number of intervening outside parties, including the United States, Russia, Turkey, Iran and Gulf states continued.[4]

ARBITRATION AND JUDICIAL SETTLEMENT

Arbitration and judicial settlement of disputes by special judicial tribunals or the International Court of Justice is frequent. An attractive aspect is that judgments are never regarded as a humiliation of losing parties. They have not been forced by an adversary to make concessions, but the outcome is a judicial institution's impartial application of law. As of the second half of the nineteenth century, settlement of differences through the application of law rather than force has had the support – but rather limited use – of governments. Through Art. 14 of the Covenant of the League of Nations, the first standing world court – the Permanent Court of International Justice – came into being and through Art. 92 of the UN Charter it was reborn as the principal judicial organ of the United Nations, now named the International Court of Justice.

Many vexing interstate problems have been eliminated through the court and – of great importance – judgments and advisory opinions have contributed in a major way to the growth and precision of international law.

Many judgments by courts and arbitration tribunals have been about boundaries, delimitation of maritime space or limited areas of territory, such as islands. In 1953, the ICJ adjudicated a dispute between the United Kingdom and France about two groups of tiny islands in the English Channel – the Minquiers and Ecrehous.[5] In the 1933 Eastern Greenland case, the Permanent Court of International Justice settled a dispute between Denmark and Norway by recognizing that all of the world's biggest island, Greenland. belonged to

---

[3]   Ahtisaari was later awarded the Nobel Peace Prize and elected President of Finland 1994–2000.

[4]   www.britannica.com/event/Syrian-Civil-War. See Zartman, I. William (2019) 'UN Mediation in the Syrian crisis. From Kofi Annan through Lakhdar Brahimi to Staffan de Mistura' in *Syrian Studies* 11(2).

[5]   For further reference, see www.icj-cij.org/en/case/17.

Denmark.[6] The ICJ has also settled a number of disputes between developing countries about territory and borders. An arbitration about a big piece of land took place between India and Pakistan (1968) regarding the 'Rann of Kutch' and its vast areas of salty marshes and deserts. The judgment was accepted by both parties and the risk for future use of force relating to this territory was averted.[7] In a recent case, the Permanent Court of Arbitration approved the claim of the Philippines to sovereignty over certain islands (Spratly Islands) claimed – and partly occupied – by China. However, China declined to accept the jurisdiction of the Court and rejected the judgment.[8]

Many specialized judicial tribunals have been established within the UN system. Several of them were created to try crimes relating to particular armed conflicts. In well-publicized proceedings they have, for instance, convicted Charles Taylor, Slobodan Milosevic and Radovan Karadžić.[9]

Even more important than the ad hoc tribunals for war crimes is the International Criminal Court – a permanent tribunal – that has been created (2002) to try crimes of genocide, war crimes, crimes against humanity, and crimes of aggression.[10] Thus, the Nuremberg tribunal has not stayed an isolated event, but rather the first international judicial grappling with personal criminal responsibility even at the highest levels of state for certain breaches of international law.[11]

---

[6] See https://jusmundi.com/en/document/decision/en-legal-status-of-eastern-greenland-judgment-wednesday-5th-april-1933.

[7] https://legal.un.org/riaa/cases/vol_XVII/1-576.pdf.

[8] See above, Chapter 3, p. 52 and 'The South China Sea Arbitration', Permanent Court of Arbitration, 2016, https://pca-cpa.org/en/cases/7/.

[9] Former Yugoslavia: www.icty.org; See also Donlon, Fidelma. 2011. 'Hybrid Tribunals'. in Routledge *Handbook of International Criminal Law*, 85–105. On international war crimes tribunals more generally, see: ICRC. 2013, *International Criminal Justice: The Institutions – Factsheet*. Geneva: ICRC. Advisory Service on International Humanitarian Law. www.icrc.org/en/document/international-criminal-justice-institutions. And: www.beyondintractability.org/essay/int_war_crime_tribunals.

[10] Further discussion of the ICJ is available at www.cfr.org/backgrounder/role-international-criminal-court (2022). Also see 'The Court Today. The Hague: ICC. Factsheet', www.icc-cpi.int/Publications/TheCourtTodayEng.pdf.

[11] For instance, in 2012 Charles Taylor, former President of Liberia and leader of a revolutionary front in Sierra Lone, was sentenced to 50 years in prison by the Special Court for Sierra Leone for war crimes and crimes against humanity. See www.nytimes.com/2012/05/31/world/africa/charles-taylor-.

The International Criminal Court at the Hague has issued two warrants for arrest – in 2009 and 2010 – for former head of state of Sudan [al-Bashir] for responsibility in atrocities committed in the region of Darfur. Reference on Bashir case: www.icc-cpi.int/darfur/albashir. In August 2021, Sudan's cabinet agreed to extradite al-Bashir (who was ousted in 2019) to the ICC www.nytimes.com/2021/08/12/world/africa/darfur-omar-al-bashir-sudan.html. It is somewhat unclear what will happen after a coup in October 2021. However, in January 2022, the

Special international judicial authorities have also been established for some other fields. One is the International Tribunal for the Law of the Sea, located in Hamburg and with the central competence to take up cases submitted to it in accordance with the law of the sea conventions.[12] It is remarkable that the United States that relies on these conventions and invokes them has not yet ratified them. Perhaps it testifies to the standing of some conventions – other examples are the convention on the law of treaties and the outer space convention – but it is an unhealthy situation introducing some uncertainty in relations.

A highly significant, innovative Dispute Settlement Mechanism was established within the World Trade Organization for international conflicts involving governments and/or private law subjects in the commercial field.[13] It is no small thing that major trade and financial disputes can be authoritatively settled with the help of a special impartial third party. According to the WTO, 607 disputes have been brought since 1995.[14] A major case handled by the Mechanism was the dispute between the Boeing Corporation and Airbus. It opened in 2004 and now seems to be finally settled.[15]

One interesting feature of the WTO Mechanism is that judgments may authorize a winning party to take measures of retaliation against actions found unlawful. Regrettably, the WTO Mechanism was paralyzed in 2019 when, following the US Trump administration's refusal to nominate a member, it lost its quorum.[16] The Biden administration has not yet (Sept. 2022) remedied the situation but appears to be taking part in talks regarding reforms within the WTO.[17]

In conclusion, there has been a remarkable expansion of matters that may be adjudicated by judicial authorities. Many new states have submitted cases to the International Court of Justice and the rate of compliance with judgments has been high.[18] The outlook for the settlement of interstate differences

---

Prosecutor of the ICC reported to the UN Security Council that the government had assured him of its continuing commitment to working together with the ICC: www.un.org/press/en/2022/sc14766.doc.htm.

[12] See www.itlos.org/en/. 'Tuerk, Helmut 2016'. 20 years of the International Tribunal for the Law of the Sea (ITLOS). Overview *Revue Belge de Droit International* 49 (2), 449–486.

[13] Jackson (2006).

[14] WTO, 'Dispute Settlement', www.wto.org/english/tratop_e/dispu_e/dispu_e.htm.

[15] See 'Highlights of the 17-Year Airbus, Boeing Trade War', Reuters, 16 June 2001, 2021. www.reuters.com/world/highlights-17-year-airbus-boeing-trade-war-2021-06-15/.

[16] https://crsreports.congress.gov/product/pdf/LSB/LSB10385.

[17] See www.atlanticcouncil.org/blogs/new-atlanticist/for-wto-reform-most-roads-lead-to-china-but-do-the-solutions-lead-away/ and Aarup, SA (2021). '"All Talk and No Walk": America Ain't Back at the WTO'. *Politico Europe*. www.politico.eu/article/united-states-world-trade-organization-joe-biden/.

[18] See Schulte (2004).

by judicial means looks positive. Yet, there has never been a sign of readiness of governments to allow disputes of high political significance to be submitted to settlement by judicial authorities. Under Art. 36:3 of the UN Charter, the Security Council may recommend parties to use appropriate means to settle disputes and 'should take into consideration that legal disputes should as a general rule be referred to the International Court of Justice...'. The Charter language accepts by implication the view that not all disputes are regarded as 'legal' or, as it used to be said 'justiciable' – or suitable for judicial settlement.

While some might argue that any interstate dispute can be settled through the application of law, governments remain reluctant. Up to January 2022, only 73 states had accepted the so-called 'optional clause' under Art. 36:2 of the Court's statute. The clause allows states to declare that they accept the jurisdiction of the Court as compulsory in 'legal disputes' in relation to any other state accepting the same obligation.[19] Many acceptances have been limited or severely qualified. The United Kingdom is the only state among the P5 that currently has accepted the optional clause.[20]

Thus, despite a much-expanded use of international tribunals, the settlement of interstate disputes by judicial means has been chosen far less often than was hoped ever since the second half of the nineteenth century. While removing many vexing differences and easing relations, it may not have often removed any risk of the use of force.

FACT-FINDING (ENQUIRY)

Procedures for 'enquiry' – fact-finding – have existed and been in use for a considerable time. One thought behind 'fact-finding' is that an impartial collection and analysis of facts may help reduce the risk of armed conflict by deflating disputes that have become inflamed through inaccurate information, rumors and allegations. Other purposes are to provide bases for solving differences or for establishing responsibility. A chief aim behind 'fact-finding' in the shape of permanent monitoring and inspection is to deter conduct – such as proliferation and testing of nuclear weapons – that may increase the risk of nuclear war.

The Covenant of the League of Nations stipulated (Art. 12) that the Council could undertake '*inquiry*' into disputes submitted to it and the UN Charter (Arts. 33 and 34) provides in the same vein that parties to disputes may seek

[19] The ICJ reports (2021) that 73 states have recognized the court's jurisdiction as compulsory. www.icj-cij.org/en/declarations.

[20] See ICJ, 'Declarations Recognizing the Jurisdiction of the Court as Compulsory'. International Court of Justice (blog). Accessed January 12, 2022. www.icj-cij.org/en/declarations.

solutions by '*enquiry*' and that the Security Council has the authority to 'investigate' disputes. In a General Assembly resolution of 1982, the Secretary-General was given the authority to engage fact-finders.[21] In 1987, the General Assembly established the 'Secretary-General's Mechanism' to investigate allegations of the possible use of chemical and biological weapons.[22]

Through its safeguards system, the IAEA continuously verifies that fissionable material is not diverted from peaceful use in non-nuclear-weapon states and from certain peaceful nuclear activities in nuclear-weapon states.[23] Safeguards inspection aims at deterring host countries from any clandestine diversion of fissionable material for the development of nuclear weapons[24] through the risk of detection.

In 1991, it was found during the first Security Council-mandated inspections in Iraq after the Gulf War that Iraq had embarked on nuclear activities without declaring them for safeguards inspection. The Agency concluded that the safeguards system that had been used (termed full scope safeguards under INFCIRC/153) in states parties to the NPT and that gave the right of inspection only to declared installations was inadequate. Work was begun on an additional protocol under which states would assume much more extensive duties of reporting and the Agency would have much greater rights to demand information and to inspect. The protocol (INFCIRC 540) was adopted in 1997 and has been accepted as safeguards regime by most – but not all – states.[25]

The Comprehensive Nuclear-Test-Ban Treaty concluded in 1995 but not yet in force (2022), also mandates a permanent system of monitoring using seismic and other methods to verify the absence of any nuclear explosions. Curiously, the monitoring system is fully in operation although the treaty has not entered into force,[26]

There is a rich experience of the use of institutionally based and ad hoc fact-finding. In 1984, during the Iraq-Iran War, an expert group appointed by the UN Secretary-General examined charges of possible violations of the

[21] Res 37/98 specifically addressed SG investigations of possible use of CBW. For further discussion of UN fact-finding: https://legal.un.org/avl/ha/ga_46-59/ga_46-59.html.

[22] On this 'mechanism', see www.un.org/disarmament/wmd/secretary-general-mechanism/. The mechanism was used in 1992 to investigate alleged use of chemical weapons in Mozambique and Azerbaijan and also in 2013 in Syria. 'Chemical Weapons Convention, Biological Weapons Convention and UNSGM', UN Office for Disarmament Affairs fact sheet, https://front.un-arm.org/wp-content/uploads/2021/07/SGM-Fact-Sheet-July2021.pdf.

[23] See von Baeckmann, A., 'IAEA Safeguards in Nuclear-Weapon States', *IAEA Bulletin* 1/1988, www.iaea.org/sites/default/files/publications/magazines/bulletin/bull30-1/30103552224.pdf.

[24] www.iaea.org/publications/factsheets/iaea-safeguards-overview.

[25] International Atomic Energy Agency, INFCIRC 540 (1997), www.iaea.org/topics/additional-protocol.

[26] www.ctbto.org/verification-regime/background/overview-of-the-verification-regime/.

1925 Geneva Protocol banning the use of chemical and bacteriological weapons and affirmed the charge that Iraq had used C-weapons.[27] More recently, groups of experts appointed and sent by the OPCW (Organisation for the Prohibition of Chemical Weapons) have examined claims that chemical weapons have been used in the Syrian civil war. Among a good deal of denials and controversy, it was affirmed by the OPCW that chemical weapons had been used by the government side and, indeed, also by the rebel side.[28]

UN Security Council-mandated inspections in Iraq during three months before the Iraq War in March 2003 (and before that in the 1990s) offer some insights into the use of fact-finding. The main task was to find and destroy any hidden weapons and to prevent the development or acquisition of weapons. It was backed by sanctions and military threats. In March 2003 – after only some three months of intense UN inspections during which no weapons had been found – the United States and its allies launched an armed invasion – the Iraq War. It was hardly out of genuine doubts regarding the integrity and competence of the UN inspection and their freedom of access to sites and installations, but rather because of a determination to continue the crusade that after the 9/11 attack on the United States began with the war in Afghanistan against the 'axis of evil'.

When the UN fact-finding inspections had not within a few months established that there were weapons of mass destruction. (as there weren't any such weapons), the United States chose to present evidence of its own based on alleged facts.[29] The reports of the professional UN inspection were not refuted but ignored and its leadership was a 'no count'.[30] However, to the embarrassment of the US government, extensive American inspections undertaken in the months after the invasion could only – like the UN inspectors – report that no weapons could be found.[31] One lesson from 2003 is that credible international fact-finding inspections can be of great value – if they are genuinely wanted and used. While in 2003 they were ignored by the US administration they led a majority of the Security Council to refuse to authorize a war that should not have been launched.

---

[27] www.nonproliferation.org/wp-content/uploads/npr/81ali.pdf.

[28] www.armscontrol.org/act/2021-07/news-briefs/opcw-confirms-chemical-weapons-use-syria. On alleged rebel use: www.bbc.com/news/world-middle-east-22424188.

[29] On the role of Secretary of State, Colin Powell, see article by Robert Baker in *N.Y. Times Magazine*, 17 July 2020. More broadly on the United States starting of the Iraq War 2003, see Draper, Robert, To Start a War (2020). See also Greg Thielmann, 'The Cost of Ignoring Inspectors: An Unnecessary War with Iraq' in *Arms Control Now* 5 March 2013.

[30] Expression used by President Bush according to column by Maureen Dowd in the *New York Times* 18 July 2016.

[31] Duelfer (2005).

International authorities entrusted with fact-finding have to use all the relevant data that they collect through their own inspectors and technical means. They may also receive data volunteered from the outside, notably from national intelligence services. Such contributions may be helpful in putting international inspectors on tracks to be examined, but they must be critically examined for veracity.[32] The usefulness of all fact-finding, observation, and inspection hinges on the professional competence and integrity of the observers and their full access to the areas or objects to be observed and information relating to them. Deficiencies in inspection efforts may create false confidence and render fact-finding misleading and dangerous. The 'Additional Protocol' that was adopted by the IAEA in 1997 extended the rights of the Agency and its inspectors to information and access.[33]

DIPLOMACY TO HELP PREVENT THE USE OF FORCE. BALANCE OF POWER

While voicing pessimism about the means of preventing the interstate use of force in the era of nuclear weapons, Hans Morgenthau placed his hope on 'diplomacy'.[34] What he and Henry Kissinger, another champion and practitioner of diplomacy, have had in mind is not the everyday activities of diplomatic missions but rather 'statesmanship' in the foreign policies of states.[35] In a similar vein advocates of the notion 'peaceful change' look to farsighted diplomacy (foreign policy) to design and propose territorial or other changes that may be acceptable – without pressures – to parties to possible future conflicts and to forestall such conflicts. The 'Ostpolitik' championed by Chancellor Willy Brandt of Germany could perhaps be cited as an example. It has been given a good deal of the credit for making the reunification of Germany possible – but also, after Russia's aggression on Ukraine, been criticized for naïve reliance on Russia.

Kissinger notes that when after the 30 years' war and the Peace of Westphalia in 1648 the 'Holy Roman Empire' lost its power to uphold peace and order in Europe, states sought through their diplomacy (foreign policies) to maintain a balance of power to deter the use of force and to prevent any state to dominate. Kissinger does not suggest that 'balance of power' is an agreed *'organizing principle'* to discourage the use of force, but rather a *political strategy* to keep

---

[32] Porter (2014).

[33] For additional information, see www.iaea.org/topics/additional-protocol. And see above, p. 157.

[34] See above, Chapter 1, p. 7.

[35] See above, Chapter 10, p. 159 and see Kissinger, *Diplomacy*.

all within their bounds. The best-known historical use of the strategy has been the ambition in British foreign policy to ensure that no single power should grow strong enough to dominate the European continent.

Obviously, the strategy of seeking a balance of power is just as interesting in foreign policy (diplomacy) in today's world: acting individually or in alliances, states seek to prevent any other nation or group of nations to become dominant regionally or globally. While the modern interdependence of states makes their strength in the economic, financial and other fields increasingly significant in the balance of power equations, their military strength still forms a key element. The spectre of 'threat equilibrium'[36] has not lost its relevance even though after the collapse of the Soviet Union the United States has shown less affinity to a balance of power than to American dominance.

As Kissinger notes, striving for a balance of power does not exclude support for and adherence to *'organizing principles'* in the community of states.[37] One such set of principles – that of 'just and unjust war' – was, indeed, propagated for hundreds of years by European legal and theological doctrine, but governments never espoused it, insisting on their freedom to wage war. Another set of 'organizing principles' – also fully compatible with the pursuit of a balance of power – was that of upholding monarchic legitimacy as the internal order of European states. This was the mission of the rulers of the 'Holy Alliance' of Russia, Austria and Prussia after the 1814–1815 conference in Vienna.[38]

It was only in the twentieth century with the Covenant of the League of Nations and the Charter of the United Nations that states accepted and declared – but often violated – the 'organizing principle' that the threat or use of force must not be used to violate the territorial integrity or political independence of other states. Again, there need be no contradiction between respect for this principle and the diplomatic pursuit of a foreign policy aiming at a balance of power regionally or globally.

The idea of spreading and balancing power to promote peace and order globally is, of course, not in line with Hobbes' idea *for state communities* that a strong ruler – a Leviathan – is key to the creation and enforcement of peace and order. However, even in the seventeenth century, Hobbesian Leviathans could perhaps have needed some countervailing power to prevent them from turning the desired peaceful communities into prisons. Montesquieu's eighteenth-century advice was a distribution – balance – of power. Of course, neither Hobbes nor Montesquieu was wrestling with the question of peace

---

[36] See above, p. 6.
[37] Chapter 5, footnote 22, p. 93.
[38] See above, Chapter 5, p. 97.

in a distant international community. Yet, it would seem that the international community, like the national communities they were thinking of, will need the key advice of both god-father Hobbes and god-father Montesquieu: Leviathan is needed for peace and order and a balance of power is needed to avoid oppression.

DIPLOMACY IS BOTH STATESMANSHIP AND A CRAFT

Although there is a rich literature of diplomatic memoirs, no repertory exists of methods through which diplomacy can help prevent the use of force between states.[39] A few points are nevertheless submitted as relevant.

Perhaps the first point to make is that diplomacy is fundamentally an attitude of seeking to avoid, forestall, reduce and, if possible, resolve differences. It can be applied just as well at the kitchen table as under crystal chandeliers or in back rooms. A second point is that some differences may not be susceptible to solutions through diplomacy. One party or another may not want solutions or positions may be such that they cannot be reconciled. If this is the case – as in the East-West conflicts during the Cold War – a tolerable process may be to let differences ache out while looking hopefully to mutual deterrence or other restraints to prevent any resort to armed force. In the long run, biology guarantees regime changes.

Third, designing diplomacy requires good knowledge and understanding of the facts, interests, powers, and aims of respective parties. This includes an understanding of the economic, political, and military leverages (for instance, 'diplomacy backed by force' or economic power) that may exist and may be brought to bear by parties. Which are the greatest needs of the different parties and who has the greatest need of a solution? Points of common interest need to be identified as well as points on which mutual concessions might open the way for rapprochement and conciliation. Good diplomacy needs a keen ear. To build stable relations through military deterrence the parties need not trust each other, but to succeed in doing it diplomacy needs to inspire reliability. It cannot mislead or lie without undermining its own chances of success.

In most countries, significant constituencies can be found supporting reliance on strong military deterrence.[40] The same support is not guaranteed for diplomacy. People advocating negotiations and possible concessions in international differences often risk being branded as 'soft', or as proposing 'surrender' or 'another Munich'.

---

[39] See Bunde (2022).
[40] See above, Chapter 7, p. 123.

Considering the cost of military forces and the size of military budgets today one might have expected taxpayers to be critical, but a majority of taxpayers both in rich and poor countries seems ready to go along when influential groups and media evoke new or growing external threats from other states or from terrorists.[41] Nevertheless, many are sceptical about reliance on deterrence as an all-dominant means of preserving peace. Especially the arms race in the field of nuclear and other non-conventional weapons, and ongoing (2022) increases in readiness for armed conflict, lead many to ask for a greater role in diplomacy.

One modern development facilitating diplomacy at the highest level is the opportunity for government leaders to communicate. A 'hot line' was one valuable result of the 1962 Cuban missile crisis. Today, leaders can reach and talk to each other directly and instantly, face to face by phone or by video calls. And they do use phones! Modern digital communications also give full opportunities for instant multilateral talks between leaders of governments, allies or groups. Leaders of great powers meet regularly in limited groups like the G7 to align positions and to reach possible agreements on political initiatives. At G20, leaders meet for similar aims on economic issues. While these two groups are – reasonably – like-minded and serve to forge common group positions, bilateral summit meetings are from time to time nearly obligatory for leaders of great powers with uneasy relations and present opportunities for high level diplomacy. Nevertheless, the UN Security Council and the very frequent informal meetings of the New York representatives of the five permanent members of the Security Council remain a place where today's three main powers (plus France and the United Kingdom) remain in constant communication.

AREAS OF DÉTENTE ARE OFTEN FAVOURED BY DIPLOMACY BUT REGARDED WITH CONCERN BY THOSE FAVOURING DETERRENCE

Both diplomacy and deterrence recognize the stability value of clear geographic and other lines for national control. Yet, both may – for different reasons – accept various kinds of areas of détente. While voices for deterrence have a general liking for red lines and concern about 'grey areas' – like seas and airspace beyond mutually recognized borders, they may conclude that in specific areas or near specific lines a desirable reduction of risk of live conflict may be achieved by a reduction in the deployment of arms and forces facing each other.[42]

---

[41] See above, Chapter 7, p. 119.
[42] See above, Chapter 7, p. 125.

Diplomacy, on the other hand, has a general concern about the risk of sparks at red lines where adversaries nervously observe each other. It may favour a reduction in armed presence or withdrawal of armed forces and weapons from such lines and areas to achieve reductions in tension. To give two examples: to avoid raising tensions and provoking Russia, nuclear weapons have not been deployed in European states that joined NATO but were once under Soviet control. For the same reason Denmark and Norway, two NATO members, will not accept the stationing of nuclear weapons on their territories in peace-time. A similar rationale was behind the restraints shown in the rotation rather than a permanent stationing of foreign troops in the Baltic States.

SOME INSTANCES IN WHICH MULTILATERAL DIPLOMACY HAS BROUGHT AGREEMENT ON SPECIAL AREAS OF DÉTENTE TO REDUCE THE RISK OF FUTURE CONFRONTATIONS

In the Antarctic Treaty of 1959, states – including the United States and the Soviet Union – succeeded through remarkable diplomacy despite the Cold War to agree on rules excluding military and commercial activities in the vast region and freezing national territorial claims. The Antarctic thus became the first nuclear-weapon-free zone and the treaty and the Secretariat established in Buenos Aires are still of high value.[43]

Similarly, through diplomacy and despite the Cold War, the 1967 Outer Space Treaty (or more fully the Treaty on Principles Governing the Activities of States in the Exploration and Use of Outer Space, including the Moon and Other Celestial Bodies) established a number of basic rules regarding states' exploration and exploitation of outer space. The treaty has been useful for many decades to avoid controversy among states active in space. For instance, it prohibits the stationing of nuclear weapons in space. However, the treaty was agreed early in the space age. With more and more satellites of great military importance and more and more space activities vital for states' security and welfare, the treaty is no longer sufficient. The additional agreement is needed but not attained.

A third case to cite in this context is that through many years of patient diplomatic negotiations, the United Nations Convention on the Law of the Sea (UNCLOS) was adopted in 1982. It confirmed and offered rules regarding the freedom of the high seas and has constituted the legal regime for the Arctic Ocean. It has been remarkably helpful to prevent conflicts between

---

[43] www.ats.aq/index_e.html.

states on practical and economic matters such as the delimitation of continental shelves and economic zones. It was for instance relevant in the settling of the Norwegian-Russian border in the Barents Sea in 2010.[44] Yet, for a prudent and sustainable use and exploitation of the seas beyond national jurisdictions, further agreements are needed.

MECHANISMS FOR GLOBAL DIPLOMACY

The three instruments cited in the preceding section on areas/space that cannot be appropriated by any state were all the fruits of diplomacy within the framework of the United Nations. The organization is, indeed, the most evident and natural place for global diplomacy. All states and innumerable governmental and non-governmental organizations are represented in New York and engage in the myriad of differences and conflicts that simmer or boil around the world.

However, besides the United Nations, intergovernmental regional organizations play important roles in diplomacy. The Organization of African Unity (OAU, later called African Union) has been highly active to solve many conflicts and the Organization for Security and Cooperation in Europe (OSCE) has been a forum for post-Cold War East-West diplomacy and the organizer of important peacekeeping operations in former Yugoslavia, in Georgia and in the Ukraine. Other regional organizations involved in the peaceful settlement of disputes include the Organization of American States (OAS) and the Association of Southeast Asian Nations (ASEAN). Diplomatic projects of importance are also often initiated at meetings of informal high-level groups of states, like the G7, G20, and G77.[45]

Individual governments – like those of Norway, Sweden, Austria and Switzerland – are also known for efforts to offer ideas, go-betweens, or simply meeting places for diplomacy between disputing parties. The 'Oslo' accord on Palestine, the Camp David Agreement or the 'Stockholm' talks between parties to the civil war in Yemen bear witness to such assistance.[46]

---

[44] www.theguardian.com/world/2010/sep/15/russia-norway-arctic-border-dispute.
[45] The G7 is an informal group of industrialized democratic states + the EU as participant. It shrunk from G8 to G7 as Russia was excluded after its occupation and annexation of the Crimea. It adopts 'understandings' and has working groups and task forces for specific problems. See Dobson (2007). The G20 is an intergovernmental forum consisting of 19 countries and the EU that addresses diverse issues relating to the global economy. The G77 consists of 134 developing countries that form a loose and rather heterogenous alliance to promote the interests of developing countries. It meets once a year at foreign minister level. Website: www.g77 org/doc.
[46] Oslo: https://history.state.gov/milestones/1993-2000/oslo. Camp David: www.history.com/topics/middle-east/camp-david-accords. Yemen: www.mei.edu/publications/stockholm-riyadh-breaking-yemen-peace-process-deadlock.

The modern world has many non-governmental groups of experienced statesmen (and women) or experts who engage in exploring and proposing ways to defuse burning differences.[47] Religious movements acting individually (the Pope) or in groups, such as the Organization of Islamic States, also weigh in to seek to conciliate in various state differences.[48]

CASES OF DIPLOMACY AIMING TO PREVENT THE USE OF FORCE

The proof of the diplomatic pudding is in the eating. We shall first describe two very different major cases of diplomacy defusing the risks of nuclear weapons. Thereafter, to illustrate the role of diplomacy, we shall list a number of arbitrarily selected cases of successes, failures and stalemates of diplomacy.

The Cuban crisis of 1962 offers a demonstration both of the force and danger of deterrence and the value of diplomacy in defusing risks of the use of nuclear weapons. The Soviet deployment of nuclear missiles in Cuba may have had the aim to establish a tool of deterrent against a US invasion of Cuba and, at the same time, a threat against the United States. When the US felt the proximity of the threat was provocative and could not be tolerated the move proved to be miscalculated and dangerous.

All sensed the risk of war and mutual devastation. It is frightening to note that practically all the military and civilian advisers who surrounded President Kennedy urged him to order military action to stop the Soviet delivery of missiles and nuclear weapons to Cuba despite the horrendous developments that such armed action might have caused.[49] Then, through the determined leadership of President Kennedy, a diplomatic way out was found. The Soviet Union interrupted its nuclear deployment in Cuba and the US committed to withdraw missiles from Turkey and to refrain from attacks on Cuba.

This 'mother of all diplomacy' is believed to have prevented nuclear war and even led to a period of détente and important subsequent agreements.[50] Among many lessons, the settlement of the Cuban crisis illustrates one important and often overlooked feature of diplomacy – that of observing respect between adversaries. Conventional diplomatic procedures and approaches are sometimes ridiculed as overly courteous. This view ignores

---

[47] For instance, 'The Elders' composed of former government leaders. For further information on The Elders, see https://theelders.org/.

[48] www.oic-oci.org/home/?lan=en.

[49] Kennedy (1969).

[50] Cf. above Chapter 3, p. 37 and Chapter 8, p. 133.

the reality that peoples and their representatives – whether saintly or villainous – mostly become less cooperative and conciliant if they are humiliated. Showing contempt for government leaders of another country and its people might gain points in domestic politics but it is a sure way of reaping resentment and rigidity in relations.

In the Cuban case, the concessions made by the US were a vitally important feature to attain the agreement. It helped to avoid the humiliation that a one-sided Soviet retreat would have caused. It should be added that the US public opinion might not have shared the understanding that diplomacy required some concessions to the other side. Full information about them was made public only many years after the settlement.

The Joint Comprehensive Plan of Action (JCPOA) drawn up with Iran in 2015 and described above in Chapter 2 offers another insight into successful diplomacy. Unlike the Cuban case, it took many years of patient work rather than a few dramatic days to achieve. It needed understanding not between two nuclear-armed states but between five nuclear-armed states (plus Germany and EU) and Iran – a non-nuclear-weapon state. There are also some similar features.

Behind the JCPOA there was a jointly identified fear: that an unrestrained and unverified Iranian nuclear program could develop quickly into an arms program and trigger regional proliferation and conflict. A solution defined during years of diplomatic talks traced a way through which economic and other sanctions on Iran were lifted and Iran could continue a nuclear program satisfying its peaceful needs but committed to an important scaling down of its program and accepted comprehensive verification. To avoid the impression that any party had made concessions – and perhaps to avoid national demands for approval by legislatures or other reasons – the term 'agree' was almost consistently avoided! Instead – with their steadfastness and dignity intact – the parties made parallel statements that 'they will' do this and that...'.

The 'deal' was not packaged as an 'agreement' – which, in fact, it was – but as a 'joint comprehensive plan of action'. It received its binding force not by signatures and ratifications but through being endorsed by a unanimous resolution of the UN Security Council. It was hailed as a major success and led to a short period of relaxed relations. However, the diplomacy proved of little avail when in 2018 the US Trump administration, in a move that severely undermined the authority of the Security Council, ignored the plan and the resolution.[51]

---

[51] See *American Journal of International Law*, www.cambridge.org/core/journals/american-journal-of-international-law/article/abs/president-trump-withdraws-the-united-states-from-the-iran-deal-and-announces-the-reimposition-of-sanctions/51C49F518A0FB1A576FA101925493727.

This prompted Iran to a step-by-step departure from the plan in retaliation. Diplomacy came back in 2021 when the Biden administration in the United States went along with talks to revive the plan. Such talks were carried out through intermediaries during the whole of 2021 but were not successful even by December 2022.

Some instances in which diplomacy (statesmanship) by one or more states had significant peaceful impacts:

- The 1814–1815 Conference in Vienna restored peace in Europe after the end of the Napoleonic Wars.
- The 1925 Locarno Pacts through which a number of thorny European security problems were – temporarily – resolved.
- The Marshall Plan of 1947 contributed significantly to stabilize the national economies in Europe after World War II.
- The European Coal and Steel Community 1951 developed by European Union.
- The Austrian State Treaty 1955 ended the four-power military occupation.
- The reunification of Germany 1990.
- The withdrawal of the Soviet Union from satellite states in 1991.

INSTANCES OF DIPLOMATIC MOVES TO STABILIZE BALANCE OF POWER

- President Nixon's opening to China in 1972 to better balance Soviet power.
- President Putin's efforts nearly fifty years later to increase Russian-Chinese cooperation to balance US global dominance.
- US efforts to establish close links with India, Australia and Japan (the Quadrilateral Security Dialogue, QUAD initiated in 2007) to build a stronger balance for the containment of China.

INSTANCES WHERE RESULTS OF DIPLOMACY HAVE BEEN DENOUNCED

- The Munich Agreement of 1938 was seen by many as encouraging Nazi Germany to make further demands.
- The Yalta Agreement of 1945 was seen by many as giving too great concessions to the Soviet Union.

INSTANCES OF ENDLESS DIPLOMACY WITHOUT RESULT

- Efforts through diplomacy to find a solution to the dispute between India and Pakistan about Kashmir have gone on without result since the division of India in 1948.
- Talks under UN auspices to bring unification of Cyprus have gone on without success since 1974.
- Efforts since the middle of the 1970s to solve the conflict regarding the Western Sahara.
- Talks about a 'two-state solution' in the conflict over Palestine have taken place on and off without result since the Oslo process began in 1993.
- Talks took place after 2015 in the 'Minsk process' between Ukraine, Russia, France, and Germany to find arrangements acceptable to both Ukraine and Russia. They did not succeed. Russia invaded Ukraine in February 2022.

As a last case of 'endless' diplomacy, we may note talks about the nuclear weapons program of North Korea. One round began in 2018 following an autumn (2017) during which tension between the United States and North Korea (DPRK) was high and both parties talked in a menacing manner about their nuclear weapons capabilities. Through diplomacy between North and South Korea, the situation had eased in 2018. Most important was that North Korea – without presenting it as a concession – had declared that all tests of nuclear weapons and long-range missiles had been completed. Hence, the stopping of further tests was not presented as a concession.

At a meeting in Singapore in 2018 between Presidents Trump and Kim Jong Un agreement was reached to aim for denuclearization. President Trump declared – in an off-handed way that avoided it looking like a response to the North Korean stopping of tests – that the big joint US-ROK military manoeuvres would be terminated – as they were 'costly and unnecessary'. However, further diplomatic steps did not follow from this hopeful point. A second summit held in Hanoi in March 2019 marked a deadlock. In early 2022 North Korea resumed the testing of missiles. The choice remains one between renewed diplomacy and further military tension that affects the whole region of North-East Asia.[52]

---

[52] For further information, see Congressional Research Service, 'Diplomacy with North Korea: A Status Report', 30 July 2021, https://sgp.fas.org/crs/row/IF11415.pdf.

DIPLOMACY AIMING AT DÉTENTE

To aim at détente is even more ambitious than to aim merely at the absence of the use of force. Relaxed international relations – including 'positive peace' – is the goal that the UN Charter preamble pronounces, when it declares that the Members are determined 'to practice tolerance and live together in peace with one another as good neighbours'.[53] It is evident that while deterrence and mutual deterrence may, indeed, lead to non-use of force it does not lead to détente. Diplomacy, on the other hand, has the potential to create détente – including the absence of the threat or use of force.

---

[53] For a discussion of different degrees of peace, see Goertz et al. (2016).

11

Restraints on the Interstate Use of Force through Legal Norms

In our search for restraints on the use of force between states, we have looked in the preceding chapters at a variety of factors and focused closely on two: military strength for deterrence and non-military means, above all diplomacy. In this and the following chapters, we shall examine the roots, contents and effectiveness of the legal norms that exist today to prevent or reduce the inter-state use of force.

We should note at the outset that there are writers who flatly deny the existence of any such legal norms, as they deny the existence of international law. Some of the arguments advanced are that there is no legislature, no courts, and no executive authorities.[1] However, others who are not wedded to a narrow definition of law find it as natural to look for international norms prohibiting states from waging war on each other as looking for national rules prohibiting people to kill each other.

Governments and their legal advisers will uniformly declare that the states they represent are bound by international law, that it is indispensable, and that on the whole, it functions well.[2] They will agree that there are many differences between the legal order of states and that of the international community and they may agree with the observation that when governments – especially great powers – feel vital interests are at play they may be tempted to bend or breach the specific international legal rules prohibiting the use of force between states. We shall see examples of that in the following chapters. Before we turn to identify these rules and examine how they fare, it may be of interest to devote a section looking at similarities and differences in the creation and role of law in national and international communities.

---

[1]   Hart (1961). These tenets are examined by Franck (2006), pp. 88–106: see also Oppenheim (1948), pp. 13 ff. and Henderson (2018), p. 41.

[2]   See Oppenheim (1948), § 10. Cf. Brierly (1944), Chapter 1.

THE CREATION AND ROLE OF LAW IN THE
NATIONAL AND INTERNATIONAL COMMUNITIES

A hundred years ago the great international lawyer L. Oppenheim, wrote: *'Wherever a demand for law and order imperiously asserts itself, rules of law arise.'*[3] There is nothing mysterious about this, nor is it difficult to see that such demands emerge not as a result of some divine intervention but out of practical needs caused mostly by proximity and frequent contacts between people and groups of people – from food gatherers at the dawn of human civilization to modern states. The legal rules will reflect the interests and values that at any given time dominate in a community – whether those held by a majority of people or those of a ruler. Hence changes in values – in what I have called 'the public mind' – are likely to cause changes in the law. An example: The Norse maxim from around 800 A.C. that 'with law shall our land be built'[4] meant law reflecting the values of the Nordic lands at the time, including law that upheld, for instance, slavery. When values changed, law changed to prohibit slavery.

In early human communities, rules arose as custom. Proximity and frequent interaction brought human cooperation, but also frictions, differences and conflicts. Some triggered the use of force, some were solved and settled through decisions within the communities. Precedents arose when decisions and solutions followed earlier decisions and solutions and customary law arose when precedents were perceived as compelling. The laws varied over the centuries as the organization and values of communities (and rulers) – the 'public mind' – evolved.[5] The laws also varied between different communities as the values prevailing in them differed.

EVOLUTION OF LEGAL SYSTEM IN SWEDEN

Looking at the emergence of law within independent communities, I will use as an illustration the legal system in Sweden, which I know best. It seems likely that people who lived during the first millennium in areas that became Sweden – like people in other early social orders – used conclusions/judgments in one case as a guide in a later similar case. Precedents accumulated

---

[3] Oppenheim (1921), p. 3.
[4] Cit. from Hathaway and Shapiro, op. cit., p. 373.
[5] Today, there are no laws that stipulate crucifixion or impalement as penalty. While in a small number of states cruel punishments are retained, more humane values prevailing in most countries have led to the abandonment of the death penalty in a vast number of states. See comments above in Chapter 1, p. 4.

to eventually form binding customary rules. A similar process was described by the famous Dr. Samuel Johnson, who observed that 'the chains of habit are too weak to be felt until they are too strong to be broken'.[6]

Violations of the customary rules – whether killings, theft or other – may have been deterred by a general awareness that they could be avenged by the family and clan of a victim, or that the community could declare a perpetrator 'outlaw'. Reliance was also placed on conciliation and the payment of compensation – outcomes that did not require developed community mechanisms for implementation.

Around 1100 A.D., bodies of regional customary law that in Sweden had until then been memorized by trusted community members, were codified and a hundred years or so later kings who had by now succeeded to assert rule over all regions of the country were able to unify and develop the regional codes and to introduce the first national Swedish code.[7] As the central government headed by the king became more powerful and wielded effective control over the use of armed force, it established courts to judge in disputes and in violations of the law and the function of enforcement and deterrence moved from the 'self-service' of victims and clans to standing governmental institutions.

With further growth and social development, the popular acceptance of laws (and taxes!) through a national assembly became increasingly important. In modern Sweden, as in other democracies, legislative power is vested in a popular assembly (parliament) elected by general suffrage. Proposed laws are introduced for adoption in this legislature whose members come from political parties representing diverse groups and opinions. If a majority of democratically elected representatives support proposed rules, there is a reasonable assurance that the rules have also a very substantial support among the voters, which will strengthen their effectiveness.

The acceptance of decisions by majority vote in national legislatures – or in any human assembly – is of crucial importance. In law-making assemblies, it means that the legislators who at any specific time form a minority have agreed in advance that they will accept and respect the rules that are adopted over their opposition. This is a high price, but the majority rule brings a tremendous common gain: communities of many people – perhaps millions or hundreds of millions – enable themselves to reach decisions and take actions

---

[6] While perhaps apocryphal, several versions of this quote have widely been attributed to Johnson, albeit without a specific textual reference. For the variations, see https://quoteinvestigator.com/2013/07/13/chains-of-habit/. This particular quote is cited in *Peter's Quotations: Ideas for Our Time* (1977) and *Barnes & Nobel Book of Quotations* (1987).

[7] See Donner (2002).

even though they comprise many people who may have preferred different or no decisions. It is paid when there is confidence that no majority will abuse its power – notably by ignoring agreed guaranteed rights.

EVOLUTION OF THE LEGAL SYSTEM FOR
RELATIONS BETWEEN COMMUNITIES

Turning from relations and rules within communities to relations between independent communities – from tribes to states – we find that a few customary rules arise early. Oppenheim, cited above, mentions the inviolability of messengers as probably the oldest customary intercommunity rule.[8] Perhaps another early rule was that agreements, including peace agreements, entered into between rulers and communities must be respected – in Roman law coined as *'pacta sunt servanda'*.

As independent states arise and transport by sea and land develops, there is new proximity between communities. Contacts and relations between them become more frequent and the 'demand for rules' increases. More customary rules evolve and are described by writers,[9] for instance, regarding territorial waters and the high seas, the treatment of foreigners, or regarding diplomatic emissaries. By the time of the peace congress at Vienna after the Napoleonic wars (1815), the existing body of customary rules that applied in the relations between European states was clearly insufficient to meet the 'demand for law and order' that asserted itself. In the absence of a legislating assembly that could adopt rules by majority, the governments of the international (European) community of states turned in a big way to agreements in which they laid down specific rules that they promised each other to follow, for instance regarding traffic on international rivers.

Treaties and conventions containing rules binding parties supplemented the customary law rules that continued to bind all. It did not take long before the amount of treaty rules in the most diverse fields – including rules for the establishment and operation of the first international organizations – by far surpassed the volume of customary law. The term 'law-making treaty' was applied to treaties that were adhered to by so many states that their rules came to cover most of the international community and serve a function similar to that of law in a national community. This feature of near universality was

---

[8] Oppenheim (1921), p. 173; see also above, Chapter 5, p. 89.
[9] The literature on the evolution of customary international law is vast. For a useful research guide, see Silke Sahl, 'Researching Customary International Law, State Practice and the Pronouncements of States regarding International Law', Hauser Global Law School Program, Columbia University, www.nyulawglobal.org/globalex/Customary_International_Law.html.

signaled by an impressive project (1931–1950), in which the Harvard Professor of International Law, Manley O. Hudson, published nine volumes of global conventions under the common title 'International Legislation'. Today, such a project would be hard to undertake. The treaties – including conventions aspiring to global adherence – registered by states with the United Nations fill more than two thousand volumes of the United Nations Treaty Series.

SIMILARITIES AND DIFFERENCES BETWEEN THE NATIONAL AND INTERNATIONAL LEGAL SYSTEMS

Ruth Donner has made the observation that the evolution of the international legal order has in several respects followed and been similar to that which took place much earlier within individual communities.[10] We might, indeed, take note of some parallelism and, again, the individual national community I choose for comparison is Sweden.

First, customary law, which marks the beginning of the legal systems of Swedish and other individual human communities, is also the starting point of the legal system for intercommunity relations. We may assume that in both cases proximity and frequency of contacts trigger the demand for rules. While these factors arise early within individual human communities, they turn up later and more sparingly *between* communities and increase if and as contacts and communications increase.

Second, central authorities to implement and enforce law were weak both within the early individual communities – like Sweden in 1000 A.D. – and in the international community. In both cases, a deterrent against actions violating rules may exist in the general awareness that potential targets of wrongdoings can be expected to defend themselves and to retaliate – alone or with allies. In individual communities, the capacity of the central authorities to implement and enforce law increased dramatically through the consolidation of the states. In the international community, it became possible only many hundred years later for aggrieved parties to lodge complaints to international organizations like the League of Nations and the United Nations, where the capacity for effective handling of complaints and enforcement still remains uneven and uncertain. Courts for the handling of breaches of international criminal law – including war crimes, the starting wars of aggression and genocide – have come to a promising if somewhat uneven start.[11]

---

[10] See a thought-provoking article by Donner (2002).
[11] See below Chapter 18, p. 292 and for information on the International Criminal Court, see https://www.icc-cpi.int.

Third, the customary law that arose within early state communities was codified at an early stage – in Sweden around 1000 A.D. Major bodies of customary international law have also become codified but it has happened almost one thousand years later – through a highly successful process under the auspices of the United Nations.[12]

The similarities that we note in the emergence and evolution of rules within and between communities may lead us to ask if the factors that have given rise to and driven this evolution – greater proximity and increasing interaction of people and communities – will continue to lead the evolution of the international order in the same or similar tracks that the national communities travelled long ago?

At the present time, there is a massive making of rules both within national communities and within the international community, but the methods of rule-making are starkly different. As described above, elected national legislatures adopt rules of statutory law by majority votes. They become binding on all concerned – '*erga omnes*' – regardless of individual consent and there are institutions ensuring effective implementation/enforcement. By contrast, the international community of states has no 'legislature' that is elected by general suffrage and entrusted with the adoption of rules binding on all by majority vote. It is constrained to adopt new rules by treaties that become binding on states only through their individually expressed consent.

An illustration is the UN General Assembly whose power is limited to adopting recommendations. While weighted voting and the adoption of some categories of rules by majority vote has become part of the system of the European Union of states, it is not yet on the horizon in the global community. The inescapable result is that where states whose participation in a treaty may be indispensable do not agree to adhere, the aim of the treaty may be beyond reach.[13]

The difficulty of assuring treaty objectives when needed state participation cannot be assured is made the worse by the fact that treaties often have withdrawal clauses enabling parties to give notice and abandon cooperation.[14] Thus, it is evident that although providing a formidable surrogate for a systematic legal system responding to the needs of the ever more closely woven international community, the fabric of treaties has grave shortcomings. To

---

[12] On codification, see Oppenheim (1948), p. 56 ff.

[13] An example is the Comprehensive Nuclear-Test-Ban treaty of 1996 to which most states in the world have adhered. It has not entered into force, as a small group of states – including the United States – whose adherence is required has not been willing to adhere (as of 2022.)

[14] The 2020 US withdrawal from the Paris climate agreement is an example. It was reversed by the Biden administration in 2021.

these, we must add uncertainties about access to impartial interpretation and questions whether reciprocity or other factors will ensure the loyal implementation of obligations.

THE RULES AGAINST THE USE OF FORCE
WITHIN AND BETWEEN COMMUNITIES

Turning to the specific rules that govern the use of force, we may assume that *within* groups of people and communities, customary rules that made it a breach of law to kill a neighbour emerged early. Awareness of clans' and tribes' protection of their members may have been a factor in helping to create respect for the rules. Operation of such rules in early societies may also often have relied on personal action by the parties, such as conciliation and the payment of damages (blood money). As societies developed and became states the upholding and implementation of criminal law and execution of penalties became the task of public prosecutors, courts and other governmental authorities. Killing and the use of force became offenses against the state. Revenge was not to be taken by individuals and their clans. The state organized the punishment – and collected the fines.

However, we should not forget that while the 'public mind' has demanded the legal rules, neither in early communities nor in modern society are these rules the primary restraint standing in the way of killing and the use of force. First, moral inhibitions against the use of force are inculcated by families, schools, churches and society, and children and grown-ups are advised to solve their differences by non-violent means.

Second, all societies acknowledge a legal right to proportionate self-defence, and just as military defence may deter international aggression the awareness that potential victims may use force in personal self-defence may deter attacks on individuals. We need not look very far back to see that national societies relied a good deal on self-defence as preventing the use of force. In the past people were armed. In pictures from even only a hundred years back, we can see how men of authority or status carried elegant swords as relics of a time when everyday life required a weapon with which they could avert attacks on themselves. Even today, men in some cultures carry daggers -hopefully – as decorations. More problematic is that in the US today many assert that carrying firearms is the surest and best way to prevent attacks.

Third, 'the public mind' in most countries has reached the opposite conclusion, namely that to help prevent killings and the use of force, we should make sure that weapons are not easily available. A state monopoly on the possession and use of arms is widely seen as a criterion of modern society.

LAWS ARE CONFLICT PREVENTING

When we look for means that prevent the killing and the use of force in society apart from the rules of law that specifically prohibit these actions, we should also note that the totality of legal rules guiding conduct in society – national as well as the international – helps to reduce the risk of conflicts and concomitant risks of a use of force. For instance, the (hopefully) habitual respect for traffic rules in society prevents not only accidents but also millions of quarrels and conflicts (including shootings!). In the international community, many provisions of the Law of the Sea Conventions have without doubt helped to avoid interstate conflicts.[15] Thus, the fabric of law in national communities – and in international treaty rules as well – serves not only as a basis for judgment in conflicts but more fundamentally as guidance for how we should act to avoid conflicts.

NATIONAL CONSTITUTIONS PROVIDING RESTRAINTS ON RESORT TO FORCE

Considering national legal rules to prevent the killing and the use of force we might note, finally, that constitutions of states frequently contain provisions that prohibit, restrict, or require parliamentary consent for the use of armed force against other states. While such rules may be revoked and governments sometimes have shown the talent to circumvent them, they may be of great practical value to restrain executive branches of national governments.[16] Even during a period of the French revolution, one constitution was in force that prohibited any declaration of war without a decree of the National Assembly.[17] Article 9 of Japan's present Constitution provides that the 'Japanese people forever renounce war as a sovereign right of the nation and the threat or use of force as means of settling international disputes'.[18]

RESTRAINTS AGAINST RESORT TO FORCE IN THE GLOBAL SPHERE

Turning now from the national to the global sphere, we must note that while from the early days of human civilization some customary rules developed regarding relations between independent communities, even by the time when

---

[15] Cf. Goertz (2016), p. 183.
[16] See Damrosch (1997) and see Kress (2016).
[17] National Assembly of France, 'The Constitution of 1791', full text (in English) available at https:// wp.stu.ca/worldhistory/wp-content/uploads/sites/4/2015/07/French-Constitution-of-1791.pdf.
[18] https://japan.kantei.go.jp/constitution_and_government_of_japan/constitution_e.html.

sovereign states began to appear at the end of the Middle Ages no such rules had emerged to restrain the use of armed force between states.[19] However, many bilateral treaties about 'friendship' and 'commerce and navigation' resulted from increasing contacts and trade and gave basic rules for peaceful bilateral relations between countries. Major peace treaties, such as the Westphalian Peace of 1648 and the treaties made at the 1814–1815 Congress of Vienna, were obviously aimed at peace but did not seek a normative approach to eliminate future wars.[20]

The absence of both customary and treaty rules prohibiting or restricting the international use of force did not mean, of course, that there were no other restraints. First of all, the military strength of a potential adversary could have a deterrent effect. The financial costs of war had to be weighed against potential gains. Public aversion to the burdens and pains of war could be another restraining factor.

As noted above, in the nineteenth-century peace movements aimed both at mitigating the cruelty of warfare war and preventing war.[21] Focus in the nineteenth century was not so much on a treaty rule prohibiting the use of armed force – which governments were not ready for – as on the prevention of war through arbitration and disarmament. Only the horrors of World War I and strong public opinion against all wars led eventually to the creation of the League of Nations and the explicit provisions in the Covenant against the use of force (external aggression.) They were not the result of the constructive passion and skill of President Wilson alone but owed much from a 'public mind' that had been building for many decades. We should note that while the legal rules contained in the Covenant constituted a central approach to the elimination of armed forces and war, it was by no means the only way. States would continue to maintain armed forces to deter aggression. Other ways of preventing war were the settling of disputes through diplomacy or arbitration and the elimination of weapons through disarmament.

Through the adoption and public support of the Briand Kellogg Pact, the Statute of the Nuremberg tribunal, and the Charter of the United Nations, the international norms first laid down in the Covenant against the interstate use of force developed and matured. Chapter 5 described the main features of these instruments. This and the following chapters are focused on the interpretation of the norms against the use of force as they have evolved from the Covenant of the League of Nations to the Charter and the practice of the United Nations and the pronouncements of the International Court of Justice.

---

[19] See above, Chapter 5, p. 91.
[20] Cf. above, Chapter 5, p. 97. See also Paulus (2011); and Devere et al. (2011), pp. 46–70.
[21] Above, Chapter 5, p. 99.

THE LEAGUE OF NATIONS 1920–1946

President Wilson of the United States was convinced that firm rules on state conduct were indispensable but also that a permanent world organization and collective action were needed to uphold the rules and maintain peace and order. He provided a blueprint and pressed it vigorously and successfully on the other victor states. The Covenant and the League was an enormous innovation. International law was declared as the norm for government conduct and a key provision was Art. 10 under which 'The members undertake to respect and preserve as against external aggression the territorial integrity and existing political independence of all Members of the League....'[22]

Implementation was foreseen through the novel principle of collective security. Art. 11 stipulated that: 'any war or threat of war... is ... declared a matter of concern to the whole League, and the League shall take any action that may be deemed wise and effectual...' and Art. 16 provided that if any member resorted to war in disregard of League obligations: 'it shall ipso facto be deemed to have committed an act of war against all other Members of the League ...'

Sadly, on major matters, the experience of the League proved dismaying.[23] In particular, Art. 10 which required respect for the territorial integrity and political independence of other members was violated many times – most gravely, of course, through Germany's, Italy's and Japan's waging of the World War II.

THE BRIAND KELLOGG PACT OF 1928[24]

On 27 August 1928 the Briand-Kellogg Pact (the Pact of Paris) was signed in Paris and subsequently ratified by 63 states. It comprised two operative articles:

> Article I. The High Contracting Parties solemnly declare... that they condemn recourse to war for the solution of international controversies, and renounce it, as an instrument of national policy in their relations with one another.
>
> Article II. The High Contracting Parties agree that the settlement or solution of all disputes or conflicts of whatever nature or of whatever origin they may be, which may arise between them, shall never be sought except by pacific means.

[22] See Walters, p. 48. Cf. Hathaway and Shapiro, p. 105.
[23] See above, Chapter 5, p. 103 ff.
[24] Cf. above Chapter 5, p. 103.

The value of the pact as a prohibition of war has been the subject of widely different assessments. While some have read the Pact with a critical eye[25] and viewed it as mainly hortatory, it has more often been understood as a legally binding norm covering 'war' as well as acts 'short of war' including any substantial use of armed force.[26] In the view of US Secretary of State, Stimson, the world had outlawed war by the Pact. He declared what came to be named the Stimson doctrine under which the US would not 'recognize any situation, treaty or agreement which may be brought about by means contrary to the covenants and obligations of the Pact of Paris of August 27, 1928.'[27]

In a recent comprehensive analysis of the efforts that led to the pact and of its effects, Yale professors Hathaway and Shapiro express the view that the pact had a decisive impact on the international order: before 1928 was the 'old world order', after 1928 was the 'new world order' in which war was no longer seen as 'an instrument of justice' – a legitimate means of 'righting wrongs'.

However, the authors' enthusiasm for the Paris Pact is coupled with the insight that rather than being the result of a single leap by governments, 'the outlawry of war' was a process in which the Pact was preceded by the Covenant of the League and followed by the Charter and judgements of the Nuremberg tribunal with the UN Charter as its latest – but not final – step.[28]

THE CHARTER OF THE NUREMBERG TRIBUNAL 1945[29]

Art. 6 of the Charter of the International Military Tribunal. provided that the Tribunal should have the power to 'try and punish persons, who acting in the interests of the European Axis countries... committed any of the following crimes (a) Crimes against peace. Namely planning, preparation, initiation or waging of a war of aggression or a war in violation of international treaties, agreements, or assurances, or participation in a common plan or conspiracy for the accomplishment of any of the forgoing.'

The premise has been broadly supported that 'wars of aggression' had become illegal. The British Prosecutor, Sir Hartley Shawcross, stated that the Charter of the Tribunal was in conformity with already existing law. He referred to evolution and practice within the League of Nations and to the

---

[25] See Walters, op.cit., pp. 384–387.
[26] See Brownlie (1963), p. 87.
[27] Quoted from Hathaway and Shapiro, op.cit. p. 167; cf. art. 52 of the Vienna Convention on the Law of Treaties, cited below at p. 292.
[28] For a detailed account, see Brownlie, p. 66 ff.
[29] Cf. above, Chapter 5, p. 104.

Briand-Kellogg Pact which 'abolished war as a legally permissible means of enforcing the law or of changing it'.[30]

Questioning the legal position of the prosecutors, Dr. Jahrreiss, in defence of the accused, argued on the other hand that by 1939 the system of the League and the Pact of Paris had collapsed and that in the years prior to the outbreak of World War II, there was 'no effective general rule of international law regarding prohibited war'.[31] It was true that the rule that was first planted in the Covenant of the League and that had grown in the 1920s had been flagrantly violated in a number of cases: as in Japan's expansion in Manchuria, the Italian invasions of Ethiopia and Albania, and the Soviet occupation of Carelia. It had hardly worked as an 'effective' rule to restrain the use of force.

However, serial violations of rules, whether international or national, need not be the same as 'collapse' of rules. The Nuremberg Charter and trials might even be seen as testimony to the endurance of rules whose time had come. Subsequent discussions and actions regarding the Charter and judgments of the Nuremberg Tribunal by the UN General Assembly confirmed general support for the position that they had a basis in international law as it had developed since the time of the Covenant.[32]

Perhaps Germany's, Italy's, and Japan's waging of World War II and land conquests ('Lebensraum') should be seen as a major relapse into once normal but now discredited state behavior rather than as eclipsing the nascent rule. As we shall see, the Charter of the UN and many measures and actions in the UN have not only confirmed the rule that began its life in the Covenant but also taken the issue of the international legal restrictions on the use of force much further. This must not, of course, blind us to the reality that many violations of these restrictions have remained without UN condemnations – mostly due to disagreement between the permanent members of the Security Council.

THE UNITED NATIONS 1945–

The main features of the UN Charter were discussed above in Chapter 5. At this point, the focus is on the United Nations as providing norms against the use of force.

Both in the League and the United Nations, the great powers have – as in the preceding centuries – seen their own role as crucial for the maintenance

---

[30] Remarks of Sir Hartley Shawcross, *Nuremberg Trial Proceedings*, vol 3, Morning Session, 4 *December 1945*. https://avalon.law.yale.edu/imt/12-04-45.asp.

[31] The account and quotes are from Brownlie, p. 168.

[32] See Brownlie, p. 191 ff.

of peace and of their own power. Nevertheless, the founding instruments of both explicitly recognize international law as the main instrument governing the relations of states in the world community. As noted above, the preamble of the Covenant proclaimed 'international law as the rule of conduct among Governments', while Art. 2 of the Charter lays down a catalogue of seven central principles of international law that members are to respect.

Of special interest to this study is that both the Covenant and the Charter use the approach – new to the world in 1920 – of laying down explicit rules to restrict the use of force between states. The preamble of the Covenant invoked the 'obligations not to resort to war', while the first lines of the preamble of the Charter declare the aim of the United Nations to be 'to save succeeding generations from the scourge of war' and Art. 2:4 lays down the obligation not to use force.

Art. 10 of the Covenant, we have noted, laid down a duty to respect the territorial integrity and political independence of other members, while Art. 2:4 of the UN Charter enjoins members to refrain in *their international relations from the threat or use of force against the territorial integrity and political independence of any state.*

While in the Covenant a right of self-defence was only implied and of uncertain reach, the Charter spelled it out in an explicit article – 51 – confirming and at the same time limiting it. We shall have occasion to come back to this point in Chapter 14.

Both the Covenant and the Charter envisage enforcement through measures taken by all members against violations of the rules – collective security. With 193 members representing a whole world in accelerating economic interdependence, the United Nations has incomparably more potential collective power than the League that remained a European-dominated club missing several great powers, notably and disastrously the United States. However, the mobilization and deployment of this UN power is dependent upon the formation of joint decisions. Above all its effective exercise is dependent upon a joint will among the great powers. In 1945, this was well understood by the great powers that had won the preceding war and reserved the leading and dominating role for themselves as, indeed, the great powers had done at Westphalia in 1648, Vienna in 1814–1815 and Paris in 1919.[33]

The effectiveness of the new construction was both promoted and undermined by the voting rules agreed upon. In the League, decisions in both the Council and Assembly were taken by unanimity (Art. 5), except that any party to a dispute should not vote. This order, which gave a veto even to small states,

---

[33] See Arechaga (1978), p. 86.

was replaced for the United Nations by an order of majority decisions that would make it more likely to reach decisions and allow effective action. At Yalta, in 1945, President Roosevelt tried hard to include a straight majority rule for the Security Council to enhance its chances for effectiveness. However, he eventually yielded to Stalin who feared that the Soviet Union could be outvoted. A compromise was accepted allowing decisions by majority vote, but unlike the other members of the Council each of the five permanent members would have a right of veto in all decisions on substance.

Evidently, the solution was not in consonance with the principle of equality of states proclaimed in art. 2:1 of the Charter and the principle that a party should not vote in its own case.[34] However, this was realpolitik. Effective economic or military enforcement measures against small or medium-sized states might be desirable and could be a realistic scenario even without unanimity, provided, however, that the decisions were supported by the five great powers sitting as permanent members.[35] On the other hand, it was hardly realistically expected in 1945 or later that the great-power winners of the world war would sign on to a system under which any majority in the Council would be able to brand them as 'aggressors' and subject them to sanctions.[36]

---

[34] See interesting accounts of the negotiations in Hathaway, op.cit. pp. 206 ff., Mazower (2012), p. 208 and Arechaga (1950), p. 25 ff.

[35] It has, in fact, played out, notably in the case of Iraq in 1990 and 1991.

[36] The economic sanctions that have been taken against Russia for her occupation of the Crimea and incursions in East Ukraine are not based on Security Council resolutions, but are based on decisions by the European Union and the United States. By contrast, acting under the Uniting for Peace resolution (Res. GA 377A(V)), the UN General Assembly did brand China as aggressor, when in 1950 during the Korean war Chinese 'volunteers' intervened to prevent US led UN forces getting close to the DPRK-China border. However, the resolution of the Assembly in February 1951 – GA Res 498 – stopped short of recommending any sanctions. On 2 March 2022, the General Assembly, facing a deadlocked Security Council, used the Uniting for Peace resolution to condemn Russia's 'Aggression against Ukraine'; *inter alia*, the new resolution 'Deplores in the strongest terms' Russia's aggression against Ukraine. General Assembly, Resolution ES-11/1, 2 March 2022, https://documents-dds-ny.un.org/doc/UNDOC/ GEN/N22/293/36/PDF/N2229336.pdf?OpenElement. A voting summary can be found in 'UN resolution against Ukraine invasion: Full text', *Aljazeera*, 3 March 2022, www.aljazeera.com/ news/2022/3/3/unga-resolution-against-ukraine-invasion-full-text. The non-binding resolution did not impose any sanctions.

12

UN Charter Articles Relating to the Use of Force

In this and the following chapters, we shall focus on several Charter articles that relate to the of force. We shall examine what restraints they were intended to impose, what use of force was to be allowed and how the United Nations has come to interpret the rules and grappled with alleged violations. We shall examine many concrete cases to reach an understanding of the current scope, contents and effectiveness of today's rules on the interstate threat or use of force. The accounts of many cases will supplement the 'panorama' of inter-state uses of force presented in Chapters 2 and 3 to illustrate the role of force in the post-World War II world.

UN CHARTER ARTICLES RELATING TO THE USE OF FORCE

- 2:4 – general prohibition of threat or use of force
- 42 – exception to 2:4 authorizing the Security Council to use force
- 51 – exception to 2:4 allowing individual and collective self-defence if an armed attack occurs
- 53 – exception to 2:4 on the use of force by regional organizations authorized by the Security Council

Art. 2:4 provides the fundamental general norm that prohibits the threat or use of force between states. It reads: 'All Members shall refrain in their international relations from the threat or use of force against the territorial integrity or political independence of any state, or in any other manner inconsistent with the Purposes of the United Nations.'

The UN Charter was adopted in 1945 and the content of the rule quoted is like other rules in the Charter affected and developed by practice and changing conditions. The Vienna Convention on the Law of Treaties (Art. 31:3) provides that interpretation of treaties shall take into account: 'any subsequent agreement between the parties regarding the interpretation of the treaty or the application of its provisions' and: 'any subsequent practice in the application of the treaty which establishes the agreement of the parties regarding its interpretation.'

The two provisions are of direct relevance to the Charter as a live treaty.[1] Its contents are constantly interpreted and applied by the members. For interpretations of Charter norms by members we may look at resolutions – especially those adopted by consensus or large majorities – in the General Assembly and the Security Council. Of particular interest is the so-called Friendly Relations Declaration that was adopted by the General Assembly in 1970. The Helsinki Declaration of 1975 is also of great interest, as the Conference on Security and Co-operation in Europe reflected a common East-West understanding of UN Charter rules.[2]

The terse language of the written rule in Art. 2:4 raises both difficulties and temptations for states assessing what they are free and not free to do legally to pursue and defend their perceived interests. The rules also leave UN organs a freedom that is both welcome and difficult, when judging whether a particular state's conduct breached or respected the rules.[3] Yet, it is the task of the Security Council, the General Assembly and the International Court of Justice to bring nuances and adjustments to the meaning of Article 2:4 and other international legal rules.

THE AIMS AND LIMITATIONS OF THE GENERAL PROHIBITION IN ART. 2:4

The scope of the prohibition in Art. 2:4 is shown through the terms used in the article itself – 'force', 'territorial integrity and political independence' and 'international relations'. Limitations follow from provisions in other Charter articles (2:7, 42, 51 and 53) and through interpretations in authoritative UN declarations and in the practical application of the rules.

A PRIMARY THRUST OF CHARTER ART. 2:4 IS TO PROHIBIT THE USE OF FORCE TO SEIZE TERRITORY

The seizing of and encroachment on the territory by war has been a staple feature in world history.[4] Art. 10 of the League Covenant sought to 'preserve'

---

[1] Franck (2002) (as all Franck notes in this chapter) writes about applying the United Nations' quasi-constitution as a 'living tree', pp. 51 and 134.

[2] For the Friendly Relations Declaration see A/Res/25/2625 on 24 October 1970; see also above Chapter 3, p. 38 and below, Chapter 12, p. 185.

[3] See below, p. 186.

[4] See above, Chapter 4, p. 55 A table showing how many of the armed conflicts between 1713 and 1789 had regard to territory is offered in Finnemore (2003), p. 109.

member states' 'territorial integrity' and 'political independence' against 'external aggression'. After a second world war, the authors of the UN Charter were as determined as the authors of the League Covenant had been to tackle the issue of war and violent encroachments on states' territory. Hence, the 'object and purpose' of UN Charter Art. 2:4 prohibiting the 'threat or use of force against the territorial integrity or political independence' is similar to that of Article 10 in the Covenant. Preventing armed action that aimed at seizing – or otherwise encroaching on – the territory of states was a central aim that the authors of the Covenant rule and the Charter rule had in common. It remains a fundamental line. The Friendly Relations Declaration of 1970 states: '... The territory of a State shall not be the object of acquisition by another State resulting from the threat or use of force. No territorial acquisition resulting from the threat or use of force shall be recognized as valid.'

Looking at the real world, we can see that during the 20 years between 1920 and 1940, events grossly contradicted the central aim of League Covenant Art. 10 – to prevent 'aggression' and the acquisition of land by force. Such, however, has not been the reality during the nearly 80 years since the adoption of the UN Charter and its Art. 2:4. Already in the Atlantic Charter on 14 August 1941 – in the beginning of World War II, President Roosevelt and Prime Minister Churchill proclaimed as principles in their national policies

First, their countries seek no aggrandizement, territorial or other;

Second, they desire to see no territorial changes that do not accord with the freely expressed wishes of the people concerned.

Since World War II, the most powerful states have, indeed, almost consistently observed the restraint that the two of them declared in the Atlantic Charter. Long-lasting and large-scale belligerencies have taken place but – with the stark exception of the 2022 Russian invasion of Ukraine – wars of conquest and about territory have not. So, what were the large wars about? The Vietnam War, fought by the United States as part of a mistaken containment of Communism, could be seen as an intervention in a Vietnamese civil war[5] but is perhaps best characterized as a colonial war inherited from France and not brought before the UN. The wars that have ravaged Afghanistan since 1979 and since 2001 were neither for the Soviet Union nor for the United States aimed at acquisition of territory. They were rather armed interventions that horribly and tragically worsened as civil wars between different competing Afghan groups.

---

5   See Falk (1966).

A number of cases have been noted, however, in which states – North Korea, Israel, Argentina, Iraq, Russia and Turkey – used force and sought to acquire territory in clear breach of the restraint demanded by the Charter norm.[6] However, violations of rules do not mean that rules are irrelevant – whether in domestic or international jurisdictions.

In the cases of North Korea's attack on South Korea and Iraq's occupation of Kuwait, the UN machinery authorized effective armed collective action that reversed the illegal seizure of land by force and upheld the UN norm in Art. 2:4. India's march into Goa and incorporation of the territory in India met no censure in the General Assembly of the United Nations. Perhaps the majority of the Assembly felt a judgment guided by Art. 2:4 in face of an intransigent and outdated Portuguese colonial rule would have been awkward.[7] The cases of the Israeli occupation of the Golan Heights and the West Bank, the Russian occupation and annexation of the Crimea, the emergence of Abkhazia and South Ossetia as states after the Russian intervention in Georgia in 2008, and the Turkish occupation and state creation in Cyprus have not been reversed but met by general non-recognition – as required in the Friendly Relations Declaration quote above.[8] The Russian invasion of Ukraine in February 2022, in flagrant violation of UN Charter Art. 2:4, may originally have aimed at installing a Moscow-controlled regime rather than an annexation of Ukraine's territory. However, if Russia were to rip off Ukrainian territory by the threat or use of force it should not be recognized as legal – according to the UN General Assembly resolution adopted on 2 March 2022. (A/RES/ES –11/1).

Many modern writers have noted that the seizing of territory by force has become rare after 1945 and that this is a remarkable development.[9] The comments seem justified not least against the background that there exist some important disputed claims to territory in the world. It is also striking that while existing great military powers indulge in arms races and tenaciously hold on to the ability to smash each other to pieces, differently from past centuries they show no inclination to grab territory from each other.

One would be naïve to suggest that the rarity of the use of force to seize territory is a direct result of the entry into force of the legal norm that was laid down in Art. 2:4 of the UN Charter. An essential factor may well be that

---

[6] See above Chapter 4, p. 55 There have also, as noted in Chapter 4, p. 56 ff been a number of border disputes and clashes, For instance, between China and the Soviet Union in 1969; between China and India; between India and Pakistan; and between Ethiopia and Eritrea. See also above, Chapter 4, p. 56.

[7] See Franck, p. 117.

[8] Ignoring that line in 2019, the US Trump administration recognized Israel's annexation of the Golan Heights.

[9] See Henderson, p. 42.

today's major military nuclear-equipped powers may regard most territorial expansion as too risky. They may look for other ways of gaining benefits and extending their influence. Other reasons for the welcome rarity of territorial conquest today may be, for instance, that in today's world of fast-moving goods, people and finances, all governments may prefer to seek 'non-owner' influence over other states rather than taking on the costs, risks and opprobrium of conquering land. Perhaps also with the general embrace of the national state, the end of colonialism and the emergence of many new states there are fewer incentives for slicing and re-slicing the global cake. Finally, one should recognize that the traditional permissive mental attitude–above termed 'the public mind' – to the international use of force gradually changed in the course of the first half of the twentieth century and that the belligerent conquest of land in particular has come to be seen as reprehensible and deserved to be outlawed.

The aim of Art. 2:4 is also to broadly prohibit interstate encroachments on territory and threats and uses of force that have other aims than the seizing of territory.[10] Employing the broad and descriptive term *'use of force'* and including *'threats'* the Charter clearly covered a wider range of actions than Art. 10 of the Covenant that referred to the concept *'external aggression'*. History offered examples of a broad range of other interstate threats or uses of force. One report states that between 1798 and 1941 there were 149 'US episodes' similar to a nineteenth-century US naval bombardment in Nicaragua undertaken after violence against US nationals and their property.[11] Throughout the nineteenth century, the Holy Alliance made generous interstate use of armed force – not to seize territory but – to stop liberal constitutional change in Europe. In 1907, as noted earlier, the Porter convention testified to and sought to limit the practice of sending gunboats threatening bombardment unless debts were paid.[12]

In 1945, such free-wheeling interstate use of force by powerful states was clearly unacceptable to a large part of the public mind and to the authors of the UN Charter. In Art. 2:4 they formulated a rule that prohibited a wide range of coercive actions.[13] The brevity and generality of this updated rule cry for clarifications and amplifications. What is today included under the prohibition and what types of actions fall outside the scope of the article?[14]

---

[10] Cf. above, Chapter 6, p. 112 on the evolution of public thinking regarding 'measures short of war'.
[11] See Franck, p. 77, note 7. A table of interventions in the period 1815–1850 is provided by Finnemore, pp. 122–123.
[12] See above, Chapter 5, p. 101, Chapter 6, p. 112, and see Brownlie, p. 225.
[13] See comment in Simma, p. 207.
[14] Cf. Henderson, p. 19.

INTERVENTION

While the seizing of territory was a normal part of the aims of traditional war, most post-World War II interstate uses of force or coercion are prompted by other aims. This has made the part of Art. 2:4 that covers actions beyond traditional war and the seizing of territory the practically most important. Today, such actions are often lumped together under the concept 'interventions'.[15] While the many different aims that interventions may have – for instance, regime change or rescue of citizens – is of no relevance in determining whether they are prohibited under Art. 2:4 the form and degree of compulsion applied is.

Three groups may be identified:

- One kind of 'interventions' that is most likely to be considered prohibited under Art. 2:4 is in a form that comprises direct or 'indirect' interstate use of 'force',
- A second kind of 'interventions' does not use such force' but comprises some measure of 'coercion'. They are likely to be prohibited – not under Art. 2:4 but – as 'intervention' under customary international law.[16]
- A third kind of 'intervention' are those that comprise neither 'force', nor 'coercion' but 'pressures'. They are not likely to fall under any ban and would more properly be termed 'interference'.

To decide whether particular actions are prohibited under one rule or another or not at all can be difficult. Guidance must be sought first of all in the meaning given to the terms used in Art. 2:4, notably the term 'force' and the term 'international relations'. While, as we shall see, the understanding that emerges from the practice of states is not straightforward, the survey of a fairly large number of concrete public cases – in Chapters 14 and 15 below – will point to several conclusions as to what kinds of interventions are today considered illegal.

SCOPE OF ART. 2:4 IS LIMITED BY THE MEANING OF ITS KEY TERMS – 'FORCE', 'THREAT' AND 'INTERNATIONAL RELATIONS'

What limitation lies in the term *'force'*? Could coercive economic *measures* be covered? Viewing, for instance, the efforts in 2020 by the US government to exert *'maximum economic pressure'* on the government of Iran through a blockade

---

[15] For a discussion of the definition of 'intervention', see above, Chapter 1, p. 5 and see Beckman, pp. 23 ff. and Finnemore, pp. 7 ff.

[16] For the analysis by the International Court of Justice, see its judgment in the Nicaragua case discussed below in Chapter 15, p. 213 ff.

of Iran's oil sales and financial transactions, one can see that economic actions might have enormous 'force' and devastating consequences. However, the legislative history of Art. 2:4 shows that an explicit reference to economic measures was proposed at the drafting stage and rejected. It may also be noted that the extensive elaboration of the prohibition of the use of 'force' in the Friendly Relations Declaration contains no word about economic pressures. Only in the Declaration's elaboration of the principle of non-intervention do we find a ban on '*attempted threats against the personality of the State or against its political, economic and cultural elements…*' While the global economic blockade that the United States has sought to inflict on Iran may thus be a violation of the norm prohibiting intervention it is hardly a breach of Art. 2:4 in which 'force' is generally recognized to denote physical coercion.[17]

The general consensus on this point has not, however, stood in the way of the recent broad international understanding that some types of cyber-attacks may be seen as equivalent to use of armed force and accordingly prohibited under Art. 2:4.[18] Some practical experiences in the last decade–including the so-called Stuxnet cyber-attacks on Iranian centrifuges for the enrichment of uranium – have fast convinced governments that 'cyber warfare' has the potential to bring catastrophic destruction[19] and notice has been given that it may be regarded as 'armed attacks' triggering the right of self-defence.[20] In 2021, the British government issued a new doctrine that could even open for use of nuclear weapons in response to an attack by cyber means.[21]

The prohibition of a '*threat*' of force which is also covered in Art. 2:4 appears to have elicited surprisingly little international discussion.[22] While the Friendly Relations Declaration does not amplify or explain the concept, the Helsinki Final Act seems to have had threats in mind when it stipulated that the parties 'will refrain from any manifestation of force for the purpose of inducing another participating State to renounce the full exercise of its sovereign rights.'

The language is somewhat cryptic, but may aim at conduct opposite to the kind of practices prescribed in the agreement on Conventional Forces in Europe (CFE, 1990) to build mutual confidence, for instance, notify each

---

[17] See Henderson (2018), pp. 52–53; D.H. Joyner argues that unilateral economic sanctions may violate customary international law, in particular the principle of non-intervention. See Joyner (2016). Cf. below, Chapter 15, p. 214 on the judgment of the ICJ in the Nicaragua case.

[18] On cyber war, see above, Chapter 8, p. 129 and see Henderson, pp. 55 ff., Gray, pp. 34–35.

[19] See Henderson, pp. 55 ff., 221.

[20] US statement cited by Henderson, p. 236.

[21] www.theguardian.com/politics/2021/mar/16/defence-review-uk-could-use-trident-to-counter-cyber-attack.

[22] See Henderson pp. 26–31. A recent monograph is Stürchler (2007).

other and mutually invite observers to military maneuvers. Naval demonstrations and army deployments near borders have been a classic kind of warning that a military attack could follow. Somewhat similar is the common military recourse to 'prodding' that consists in flying or sailing near borders or planes or ships to test the alertness and strength of a potential adversary.[23] Both practices risk increasing tension, causing sparks and unintended clashes.

With respect to specific instances that may have constituted 'threats' within the meaning of UN Charter Art. 2:4, an obvious first case would be Russia's accumulation of troops near the border to Ukraine in 2021 and early 2022. Before its armed invasion of Ukraine on 24 February 2022, Russia maintained that it was simply within its freedom to move troops around within its own territory. It seems obvious that the action aimed to threaten Ukraine to concessions. Another instance of a 'threat' arguably falling under Art. 2:4 could have been the US concentration at various times of naval power, including aircraft carriers, in the Persian Gulf with a view – one might assume – to threaten Iran. Lastly, an illustration of how differently government statements on nuclear weapons can be viewed was offered at the discussion of the outcome document for the 2022 NPT Review Conference: France, the UK and the US presented a paper that sought to distinguish between 'irresponsible' offensive nuclear threats (made by Russia during its war with Ukraine) and 'responsible' nuclear threats (made by themselves) for 'defensive' purposes. Russia chose to term its own statements 'warnings' and part of its 'deterrence' strategy.[24] Differently from the four nuclear-weapon states, the parties to the 2017 Treaty on the Prohibition of Nuclear Weapons (TPNW) had in June condemned any and all nuclear threats as violations of international law, including the UN Charter, whether they be explicit or implicit and irrespective of the circumstances.

Another question relates to the words *'territorial integrity'* and *'political independence'*. It is generally recognized that linking the ban on the threat or use of force to effects on the 'territorial integrity' or 'political independence' implied no limitation in scope.[25] Indeed, it is difficult to imagine an interstate use of force that will not injure one or the other. An operation like Israel's intervention to free hostages at the airport of Entebbe in Uganda in 1976[26] was limited in aim, time, use of force and was not directed at the Ugandan

---

[23] See above Chapter 7, p. 121.
[24] Arms Control Association, Press Release of 26 August 2022. www.armscontrol.org/aca-press-releases/2022-08/npt-review-outcome-highlights-deficit-disarmament-diplomacy.
[25] See Brownlie, p. 267, Henderson, pp. 19–22.
[26] See below, Chapter 16, p. 244 and Franck, pp. 82–86.

government. Yet, it involved an unauthorized flight into Ugandan air space and encroachment on Uganda's exclusive right to use force in the land.

A third – large and difficult – question is what limitation of the scope of Art. 2:4 follows from attaching the prohibition of the use of force only to '*international relations*'.

THE RULE IN ART. 2:4 IS LIMITED TO 'INTERNATIONAL RELATIONS'

Art. 2:4 spells out that the prohibition of threat or use of force has regard to 'international relations'. Two rules are implied:

- states must not use force against other states[27]
- states are not prohibited to use force within their own jurisdiction.

The rules are *unsurprising*. International law consists of norms that have emerged through acceptance by states and if there is something the community of states is likely to agree on it is that each one of them is sovereign – meaning *inter alia* that it has the exclusive right to use force within its own territory and jurisdiction, including, if need be an armed force to suppress civil wars, uprisings or other disturbances.

However, in a world of accelerating interdependence and increasing demands for universal respect for human rights, this tenet raises several problems. For one thing, as noted, most armed conflicts and bloodshed today take place inside states. In some cases, as in Cambodia (1975–79) and Rwanda (1994) there was genocide inside national borders. In others, as in the former republic of Yugoslavia and in Myanmar grave ethnic cleansing took place. Some internal conflicts became so long-lasting and shattering that we talk about failed states and ask in despair for ways in which the external world may help on-site to restore political and social order. It happens also – not infrequently – that the situation inside some states is perceived by other states as gravely affecting their interests and creating incentives for intervention.

Thus, the two apparently simple rules cited above are under strain and other legal rules add to the strain: A government of a state is deemed free not only to use force of its own to suppress internal uprisings – including attempts at secession – but also to ask or consent to other states helping to suppress such uprisings.[28] Foreign states can thus legally enter a non-international conflict on the

---

[27] This includes not only their territory proper but also vessels, like ships, air planes and satellites. Cf. Henderson, p. 71.

[28] Gray, p. 78, 84, 90.

basis of such request or consent. A precondition is, however, that the request or consent comes from a governmental authority that can rightly claim to act on behalf of the state.[29] A foreign state is guilty of illegal intervention if it enters an internal conflict at the request of a rebel – or secessionist – opposition group.[30] The states of the international community may thus be said to have skewed the rules in favour of the survival of incumbent governments and against rebels and secessionists who might – illegally – be receiving assistance from other countries. Moreover, The Friendly Relations Declaration provides as follows:

> Every State has the duty to refrain from organizing or encouraging the organization of irregular forces or armed bands including mercenaries, for incursion into the territory of another State.
>
> Every State has the duty to refrain from organizing, instigating, assisting or participating in acts of civil strife or terrorist acts in another State or acquiescing in organized activities within its territory directed toward the commission of such acts, when the acts referred to in the present paragraph involve a threat or use of force.

Yet in fluid situations, it may be questioned whether a government on the verge of being unseated or an armed opposition nearly in control should have the authority to speak for the state and invite foreign states to join in the contest. Judgments on the matter by other governments naturally tend to be influenced by their political preferences.[31]

The possibility of calling for assistance from outside powers raises not only the question of whether the issuer is in a position to legally act on behalf of the state but also whether a request or consent is genuine and not extorted. The answer may be negative on either or both points. Claiming that its armed intervention in Hungary in 1956 was justified the Soviet Union pointed to a request from the former Prime Minister of Hungary.[32] Similarly, the United States claimed its intervention in the Dominican Republic in 1965 was justified *inter alia* by a request from the ousted government.[33] The 'Prague Spring' government of Alexander Dubček denied in the Security Council in 1969 that it had requested armed Soviet intervention.[34]

---

[29] Gray, p. 100.
[30] See Nicaragua case, ICJ judgment, p. 99.
[31] Gray, p. 100.
[32] See Gray, p. 92 and see Chapter 15, p. 218.
[33] Gray, p. 92 and see below, Chapter 15, p. (7E p. 52).
[34] See Franck, pp. 73–75 and see below, Chapter 15, p. 218. A stark early case was the Kuusinen revolutionary government purporting to represent Finland during the Finno-Russian war of 1939–1940 and requesting military aid from the Soviet Union. At the time Mr. Kuusinen's 'Finnish People's Government' was located on a small fraction of territory occupied by the Soviet Union. See Blix (1960), p. 143.

THE CIVIL WAR IN SYRIA AND INTERNATIONAL
INTERVENTIONS 2011–PRESENT

Several writers[35] have ably described and analyzed cases of foreign interventions in internal conflicts. We shall focus on the conflict in Syria that began in 2011 and that shows heavy foreign participation ignoring the international prohibition of intervention.[36] The special bombings that were carried out by the United States, the United Kingdom and France as punishment for claimed use of chemical weapons by the Syrian government are described below in Chapter 16.

As described in Chapter 2, protests in the wake of the 'Arab Spring' against the repressive Assad regime in Syria were brutally crushed by the government in 2011. The conflict inside Syria escalated and subjected to so much foreign intervention that it was sometimes described as a war between several Islamic Sunni states led by Saudi Arabia on one side and part of the Islamic Shia world led by Iran on the other side. However, with many other interested parties acting in the conflict – including the United States, United Kingdom, France, Russia, Turkey and Israel – it was more complicated than a Shia-Sunni contest.

Sunni Gulf states, the United States, some other Western states and Turkey intervened on the side of the armed uprising directly or through various rebel groups with funds, arms, advisers or volunteer fighters. On the other side, the Syrian government requested and received much assistance and support from the outside. Iran and the Lebanese Iran-allied Hezbollah movement provided fighting cadres and arms and Russia – with military bases in Syria – contributed vitally important air force support, tanks and troops.

With regard to the actions on Syrian territory by governments opposed to the Assad regime, we need to distinguish between the operations to crush the brutal and fundamentalist ISIS[37] and the operations directed against the Assad regime. Much of the fighting against ISIS on Syrian territory was waged by Syrian Kurdish groups not under government control but supported by the United States. It was further waged by Iranian troops. The United States and several other Western states claimed that defeating and eradicating ISIS

---

[35] For instance, Brownlie, p. 224, and Grey, pp. 79–119.

[36] The Syrian civil war is described above in Chapter 2, pp. 27–28. For other accounts, see Gray, pp. 88, 107–119 and Lund, A., 'Syria's Civil War: Government Victory or Frozen Conflict' (Kista. FOI, December 2018) www.foi.se/en/foi/news-and-pressroom/news/2018-12-17-foreign-interventions-freeze-the-conflict-in-syria.html.

[37] See above, Chapter 2, p. 26. The operations against ISIS prompted many letters by different participants to the UN Security Council, for example letters 2015 from the Syrian government (S/2015/718 and S/2915/719).

was their chief mission in Syria and the US air attacks on ISIS were highly significant. Although ISIS was established on Syrian territory and sought to establish a new Caliphate in the Levant including Syria, the Assad government declared that operations against ISIS without Syrian consent violated its sovereignty and protested against them. The United States and its allies asked for no such consent and justified the operations on Syrian and Iraqi territory against ISIS as United States–Iraq collective self-defence.

The heterogenous outside groups that sought to topple the Assad regime – including Al Qaeda-linked terrorist groups – do not appear to have bothered to present any legal justification for the various ways in which they intervened in Syria. Nor did the US – formally not at war with Syria – appear to have provided any legal justification for overtly or covertly joining these interventions by providing funds, weapons and advisers to selected – presumed non-terrorist – parts of the groups. Turkey assisted in the fight to topple the Assad regime by facilitating the transit of volunteers to anti-Assad rebels, by controlling rebel areas not far from the Turkish border (Idlib) and – in 2019 – more dramatically by invading and occupying a zone of Kurd-held Syrian land along Turkey's Southern border. Israel, lastly, frequently intervened by bombing Iranian targets or transports in Syria, sometimes claiming that the action was taken as reprisals for missile attacks from Syrian territory.[38]

The considerable assistance extended to the Syrian government by Iran, Lebanese Hezbollah and Russia at the request of the government slowly allowed the Assad government to prevail. Diplomacy led by Russia, Iran and Turkey (2021) – and talks under the formal auspices of the United Nations – may lead to a new constitutional compact designed to steer Syria to peace. On 21 December 2021, the three states concluded their 17th round of talks in Astana 'for the purpose of ensuring peace in Syria'. The declaration reaffirmed Syria's 'sovereignty, independence, unity and territorial integrity'. The statement also reaffirmed their joint commitment to fighting terrorism and to 'improve the humanitarian situation'. However, even by December 2022, no solutions to the constitutional problems had been agreed.

It is striking that – forgetting the ISIS aims for a big Caliphate – the long war in Syria was not about land. Turkey's military invasion of a strip of Syrian land bordering Turkey caused a justified universal outcry. It was probably driven by Turkish concerns about Kurdish power rather than an aim to defeat the Assad government and grab land and the occupation has been explained as a temporary measure. It was agreed by all – including Turkey – that the war should not modify Syria's borders. For all intervening parties – possibly except

---

[38] See Chapter 2, p. 28.

Israel – the war was with varying motivations for or against regime change. Israel was certainly no friend of the Assad regime, but that regime was at least a known quantity with which relations were stable. A replacement might be less predictable. The main purpose of Israel's air interventions was to hit the Iranian military presence in Syria and Iranian transports of arms to Hezbollah in Lebanon.

It is also striking that the opponents of the Assad government – including the Western states – do not seem to have questioned the government's right to ask for assistance and the right of Russia, Iran and Hezbollah to intervene. While some would like to deny authoritarian governments a right to call for armed foreign assistance, the broad acceptance in the case of Syria suggests that the permissive rule regarding help to established governments is firm.

None of the states that intervened to help remove the Assad regime – including the United States and the Gulf states – considered themselves to be at war with Syria. They avoided sending any regular national military units to take part in ground operations against the government side. The determination of the United States and other states to keep their intervention against Assad at relatively low visibility may have flowed more from concerns about the risk of triggering another Middle East War than from an intention to avoid a glaring disregard for Art. 2:4. Nevertheless, one cannot ignore that the Charter article's legal ban on the use of armed force may have presented a threshold that together with strategic concerns resulted in a degree of restraint.

A last comment is that multiple foreign interventions with widely different aims transformed the original rather small-scale indigenous uprising into a complex long-lasting war that caused several hundred thousand casualties and many millions of refugees and internally displaced persons. Had the rules prohibiting outside intervention in support of uprisings been respected by Gulf states, the United States and Turkey, the Assad regime would probably have won an early victory. The various aims of the intervening parties would not have been pursued. In the real world, they were, indeed, pursued with the result that a decade of war and anarchy was added to tyranny and oppression.

INTERVENTIONS HAVE LED TO THE
MAJOR USES OF ARMED FORCE

The Syrian conflict is not the first civil war that has been enlarged and prolonged through armed foreign interventions – whether lawful or unlawful. We have noted that both the Vietnam War and the war in Afghanistan could be viewed as internal conflicts that were transformed through interventions from the outside. We might add Libya, where a UN-authorized action developed into a long civil war through interventions.

To prevent conflicts inside states requires other approaches than the elimination of interstate conflicts. Internal conflicts flow from defects in 'nation building'. The foreign intervention of the kind witnessed in Syria, Afghanistan, or Libya has not offered a desirable path to nation-building. What could be done?

In the case of 'failed states', the question is acute, but many other states in the process of 'failing' by sinking into strife, narcotics trafficking, corruption, or ethnic conflicts would also need help. The world community – acting through the United Nations or regional organizations or civic movements – should be ready to decisively step up its assistance, but a troubling question is whether help from the outside is at all possible – except in the form of food, shelter and the receipt of refugees. If this assistance fails to materialize, it will become clearer than ever that not only have states failed, but so has the international community as a whole.

13

The Security Council May Use or Authorize
States or Regional Organizations to Use Force

The scope of the general prohibition in Charter Art. 2:4 of the use of force is limited by the right of the Security Council to take enforcement measures under Art. 2:7, to use force under Art. 42, and to authorize regional organizations to use force under Art. 53.

THE UN MAY INTERVENE INSIDE
STATES – EVEN WITH FORCE – UNDER ART. 2:7

The prohibition in Art. 2:4 for states to use force against other states and the implicit recognition of their right to use force within their own domestic spheres aim to protect their sovereignty. In Art. 2:7 we find that this sovereignty is given an even wider protection through a ban also for the UN to *'intervene in matters that are essentially within the(ir) domestic jurisdiction'*. As discussed above, the term *'intervene'* comprises uses of force prohibited in Art. 2:4 but also coercive actions that do not include physical force and even non-coercive actions that might better be labeled 'interference'. Beginning with the consideration of South Africa's apartheid policies, majorities in UN organs have increasingly come to the view that verbal criticisms and even condemnations, especially in questions regarding human rights, do not constitute unlawful 'intervention'.

One line in Art. 2:7 limits the shell of sovereignty around the domestic sphere. The awareness that at times policies and actions within states may constitute a threat to international peace and security led the authors of Art. 2:7 to stipulate that the article does not stand in the way of the UN applying *'enforcement measures'* under the conditions laid down in Chapter 7: the Security Council is always entitled to use or authorize the use of force in conformity with Art. 42.[1]

---

[1] See Franck (2002) (as all Franck notes in this chapter), pp. 136–137. An authorization to intervene by force could conceivably also come in the shape of a recommendation from the General Assembly under the Uniting for Peace resolution. See Franck, pp. 24 ff.

The R2P Doctrine

The doctrine '*Responsibility to Protect*' (R2P)[2] may also lead to a use of force authorized by the Council. The doctrine emerged through the adoption of the 2005 UN World Summit Outcome Document.[3] It is created for cases where some government utterly fails in its duty to protect people against – or is itself the author of – large-scale violence within its territory. The doctrine foresees a number of non-coercive ways through which the UN may act to help remedy the situation but opens also for intervention by the use of force authorized by the Security Council.[4]

Perhaps the argument may be advanced that events within the domestic sphere may be such as to affect international peace and so justify enforcement action by the Security Council under Chapter 7 and Art. 42. However, the explanation of why the UN Summit endorsed an expansive role for the United Nations in these cases is probably a wide-spread feeling that the international community must not stand passive and watch large-scale cruelties behind national borders, as was done to the shame of the world and the UN in the cases of the genocides in Cambodia (1975) and Rwanda (1994) and – in the view of many – is done in the case of the Rohinga *people* in Myanmar (from 2017).

The R2P doctrine has been cited in several UN resolutions but has not been relied on for action except in the case of Libya in 2011. Based on a Security Council resolution[5] and led by NATO, the intervention resulted in the toppling of the erratic and oppressive dictatorial regime of Gaddafi. Sadly, for over ten years (2022) it resulted not in a stable order but in a civil war and anarchy and intervention by several foreign states. The doctrine is viewed with suspicion by many developing countries fearing that it can be misused by great powers concealing political intentions behind a humanitarian mantle. It has been hailed by many others as an instrument for upholding basic norms of human rights in the modern world community. It may yet prove its value.

---

[2]   See Henderson, pp. 125 ff.; Franck, pp. 40 ff. discussing cases relating to Congo, Côte d'Ivoire, Yemen, Iraq, former Yugoslavia, Somalia, Haiti and Sierra Leone and other states.

[3]   General Assembly, A/60/L.1, 24 October 2005, www.globalr2p.org/resources/2005-world-summit-outcome-a-60-l-1/. For further discussion, see Gareth Evans, *The Responsibility to Protect: Ending Mass Atrocity Crimes Once and for All* (Washington, DC: Brookings, 2008).

[4]   For the Secretary-General's report on implementing R2P, see UN General Assembly, report A/63/677, 12 January 2009, https://documents-dds-ny.un.org/doc/UNDOC/GEN/N09/206/10/PDF/N0920610.pdf?OpenElement.

[5]   S/RES/1973 (2011). For a detailed analysis of the case and the doctrine, see Henderson, pp. 137 ff., 154 and 163 ff.

THE SECURITY COUNCIL MAY USE OR
AUTHORIZE THE USE OF FORCE – ART. 42

The foremost function of Art. 42 is to confer authority on the Security Council to take action by the use of force in interstate conflicts that comprise threats to the peace, breaches of the peace or acts of aggression. The article marked a leap forward from the security system of the League of Nations. It assumed originally that agreements would be reached with UN Member states to make armed forces and facilities available to the Council (Art. 43) and that a Military Staff Committee would assist the Council (Art. 47). As no agreements were concluded to provide armed forces the Council has chosen to interpret the Charter as allowing it to authorize member states to use their armed forces on its behalf.[6]

While the Security Council has very often authorized peacekeeping operations involving armed forces but not enforcement,[7] cases of Security Council-authorized enforcement action in interstate conflicts have been few. Some feel that permanent members that claim the privilege of the veto on account of their special responsibilities owe it to the rest of the world to act with the world's interest in mind and not lightly bring the Council to paralysis by using their veto.[8] It is easy to agree with this view. A rare measure to restrain the use of the veto was adopted by the General Assembly on 26 April 2021 through Resolution 76/262. The gist of the resolution that had been championed by Liechtenstein, was called the 'veto initiative' and was adopted by consensus was that whenever a resolution in the Security Council was stopped by a veto the matter could be automatically taken up within 10 working days for discussion in the General Assembly. The country responsible for the veto would be invited to be the first speaker in the discussion to be enabled to explain the reasons for the country's negative vote. It was argued that this procedure – which does not limit the right of veto – will enhance the global public scrutiny of the actions of the permanent members and give them reasons to exercise more restraint on using the veto. The new procedure should be welcomed and can perhaps deter permanent members from frivolous uses of veto. However, one should be cautious to assert that the veto power *per se* is the great wall that blocks the way for the Council to intervene effectively to prevent or stop the use of force between states. The veto is a procedural stopping card that sends

---

[6] See Franck, p. 24.

[7] See Gray, pp. 262 ff., Henderson, pp. 167 ff.

[8] For further discussion of the Security Council, the veto and R2P, see Global Centre for the Responsibility to Protect, 'UN Security Council and the Responsibility to Protect' [n.d.], www.globalr2p.org/calling-for-a-unsc-code-of-conduct/.

a signal about the opposition of a permanent member that could use its power on the ground to stop a proposed UN action.[9]

SECURITY COUNCIL AUTHORIZING ENFORCEMENT ACTION IN KOREA 1950 AND KUWAIT 1991

In June 1950, North Korea attacked South Korea and the Security Council recommended that members provide assistance to South Korea and make their forces available to a unified command headed by the United States and operating under the UN flag. The resolution was adopted with three abstentions. The Soviet Union, which would certainly have cast a veto, was absent from the Council as a protest against China being represented by the government in Taiwan.[10] The Soviet Union did not proceed to use its military power to stop the collective action that through its absence from the Security Council it had accidentally failed to stop by a veto. Ironically, instead, the collective action came to a halt and a diplomatic process was initiated, when the People's Republic of China, which had been excluded from the Council and the opportunity to veto decisions showed its opposition to the Council recommendation and UN action by sending an army of 'volunteers' and engaging in a bloody war until an armistice was reached.

The second case was the collective action that was taken under the US leadership following Iraq's attack and occupation of Kuwait in 1990. It is an example – a lonely one – of the UN Security Council authorizing the use of force against an act of aggression and occupation.[11] East-West détente prevailing in 1990 enabled Russia to join a Council majority asking member states to use all necessary means to reverse the occupation – which happened through operation 'Desert Storm' under US command.

SECURITY COUNCIL DECISIONS OF 1990 CLAIMED AS PROVIDING AUTHORITY FOR THE INVASION OF IRAQ IN 2003

In the case of the 2003 invasion of Iraq by a coalition of willing states, it was argued by the United Kingdom and the United States that the authorization

---

[9] The case of ignoring the opposition of permanent members in the case of NATO's Kosovo bombings is discussed below in Chapter 16. See also below how in the Korean war action by Beijing – without yet access to the China seat and veto power in the Security Council – brought about an end to UN/US operations moving near the border to China. Cf. above, Chapter 3, p. 35.

[10] See Franck, p. 25.

[11] UNSC Res 678 of 29 Nov. 1990. An excellent account of the diplomatic-political work leading to the resolution and action is found in Sjöberg (2006) pp. 267 ff.

that the Council had given for the use of armed force in 1990 and that had
been relied on for several subsequent limited armed actions in Iraq remained
a valid legal ground for the armed action in 2003. The reasoning has generally been deemed strained.[12] The aim of the Council authorizing the use of
force in 1990 had been to reverse the occupation of Kuwait. Although in 2003
a variety of aims were advanced publicly in the United States for the invasion it seems most likely that the dominant motivation this time was regime
change.[13] The removal of Saddam Hussein had not been the aim and had
not been sought in 1990 and the mandate from that time to use force could
hardly be relevant in 2003. It would have been all the more unreasonable as it
was evident that in March 2003 less than nine members of the Council would
have voted for a decision to invade, while negative votes would have been cast,
including vetoes by China, France and Russia.[14]

THE GENERAL RULE AGAINST THE USE OF FORCE IS QUALIFIED BY THE SECURITY COUNCIL'S RIGHT TO AUTHORIZE REGIONAL ORGANIZATIONS TO USE FORCE

Under Art. 53 of the UN Charter: 'The Security Council shall, where appropriate, utilize (such) regional organizations or agencies for enforcement
action under its authority. But no enforcement action shall be taken under
regional arrangements or by regional agencies without the authorization of
the Security Council ....'

At the drafting of the UN Charter in San Francisco, there was a good deal
of enthusiasm for relying on regional organizations to share equally with the
United Nations the responsibility for the maintenance of peace. Nevertheless,
the conference decided that prior authorization by the Security Council
would be required for them to take enforcement action.[15] There are conflicting views as to which organizations and agencies may qualify as 'regional'[16]
under Art. 53. and there have been only a few occasions on which Art. 53 has
been relevant.[17]

The first case was provided by the action of the Organization of American
States (OAS) in the 1962 Cuban Missile Crisis. Having learnt about the Soviet

---

[12] See Sjöberg (2006), p. 388.
[13] See above, Chapter 2, p. 39 and below Chapter 16, p. 241.
[14] For a detailed examination of the UK/US argument, see Henderson, pp. 131 ff. and see
    Simpson (2005).
[15] See Franck, pp. 157–158.
[16] See Stone (1954), pp. 247–251.
[17] Ibid.

installation of missiles in Cuba and of the quarantine declared by the United States on the Soviet ships approaching Cuba, the Permanent Council of the OAS, acting without any prior authorization of the Security Council, recommended the members to '*take all measures, individually and collectively including the use of armed force which they deem necessary* ....."[18] No member of the OAS had occasion to proceed practically to use armed force and actually ignore the need for prior Security Council authorization. Hence the issue of breach of Art. 53 never came to a head.

In two other cases, a ceasefire and monitoring group established by the Economic Community of West African States (ECOWAS) intervened with armed forces to end brutal and complex internal hostilities in Liberia and Sierra Leone from 1990 to 1998. In both cases, the Security Council commended the actions *post facto* despite the absence of prior authorization.[19] Yet another case of the use of armed force by a regional organization without prior authorization of the Council was the much-debated NATO bombing to end Serbian atrocities in Kosovo in March 1998. The extreme humanitarian situation was invoked as justification but the action and the failure to seek authorization by the Council were fiercely criticized by China.[20]

It can hardly be concluded from the cases cited above that the Security Council should be on its way to a practice ignoring the requirement in Art. 53 that regional organizations must have prior authorizations from the Council for enforcement action.[21] The rationale for Art. 53 – to let regional organizations take care of and stop regional conflicts – seems still valid.[22] The organizations may be expected to have expertise, experience and, indeed, the interest of their own to tackle and solve problems of their regions.

Some armed conflicts in Africa or possibly South America might not affect strong outside interests and the outside world might simply be grateful if the African Union (formerly OAU) or the OAS were ready to handle them. However, in a world of accelerated integration, no region escapes being the subject of strong political, strategic, and economic interests of other regions and states of other regions. Conflicts in one region – say Africa – might be of great interest to states outside.

---

[18] On 23 October 1962-See Franck. p. 99. Cf. Pirrone (1986), pp. 227–228. See discussion by Schwebel (1972).

[19] See Franck, pp. 155–162; Henderson, p. 151.

[20] A detailed account of the case is given below, Chapter 16.

[21] Franck, p. 162; Henderson, p. 120.

[22] In his book *World Order*, Kissinger stresses the importance that regional order has for world peace. See p. 371.

Accordingly, it is unlikely and would be unwise for the United Nations which is responsible for world peace to move to a practice that would allow regional organizations to use force within their regions without prior authorization by the Security Council. Even more unlikely and unwise would it be for the United Nations to acquiesce in any development allowing regional organizations to take enforcement action without prior Council authorization in conflicts beyond their own regions or against other regions.[23] NATO has several times been authorized by the Security Council to perform or take part in enforcement actions – as in Afghanistan and Libya and against ISIS – but there is no likelihood for a UN practice leaving NATO free to take armed action without Security Council authorization, except in the case of self-defence. Kosovo was not the beginning of such a practice and the claim is no more heard that NATO authorization of armed actions could replace Security Council approval.[24]

---

[23] See Gray, p. 452.
[24] See Henderson, p. 120.

14

The Right to Individual and Collective Self-Defence as an Exception to Art. 2:4

The rule in UN Charter Art. 2:4 is qualified by the right to individual and collective self-defence under Art. 51, which reads:

> Nothing in the present Charter shall impair the inherent right of individual and collective self-defense if an armed attack occurs against a Member of the United Nations, until the Security Council has taken measures necessary to maintain international peace and security. Measures taken by Members in the exercise of this right of self-defense shall be immediately reported to the Security Council...

The article is one of the most important and also one of the most controversial in the Charter. Looking back at the order that applied in the League of Nations may help us to understand why. The rules of the **League's** Covenant relating to collective security constituted great steps toward modernity but had grave loopholes. The right to self-defence was assumed but not spelled out and defined. If, in an unresolved conflict, the Council 'failed to reach a report', members were free to *take such action as they shall consider necessary for the maintenance of right and justice'*. (Art. 15(7)). This freedom included the option to use force under a right to self-defence that the member itself defined.

The architects of the UN Charter sought to learn from the past and to create a firm security order: the member states undertook the broad and categorical obligation not to threaten or use armed force against each other (Art. 2:4) and this abdication of state power was matched by a collective security system that conferred extensive powers on the Security Council to intervene in cases of threats or breaches of the peace. Theoretically, there should never arise a need for states to act in self-defence!

However, the authors of the Charter were aware that in the real world, the Security Council might not have an armed force ready for action at the instant when it was needed and might not have the power to order its members to take part in collective military actions. Against this background, they decided at the San Francisco Conference to leave freedom to states victims of breaches of the peace to defend themselves until the Security Council had taken sufficient action.[1] Art. 51 was inserted and stipulated that *'if an armed attack occurs'* no provisions of the Charter (notably Art. 2:4) were to impair member states' 'inherent right' of self-defence *'until the Security Council has taken measures necessary to maintain international peace and security.'*[2]

The term *'armed attack'* suggests that the authors primarily thought of breaches of the peace like traditional armed attacks across international borders. However, as the world moved into the post-World War II era, many uses of force began differently. Moreover, the Security Council, which had been given the legal authority to intervene in a wide range of conflicts, was mostly paralyzed. Yet, while states were placed before a variety of threats and encroachments, they were allowed to use armed force only in individual or collective self-defence and then only in face of 'an armed attack'.

What could states do if faced with lesser or different threats or infractions and an inactive Security Council? Some felt there was a loophole in the Charter.[3] Could it be fixed by a 'constructive' – flexible – interpretation of Art. 51?

Efforts failed to bridge the gap between the claims on the one hand for greater 'elbow room' for action in individual and collective self-defence and, on the other insistence on a strict reading of the strong tenor of the Charter restrictions.[4] In the Friendly Relations Declaration the question was dodged. It was devoted only a few lines under the principle of non-use of force and their glaring emptiness testifies to the failure to reach a consensus on any modification or amplification of Art. 51: 'Nothing in the foregoing paragraphs shall be construed as enlarging or diminishing in any way the scope of the provisions of the Charter concerning cases in which the use of force is lawful.'

However, there has been no lack of governments and writers that have presented arguments for interpretations that would give more 'elbow room' for states to use force and to invoke self-defence as justification for armed action. For instance, it has been contended that Art. 51 should be read primarily as a confirmation of an *'inherent right of individual and collective self-defence'* and that the case of 'armed attacks' was only one of several possible contingencies

---

[1] For detailed analyses, see Brownlie, pp. 270–275; Franck, pp. 48–51 and see Goodrich and Hambro, pp. 106–107.
[2] See Brownlie, pp. 270–272; Franck, p. 48.
[3] See Henderson, p. 224.
[4] Gray (2018), p. 170.

that could trigger this right.[5] Another way of creating greater freedom for the use of force in self-defence has been to interpret the concept 'armed attack' with imagination. How plausible are these interpretations?

First, did Art. 51 simply confirm an 'inherent right' of self-defence that existed under customary international law before the Charter was adopted? Action – whether by individuals or states – to avert attacks that are starting or ongoing must always have been found natural and irreproachable by society. In this general sense, it may be reasonable to talk about an 'inherent' legitimacy. However, so long as such a general notion is not made more specific by legislation or precedents it gives little guidance. This was the situation under the League Covenant.

The wording chosen for Art. 51 suggests that the authors wanted to avoid issuing broad and elastic permission for the use of force in self-defence. They refrained from using the abstract term 'aggression' that had historically been given many meanings and landed instead on the concrete and descriptive words 'armed attack' that might have been thought less susceptible to fanciful interpretations. They may also have felt that they were introducing important limits to the right of self-defence, when they explicitly stipulated that it would last only until the Security Council took necessary measures to maintain peace and security.[6] It is submitted that by including the word 'inherent' the authors signalled that they did not question that there had always existed a right to self-defence – not that they could not regulate it, which they thought they had to do and did. They chose not to issue a license for self-defence whenever a state was affected by another state resorting to 'the threat or use of force' that they had prohibited in Art. 2:4. Thus, no threats and only coercive acts of gravity on par with an 'armed attack' would trigger a right to self-defence.

The authors of the San Francisco text of Art. 51 attained a good deal of precision to which member states subscribed when they adhered to the Charter and it has been a desirable barrier against attempts to push the gates open for using self-defence as a justification for resorting to armed force. At the same time, 75 years of experience has also shown that the limited license formulated can be awkward.

Through a slow evolution brought about by resolutions of the Security Council and the General Assembly and judgments by the International Court of Justice – there have been minor adjustments in the reading of the rule to make it better fit the contemporary world. In this process, as we shall see,

---

[5] See Bowett, 'The use of force for the protection of nationals abroad' in Cassese (1986), pp. 39–55.

[6] On the effect of the term 'until ...' see Henderson, pp. 366–271.

many claims for adjustment have been refuted, some affirmed and yet others left hanging in the air.

Going through cases brought before the UN, one cannot avoid the impression that, in many conflicts, states tried to put the stamp of 'self-defence' on actions which they no doubt deemed urgent and important to themselves but which did not look much like an armed attack. For example, in 1971 at the break-up of Pakistan, millions of refugees inundated India to escape the brutality of the civil war. Though India was clearly not the subject of an armed attack it had an urgent interest in the war being ended and the UN was unable to do this. India chose to take armed action to help end the war and – at the same time – to weaken its neighbour Pakistan through the emergence of the new state of Bangladesh. The argument was advanced by India that the action was justified to meet a 'civil aggression'. As on many other occasions, the UN General Assembly avoided a legal stand. In a strong majority vote, the Assembly simply called for the withdrawal of Indian armed forces, neither condemning the action nor accepting the idea that 'civil aggression' could be tantamount to 'armed attack'.[7]

A right of 'self-defence' – whether claimed to be inherent or not – has been invoked somewhat like a *default* argument by states using force that was hard to associate with any armed attack. Christine Gray writes about states creating 'a veneer of legality' by invoking Art. 51 and self-defence.[8] She terms it 'a ritual incantation of a magic formula, not expected to be taken seriously' even when it seems entirely implausible.[9]

Nevertheless, on some points general understandings seem to have developed that take us beyond the bare terms of Art. 51. One is that to justify the use of armed force in self-defence there must exist an action of some gravity. The argument is not accepted that any trivial injury that a state suffers gives rise to a right of armed self-defence that is proportionate. Border 'skirmishes' are given as examples. A rationale is that otherwise serious conflicts could escalate out of minor border incidents.[10] Another point of agreement is that although hostile economic action might constitute unlawful intervention it is not equivalent to the use of force under Art. 2:4.[11]

---

[7] Eric Pace, 'UN Assembly, 104–11, Urges Truce', *New York Times*, 8 December 1971, www .nytimes.com/1971/12/08/archives/un-assembly-10411-urges-truce-un-vote-follows-pleas-for-action.html. The text of A/RES/2793 (XXVI), adopted 7 December 1971, is available at https://documents-dds-ny.un.org/doc/RESOLUTION/GEN/NR0/328/09/IMG/NR032809. pdf?OpenElement.

[8] Gray (2018), p. 175.

[9] Gray (2018), p. 125.

[10] Gray (2018), p. 157.

[11] See above, Chapter 12, p. 189.

Even when in 2018 the United States ignored a binding Security Council resolution (SC/2231) and used its considerable economic and financial power to bring 'maximum pressure' on Iran the measures though widely seen as violating a binding Security Council resolution were not regarded as an 'armed attack'.[12]

REPRISALS

A distinct type of action that is generally deemed to be prohibited and not possible to justify as self-defence are reprisals involving the use of force.[13] They are singled out in the Friendly Relations Declaration: 'States have a duty to refrain from acts of reprisals involving the use of force'

The rationale for this rule is simple: self-defence is the action to stop or to avert ongoing or initiated offensive actions of physical force. By contrast, reprisals do not stop or avert an attack. They are taken subsequently to attacks as an act of revenge – a tit for tat – for attacks. The argument is advanced, acted upon and sometimes probably valid that predictable armed reprisals may serve as a deterrent. However, reprisals also risk developing into chain reactions and escalations of force levels. In national contexts, central governments have always sought to prevent vendettas and the international community evidently seeks to follow a similar line. A difference, however, is that the international community mostly does not have the ability to react with sufficient vigour against the use of force to satisfy a victim's perceived need for retribution. So long as this is the case it will be difficult to consistently uphold the rule against reprisals in the international sphere.[14]

A much-publicized example was the US drone attack on 3 January 2020 at Baghdad airport killing the Iranian General Qasem Soleimani who had just landed for talks with the Iraqi government. The US claimed that the attack was taken in self-defence under Art. 51 and served to deter Iran from instigating attacks on US forces in Iraq. After a few days, Iran fired missiles inflicting damages but killing no one at two US military bases housed in Iraq. Iran characterized these attacks as a measured and proportionate action in self-defence and in response to the US action. It seems more natural to say that the United States and Iran were engaged in a chain of actions more properly termed reprisals than acts of self-defence. It was striking that after the attack on

---

[12] See above, Chapter 2, p. 26 and Chapter 12, p. 190

[13] See Henderson, p. 240 ff., Gray (2018), p. 160 and 162 and see G.A Res. A/RES/68/268, 9 April 2014. www.ohchr.org/Documents/HRBodies/TB/HRTD/A-RES-68-268_E.pdf.

[14] See below, p. 211 ff.

Baghdad, the whole world saw it as inevitable that Iran would act in reprisal. When it did occur, the world was relieved that it was restrained and did not trigger the United States to yet another attack.[15]

The general understanding was cited above that some types of adversarial action are not seen as equivalents of 'armed attack' – for example skirmishes or economic measures. Hence, they do not justify armed action in self-defence under the narrow licence for self-defence given in Art. 51. There have also emerged understandings that go in the opposite direction and conclude that some actions that do not obviously fit the term 'if an armed attack occurs' may nevertheless justify the exercise of self-defence. The first is cyber-attacks. We have noted that where they are of a kind that will cause physical damage they have come to be regarded as possibly equivalent to a use of force prohibited under Art. 2:4.[16] Military leadership all over the world is now analysing how this potential game changer may be used, to what extent shields can be created against cyber-attacks and to what extent capacity for retaliation in kind or with different weapons may serve to deter. They do not seem to doubt that cyber-attacks could be of a gravity equivalent to 'armed attacks' and justify self-defence.[17]

A broad understanding seems further to exist, though not clearly borne out by any state practice,[18] that the expression *'if an armed attack occurs'* need not necessarily refer to attacks that are ongoing or have begun but could be 'imminent' – about to occur. The argument is that an armed attack 'occurs' not just when armed forces cross territorial borders or bombs explode but already when lethal weapons are irretrievably on the way to their targets. Victims should not be obliged to delay interception until missiles, bombs or grenades impact or cross territorial borders but be able to 'preempt' the attack. The *Caroline case* is invariably cited not only as offering a definition of self-defence but also as justifying self-defence against 'imminent attacks'. When the British destruction of the American ship Caroline in 1837 was discussed between the two states at the highest level and they spoke about *'a necessity of self-defense, instant, overwhelming, leaving no choice of means and no moment for deliberation'*[19] the concrete question they had in mind was the admissibility of military defensive action to forestall an 'action' that had not yet begun but was deemed certain to taken within a very short time.

---

[15] For a description and analysis see note in *American Journal of International Law*, vol. 114 (2020), pp. 313–323; the case is described below, Chapter 15, p. 234.

[16] See Chapter 8, p. 129 and Chapter 12, p. 190.

[17] See Gray (2018), pp. 34–35.

[18] See Gray (2018), p. 175.

[19] https://avalon.law.yale.edu/19th_century/br-1842d.asp.

The Caroline formula may have slumbered for a long while but came much alive in the early years of 2000. It was supported in a 2004 report by a (truly) High-level Panel set up by the UN Secretary-General and comprising a former national security adviser of the US (Scowcroft) a former foreign minister of China (Qian) and a former prime minister of the Russian Federation (Primakov): '...a threatened State, according to long established international law can take military action as long as the threatened attack is imminent, no other means would deflect it and the action is proportionate.'[20]

In his report *'In larger freedom'* the Secretary-General endorsed the position of the High-level Panel.[21] However, neither the High-level Panel nor the Secretary-General has accepted a US claim that 'preventive action' against non-imminent threats could be justified as self-defence. This question will be discussed below.[22]

In the next two chapters, a large number of concrete cases of international interventions will be surveyed illustrating the variety of justifications states have offered despite the fact that self-defence against an armed attack is the only exception open to them under the Charter. It will also be noted how claimed justifications have been judged by the Security Council, General Assembly or the International Court of Justice.[23] It will be seen below that the judgments reflecting their interpretation of the relevant rules, mostly did not relent from a strict reading of the Charter rules even though it sometimes seemed awkward.

---

[20] UN (2004), para. 188.

[21] Doc. A/59/2005, 21 March 2005, https://documents-dds-ny.un.org/doc/UNDOC/GEN/No5/270/78/PDF/No527078.pdf?OpenElement.

[22] See Chapter 15, p. 230 on the 2002 US national security strategy and 'anticipatory self-defence' and Chapter 17, p. 267 on war against terrorism and strikes against the risk of future weapons of mass destruction.

[23] Other writers have painstakingly examined an even larger body of cases. I draw on their work and pay my respect to them. See Brownlie; Franck; Gray; Henderson.

15

Interventions Triggered by Factors Unforeseen at the Adoption of the Charter's Ban on the Interstate Use of Force

In the preceding chapters, we have discussed the aims and limitations of the UN Charter's general prohibition of the interstate use of force. Against that background, we shall in this and the following chapter examine a number of concrete cases of states resorting to the use of force, notably interventions. We shall see how they were justified by the states responsible and – in many cases – how they were judged by the General Assembly, the Security Council, or the International Court of Justice. The present chapter is focused on uses of force and interventions launched in some situations that were probably not contemplated at the time when the Charter's categorical general rule was adopted:

- 'Freedom fighting' during decolonization
- Cold War and post-Cold War struggle for dominance
- Terrorism
- Nuclear weapons development

USE OF FORCE IN THE DECOLONIZATION PROCESS

The decolonization process after World War II was short, and in many cases peaceful, but it also comprised armed conflicts that sometimes were assessed against the background of the UN Charter's prohibition of the use of force. In the world at large, there was much support for the process of emancipation and for 'liberation movements' and their struggle – even when it used armed force. Whether or not the struggle for independence was seen as an interstate process, there was an unwillingness to label it a violation of the prohibition in Art. 2:4 of the threat or use of force. One political approach was to call the struggle 'self-defence' against illegitimate and forcible colonialism.

In UN contexts, the political controversy was often avoided simply by the use of language that could mean different things to different readers.[1] Thus, the term 'struggle' could be used to mean (unlawful) 'armed struggle' to some and (lawful) 'peaceful struggle' to others. An example was Art. 7 of the Declaration on the Definition of Aggression, adopted by the UN in 1974. It referred to peoples deprived of their right to self-determination and *'the right of these peoples to struggle'* and *'to seek and receive support...'*[2] The Friendly Relations Declaration states in its elaboration of the general rule against the use of force: 'Every State has the duty to refrain from any forcible action which deprives peoples referred to in the principle of equal rights and self-determination of their right to self-determination and freedom and independence.'

With the completion of the decolonization process, this strain on the interpretation of the Charter's prohibition of the threat or use of force and article on self-defence was over. It has not reappeared in the context of non-colonial struggles for self-determination.

COLD WAR AND POST–COLD WAR
INTERVENTIONS FOR DOMINANCE

During the Cold War, the major powers were engaged in an intense competition for global dominance. The Soviet camp sought to spread the Communist political and economic system to more countries and continents. The US and many other states sought to preserve and promote liberal, market economy-based systems. As both were nuclear-capable (after 1949) they had a wise aversion against direct confrontations that could escalate. They pursued their ambitions by other means, such as economic aid and political propaganda, but also at times by open armed interventions, or by subversion in which they could deny authorship and state responsibility. Examples are presented below. The case of the US intervention in Nicaragua in the 1980s and the controversy it raised offers rich illustrations of the points made above.

INTERVENTIONS IN NICARAGUA BEFORE THE
INTERNATIONAL COURT OF JUSTICE

Following the overthrow of the dictator Somoza in 1979, the leftist Sandinista movement came into power. Relations with the US were at first friendly but

---

[1]   See Gray, pp. 68 ff.
[2]   Cit. from Gray, p. 70.

changed in 1981 with US claims that the Sandinista government assisted rebel groups in El Salvador. The reactions and actions of the United States should be seen against a background of years of resistance to Cuban influence and Communist penetration in the Caribbean and Central America. Invoking the right of collective self-defence under Article 51 of the UN Charter, the United States provided assistance to the government of El Salvador, including action or support for actions inflicting substantial harm in Nicaragua and support to groups that aimed to overthrow the Sandinista regime. In 1983, there were US-led aerial and naval bombardments of Nicaraguan ports and airports and in 1984 ports were mined under US leadership.[3] There was also economic coercion by the US through the blocking of bank loans to Nicaragua and a total embargo on trade.

In its judgment of the case[4] in which Nicaragua complained about US *'covert aggression'*, the International Court of Justice noted *inter alia* that US Congress had declared that the Nicaraguan government had taken *'significant steps toward establishing a totalitarian Communist dictatorship'* and that the US had stated that its policy toward Nicaragua was not to overthrow the government, nor to force on it a specific system of government. It was only to change the government's behavior, including the termination of support for insurgents in neighboring countries and severance of ties to the Soviet Bloc and Cuba and the return to those countries of their military and security advisors.[5]

The Court's judgment and many of its pronouncements are of great interest to our present discussion on international legal restraints on the use of force.

First, the Court made it clear that the rules of international law that govern the relations between states are not biased to favour any particular system of governance (market economy or Communist). The fundamental principle *'on which the whole of international law rests'* is state sovereignty and the *'freedom of choice of the political, social, economic and cultural system of a State...'*[6] This does not prevent states from exerting influence, but interference by foreign states is deemed wrongful when it uses methods of coercion, whether *'in the direct form of military action or in the indirect form of support for subversive or terrorist armed activities'* to influence the choice of the political, economic,

---

[3] Franck, p. 61.

[4] International Court of Justice, Case concerning military and paramilitary activities in and against Nicaragua, Merits, Judgment of 27 June 1986. Full text is available at www.icj-cij.org/public/files/case-related/70/070-19860627-JUD-01-00-EN.pdf.

[5] Judgment, pp. 56 and 57.

[6] Judgment, p. 133. The Court would have thoroughly disapproved of the aim and practice of the Holy Alliance to intervene against revolutionary upheavals. See above, Chapter 5, p. 97.

social and cultural system, and the formulation of foreign policy.[7] The Court explained it could not contemplate *'opening up a right of intervention by one State against another on the ground that the latter had opted for some particular ideology or political system'*.[8] The Court thus judged rather categorically that the East-West tug of war – including, presumably the aim of the US to bring Nicaragua to change its foreign policy by severing ties with the Soviet Union and Cuba – could not serve as a legal justification for intervention.

Second, the Court focused on the reality that interstate uses of force had evolved from those that the authors of the UN Charter had had primarily in mind and that foresaw direct actions across borders by national armed forces. The methods of the Cold War were well described in the dissenting opinion of Judge Sir Robert Jennings, who spoke about a *'world where power struggles are in every continent carried out by destabilization, interference in civil strife, comfort, aid and encouragement to rebels and the like'*.[9]

Adapting to and facing the new types of struggle, the US and its allies claimed that the international rules on the restraint of force, notably the UN Charter, made no distinction between what was termed 'direct and indirect uses of force'. Both were prohibited.[10] This reasoning was accepted by the Court, as it had earlier been accepted in the texts of the Friendly Relations Declaration. In the view of the court, the term 'armed attacks' in Art. 51 meant:

> not merely action by regular armed forces across an international border but also 'the sending by or on behalf of a State of armed bands, groups of irregulars or mercenaries, which carry out acts of armed force against another State of such gravity as to amount to' (inter alia) an actual armed attack by regular forces, 'or its substantial involvement therein'[11]

It was a significant amplification and updating of key Charter rules.

Third, after an examination of the support given by Nicaragua to rebels in El Salvador, the Court concluded that these had not been of a gravity equivalent to an 'armed attack'. Accordingly, the Court – by a vote of 12–3 – rejected the US claim that its actions in and against Nicaragua were justified under Art. 51 as 'collective self-defense' with El Salvador.[12] Their legality had to be assessed against the yardstick of Art. 2:4. Did they – as Nicaragua contended – violate the ban on the threat or use of force? Examining and judging the various

---

[7] Judgment, p. 108.
[8] Judgment, p. 133.
[9] Judgment, p. 543.
[10] See Judge Schwebel's dissenting opinion in the Nicaragua case, Judgment, p. 336.
[11] Judgment, p. 103.
[12] Judgment, p. 146.

actions taken or led by the United States, the Court provided an authoritative interpretation of the article: Mining Nicaraguan waters was judged to violate the UN ban on the use of force, but overflights of the country's territory were seen as mere violations of sovereignty. The recruiting, training, arming, financing and directing of military and paramilitary involving the use of force in Nicaragua were judged to be a breach of Art. 2:4, but military maneuvers held by the US near the borders of Nicaragua and the mere supply of funds to the *contras* were not. Measures of economic nature were also not seen as an illegal use of force – not even as an illegal intervention.

The judgment has been criticized and three judges dissented. Judge Jennings wrote that the Court's position was '*neither realistic nor just.*' However, in the massively legal reasonings around the judgement, his dissenting opinion also shone a little light on a political aspect of the legal license for 'collective self-defence' in Art. 51. He observed that '*the notion of collective self-defence is open to abuse ... as mere cover for aggression disguised as protection...*' He '*sympathized with the anxiety of the Court*' to define – collective self-defence in terms of some strictness, but queried whether '*perhaps the Court has gone too far*'...[13] Judge Jennings might be understood to have pointed to the question of whether through the claim of *collective self-defence* against relatively minor interventions in El Salvador by Communist camp newcomer Nicaragua, armed actions against Nicaragua had been transformed from an illegal to a lawful way of pursuing the Cold War. In his dissenting opinion, Judge Schwebel maintained that the Court had gravely underestimated the volume of Nicaraguan interventions in El Salvador[14] and Judge Jennings appeared to lean toward that view.

The mining and other significant military activities organized or supported by the US against Nicaragua were parts of efforts to stem the expansion of Communist influence in the Central American region. The Court saw no legal obstacles to various measures with this aim – such as economic sanctions. However, it refused to give 'armed attack' a meaning that would have given the US the 'elbow room' that it wanted in the Cold War and that would have comprised a license to attack Nicaragua under the label of collective self-defence. Perhaps this was not unreasonable. It is striking that in proceedings on Nicaragua's complaints before the Security Council, both France and Great Britain held back on their traditional support for the

---

[13] Judgment, p. 543.

[14] See Judgment, p. 271. See also his editorial comment entitled 'Celebrating A Fraud on the Court' that appeared in the *American Journal of International Law*, Vol. 106, Number 1 (January 2012), p. 102.

United States[15] presumably feeling that their ally abused the rule on collective self-defence.

INTERVENTIONS IN THE DOMINICAN
REPUBLIC (1965) AND GRENADA (1983)

Preceding the Nicaraguan case but following Cuba's joining the Communist camp there were two other Cold War events in which the United States successfully used armed force to prevent left-wing regimes to take control but failed to convince the UN General Assembly of the validity of its justification to use armed force.

On 26 April 1965, US troops invaded the Dominican Republic where a leftist regime had overthrown the government.[16] The matter was promptly brought to the UN Security Council, where the United States defended the action, explaining that the purpose was *'to save the lives of our citizens and the lives of all people. Our goal, in keeping with the principles of the American system, is to help prevent another Communist State in this hemisphere...'* The allusion to the Monroe doctrine excluding non-American interference in the Western hemisphere and, in particular to Communist expansion, was even more explicitly advanced in a speech by US President Johnson: *'The American nations cannot, must not, and will not permit the establishment of another Communist Government in the Western Hemisphere'.*[17] While in the Security Council, a majority of the Council failed to follow the Soviet proposal to condemn the intervention, it was condemned by the General Assembly.[18]

In the other case, US marines landed on the island of Grenada on 25 October 1983 and established control following the overthrow of the Government of Maurice Bishop and appeals for assistance from regional Caribbean organizations. In a first meeting of the Security Council, the US defended the intervention arguing that there had been a *'threat to the peace'* and a *'danger to US citizens'*. At a following meeting, the US representative made the unusually bold claim that the UN Charter rules allowed states to use force to promote democracy. He said that *'the prohibitions of the United Nations Charter are contextual, not absolute. They provide justification for the use of force in pursuit of other values also inscribed in the Charter, such values as freedom, democracy and peace'.*[19]

---

[15] Franck, p. 61.
[16] This account is based on Beckman (2005), pp. 115–125; Franck, p. 72 and Fulbright (1966), p. 82 ff.
[17] Cit. from Beckman, p. 118.
[18] Franck, p. 73. UN General Assembly Official Records (XX) 1352 meeting.
[19] Cit. from Beckman, p. 158.

Others held that the action was not compatible with the Charter. Outside the UN the UK Prime Minister, Margaret Thatcher, commented that if the rule were to be that the US would enter '*wherever Communism reigns against the will of the people ... we are going to have really terrible wars in the world*'. In the UN General Assembly, a resolution was adopted by a strong majority deploring the armed intervention '*as a flagrant violation of international law and the independence, sovereignty and territorial integrity of that State...*'[20]

It is hard to avoid the assessment that the arguments advanced to defend the armed intervention – protection of nationals, law and order, and regional action etc. – were chosen as more legally 'respectable' than any claimed right to secure a *regime change* to prevent Grenada from becoming a second Communist island in the Caribbean.

SOVIET INTERVENTIONS IN HUNGARY (1956) AND CZECHOSLOVAKIA (1968)

US armed interventions during the Cold War to prevent Communist expansion in the Western hemisphere had a counterpart in Soviet armed interventions against the crumbling of Communist regimes in their satellite states.[21] The first case occurred when Soviet troops marched into Hungary in November 1956 to oust the Imre Nagy regime that had come to power and that had declared an intention to leave the Soviet-led Warsaw Pact and be neutral in the Cold War. The intervention was promptly taken up in the Security Council, where the Soviet Union argued that the Warsaw pact was acting in self-defence against '*indirect aggression*' and that subversive Western activities had been behind the uprising that had brought Imre Nagy to power. A draft resolution condemning the intervention was supported by nearly the whole Council but was vetoed by the Soviet Union. When the matter later was taken up at an emergency session of the General Assembly, a strong majority adopted a resolution that condemned the intervention as a 'violation of the Charter' and called on the Soviet Union to withdraw.[22]

A second case occurred more than a decade later when in April 1968 an armed intervention by Warsaw Pact states under Soviet leadership ousted the government of Alexander Dubček and ended the 'Prague Spring' in

---

[20] Cit. from Beckman, pp. 159 and 162 and *Keesing's Contemporary Archives*, p. 32617.
[21] See, for instance, Ouimet (2003), pp. 11–37. Also see Rostow (1981).
[22] Account based on Franck, pp. 70–71.

Czechoslovakia and the policy of 'Socialism with a human face'. Although representatives of the ousted Dubček government denied having issued any invitation for the intervention or having received any support from the West, the intervention was defended as a right of 'collective self-defense'. Terms were used that sounded like a Russian echo of the Monroe doctrine – forbidding any foreign interference in the world of the Warsaw Pact. The Soviet Foreign Minister Andrei Gromyko declared that *'socialist States cannot and will not permit the vital interests of socialism to be infringed or encroachments to be made upon the inviolability of the frontiers of the socialist commonwealth and hence upon international peace'.*[23]

A resolution to condemn the intervention and urging the Warsaw Pact to end it was supported by a majority of the Security Council but failed adoption as the Soviet Union cast a veto.[24]

RUSSIAN INTERVENTIONS IN GEORGIA (2008) AND UKRAINE (2014 AND 2022)

With the end of the Cold War, the collapse of expansive Soviet Communism, the liberation of the East European Soviet satellite states and the general acceptance of the market-economy model, ideology-driven interventions disappeared. Nevertheless, neither nuclear superpower abandoned its ambitions to exert influence. In the case of the United States, these have been global and led to significant action ignoring UN rules on the use of force in the case of Iraq (2003).[25] Russian ambitions have been directed primarily at their own region, Central Asia, the Middle East and Africa.

The Russian armed interventions in Georgia (2008) and Ukraine (2014 and 2022) will be discussed below. The Russian armed participation in the Syrian civil war has been viewed with anger by many, but it has not been criticized as unlawful as it was requested by the generally – though often reluctantly – recognized Syrian government. Intervention through Russia-linked mercenaries (Wagner units) in Libya has taken place[26] against the (shaky) recognized Libyan regime while their presence in some African states (Central African Republic, Mali and perhaps others) are probably based on invitations by – shaky – governments.

---

[23] Andre Gromyko, plenary address to UN General Assembly, A/PV.1679, 3 October 1968, paragraph 78, https://digitallibrary.un.org/record/750011?ln=en.

[24] See Franck, pp. 73–75.

[25] See above, Chapter 3, p. 42.

[26] See Marten (2019).

THE RUSSIAN ARMED INTERVENTION IN GEORGIA (2008)[27]

As verified by an EU-appointed fact-finding commission, on 7 August 2008 an armed attack was launched by Georgia on the capital of Ossetia, Tskhinvali.[28] It followed periods of tension and conflict between Georgia and Russia. A number of people were killed including some Russian 'peace-keepers' stationed there under a 1992 agreement that provided for a ceasefire, military observers, and a mixed control commission. Russian forces were rushed in from North Ossetia and after evicting all Georgian military forces there some 25,000 Russians moved on into Georgia and took control also of Abkhazia, while the Russian navy entered Georgian/Abkhazian waters and defeated Georgian navy units.

Already on 12 August, French President Sarkozy, then Chairman of the European Council, went to Moscow and was able to bring about a ceasefire and a commitment to the withdrawal of Russian troops. A little later the two regions declared themselves independent and on 26 August 2008 they were not only recognized by Russia but also by less than a handful of other states. Russian troops were gradually withdrawn from Georgian territory, while the two non-recognized units have remained heavily dependent upon Russia. Relations between Georgia and Russia have continued edgy with Georgia strengthening its economic and political links with the EU and the US and military links with NATO.

When bringing the conflict before the Security Council on 8 August 2008, Russia claimed its intervention had been in self-defence against the Georgian armed attack on South Ossetia and to provide protection for Russian nationals. Other members of the Council were critical but no resolution was tabled. The EU fact-finding commission considered that Russia had been justified to invoke self-defence, but found the military campaign into mainland Georgia disproportionate and therefore not justified. Nor did it consider the protection of Russian nationals in South Ossetia – including a generous issuing of Russian passports – a valid ground for intervention.

One may speculate what the main reasons were that triggered Russia to embark on a use of armed force that was disproportionate (to the Georgian actions) and therefore unlawful. Some in the West interpreted the action as revanchism – a come-back of a greater Russia. It is submitted that another incentive may be more likely: A report from NATO's summit meeting at

---

[27] See above, Chapter 3, p. 43 A good account is found in Berner (2020) pp. 237–263. See also Bildt (2022), pp. 269–310 and Hafkin (2010) and Nichol (2009).

[28] For an overview, see Chris Harris, 'Europe's Forgotten War: The Georgia-Russia Conflict Explained a Decade On', *Euronews*, 7 August 2018 www.euronews.com/2018/08/07/europe-s-forgotten-war-the-georgia-russia-conflict-explained-a-decade-on.

Bucharest on 4 April 2008 – some months before the Russian action – notes[29] that the Alliance *'welcomes Ukraine's and Georgia's Euro-Atlantic aspirations for membership in NATO. We agree today that these countries will become members of NATO'*. The concise published record does not report that the sentence was a compromise: US President Bush had made a strong push for the membership of the two countries, but France and Germany had resisted. It does not seem farfetched to suggest that Russia may have wanted to demonstrate to Georgia and to NATO countries that Russia would not tolerate Georgia becoming a member of NATO and seeing the military alliance move up to its border. The Georgian ambition to join NATO as a member was not advanced by Russia as a justification for the intervention. In its 1975 elaboration of the principle of sovereignty and respect for the rights inherent in sovereignty, the Helsinki Final Act declared that the participating states: 'have the right to belong or not to belong to international organizations, to be or not to be a party to bilateral or multilateral treaties including the right to be or not to be a party to treaties of alliance; they also have the right to neutrality.'

Further, Russia could hardly argue that the deployment of NATO military installations in Georgia near Russia would constitute an 'armed attack' under Art. 51. It might have been difficult even to claim that such deployment would constitute a threat of force banned under Art. 2:4. Nor did Russia do so. Rather, without any verbal protest but through action, Russia made clear that Georgian membership and consequent NATO expansion up to the Russian-Georgian border would be seen as defiance of Russian regional domination and invite trouble. As seen already in the Cuban crisis in 1962, a military deployment at arm's length distance (from the US) may be a measure perceived as a provocation and an unacceptable threat. Russia, not perceiving any risk of Western military reaction to an intervention in Georgia, evidently did not feel restrained by the norm in UN Charter Art. 2:4. Nor did concern for negative international political reactions prove a hurdle. A price materialized in the shape of the non-recognition of South Ossetia and Abkhazia as states and a deterioration in the climate for East-West cooperation.

THE RUSSIAN ARMED INTERVENTIONS IN THE UKRAINE (2014–PRESENT)

Like the intervention in Georgia, Russia's seizing of Crimea in 2014 and engineering and support of uprisings in East Ukraine, were parts of efforts to retain

---

[29] NATO, 'Bucharest Summit Declaration', 3 April 2008, para. 23, www.nato.int/cps/en/natolive/official_texts_8443.htm.

regional dominance and influence. Different from the case of Georgia, however, Russia did not claim a right to use force in self-defence in Ukraine. Rather, Russia flatly denied that it had used force: it had sent no soldiers to Crimea, and Russians in Donbas might have been 'volunteers' but not Russian soldiers. The world's reading of the events was different. What were the incentives for the Russian intervention in 2014?

In both Georgia and Ukraine, the economic and political system of the West and membership in both the European Union and NATO as well as greater independence from Moscow held an attraction. In Ukraine, an agreement on economic association with the European Union was ready toward the end of 2013. Russia viewed it with increasing concern as a tool that would make the Ukraine ship drift away from the quay to which it had historically been moored. In November 2013, President Yanukovych's refusal to sign the agreement set in motion a drama that led to his own ousting in February 2014 and to the Russian seizure of Crimea and the fomenting and support of upheaval in East Ukraine.

In the Crimea that had been given by the Soviet Union to Ukraine in 1954, Russian forces blockaded several airports. Armed Russian soldiers in uniforms without nationality markings – 'little green men' – moved to control strategic points. After a referendum had been organized showing majority support for Crimea to join Russia, a vote in the Crimean parliament requested incorporation of the Crimea into Russia. At a session on 16 February 2014, the Russian Duma responded positively and Crimea was again in Russian eyes a part of Russia. Ukraine protested and most countries refused recognition.

The other Russian action consisted in the offering of Russian passports to many people in East Ukraine (in the same way as had been practiced in South Ossetia in 2008) and the organization of and assistance to pro-Russian separatists in Donetsk and Lugansk that took control over areas bordering to Russia. In 2014 they held (unrecognized) referendums for the independence of the region. Independence of the Donetsk and Lugansk People's Republics was declared on 12 May 2014. A low-level armed conflict followed that caused many thousands of casualties and came to an uncertain ceasefire only by 2020.

It seems likely that Russia considered it a vital interest to maintain a continued dominant influence both in Georgia and Ukraine and, in particular, that neither state should become a member of NATO. There was a conviction (in Russia) that the West had helped to engineer the ousting of President Yanukovych and a concern that the proud Russian naval Black Sea base in Sevastopol could become a naval base for NATO. The long-term interest in upholding the international order of the UN Charter and the Helsinki Declaration yielded to the perceived immediate vital interest. The risk that the West would go to an armed confrontation in Russia's neighbourhood was deemed to be very low.

The shrouded manner in which the intervention has been pursued in Ukraine shows that the subversive approaches that we associate with the Cold War were still alive. They make it possible for author states to deny any formal state responsibility for actions they know are breaches of legal obligations under the UN Charter. The calculation becomes ineffective, however, when the pretense is not believed by anybody. Most states saw the chain of events as an illegal annexation (of Crimea) and a violation of the UN Charter prohibition of the threat or use of force. It was not made less so by the surreptitious manner in which it was carried out. In a resolution adopted by a vote of 100–11–24 on 27 March 2014 the UN General Assembly affirmed the territorial integrity of Ukraine and declared the referendum in Crimea invalid.[30] Individual states and the EU followed with condemnations, economic sanctions and non-recognition.

The Russian actions in Ukraine in 2014 may have been designed to serve several perceived vital aims – including that of preventing integration of Ukraine into NATO. However, the violations of the international legal order – even though denied – were costly. Rather than retaining great influence in Ukraine, the actions alienated Ukraine from Russia. They also led the West to reduce relations with Russia, adopt economic sanctions and suspend Russia from membership in the G8.

The Russian Invasion of Ukraine in 2022

Copying its line of action at the intervention in Georgia in 2008 to recognize Ossetia and Abkhazia as independent states, Russia officially recognized the two self-declared republics Donetsk and Lugansk People's Republics as states on 21 February 2022. After the long period during which Russia had amassed troops along its border with Ukraine, it launched a military invasion of Ukraine on 24 February 2022. Contradicting all reports about extensive hostilities, President Putin, declared that it was not 'war' but a 'special military operation'. His choice of language testified to his effort to play down a military adventure that he must have realized violated the UN Charter and perhaps would be unwelcome to a part of Russian public opinion. Purporting to respond to the requests of the newly recognized states for armed help against alleged attacks by the central Ukrainian government, Russia could now claim that its invasion was collective self-defence. As the offensive action proceeded,

---

[30] UN General Assembly, A/Res 68/262, adopted 27 March 2014.

the objective declared was 'denazifying and demilitarizing' Ukraine, and no efforts were made to hide that the 'special military operation' was pursued with the aim of conquering or in some way controlling Ukrainian territory. The UN General Assembly condemned the 'violation of the territorial integrity and sovereignty of Ukraine' and demanded Russia reverse its recognition. The resolution A/RES/ES-11/1 was adopted with the support of 141 countries.[31]

At the end of September 2022, when Russia had suffered serious setbacks in its 'special military operation' a dramatic shift occurred. As described in Chapter 3, the Russian government decided on partial mobilization, and arranged sham referenda in which inhabitants in occupied regions were asked to approve their regions' joining Russia and the Russian Duma approved annexation. The 'special military operation' could no longer be seen by anyone as an 'intervention' with limited objectives, but only as a war of conquest.

THE USE OF ARMED FORCE AGAINST TERRORIST GROUPS HAS PUT UN CHARTER RULES ON SELF-DEFENCE UNDER STRAIN AND LED TO SOME NEW READINGS

The 9/11 2001 attack on the New York World Trade Center and the other targets in the US-led President Bush to declare 'war on terror' – a term foreshadowing that the US would base its future actions against terrorists and terrorism not only on national criminal law but also on rules governing the use of armed force between states. In the years that have followed the 9/11 events, the US and some other states have sought, as we shall see, to widen these rules to give greater freedom for the use of military force in the combatting of terrorism. However, even prior to 9/11 2001 terrorist activities had led to pressure for more legal elbow room for military action. A few cases described below will show what was demanded.

When the authors of the UN Charter provided in Art. 51 that states had an inherent right of self-defence if an attack occurs, they were not thinking of an attack by non-state terrorists. They had states in mind. Did they then mean that states had no right to defend themselves against 'attacks' by non-state actors? Surely not. Terrorism has deep roots in history and so have states' means of defending themselves against it. Politically motivated attacks by non-state actors aiming at creating fear or disruption or hitting rulers or a government have a long tradition. Examples from the 20th century are the 'red brigades'

---

[31] See Matt Robinson and Alessandra Prentice, 'Rebels Appeal to Join Russia After East Ukraine Referendum,' Reuters, May 13, 2014, www.reuters.com/article/us-ukraine-crisis-idUSBREA400 LI20140513.

in Italy and the 'red army' (Baader-Meinhof group) in Germany. Defences against such groups have traditionally been provided by national police and security and the terrorists have been prosecuted under domestic law regardless of whether they perpetrated their acts in their home country or in another country. Most terrorist acts continue to be handled in this way – for instance the large attacks in the London subway on 7 July 2005. Although combating and investigating such actions often call for international cooperation, the actions are judged under national criminal law and the legal status of the terrorists remains that of national wrongdoers unless they develop into organized revolutionary movements with armed forces under responsible command, carrying their arms openly and respecting the laws of war.[32]

Nevertheless, with increasing globalization several non-state groups and movements have emerged with international networks and aim to hurt particular governments through isolated violent actions. Al-Qaeda located mainly in countries in the Middle East but with cells in many countries and with an agenda to hit the US and some other countries is the best-known example. Countering the actions of such groups remains a task for national police and security in victim and target states and their cooperating counterparties in other countries – including countries where groups perpetrating terrorist actions are located. However, as we shall see in this section, in some situations even before 9/11 terrorist actions have triggered countermeasures that are regulated under international law, notably the use of military force across national frontiers.

CASE OF US USING FORCE IN SELF-DEFENCE IN RESPONSE TO LIBYAN TERRORISM (1986)[33]

This is an exceptional case of a state that acts like a terrorist group of non-state actors and performs sporadic violent attacks on targets in various countries. Libya under Gaddafi organized such attacks on targets linked to the US. The actions were investigated and pursued legally not only under the laws of the countries where they occurred. As described below, they were responded to also by the use of military force – through the US bombing targets in Libya.

On 5 April 1986, a bomb exploded in a Berlin night club that was frequented by American soldiers. Two Americans were killed and a large number of

---

[32] For a review of treaties relating to the combat of terrorism, see United Nations Office of Counter-Terrorism, 'International Legal Instruments', www.un.org/counterterrorism/international-legal-instruments.

[33] The account is based on the description in Franck, op.cit., p. 89 and an article by Intoccia (1987).

people were injured. The attack was traced by the US to agents sent by Libya. It had been preceded by a period of violent terrorist activities sponsored by Libya and directed especially against US targets. Two weeks after the attack – on 15 April 1986 – the US sent bombers from bases in the UK (but not permitted overflight by Spain and France) to attack Libyan targets that included President Gaddafi's headquarters. The attack lasted only half an hour but 37 people were killed. The case was brought before the UN Security Council, where the US made a reference to retaliation, but as the main justification for the use of force against Libya, the US invoked self-defence to deter ongoing and further terrorism. In the Security Council, a resolution condemning the US was stopped by three Western vetoes, but in the General Assembly, a resolution with a similar condemnation was adopted by 79 votes in favour, 28 against and 51 abstentions.[34]

The US emphasis on *self-defence* was understandable given the terrorist activities that had repeatedly been directed against US-related targets by the Gaddafi regime. Yet, it strained the meaning of Art. 51 to claim that armed actions taken two weeks after attacks could be 'self-defence'. They did not prevent or avert attacks. The response looks more like revenge – reprisals – and perhaps a signal meant to deter further acts of terrorist violence. However, in view of the declared UN consensus that reprisals are prohibited, the US could not invoke this line as justification.[35]

In the circumstances, the US chose to stretch the meaning of the letters of Charter Art. 51. While relying on German authorities to investigate the terrorist deed as an isolated action in Berlin and to persecute the actors under German law, the US – not unreasonably – viewed the terrorist use of armed force against US related targets in Berlin and elsewhere also as the latest part of a chain of sporadic armed attacks by the state of Libya. This, it was claimed, made it part of an ongoing armed action against the US and justified US action in self-defence – under Art. 51 – against the state of Libya.

Could the United States have used some non-armed response, as urged in the General Assembly resolution? Maybe. The French and Spanish refusals to allow overflight for the US bombers suggest at least unease over the belligerent response that the US chose. However, to the United States the matter looked different. The action chosen did not run any significant political or military risk (but one of the US planes was lost). While it was uncertain whether punishment would make Gaddafi change his ways, the United States

---

[34] UN General Assembly, A/RES/41/38 adopted on 20 November 1986.
[35] See above, p. 209, and see Gray, p. 205, who notes that the prohibition of reprisals has led the US and Israel to try to stretch the meaning of Art. 51.

would at least have shown all that it was not a paper tiger. The straining of a UN Charter provision regarded as unresponsive to needs in times of terrorism may not have caused any qualms in the US. Nothing more serious than a reprimand by the General Assembly could be expected.

The General Assembly also faced a dilemma given the facts and the rules of the book. The voting figures probably reflected some ambivalence to condemn the US attack as a use of force in violation of the Charter. The terrorist types of violence sponsored by Gaddafi's Libya enjoyed no sympathy in the world. Perhaps many of the votes condemning the US attack could be ascribed to a common wish to tell the guy with the big stick that, even if terror acts prompted him to seek revenge by the use of force, he should carefully consider at least the requirement of proportionality when reacting. Be that as it may, it is clear that Gaddafi's practice of terrorism drove the US to use armed force and pursue legal arguments designed to soften the rigid rule of Art. 51 drafted some thirty years earlier. The US reprisal action did not make Gaddafi change his ways: sabotage on his instructions led to the crash at Lockerbie in Scotland on 21 December 1988 of a Pan Am airliner on its way from Frankfurt to the US.

The case of US reprisal against Libya was one in which armed action taken was claimed to be *self-defence* although it was separate from and taken much after the terrorist attack that it was supposed to defend against, The General Assembly condemned the US attack but expressed no view on this specific legal issue. Nor was any light shed on it in the case described below where the focus was on the condemning of terrorist actions – not on the US attacks that were launched two weeks after these actions and claimed to have been justified as self-defence.

US ATTACKS IN AFGHANISTAN AND SUDAN FOLLOWING AL-QAEDA ORGANIZED ATTACKS ON US EMBASSIES NAIROBI AND DAR-ES-SALAM (1998)

On 7 August 1998, the terrorist group al Qaeda carried out actions that destroyed the US embassies in Nairobi and Dar es Salaam, killing hundreds of people.[36] The attacks were promptly condemned by the Security Council.[37] Two weeks later – on 21 August 1998 – the United States launched an attack by air on targets in Afghanistan thought to be a training camp for members of Al-Qaeda. Another attack was launched on a pharmaceutical factory that was

[36] The event is described in Franck, p. 94.
[37] S/RES/1189, 13 August 1998

located near Khartoum in Sudan and – erroneously – suspected to be linked to Al-Qaeda and engaged in the production of chemical weapons. The US reported its attacks to the Security Council and justified them as self-defence under Art. 51. Libya and Iraq condemned the US attacks but no further resolution was adopted. Although Sudan complained to the Council about the – erroneous – US attack the issue was not placed on the agenda and a Sudanese lawsuit seeking compensation was dismissed by a federal US court as under the US 'political question doctrine' the courts 'cannot assess the merits of the President's decision to launch an attack on a foreign target...'.[38]

Like the US attack in Libya in 1986 the attacks in Afghanistan and the erroneous attack on the factory in Sudan were not self-defence in the sense of impeding or preventing ongoing actions. Launched sometime after the terrorist actions, they looked more like punishments or reprisals. However, no view was expressed by the Council on the issue of whether subsequent isolated responses directed against non-state actors could qualify as 'self-defense'.

As in the case of Libya, the US faced a dilemma. On the one hand, it had a stark and understandable political need for revenge. On the other hand, there was a prohibition of reprisals, a paucity of plausible non-armed responses and an Art. 51 that offered no obvious line on which the US could rest its action. With respect to Sudan, Afghanistan and Libya, the US chose to show that it was no paper tiger and recognized that its actions as a great military power raised little physical and political risk. Again, the United States claimed the right of self-defence on a strained reading of Art. 51, a provision that undoubtedly was felt inadequate and too rigid by a US leadership facing a world with many terrorist groups with their eyes fixed on the United States. Any hope on the US side that its response would help to deter Al-Qaeda from further terrorist acts was sadly negated three years later when the group launched history's most infamous terrorist action – the 9/11 attack on targets in New York and Washington.

THE 9/11 2001 TERRORISM-GENERATED ARMED RESPONSE AND IMPACTED ON THE READING OF THE RULE PROVIDING A RIGHT OF USING FORCE IN SELF-DEFENCE

Sharing universal shock and indignation over the 9/11 attack the Security Council promptly and unanimously adopted a resolution in which *inter alia* it

---

[38] 'El-Shifa v. United States', US Court of Appeals, District of Columbia Circuit, 27 March 2009, https://casetext.com/case/el-shifa-pharmaceutical-v-us; 'US court dismisses 1998 Sudan missile strike suit', Reuters, 9 June 2010, www.reuters.com/article/ozatp-usa-sudan-lawsuit-20100609-idAFJOE65805A20100609. The Supreme Court later refused to reconsider the dismissal of the case: www.cbsnews.com/news/court-wont-reconsider-sudan-lawsuit-dismissal/.

recognized the *'inherent right of individual and collective self-defense in accordance with the Charter'* and called on all states *'to bring to justice the perpetrators'* and stressed *'that those responsible for aiding, supporting and harboring the perpetrators...'* should be *'held accountable'*.[39] Although this resolution was adopted several weeks before the US invasion of Afghanistan on 7 October, the explicit recognition of the right to self-defence looked, in the situation that had arisen, almost like a prior authorization of an armed response. It also settled some issues that had not been answered in the cases discussed above and it became a starting point for assertions of several rights that allegedly were or should be included in the right to 'self-defence' against terrorism.

A first point settled was that Art. 51 does not only limit a right of self-defence to cases where armed attacks have been performed by states but also extends to cases of terrorist actions carried out by non-state actors. A second point settled was that, provided terrorist actions were of sufficient gravity, they could be seen as 'armed attacks' giving a right to self-defence regardless of whether they were carried out as isolated sporadic acts or as parts of a chain of hostile actions.

While these conclusions of the Security Council served to soften some of the rigidity of Art. 51, it should not be overlooked that what the resolution of 12 September 'recognized' was a right to self-defence *'in accordance with the Charter'*. Only resolutions adopted after the US invasion could – and did – imply the settling of a third point, namely, that the action of 'self-defense' authorized by Art. 51 could come weeks after the armed terrorist attack.

A fourth and crucial point settled by these resolutions although by implication rather than by express language was that the specific US armed actions on Afghan territory – in particular attacks on areas where Al-Qaeda was thought to locate – were justified as self-defence even though the US was not at war with the state of Afghanistan. It cannot be concluded, however, that the Security Council implied that such a right could be exercised on any sovereign state's territory from which terrorists were thought to have operated or been present. The mistaken US attack on the chemical factory in Sudan described above was a telling example of where such unrestricted rights might lead.

Apart from the case where a state has given its consent to an attack on its territory – which Sudan had not – and in the case of Afghanistan – it is not easy to identify in which cases and conditions armed action in self-defence could be directed to territory in states with which the victim state is not at war. In its resolution the day after 9/11, the Council mentions one circumstance that might more generally offer valid reasons for armed action against the territory of a non-consenting state: it stresses that those *'responsible for aiding,*

---

[39] S/Res/1368 (2001), 12 September 2001. Emphasis added.

supporting or harboring the perpetrators ... will be held accountable'. In a resolution somewhat later – on 28 September – but still before the US began its
armed action, the Council quoted the Friendly Relations Declaration: *'every
State has the duty to refrain from ... assisting ... in terrorist acts in another
State or acquiescing in organized activities in its territory directed toward the
commission of such acts'.*[40]

Such considerations have been advanced for widening the right of using
force in self-defence against terrorist armed attacks to apply to states 'unable
or unwilling 'to take action against terrorists within their borders. While the
claim of such a right, like a right to the hot pursuit of terrorists into foreign
territory,[41] may not sound unreasonable, it has neither received broad nor
authoritative support. It raises concerns about the risk of unrestrained use
of force by strong states using the most modern techniques. The attack in
Sudan following erroneous intelligence[42] is a case in point. Another illustration of this risk was seen in the claim of the US and other states that they were
free to take armed action in Syrian territory in collective self-defence with
Iraq against the terrorist ISIS movement. The Syrian government, which was
ignored by the intervening states, objected that it was not unwilling to combat
the ISIS terrorists and demanded to be consulted.[43]

Another – controversial – way of generally widening the freedom to use armed
force in self-defence has been to argue that the broadly supported right to the
action in self-defence against *'imminent threat'*[44] should extend to *'anticipatory'*
action. This argument will be discussed below. In the present context, it suffices to note that if the argument were accepted in conjunction with the notion
that terrorist movements can constitute *'continuing imminent threats'* the consequence would appear to be constant freedom for military action, for instance
'targeted killings' of any alleged terrorists without consent of a territorial state.[45]

THE USE OF FORCE UNDER THE US
NATIONAL SECURITY STRATEGY 2002

The drive to widen the right to self-defence against terrorist organizations and
'rogue states' was nowhere more bluntly articulated than in the US National

---

[40] S/RES/1373, 28 September 2001.
[41] Turkey's pursuit into Iraq of allegedly terrorist Kurdish units evoked protests by the Government
of Iraq. See Gray, p. 144. For a detailed study of the question, see Mahmoudi (2021).
[42] Above, p. 227.
[43] See Gray, pp. 116 and 238.
[44] Gray, p. 250.
[45] Gray, pp. 233 and 234.

Security Strategy of 2002. It was issued on 17 September, about one year after the 9/11 attack that caused the death of thousands of people and the humiliation of the lone superpower. The administration of President Bush the younger, aspiring to lead the world, declared that

> For centuries, international law recognized that nations need not suffer an attack before they can lawfully take action to defend themselves against forces that present an imminent danger of attack. Legal scholars and international jurists often conditioned the legitimacy of preemption on the existence of an imminent threat – most often a visible mobilization of armies, navies and air forces preparing to attack.
>
> We must adapt the concept of imminent threat to the capabilities and objectives of today's adversaries. Rogue states and terrorists do not seek to attack us using conventional means. They rely on ... the use of weapons of mass destruction – weapons that can be easily concealed, delivered covertly, and used without warning. (Emphasis added)

The central message was that:

> The United States has long maintained the option of preemptive actions to counter a sufficient threat to our national security. The greater the threat, the greater the risk of inaction – and the more compelling the case for taking anticipatory action to defend ourselves, even if uncertainty remains as to the time and place of the enemy's attack. To forestall or prevent such hostile acts by our adversaries, the United States will, if necessary, act preemptively (Emphasis added)

Thus, the US had contented itself with the right to take armed action in self-defence before an attack, when such an attack was '*imminent*', terming this '*preemption*'. However, in a world with terrorists (Al-Qaeda), rogue states (Libya) and weapons of mass destruction (Iraq) the US now chose to claim a right to use force in self-defence in case of attacks that were '*sufficient*' and '*anticipated*' although there was '*uncertainty as to time and place*'.

The strategy termed such action, too, '*preemptive*' though most writers would call them '*preventive*'. This purported replacement of the notion of 'imminent threats' with 'potential threats' or 'continuingly imminent threats' (!) also appears to be a significant extension of the *Caroline* doctrine (discussed in Chapter 14) and has been viewed with general skepticism in the context of the fight against terrorism.[46]

As illustrations of when claimed widened rights of use of force in self-defence against terrorism have led the United States, two much publicized

[46] Gray, p. 248 ff.

cases – the killing of Osama bin Laden, leader of the non-state terrorist group Al-Qaeda and Qasem Soleimani, the head of Iran's Quds Force that the US – but not other states – had branded as 'terrorist'.

THE KILLING OF OSAMA BIN LADEN[47]

On 1 May 2011, a group of US Navy Seals carried out a spectacular operation at a compound in Abbottabad in Pakistan, some 60 km North-East of Rawalpindi. This was the secret residence of Osama bin Laden, the leader of the non-state terrorist movement Al-Qaeda, that had been responsible for the attack ten years earlier on the World Trade Center in New York and the Pentagon in Washington. Raiding the house, the group killed Bin Laden.

Leaving aside questions relating to the laws of war and human rights, we ask if and how a US armed operation into Pakistan could be justified? In the absence of a specific justification an armed lethal operation into the territory of a sovereign state with which the US was at peace would constitute a violation of the UN Charter's prohibition of the 'threat or use of force'.

One sufficient answer would be consent to the operation by Pakistan. Was there some prior consent or post-action acquiescence by Pakistan's government? The evidence seems somewhat contradictory. The flight into Pakistan by US helicopters appears to have been authorized, but whether there had been consent by the government of Pakistan to the armed action is less clear. Pakistan's prime minister at the time appears to have warned the US that Pakistan would defend its air space if American forces were to mount '*another*' raid on terrorists suspected of hiding inside the country. There is no evidence of Pakistani protests. The Security Council issued a statement in which it '*recognize(d) this critical development and other accomplishments made in the efforts in the fight against terrorism*'.[48] Calling the action an 'accomplishment' must mean that there was no concern in the Council that the action constituted an unlawful use of armed force

Curiously, the US Attorney-General at the time, Eric Holder, claimed that the raid and the killing were lawful as actions of '*national self-defense*'. The claim shows how widely the US thought the plea of self-defence could be used in connection with terrorism. At the time of the lethal action, the US was

---

[47] Much has been written about the case. See, for instance Deeks, 'Pakistan's sovereignty and the killing of Osama Bin Laden' in ASIL, *Insights* vol. 15, issue 11, 5 May 2011 and see paper by Arabella Thorp. 'Killing Osama bin Laden: has justice been done?' UK House of Commons Library, Standard Note SN/IA/5967, 16 May 2011.

[48] UN SC Press Notice SC/10239.

still actively engaged in the armed struggle against the Taliban movement in Afghanistan and in Pakistani areas bordering Afghanistan. However, although Al-Qaeda still existed and was active in several states, including Syria, it was no longer a major active adversary and it appears uncertain whether in 2011 bin Laden exercised any real control or had been placed in forced exile by the movement.[49]

Was it the US view that the action could be justified as self-defence against current, imminent or potential armed attacks, or a ten-year delayed response to 9/11? The reference to self-defence appears like a mere construction to deny wrongdoing but it shows also how elastic and permissive the US interpretation of the right to self-defence had become. The real explanation for the action in Pakistan was not, of course, a need for self-defence – or even deterrence – but a strongly and understandably felt need in the US for retribution for many acts by Al-Qaeda against the US, notably the 9/11 attack.

A news article in the *New York Times* in 2015 sheds some interesting light on legal considerations in Washington before the bin Laden action.[50] It appears that several legal memoranda were prepared. One discussed the problem that '*when two countries are not at war, international law generally forbids one to use force on the other's soil without consent*'. True. That the question was raised suggests that there existed no clear prior consent by Pakistan. Nor was it suggested that one should be asked, because if Bin Laden's presence was, in fact, authorized he might have been helped to escape. So the lawyers recommended a '*unilateral military incursion*' – an armed intervention – that could be claimed to be lawful if a state to be invaded was '*unwilling or unable*' to suppress a threat to others coming from its soil.

It was seen as an awkward line to argue vis-a-vis Pakistan and, the lawyers noted, also a line that did not have general recognition. Yet, they saw no other way out. Interestingly, the article states that '*while the lawyers believed that Mr. Obama was bound to obey domestic law, they also believed that he could decide to violate international law when authorizing a "covert" action...*' Whether correct or not their assessment suggests that in Washington US domestic law inspired greater respect than international law – at least for covert actions. It is not daring to guess that the political consequences of a disregard for international law were seen as more manageable – at least for a superpower – than those of domestic law.

---

[49] See Gareth Porter, 'Exclusive Investigation: The Truth Behind the Official Story of Finding Bin Laden', Truthout, 2 May 2002, https://truthout.org/articles/finding-bin-laden-the-truth-behind-the-official-story/.

[50] Charlie Savage, 'How 4 Federal Lawyers Paved the Way to Kill Osama bin Laden', *New York Times*, 26 October 2015, www.nytimes.com/2015/10/29/us/politics/obama-legal-authorization-osama-bin-laden-raid.html.

THE KILLING OF IRANIAN GENERAL QASEM SOLEIMANI ON 3 JANUARY 2020 AT BAGHDAD AIRPORT, IRAQ[51]

On 3 January 2020, the US using a drone killed the head of Iran's powerful Quds Forces, General Qasem Soleimani and several other high Iranian military and Iraqi Shia-related militias as they were leaving from Baghdad International Airport and on their way to meet with the Iraqi government. In the period before the action, there had been various missile exchanges between US forces based in Iraq and Iraqi militia groups that may have been supported by the Quds Force. The US attack was then followed by the state of Iran some days later firing missiles from Iranian territory on Iraqi military bases hosting US forces. The US operation at Baghdad was as dramatic and sensational as that which had killed Osama Bin Laden nine years earlier at Abbottabad, but there were important differences. In particular, what prevented the operation in Pakistan from being an encroachment on the country's sovereignty and a breach of the use of force in international relations was the apparent acquiescence by the state. Such consent was missing in Iraq, both before and after the action at Baghdad.

In separate letters to the Security Council on 8 January, both the US and Iran claimed that their actions had been taken in self-defence. The US letter stated that the aim of its attack on Soleimani had been to deter Iran from carrying out or supporting attacks on US forces. The letter from Iran claimed that, in targeting an American air base in Iraq, it had given a measured and proportionate military response to the US attack. There was no letter to the Council from Iraq, but it was public knowledge that after the US attack, Iraq's government had expressed support for a resolution in the Iraqi parliament that the US forces should be expelled from Iraq.

Was the US blanket justification of the Baghdad attack as 'self-defence' valid? The somewhat complicated background was as follows:

Iraq had a close relation with Iran but also with the United States with which it was united in collective self-defence to fight the utterly brutal ISIS (Daesh) movement that sought to establish a new Caliphate and controlled territory both in Iraq and Syria. In the fight against ISIS, Iraq was joined by the Iranian Quds forces that played an important role. As the suppression of ISIS in Syria was drawing to a successful close, some American troops were deployed to bases in Iraq on the legal basis of an (it seems reluctant) Iraqi invitation.[52] Elements

[51] For an overview of the event, see www.nytimes.com/2020/01/02/world/middleeast/qassem-soleimani-iraq-iran-attack.html.

[52] For a brief history of the role of US forces in Iraq in fighting ISIS, see 'US-Led Combat Mission in Iraq Ends, Shifting to Advisory Role', *Al Jazeera*, 9 December 2021, www.aljazeera.com/news/2021/12/9/iraq-official-says-us-combat-mission-in-the-country-has-ended.

of Iranian forces may at the same time have joined bases of Shia-affiliated militia groups formally under the Iraqi government. We can be sure that the Iraqi government expected the invited US forces as well as the Iranian Quds to give continued help in finishing off ISIS but also that it had given no license to them to fight each other.

Nevertheless, in the somewhat chaotic conditions in which the Iraqi government did not have full control over the country and the various armed groups within its borders, repeated missile exchanges occurred between the two. The US pointed to one such attack that had come from a Quds-supported Iraqi Shiite base and that had killed a US civilian contractor at an Iraqi base. This, it was claimed, triggered the US right to self-defence. In addition, however, the US embassy in Baghdad had been subjected to a brief siege by demonstrators apparently organized by Shia-linked militias. It was against this background that the drone strike was carried out by the United States at Baghdad's airport.

While we do not have access to any US legal memoranda – if there were any – the political reasoning behind the action is not hard to imagine. Tit-for-tat actions had taken place between US and Iranian Quds forces for quite some time and Iranian support could be seen behind several military activities that the US opposed in Syria and Yemen. While the United States presumably wished to show Iran its striking power, the killed US contractor was hardly what triggered the drone over Baghdad. More likely it was the Shia-dominated demonstration outside the US Baghdad embassy. If there were to be a siege, it would remind the US public and the world of the year-long humiliating siege of the US embassy in Teheran for 444 days from November 1979 to January 1981. It is hard to avoid the conclusion that the international legal rules relating to the use of force and self-defence hardly played any role in the operation to kill the Iranian General. No UN body considered the question.

SELF-DEFENCE ARGUED AS JUSTIFICATION FOR ATTACKS ON ALLEGED DEVELOPMENT OF NUCLEAR WEAPONS

Art. 51 of the UN Charter was written above all with old-fashioned wars in mind. It affirms a right to self-defence against an armed attack that occurs. When? The formulation '*if an armed attack occurs*' in the present tense suggests that time is the moment when borders – land, sea, or space – are hit. However, action to stop incoming missiles need not have to wait until they reach a territorial border. A claim to a right of self-defence from the moment when an attack is irreversibly on the way to its target would no doubt be accepted. The *Caroline* case cited above has been interpreted to go further and justify actions in self-defence when an attack is imminent – which is not exactly the same as when it is irreversible. While this rule now seems rather generally accepted[53] the US National Security Strategy of 2002 described the notion of 'imminence' as insufficiently permissive.[54] It is not surprising that one year after the 9/11 event, the US government wished to be free to take defensive measures even before an attack is 'imminent'. How long before? President Bush is quoted as saying that *'when a threat is "imminent" it is too late'*. Instead, the 2002 US Strategy emphasized the gravity of 'emerging threats' rather than their imminence.

With modern techniques of swift and smart delivery of weapons to targets, the time between launching and impact has gone down giving target countries little time for measures of detection, decision and preparing for a response. However, to allow the start of any such response before the foreign attack is launched is problematic. It would risk being erroneous and becoming a first strike. The US strategy's claim to freedom to take anticipatory action is likely to have aimed at terrorists and 'rogue' states, but not at established nuclear weapon states. Being written at a time filled with US allegations that Iraq retained weapons of mass destruction and was preparing a new nuclear weapon program, the US claims to anticipatory action must have been aimed at Iraq.

In a famous statement US National Security Adviser, Dr. Condoleezza Rice, said that there was *'no need to wait for the smoking gun to become a mushroom cloud'*, implying that, in her view, a right of using force to take out an Iraqi nuclear weapons program arose even long before a weapon is tested. There is no doubt that in 2002 the US meant also to claim a right to launch attacks in anticipatory self-defence on Iran. Even in recent years, the US government has frequently declared that it will not 'allow' Iran to develop a nuclear weapon and implied that armed action might be taken.[55] The US government undoubtedly also includes North Korea (the DPRK) among 'rogue states' that it will feel free to attack in anticipatory self-defence.[56]

---

[53] See above, Chapter 14 p. 211 and see the UN Secretary-General's High-Level Panel on Threat, Challenges and Change, and see Henderson, p. 277.

[54] See above, this chapter, p. 231.

[55] For example, see 'Biden declares Iran will never get a nuclear weapon "on my watch"', Politico, 28 June 2021, www.politico.com/news/2021/06/28/biden-iran-nuclear-weapon-496801.

[56] In 2018, there was much publicity about the leader of North Korean, Kim Jong-Un and US President Trump, exchanges messages about having fingers on the 'nuclear buttons' and the latter promising 'fire and fury'. See for example, BBC, 'Trump to Kim: My nuclear button is

While US statements have indicated readiness to take military action both on North Korea and Iran on account of their nuclear programs, it has not actually done so (up to present writing in 2022) except in its probable participation in the 2010 Stuxnet cyber-attack in Iran.[57] One state, however, has shown that it feels free to justify armed action by a right to anticipatory self-defence – Israel. As noted above, in 1981, Israel invoked self-defence to justify its bombing of the Iraqi nuclear research reactor Osirak.[58] As the reactor had not even been loaded with fuel at the time (and thus could not cause a spread of radioactive debris), the possible threat of an Iraqi nuclear bomb was distant and hypothetical. The Security Council strongly condemned the Israeli action as a clear violation of the UN Charter.[59]

Israel's extreme concern about any incipient nuclear capacity in its region was again in evidence when in September 2007 Israeli planes bombed a building at al-Kibar in the desert in Eastern Syria.[60] Neither Israel nor Syria made the attack publicly known for some time. In a letter to the UN Secretary-General, Syria acknowledged the attack and called the Israeli air incursion a breach of the airspace of Syria.[61] While Israel has claimed that the destroyed building had been the shell of a nuclear installation, Syria asserted that it was an empty military complex still under construction. There is still some mystery about the function of the building. Syria never requested a meeting of the Security Council, but in 2012 the non-aligned movement condemned the attack as a flagrant violation of the UN Charter. In the context of the present survey, it suffices to note that Israel in all likelihood would justify the force used as *anticipatory self-defence* against a nuclear threat to Israel.

"bigger and more powerful"', 3 January 2018, www.bbc.com/news/world-asia-42549687; and Megan Kineally, 'From "fire and fury" to "rocket man", the various barbs traded between Trump and Kim Jong Un', ABC News, 12 June 2018, https://abcnews.go.com/International/fire-fury-rocket-man-barbs-traded-trump-kim/story?id=53634996.

[57] Though it has not been invoked in these cases, the US doctrine of 'counter-proliferation' has provided a rationale for military action in similar circumstances. For a discussion of the 1993 US Counterproliferation Initiative, see https://irp.fas.org/offdocs/pdd18.htm. Variations of this doctrine have also 'proliferated' to Britain and Australia.

[58] Above, Chapter 4, p. 73, and see Braut-Hegghammer (2011), pp. 101–132.

[59] S/Res/487 (1981), 19 June 1981. Also see 'Israeli Attack on Iraq's Osirak 1981: Setback or Impetus for Nuclear Weapons?' (Washington D.C.: National Security Archives, 7 June 2021), at https://nsarchive.gwu.edu/briefing-book/iraq-nuclear-vault/2021-06-07/osirak-israels-strike-iraqs-nuclear-reactor-40-years-later; and Vargo, Marc, *The Mossad: Six Landmark Missions of the Israeli Intelligence Agency, 1960–1990* (Jefferson, North Carolina: McFarland, 2014).

[60] Note: Cf. above, Chapter 4, p. 73.

[61] Letter to the Secretary-General and the President of the Security Council, S/2021/197, 3 March 2021, www.securitycouncilreport.org/atf/cf/%7B65BFCF9B-6D27-4E9C-8CD3-CF6E4FF96FF9%7D/s_2021_197.pdf.

In the case of Iran, both the Israeli and the US governments have repeatedly threatened to use force to prevent the possible development of an Iranian nuclear weapon. While no bombing as in Iraq and Syria has so far occurred, in 2010, a large number of centrifuges were destroyed in an Iranian plant for the enrichment of uranium through a cyber operation named *Stuxnet* widely believed to have been a joint Israeli/American operation. The same enrichment plant was hit by sabotage several years later. Further, several Iranian nuclear scientists have been assassinated presumably in order to disturb Iran's nuclear program. Thus, Iranian authorities reported that on 27 November 2020, a prominent nuclear scientist had been killed in an attack presumed to have been organized by Mossad, the Israeli security service.[62] 'Anticipatory self-defense' may have been the legal doctrine behind both the cyber-attack and the assassinations. However, no one has admitted responsibility for any of the actions, which suggests awareness that it would incur disapproval by the international public.

Despite claiming the right to anticipatory self-defence in 2002, the US is not known to have acted on such basis against any nascent nuclear weapons capacities, except probably taking part in the Stuxnet operation against Iran in 2010 and there are reasons to think that governments generally will not stretch further than a *Caroline* standard, i.e. accept self-defence against attacks that are 'imminent.' In a memorandum of 7 March 2003, the UK Attorney-General recognized that 'force may be used in self-defence if there is an actual or imminent threat of an armed attack' but he rejected such a right in other cases:

> … in my opinion there must be some degree of imminence. I am aware that the USA has been arguing for recognition of a broad doctrine of a right to use force to pre-empt danger in the future… this is not a doctrine which, in my opinion exists or is recognized in international law.[63]

The issue was also taken up in the UN Secretary-General's High-level Panel on Threats, Challenges and Change. It discussed specifically the case of a state acquiring nuclear weapons-making capability with possibly hostile intentions. Following the Caroline case[64] the Panel considered that:

> a threatened State, according to long established international law can take military action as long as the threatened attack is imminent

However, it saw the acquisition of a nuclear weapons-making capability as a non-imminent threat and rejected any right to anticipatory – preventive – self-defence. In its view, there would be time to submit the matter to the

---

[62] See Bergman (2018).
[63] Cit. from Henderson, p. 294. See also Gray, pp. 248 ff. and see below, Chapter 17, p. 258.
[64] Cf. above Chapter 14, p. 210.

Security Council, which could authorize suitable action including in the last resort, military action. Even in the case that the Council remained unwilling or unable to remove the alleged threat, the Panel rejected unilateral armed action, stating:

> ... in a world full of perceived potential threats, the risk to the global order... is simply too great for the legality of unilateral preventive action, as distinct from collectively endorsed action, to be accepted. Allowing one to act so is to allow all.
>
> We do not favour the rewriting or reinterpretation of Article 51.[65]

In his report '*In Larger Freedom*' UN Secretary-General Kofi Annan concurred with the advice of the Panel. Thus, while in his view Article 51 fully covers the right for states to use armed force in self-defence against imminent threats, for responses to non-imminent threats he points to the power of the Security Council.[66]

Accordingly, it seems very unlikely that there will be any new reading of the prohibition of the use of force to allow attacks on nascent nuclear installations on account of the threat that they might pose in the future.

---

[65] A *More Secure World*, UN (2004), p. 63, paras. 191 and 192.
[66] See UN Doc A/59/2005 of 21 March 2005, Sec. E.

16

Interventions Seeking Regime Change, Protection of People or Punishment

THE SCOPE OF THE PROHIBITION IN ART. 2:4
ON THE USE OF FORCE. FURTHER CASES
OF INTERVENTIONS. MOST JUSTIFICATIONS
CLAIMED NOT ACCEPTED

The survey in the preceding chapter looked at a large number of cases in which interventions and interstate armed force were used in circumstances that had not been contemplated when the relevant UN Charter articles were drafted. We have seen that the changed circumstances– use of subversion and terrorism – led UN organs to a reading of the concept of 'armed attack' in Art. 51 that somewhat widened the right of self-defence. In most cases, however, the claims of self-defence as justification for interventions were not accepted. Indeed, the claims often appeared far-fetched and advanced mainly because a government aware that it had ignored the law felt that some justification had to be on the table.

Even though 'self-defence' has been a kind of default plea by states to justify interventions there are many cases that do not fit neatly into this group. To give a broad picture of post–World War II interventions a number of such cases and their judgment of them will be described below. Not surprisingly, states seek grounds they think may sound reasonable and persuasive to a home audience or an international public, for instance, the protection of nationals in peril.

INTERVENTIONS SEEKING REGIME CHANGE

Many cases of interventions have taken place in which states – mostly great powers – have used force or subversion to bring about regime changes in other states. In some cases, the action has aimed at the elimination of specific rulers – even through assassinations.

Thus, in the 1960s, Cuban President Fidel Castro and his brother Raul were targets of presumed foreign state-instigated attempts of assassination.[1] A US commission headed by Senator Frank Church reported in 1976 on alleged assassination plots involving foreign leaders, including Fidel Castro.[2] Although President Ford issued an executive order on 19 February 1976 banning US-sanctioned assassinations of foreign leaders, subsequent executive actions have authorized 'targeted killings' of 'high value' victims. More often the United States has intervened by non-lethal subversive means to eliminate foreign government leaders.

Thus, the US participated in the toppling of the Iranian Prime Minister Mossadegh in 1953, in the ousting of Prime Minister Cheddi Jagan of Guyana in 1964, and Chilean President Salvador Allende in 1973.[3] While perhaps not violating the Charter Art. 2:4 prohibiting the interstate use of force, such subversive actions – none of which was brought before the UN – are likely to be breaches of the rule of non-intervention.[4] We may note in this context that the UK Prime Minister Tony Blair, who in 2003 shared the US aim of eliminating Iraq's 'evil' dictator, Saddam Hussein, was briefed by the British Foreign Office that it was the established position of the UK (Foreign Office) that however odious or hostile a foreign government was it was not legal for foreign states to use force to topple it.[5]

Despite the principled position of the British Foreign Office, there are, as will be shown below, some cases in which rulers toppled have been so odious that the world refrained from criticism or looked away. Application of the Charter rules would have been awkward.

---

[1]　See CIA Targets Fidel: Secret 1967 CIA Inspector General's Report on Plots to Assassinate Fidel Castro (New York: Ocean Press, 1996); and 'CIA Assassination Plot Targeted Cuba's Raul Castro' (Washington, DC: National Security Archive, 16 April 2021), https://nsarchive .gwu.edu/briefing-book/cuba/2021-04-16/documents-cia-assassination-plot-targeted-raul-castro.

[2]　https://churchcommittee.voices.wooster.edu/documents/document-9/.

[3]　Mossadegh: James Risen, 'Secrets of History: The CIA in Iran', New York Times, 16 April 2000, www.nytimes.com/2000/04/16/world/secrets-history-cia-iran-special-report-plot-convulsed-iran-53-79.html. Jagan: 'CIA Covert Operations: The 1964 Overthrow of Cheddi Jagan in British Guiana' (Washington, D.C.: National Security Archive, 6 April 2020), https://nsarchive .gwu.edu/briefing-book/intelligence/2020-04-06/cia-covert-operations-overthrow-cheddi-jagan-british-guiana-1964. Allende: 'The CIA and Chile: Anatomy of an Assassination' (Washington, D.C.: National Security Archive, 22 October 2020), https://nsarchive.gwu.edu/briefing-book/ chile/2020-10-22/cia-chile-anatomy-assassination.

[4]　See the Friendly Relations Declaration, above, Chapter 12 p. 185.

[5]　See Blair (2010), p. 400 and Sands (2006), p. 182; and see Blix (2011).

OUSTING OF EMPEROR BOKASSA OF THE
CENTRAL AFRICAN REPUBLIC (1979)

Emperor Bokassa of the Central African Republic was expeditiously ousted with little international regret in September 1979, when he was on a state visit to Libya. A month before he was deposed, a commission of inquiry established by the OAU had determined that he had ordered and participated in the massacre of 100 schoolchildren. In a quick and bloodless operation, former president of the country, David Dacko, and 800 French soldiers were flown into Bangui and declared the emperor deposed, while French authorities made it clear that it had not acted with the aim of seeking any territorial or other concessions. A few African states and the Soviet Union criticized the action, but no initiative was taken to submit the case to the Security Council or to the General Assembly that was in session. The categorical rules of the Charter would hardly have allowed the General Assembly to declare the French intervention justified. Thomas Franck rightly comments that the UN 'system quietly, but eloquently, looked the other way'.[6]

THE OUSTING OF IDI AMIN OF UGANDA (1978)

Another reckless ruler toppled was Idi Amin, President of Uganda, infamous for shocking human rights abuses. In October 1978, his troops made incursions into neighboring Tanzania. The infractions were not only fended off but Tanzanian troops moved on to liberate Uganda from Amin, who fled as a new provisional government took power. By mid-April 1979 the country was pacified, the new government was recognized and in May the Tanzanian troops left the country – while the UN appeared to have ignored the whole affair. Tanzania's reference to the right of self-defence was not very convincing considering the minor violation of its borders and the campaign through Uganda to overthrow the government. Thomas Franck, who chooses to list the case among 'purely humanitarian' interventions, is probably right to say that the international community felt that it was 'time for Amin to go' and that Tanzania simply performed the task. The UN's refraining from even taking note of Tanzania's use of armed force must be seen as a way of condoning the action. As in the case of Bokassa, the UN's silence in the Amin/Uganda affair showed a preference to blink rather than to acknowledge in one way or the other that the UN prohibition of the use of armed force was too rigid to fit the situation.[7]

[6]   See Franck, pp. 151–152.
[7]   See Franck, pp. 143–145.

VIETNAM'S INTERVENTION OUSTING
THE REGIME IN KAMPUCHEA

The same year that Tanzania marched into Uganda and chased away Idi Amin, another odious regime, that of Pol Pot, head of the Khmer Rouge that had been responsible for murdering a million people, was expelled. Claiming that Cambodia had made incursions into Vietnam and invoked the right of self-defence, Vietnam marched into Cambodia in December 1978, chased away the Pol Pot government and helped to install a new regime. As in the case of Tanzania, the claim of self-defence was not persuasive.

However, while the international community showed a good understanding of Tanzania, it was critical of Vietnam. The intervention in Uganda was seen as an action by a much respected, independent-minded African country. By contrast, the intervention by Vietnam, allied with Moscow, was perceived as part of the struggle between the Soviet Union and China. The hands of the regime of the Khmer Rouge were indeed dripping with blood but the hands of the Hanoi government were not shining clean. In January 1979, several non-aligned members of the Security Council tabled a resolution that implicitly criticized Vietnam's armed intervention by calling for the preservation of the sovereignty, territorial integrity and political independence of Cambodia and the withdrawal of all foreign forces. The resolution failed adoption by 13–2 (including a decisive Soviet veto). A resolution of a similar tenor tabled in the General Assembly was adopted by 90-21 with 29 abstentions.[8]

Thomas Franck explains the criticism of Vietnam as the Assembly majority's 'residual adherence to the priority of peace and the non-use of force, absolute sovereignty and territorial integrity'. In his view, the need to turn against regimes of horror should have led the Assembly to bend the rigid frame of Art. 2:4.[9] It is hard to know whether humanitarian considerations contributed to Vietnam's determination to topple the ignominious ruler. In any case, the UN General Assembly majority did not let such considerations lead to a soft reading of the article.

PROTECTION OF NATIONALS AS
JUSTIFICATION FOR INTERVENTION

Armed interventions to save nationals in peril have been a common practice in the past, sometimes taking the form of 'gunboat diplomacy'.[10] Although the

---

[8] A/RES/34/22 (14 November 1979), at https://documents-dds-ny.un.org/doc/RESOLUTION/GEN/NR0/376/49/IMG/NR037649.pdf?OpenElement.

[9] Franck, p. 150.

[10] Franck, p. 76.

categorial language in Art. 2:4 of the UN Charter should cover such uses of force, the practice has not disappeared. Most cases appear to be connected with chaotic situations when the national order has broken down. They do not seem to occasion complaints to the Security Council or lead to international incidents. Nevertheless, there are a number of instances where such interventions have been opposed and denounced as violations of the ban on the use of force.[11]

Sometimes the purpose of claiming the protection of nationals as principal or partial justification may have been to obtain greater domestic or international acceptance for an action the main aim of which may have been to achieve regime change. The United States referred to the protection of nationals in connection with armed interventions in the Dominican Republic (1965), Grenada (1983) and Panama (1989).[12] The United Kingdom did the same in several cases, including the intervention in Kosovo.[13] Russia, which had long rejected the protection of nationals as a justification for intervention, changed its position and invoked it as a ground for its intervention in South Ossetia (2008) and activities in Ukraine[14] and sought in both cases to further explain that persons protected had Russian passport (recently issued to them).

THE ENTEBBE CASE (1976)

Two cases of military interventions to free nationals who were hostages may be noted. The first case was that of Israel's liberation of hostages at the Entebbe airport in Uganda in 1976.[15] On 27 June 1976, an Air France jet on the way from Israel to Paris was hijacked by a group of pro-Palestinians and directed first to Libya and then on to Entebbe in Uganda. Several Israelis were made hostages and demands were made that fifty-three Palestinians imprisoned in Israel and some other countries should be released. In an Israeli aerial military action that cost a number of lives and destroyed part of the Entebbe airport, the hostages were released. The Israeli government promptly notified the Secretary-General of the UN about the action stressing that there had been a need for fast action and that Israel had acted exclusively in self-defence against terrorist organizations. The Ugandan government responded by complaining that Uganda had been 'attacked' by Israel and demanded that Israel should be condemned.

---

[11] See Gray, pp. 165 ff; Henderson, pp. 248 ff. and see Bowett, 'The use of force for the protection of nationals abroad' in Cassese (1986), pp. 39–55.

[12] See above, Chapter 15, p. 217.

[13] On the Kosovo intervention, see below, p. 245.

[14] See above, Chapter 15, p. 219.

[15] The account below is a based on the description of the case in Franck, pp. 82–86.

In the Security Council, three African states sought to condemn Israel's violation of Uganda's sovereignty and territorial integrity and demanded compensation, while the United States and the United Kingdom would only condemn the hijacking. Israel noted that Uganda had failed to exercise sovereignty over its own territory. African states generally sided with Uganda. A Western-sponsored draft resolution obtained only 6 (Western) votes in favour, 0 against and 2 abstentions (Panama and Romania). However, USSR, China and some developing countries boycotted the meeting. Not having attained the required majority of 9 the Western draft resolution failed and neither a condoning nor a condemning of the intervention was obtained.

The other case was a US operation connected with Iranian students' siege of the US embassy in Teheran in 1980.[16] In a daring but unsuccessful helicopter operation justified as self-defence, the US government sought to liberate 53 US nationals who were held hostage. The affair was neither considered by the UN Security Council nor by the General Assembly. Considering the Entebbe case, it seems unlikely that a majority could have been found that would have held the intervention acceptable under Art. 2:4.

HUMANITARIAN INTERVENTION: KOSOVO (1999)

Humanitarian intervention is a much-discussed concept claiming that states singly or severally have the right to undertake armed interventions to protect or rescue groups of people – nationals and residents alike – in places where they run acute risks to their lives. The right is said to be based on customary international law and to form an exception to the UN Charter prohibition of the interstate threat and use of force (Art. 2:4). It thus differs from the claimed exception that states can intervene to protect their own nationals (above), which is said to be based on the UN Charter-based right to self-defence (Art. 51).

Reference is sometimes not only made to historical instances where some states saved Christians from peril in Ottoman Turkey but also to modern cases in which governments took armed action in chaotic areas to rescue people regardless of their creed and ethnic belonging.[17] At the centre of the discussion is the bombing of the Federal Republic of Yugoslavia (F.R.Y.) to force its ruler Milosevic to end oppression and brutal ethnic cleansing in the region of

---

[16] For a detailed documentary history, see National Security Archive, 'Iran Revolution and Hostage Crisis, 1979–1981', 5 November 1999, https://nsarchive.gwu.edu/events/iran-revolution-hostage-crisis-1979-1981.

[17] See Vervey, p. 60.

Kosovo. The bombing that started on 24 March 1999, after long periods of tension and conflict, was carried out on the basis of decisions in NATO without any prior authorization of the Security Council. Many authors have sought to justify the action with the notion of humanitarian intervention. The preponderant reaction to this claim has been negative.[18]

A speech by UK Prime Minister Tony Blair, in Chicago on 22 April 1999 during the Kosovo crisis explains the ideological and political background of the concept of humanitarian intervention and NATO's action. Looking at the then current international situation he said that:

> Many of our problems have been caused by two dangerous and ruthless men – Saddam Hussein and Slobodan Milosevic. Both have been prepared to wage vicious campaigns against sections of their own community. As a result of these destructive policies both have brought calamity on their own peoples…[19]

He argued that the ongoing armed intervention in the F.R.Y. was 'a just war' against 'an evil dictator'. It was based not on territorial ambitions but 'on values'. He noted that there was no longer a threat to states' existence (the cold war was over) and that the United States 'was by far the strongest state and the "sole superpower". A *"new framework"* was needed, he said, with action guided by *"a subtle blend of mutual self- interest and moral purpose"* to spread the values of liberty, the rule of law, human rights…' He recognized that the forces of good could not intervene everywhere but must *'identify the circumstances in which we should get actively involved in other people's conflicts.'*

He recognized that:

> Non-interference has long been considered an important principle of international order. And it is not one we would want to jettison too readily. One state should not feel it has the right to change the political system of another or foment subversion or seize pieces of territory… But the principle of non-interference must be qualified in important respects. Acts of genocide can never be a purely internal matter. When oppression produces massive flows of refugees which unsettle neighboring countries…

He recognized further that: 'Looking around the world there are many regimes that are undemocratic and engaged in barbarous acts … So how do we decide when and whether to intervene?'

Tony Blair presented five tests that would need to be considered. The first was the presence of *'humanitarian distress'*. Among the other tests, one

---

[18] See Gray, p. 56; Henderson, p. 396 ff. and Menon, pp. 60 ff.
[19] Tony Blair, 'The Blair Doctrine', Chicago: Public Broadcasting Service, 22 April 1999, https:// archive.globalpolicy.org/empire/humanint/1999/0422blair.htm.

looks in vain for one that required the action to be permitted under the UN Charter. Professor Lawrence Friedman who prepared the first draft of this part of the speech has commented that he had been struck by views expressed by former US Secretary of State, Dean Rusk, that democratic states faced problems *'when they were perceived to be acting illegally'*, as the UK was when it intervened in Suez (1956) and the US was over the attempted and failed Bay of Pigs invasion in Cuba (1961). Freedman comments that the consideration of legality had not been well conveyed in his draft and was lost in Blair's speech.[20] However, without directly mentioning the UN Charter, Tony Blair showed a clear awareness that his new *'framework'* of new rules:

> will only work if we have reformed international institutions with which to apply them. If we want a world ruled by law and by international cooperation then we have to support the UN as its central pillar. But we need to find a new way to make the UN and its Security Council work if we are not to return to the deadlock that undermined the effectiveness of the Security Council during the Cold War. This should be a task for members of the Permanent Five to consider once the Kosovo conflict is complete. (Emphasis added.)

Blair was obviously aware that among the P5 in the Security Council, Russia and China were adamantly opposed to the armed NATO intervention and considered it a breach of the UN Charter. He was ready to ignore their objection in the case underway and left the question for a solution after the Kosovo affair. However, only four years later he faced the same problem when three of the P5 – China, France and Russia – opposed the alliance of willing states led by the United States and the United Kingdom invaded Iraq in March 2003. One reason why Mr. Blair was ready to ignore the need for Security Council authorization – and Chinese and Russian consent – to the Kosovo action was alluded to by himself when he noted that the US was the most powerful state in the world and its only superpower. This was in 1999 and although China and Russia had veto power in the Security Council, NATO had hardly any reasons to fear any significant counteraction. This was a correct calculation. Mr. Blair had said that the principle of non-interference could not be jettisoned 'too readily', but jettisoned it was. In 1999, facing Milosevic in F.R.Y. as in 2003 facing Saddam Hussein, an Anglo-American 'holy alliance' could and did intervene against 'evil' rulers and ignored the legal need for P5 approval in the Security Council. Finding ways to achieve P5 unity and cooperation was – and still is – left to the future.

So, how was the NATO Kosovo armed intervention justified in intergovernmental language rather than in passionate political Chicago language? And

---

[20] Freedman (2017), pp. 107–124.

what was the reaction?[21] In a meeting of the Security Council in October 1998 the US representative declared simply that NATO held it had the authority to use force. The dramatic humanitarian situation was invoked as a background more than a ground for such action:

> The NATO allies, in agreeing on October 13 to the use of force, made it clear that they had the authority, the will and the means to resolve this issue. We retain that authority. We will not tolerate the continued violence that has resulted in nearly a quarter of a million refugees and displaced persons and thousands of deaths, and has jeopardized the prospects for peace in the wider Balkans.[22]

The US stand was challenged by China and Russia. On 24 March 1999, when NATO forces had started to attack targets in the Federal Republic by bombings and cruise missiles, Russia called for an emergency session of the Security Council, where it declared that *'attempts to justify the NATO strikes with arguments about preventing a humanitarian catastrophe in Kosovo are completely untenable...'*[23]

The representative of China declared that: '...it is the Security Council that bears primary responsibility for the maintenance of international peace and security. And it is only the Security Council that can determine whether a given situation threatens international peace and security and can take appropriate action'.

The Netherlands representative, while recognizing the central role of the Council, did not think it acceptable for the Council to be paralyzed: 'The Secretary-General is right when he observes ... that the Council should be involved in any decision to resort to the use of force. If, however, due to one or two permanent members' rigid interpretation of the concept of domestic jurisdiction, such a resolution is not attainable, we cannot sit back and simply let the humanitarian catastrophe occur'.

The UK representative was more cautious and argued that 'as an exceptional measure on grounds of overwhelming humanitarian necessity, military intervention is legally justified'.

---

[21]　The account below of the events and statements in the Security Council is based on the description of the case in Beckman, pp. 207–222. There are many other detailed and excellent discussions of the Kosovo conflict. See Gray, pp. 45–58; Henderson, pp. 393–396; and Franck. pp. 163–170.

[22]　Cit. From Beckman, p. 213.

[23]　Remarks of Sergei Lavrov, S/PV.3988, UN Security Council meeting of 24 March 1999, www .securitycouncilreport.org/atf/cf/%7B65BFCF9B-6D27-4E9C-8CD3-CF6E4FF96FF9%7D/ kos%20SPV3988.pdf. The following quotes from China, Netherlands, and the UK are from this same document.

A draft resolution was presented by Russia declaring that NATO's '*unilateral use of force constitutes a flagrant violation of the United Nations Charter*'. It was rejected by a vote of 3 in favour (China, Namibia and Russia) and 12 against. The vote reflected an unwillingness to brand the Kosovo intervention as a 'flagrant violation' of the UN Charter, but hardly signaled approval of the operation or of a rule permitting humanitarian intervention.[24]

After the extensive NATO bombing campaign and the meeting in the Security Council there followed a period of negotiations including talks in May 1999 in which Russian Prime Minister Chernomyrdin and Finnish President Ahtisaari brokered an agreement that was accepted by NATO and Belgrade. Kosovo declared itself independent in February 2008, but a number of states do not accord recognition.

What light does the handling of the Kosovo events in 1998 and 1999 throw on the scope and effectiveness of the norm laid down in UN Charter Art. 2:4 to restrain the interstate use of force? It is hard to avoid the impression that once the NATO countries felt politically impelled to engage in the settlement of the conflict in Yugoslavia, felt they had exhausted all conceivable non-violent means, and had concluded that the humanitarian situation resulting from the armed action of Milosevic' armed forces was catastrophic, they no longer saw the prohibition in Art. 2:4 as a restraint but as an obstacle to ignore.

It has been commented that intervention by NATO troops on the ground would have been a far more effective action than an 11-week-long bombing campaign exacting an estimated toll of some 10,000 people. One reason, one would surmise, for undertaking the operation from high altitudes may have been that it could be done without causing any casualty on the NATO side. Perhaps another reason was that 'boots on the ground' would have signaled intervention even more concretely: NATO did intervene to stop an ongoing horror but at the same time the alliance kept its distance from the fighting parties.

The Kosovo intervention was decided at a time when the leading member of NATO, the United States was at the peak of military dominance and Russia at a low of military readiness. From this position of world leadership, the states leading NATO simply laid down that the NATO Council could order an armed intervention without needing any authorization from the UN Security Council.

Tony Blair in Chicago had been aware of the Chinese and Russian resistance to intervention and had talked about a new way to make the UN and its Security Council work and avoid paralysis. However, that effort was for after Kosovo. For Security Council use, his Chicago plea that a new 'framework'

---

[24] See Gray, p. 47.

should allow – even mandate – exceptions from the non-intervention rule to allow action against 'evil' was evidently too sweeping and high-strung. Instead, intervention based on 'humanitarian necessity' was advanced as a somewhat more specific permissible exception from the rule in Art. 2:4. It was easily understood and appealing to many at the time. What caused convulsions was not per se contemplating an exception to Art. 2:4. It was rather that such an exception would add a second category of permissible armed action – beyond self-defence – in which approval by all P5 of the Security Council would not be required. The resolution tabled by China and Russia to declare the intervention a violation of the Charter had been defeated (see above), but the UK had preferred to defend the action as exceptional, suggesting that it was a one-off and that the prohibition in Art. 2:4 remained. Both Germany and the US subsequently expressed the view that the Kosovo intervention should not be seen as a precedent.[25] On reflection, it was perhaps realized in the NATO camp that if accepted as a precedent modifying the categorial Charter rule, humanitarian intervention would be available not just to NATO but to all, including China and Russia. In his 1999 *Report on the work of the organization*, UN Secretary-General wrote: 'What is clear is that enforcement action without Security Council authorization threatens the very core of the international security system founded on the Charter of the UN. Only the Charter provides a universally accepted legal basis for the use of force'.[26]

The rule of unanimity – the veto – was not included in the Charter on the basis of a belief that collective judgments including all five permanent members of the Security Council would necessarily bring wiser decisions. Rather it was plugged in as a procedural obstacle to a use of armed force that might be contrary to the interest of a permanent member and that could – in a worst case – lead such member to take armed or other drastic action.[27] When the NATO countries proceeded to intervene in Kosovo against the known objections of China and Russia, they did so in the conviction that neither of these states was in a position at the time to take significant counteraction but would limit themselves to protests. That calculation was correct. Paralysis at the United Nations was avoided by disregarding a central requirement of the UN security order and a new situation was brought about in the F.R.Y. ignoring the need for support by China or Russia.

Other costs of the application of humanitarian intervention will be discussed below, but it should be noted in this context that the sentiment voiced

---

[25] Gray, p. 52.
[26] Cit. from Gray, p. 53; UN doc A/54/1 (1999) at para 66; 1999 UNYB 3 at 10.
[27] On the veto, see also Chapter 13, p. 200.

by Tony Blair that it is unacceptable for the UN to stay paralyzed in face of humanitarian catastrophes – as it was in Cambodia or Rwanda – led a few years later to the R2P doctrine[28] that recognizes such disasters as matters of international concern requiring UN to act. Yet, the doctrine has not overcome the question that Tony Blair left for after Kosovo: how to ensure cooperation between the P5 in the Security Council. For decisions about an enforcement action, the R2P still requires Security Council approval – hence unanimity among permanent members.

INTERVENTION TO PUNISH – ANOTHER EXCEPTION TO THE PROHIBITION OF THE USE OF FORCE? CHEMICAL WEAPONS IN SYRIA 2013–2018[29]

On 14 April 2018, the civil war still raging, the United Kingdom and France joined the United States in bombing government-controlled targets in Syria. The attacks followed claims that units under Syrian government control had used chemical weapons in the civil war. Viewed against the position of the three governments that they did not intervene in the civil war, that they did not claim self-defence, and that they had no authorization from the UN Security Council, the action stood out. While punishments for war crimes have often been meted out – after the end of armed conflicts – by victor states – the appearance from the outside of great powers not as belligerents but as sheriffs and guardians of the laws of war during an ongoing civil war was something new.

It amounted to telling the Syrian government: 'you can go on fighting your civil war in which we do not intervene against you openly – but keep the fighting clean!' Did the action of the three great powers constitute a claim to a novel exception to the rule in Art. 2:4 or did they simply ignore the rule? Below is an account and a discussion of the events.

Reports about the use of chemical weapons came early in the Syrian civil war. The reactions were sharp, not least in the United States and other Western countries that were strongly opposed to the dictatorial Assad regime. President Obama took the step of warning the regime in Damascus. In a speech on 20 August 2012, he said: '*a red line for us is we start seeing a whole bunch of chemical weapons moving around or being utilized. That would change my calculus. That would change my equation*'.[30]

---

[28] See above, Chapter 13, p. 199.
[29] The subject is mentioned briefly above in Chapter 4 at p. 68 and described in Chapter 12, p. 194.
[30] Barack Obama, Remarks by the President, 20 August 2012, https://obamawhitehouse.archives .gov/the-press-office/2012/08/20/remarks-president-white-house-press-corps.

Almost exactly a year thereafter, on 21 August 2013, a large-scale attack with the chemical nerve agent sarin took place at Ghouta, a suburb of Damascus, killing some 1,400 civilians. The horrible event shocked the world and for President Obama, it raised the acute question of how to follow up on the warning he had issued. In the United States, groups that had long wanted to see stronger American support for anti-Assad groups in the civil war now pressed for the United States to take some military action against the Syrian regime that was thought to be responsible for the attack. Among many others, Secretary of State Kerry took the line that Assad should be punished in part because *'it matters deeply to the credibility and the future interests of the United States of America and our allies...'*[31] Especially the argument about credibility came to be a central point for all who wanted to see action. However, there were also important voices cautioning against an armed attack without prior authorization by the US Congress and the UN. Secretary-General, Ban Ki-moon said: 'The use of force is lawful only when in exercise of self-defence in accordance with Article 51 of the United Nations Charter and/or when the Security Council approves such action.'[32]

In a major article in the *New York Times*, two professors at Yale Law School argued that an attack by the United States without prior Security Council authorization 'will flout the most fundamental international rule of all – the prohibition of the use of military force, for anything but self-defense...' and further: '...If we follow Kosovo and Iraq with Syria, it will be difficult, if not impossible to stop others from a similar use of force down the line....'[33]

President Obama, himself, keeping his options open, said that he was 'comfortable going forward without the approval of the United Nations Security Council that so far has been completely paralyzed and unwilling to hold Assad accountable'.[34]

Nevertheless, Obama did ask Congress for support for limited strikes on Syria to punish Assad and he asked some Western governments if they were prepared to join in punitive action. In neither quarter did he get any support. In an extensive interview in *The Atlantic* on 15 March 2016, Jeffrey Goldberg reports *that* Obama recoiled from the idea of an *'attack unsanctioned by international law or by Congress'.* The German Chancellor, Angela

---

[31] Remarks on 30 August 2013, full transcript at www.washingtonpost.com/world/national-security/ running-transcript-secretary-of-state-john-kerrys-remarks-on-syria-on-aug-30/2013/08/30/ f3a63a1a-1193-11e3-85b6-d27422650fd5_story.html.

[32] Reuters, 3 September 2013.

[33] Oona A. Hathaway and Scott J. Shapiro, 'On Syria, a UN Vote Isn't Optional', *New York Times*, 3 September 2013, www.nytimes.com/2013/09/04/opinion/on-syria-a-un-vote-isnt-optional.html.

[34] 'Obama statement on decision for US strikes on Syria', Reuters, 31 August 2013, www.reuters .com/article/us-syria-crisis-obama-text-idUKBRE97U0DC20130831.

Merkel had said that Germany would not participate and on 29 August the UK parliament – no doubt with unhappy memories of how the country had been drawn into the 2003 invasion of Iraq through cooperation with the United States – voted against UK participation.[35]

Through a surprising turn of events, Obama was taken out of his dilemma by the plan jointly worked out with Russia to persuade Syria to join the Chemical Weapons Convention and agree to surrender its stock of chemical weapons. The remarkable plan was gladly supported by a unanimous Security Council and carried out in an equally remarkable UN – OPCW 'joint mission'.[36] Sadly, this was not the end of the use of chemical weapons in the Syrian civil war. Although a quantity of some 1308 tons of chemical agents was collected, transported out of Syria and destroyed it appears that some were left or newly produced – and used. On a number of occasions, chemical weapons were used by anti-government forces as well as by the government side. After an attack in April 2017, US President Trump ordered the bombing of a Syrian air base (Shayrat) from which the chemical weapons were thought to have been flown to the target.[37] He claimed that differently from President Obama he had acted to maintain US credibility.

A year later, on 14 April 2018, in response to another possible use by the government of chemical weapons against civilians at Douma, an attack was launched by the Unitd States together with the United Kingdom and France and directed at sites alleged to be linked to the production or storage of chemical weapons. In a TV interview, Trump explained that the action was meant as a deterrent against the production, spread and use of chemical weapons. There was, he said, a vital US interest involved and readiness to continue such action until Syrian troops stopped its use of chemical weapons.[38]

The concerns that President Obama had had about punitive US bombing without Security Council authorization were probably absent in the mind of

---

[35] 'Syria crisis: Cameron loses Commons vote on Syria action', BBC, 29 August 2016, www.bbc.com/news/uk-politics-23892783.

[36] See, for instance. SC Res 2118 and letter of 7 October 2013 from the SG of the UN to the President of the SC. UN DOC. S/2013/591.

[37] For a full text (video and print) of his statement, see 'WATCH: President Trump's full statement on US missile attack on Syria', 6 April 2017, www.pbs.org/newshour/politics/listen-president-trumps-full-statement-u-s-missile-attack-syria.

[38] A controversy arose about who had performed the C-weapons attack at Douma. A special inquiry was undertaken within the OPCW and it concluded in 2020 that government forces had been responsible. The OPCW also disputed claims by two inspectors who performed the first OPCW inspection that their report was not correctly reflected. 'Inquiry strikes blow to Russian denials of Syria chemical attack', *The Guardian*, 2 February 2020, www.theguardian.com/world/2020/feb/07/inquiry-strikes-blow-to-russian-denials-of-syria-chemical-attack.

President Trump. More likely he wanted to look resolute to the public and different from Obama who had used diplomacy vis-à-vis a brutal regime. He was probably right in thinking that a forceful global sheriff would be liked by the public and that many in the political elite would feel that the US sheriff was now credible again. It is harder to guess why the governments of the UK and France joined the US in performing the second strike. Perhaps there was a wish – in line with Tony Blair's pleas in Chicago in 1999 – that decent governments should act against evil.

Yet, arguments were advanced against the action. We have recorded above the negative statement by the UN Secretary-General and the comments by two Yale professors. In an article disseminated by the BBC and dated 14 April 2018 Marc Weller, Professor of International Law at Cambridge University, wrote

> Legally, the claim to enforce international law on chemical weapons by violent means would return the world to the era before the advent of the UN Charter. The Charter allows states to use force in self-defence and, arguably, for the protection of populations threatened by extermination at the hands of their own government. The use of force for broader purposes of maintaining international security is also possible. However, such action is subject to the requirement of a mandate from the Security Council.[39]

Russia, as a member of the Security Council, tabled a resolution condemning the strike in 2018.[40] It was supported by China and Bolivia but opposed by 8 members including the three behind the criticized action – the United States, the United Kingdom and France. Four states abstained.[41] The UK sought to justify the action as a '*humanitarian intervention*'. Although the proposed condemnation was rejected the result can hardly be interpreted as expressing views on the legal issue.

Many governments and people felt undoubtedly that the use of chemical weapons deserved a strong reaction and they may have approved the action. However, different from the US attack in Libya in 1986 that responded to Libyan-sponsored terrorist acts directed against the US, the punitive action after the Douma event had not been preceded by any Syrian action – chemical or other – directed against any one of the three states that performed

---

[39] Marc Weller, 'Syria air strikes: Were they legal?', BBC, 14 April 2018, www.bbc.com/news/world-middle-east-43766556. An article on the 2017 air strike is found in the *American Journal of International Law*. vol. 111 (2017), pp. 781–787.

[40] S/2018/355, Russian draft resolution, 14 April 2018. www.nytimes.com/2018/04/14/world/middleeast/un-security-council-syria-airstrikes.html.

[41] See *American Journal of International Law*, Vol 112/July 2018, pp. 522–527.

the action. It was in no way self-defence. It also stood in stark contrast to the absence of forceful reaction from the same states against the extensive and horrible Iraqi use of chemical weapons that is calculated to have led to a million Iranian casualties in the Iraq-Iran war in the 1980s.

The different attitudes could hardly have been due simply to the fact that the Chemical Weapons Convention did not exist in the 1980s. The Geneva Protocol of 1925 existed. A more likely explanation is that there had been no political eagerness to punish war crimes against Iran, but there were strong political incentives to demonstrate anger with the Assad regime. The actions for which President Obama was so fiercely criticized in the United States – to work with Russia in persuading Syria to join the Chemical Weapons Convention and to cooperate in a Security Council-mandated elimination of weapons – seems more purposeful. There is the possibility that the Syrian governmental side did not surrender 100 per cent of its chemical weapons and may have later used some or produced new ones does not detract from this judgment.

17

Findings Regarding the Role of Norms to Restrain the Interstate Use of Force

The preceding chapters have shown how in the last hundred years international rules have emerged and developed with the aim of restraining the use of force between independent communities. While it is difficult to ascertain whether and what restraint the rules – separated from other factors – may actually have had on governments, we have examined cases where governments have used force, asked what the aims and claimed justifications were and how UN organs assessed the actions (post–World War II) against the background of the norms they considered governing. In this chapter, we shall try to describe where the evolution of the rules has led so far, examine what kinds of interstate use of force have remained so far, and how the state community – as represented by UN organs – has considered them.

A first observation that emerges from the preceding chapters is that while over time the world has come a long way in developing a broad fabric of law for relations between its independent members, specific rules on the resort to force have emerged only in the 20th century. Hobbes (1588–1679) taught that only through Leviathan – a strong central order – that provided laws, ensured trials, judgments and executive action could the use of force be prevented and social peace be attained.[1] As no such order existed among sovereign states, no peace and order could be expected between them.

If Hobbes had lived today, he would have been amazed to see that even without a Leviathan a complex modern world community can operate with relative efficiency and harmony and that this is decisively helped by some rules of customary law and a massive body of rules in bilateral and multilateral treaties.[2] However, he would also have noted many breaches of the rules requiring restraint in the use of force and probably said that a Security

---

[1] See above, Chapter 5, p. 92.
[2] Cf. above, Chapter 5, p. 93.

Council dominated by five independent great powers was not a real Leviathan that could uphold law and world order.

He would have been right. Failing consensus among the five permanent members and an armed force at its disposal the Council has often been a scene of paralysis rather than a world authority upholding peace. What Hobbes could not have foreseen was that some four hundred years after his time many factors, including the deterrence of mutual assured destruction through nuclear weapons (MAD), mutual economic dependence (MED), the benefits of extensive cooperation, diplomacy and common rules reflecting a 'public mind' have nevertheless combined to bring restraints on the interstate use of force.

USE OF ARMED FORCE TO SEIZE LAND IS BECOMING UNCOMMON

A second observation that stands out is that after the end of World War II, the age-old practice of states using force to seize territory has been on the way out – an exception being made notably for Russia's actions in Ukraine in 2014 and 2022. As noted above, many circumstances may have combined to bring this result.[3] The legal rule in Art. 2:4 of the UN Charter and the 'public mind' that it reflects may be a part of the explanation for the changed attitudes and conduct of states. If the rule in Art. 2:4 were to be likened to a national criminal law ban on 'assault and robbery', the cases under the robbery part – grabbing of land by the use of force – have not been many. Moreover, even without an almighty Leviathan they have been successfully resisted in some cases and the results remained non-recognized by states in most others.

ARMED INTERVENTIONS WITHOUT SEIZURE OF LAND ARE STILL NUMEROUS

The third observation is that interventions – that do not involve the seizure of land and – that may or may not violate the broad reach of Art. 2:4 have remained numerous. As these actions form a major part of the active interstate use of force in today's world, it is important to try to understand what has caused them and why there has not been more restraint. The survey in the preceding chapters of many cases of intervention and justifications offered for them, tell us something about whether and how seriously the rules of restraint were taken, how appropriate the applicable norms have been, and how some adjustments have occurred in the reading of them to make them more appropriate in the current world.

---

[3]   See above, Chapter 6, p. 107 ff and Chapter 12, p. 185 ff.

A fourth observation is that the ban on the use of force in Art. 2:4 of the UN Charter extended to action far beyond the conquest of territory and included not only interventions by force but also the threat of use of force. The authors wanted a sweeping prohibition and assumed that the broad competences they gave to the new world organization would enable it to cope with all kinds of breaches of and threats to the peace. Accordingly, the right to use force in self-defence in cases of armed attacks was opened but narrowly – allowing such action only until the Security Council had taken necessary measures. It was a design based on optimism – some would say naïveté. With developments like 'wars of national liberation', 'indirect aggression', globalized terrorism, nuclear weapons and a frequently paralyzed Security Council, the proclaimed rules came to apply in a reality that in important respects was unforeseen and sometimes placed states under strain.[4]

It is no surprise to find great powers of the Western world, in particular the United States, often pushing for and acting on readings of the rules that would give themselves more elbow room for the use of force to protect and pursue their interests. It is also no surprise that many small and weak states have been reticent to soften the reading of restrictive rules, fearing they could become targets of intervention.

The result? Some limitations of the scope of the prohibitions have resulted from generally agreed interpretations and in a few cases the rules have proved awkward and been ignored. However, as the survey of cases has shown and as the sections below will summarize, the restraints stipulated have mostly been upheld rigidly by UN organs, while the reading of some of them has been adjusted to prevent them from posing demands that would be unrealistic and unreasonable in the brave new unforeseen world.

SCOPE OF CHARTER'S RESTRAINTS ON INTERSTATE USE OF FORCE IS LIMITED BY SOME AGREED INTERPRETATIONS

It seems generally agreed that the UN Charter's prohibition of the interstate use of force is aimed primarily at physical force.[5] Economic pressure may constitute prohibited intervention but is not regarded as 'force' under Art. 2:4 nor, indeed, as 'armed attack' that may give rise to a right of armed self-defence under Art. 51.[6] The point is of increasing importance at the present time when the use of economic force seems often to be chosen rather than kinetic force.

---

[4]   See above, Chapter 14. p. 206.
[5]   See above, Chapter 12, p. 185.
[6]   See above, Chapter 14, p. 206.

It further seems generally understood that the use of force in self-defence under Art. 51 must be proportionate and that an 'armed attack' to give a right to the use of force in self-defence – while it may be only imminent – cannot be a minor border skirmish but must be of significant gravity.[7]

An authoritative resolution of the General Assembly has declared that armed reprisals fall under the prohibited 'use of force', but no agreed understanding seems to have emerged on the precise meaning of the explicit prohibition in Art. 2:4 of threats of the use of force.[8] The bans are understandable as reprisals pose a risk of prolonged use of force and both threats and reprisals pose a risk of escalating tensions. However, the bans do not seem likely to be effective to restrain strong incentives to retaliate or to threaten. We may note the paradox that although retaliation is generally prohibited the perhaps most serious restraint against a first strike with a nuclear weapon is the fear of a second retaliatory strike.

SEEKING 'REGIME CHANGE' IS NO JUSTIFICATION FOR USING INTERSTATE FORCE

While states are unhindered to criticize and oppose regimes of foreign states, cases examined in Chapter 15 tell us that they are prohibited from using force – whether styling it individual or collective self-defence – to engineer or resist regime change. Some cases of US interventions to prevent the spread of Communist regimes, and two cases of Soviet interventions to prevent Communist regimes from collapsing, were discussed above in the context of pressures that the Cold War brought on the UN Charter.[9]

Only rarely did the United States or Russia admit the obvious fact that the nature of a regime was the cause of their interventions. The US has even sometimes expressly disassociated itself from the idea of a license for intervention in favour of the democratic rule. The judgment of the International Court of Justice in the Nicaragua case noted that the United States argued it had not sought to force a specific form of government on Nicaragua – only to change the government's behavior, including the breaking of ties with the Soviet Bloc.[10] After the US intervention in Panama in 1989 to depose President Noriega, the US representative in the Security Council said: *'I am not here today to claim a right on the behalf of the United States to enforce the will of history by intervening in favour of democracy... We are supporters of democracy*

---

[7] See above, Chapter 15, p. 235.
[8] See above, Chapters 12, p. 189.
[9] See above, Chapter 15, p. 218.
[10] See above, Chapter 15, p. 213.

*but not the gendarmes of democracy, not in this hemisphere or anywhere else ...
We acted in Panama for legitimate interests of self-defence and to protect the
integrity of the Canal treaties'.*[11]

In two cases – Bokassa and Amin[12] – we have seen how the United Nations
and the world looked the other way when two outrageous government leaders
were ousted through foreign interventions. However, the General Assembly's
criticism of Viet Nam's intervention in Cambodia (1978–79) to chase away the
blood-stained Pol Pot regime shows what reluctance there is to tolerate that
individual states intervene by force to topple any regime.[13] In his speech in
Chicago in 1999, Tony Blair pleaded for ways of intervening and removing 'evil
dictators' like Saddam Hussein and Slobodan Milosevic but recognized the
legal obstacles to do so in the absence of agreement in the Security Council.[14]

Russian Invasion of Ukraine 2022

The Russian invasion of Ukraine in 2022 is in a category of its own. The
announced aim to 'demilitarize' and 'denazify' Ukraine may be assumed to
have comprised an intention to change the regime. But to what? Not – as
under the Brezhnev doctrine – to become and forever remain a member state
of a Socialist commonwealth, but perhaps to become a state building on an
economic, political and cultural model akin to that of Russia, but without
an independent military force. Whatever the aim, the means used were illegal: armed force against the territorial integrity and political independence of
a UN member, and the action was promptly censured by an overwhelming
majority of the UN General Assembly[15] and followed – not by UN enforcement action – but by crippling economic measures adopted by member states
and large-scale supply of arms to the Ukrainian forces.

ADJUSTMENT OF RULES RESISTED: NO EXCEPTION
FROM THE PROHIBITION OF THE USE OF FORCE
FOR THE PROTECTION OF NATIONALS

The protection of nationals has deep roots as a justification for armed interventions. It was a part of 'gunboat diplomacy' practiced by strong states in

---

[11]   Cit. from Gray, p. 66. But see the statement in opposite direction by a US representative in the
      Security Council in the case of the 1983 intervention of Grenada. Above, Chapter 15, p. 217.
[12]   See above Chapter 16, p. 242 m.
[13]   See above, Chapter 16, p. 243.
[14]   See above, Chapter 16, p. 246.
[15]   A/RES/ES-11/1, adopted 18 March 2022.

the past.[16] In the -post-World War II period, it has been used to help nationals in peril but also as fig leaves for other aims and it is opposed or met with suspicion by many states. It is no longer accepted as a ground for armed interventions.[17]

The United States invoked self-defence for its (failed) attempt in 1980 to rescue 53 US citizens hostage at the US embassy in Teheran. Had the case been dealt with in the Security Council – which it was not – the plea of self-defence would probably have had as little support as that which met Israel's plea of self-defence in the case of its armed intervention to save hostages at the Entebbe airport in Uganda in 1976.[18] Thomas Franck comments that *'The opposition of so many states ... illustrates the depth of fear of opening the door, however narrowly to unilateral use of force, even where the justification for intervention is strong.'* Franck would like to keep that door at least ajar where there are specific 'mitigating circumstances'.[19]

ADJUSTMENT OF RULES RESISTED: NO EXCEPTION FROM THE PROHIBITION OF THE USE OF FORCE FOR 'HUMANITARIAN INTERVENTIONS'[20]

In the case of 'humanitarian intervention', it is claimed that in extreme cases the prohibition of the use of force in Art. 2:4 exceptionally allows the use of force. NATO's bombings in Yugoslavia during the conflict over Kosovo (1999) caused a flood of arguments and writings for and against the tenet – and the action.

Many years after the absence of any international intervention to stop the genocide in Rwanda in 1994, and after the controversial NATO intervention in Kosovo in 1999, it is easy to see that the political and legal controversy does not lie in disagreement with the argument that a 'framework' for action is needed.[21] The proximity between peoples in the modern world makes inaction in face of massacres unbearable. At the same time, claiming that force

---

[16] Examples include, among others, threats of British gunboat diplomacy during the first Opium war (1839–42), the Don Pacifico affair (1850, Great Britain), the Paraguay expedition (1858–59, USA), the Venezuela Crisis (1902–03, Great Britain, Germany, Italy), or the Agadir crisis (1911, Germany).

[17] See above, Chapter 16, p. 188 For an extensive discussion of the subject, see Brownlie, pp. 289–301: Franck, pp. 76–96; Gray, pp. 165–159; Henderson, pp. 247–256.

[18] Described above Chapter 16, p. 244.

[19] See Franck, pp. 85 and 96.

[20] See above, Chapter 16, p. 245 and see the excellent treatment of the subject in Gray, p. 40 ff.; Henderson, p. 379 ff. And see Menon (2016), pp. 60 ff.

[21] See above, Chapter 16, p. 246.

used in the humanitarian intervention should be an allowed special exception from the prohibition of the use of force by states is to ignore a fundamental basis of the UN security system: the need for Security Council authorization of enforcement actions.[22] The conscious ignoring by NATO of the requirement of such authorization in the case of Kosovo had a cost. It made it less difficult for Russia to claim freedom of action when it later unilaterally intervened by force in Georgia and Ukraine.

As noted, the UN sought a way out of the dilemma by placing a new emphasis on the duty of the states to protect all persons within their jurisdictions and – when the state fails – recognition of the duty of the world community to act. However, on the crucial point of use of force, the R2P doctrine came back to square one: it does not open for unilateral humanitarian action by individual states or alliances but requires authorization by the Security Council. Thus, the world still cries for the talks between the P5 members of the Council that Tony Blair realized were necessary.[23]

ADJUSTMENT OF RULES RESISTED: NO EXCEPTION FROM THE PROHIBITION OF THE USE OF FORCE FOR ATTACKING A NASCENT NUCLEAR WEAPONS CAPACITY

The authors of the UN Charter were aware, of course, that the prohibition of the use of force would apply in the same way to all weapons. Yet, as no nuclear weapons had yet been used when the Charter was adopted in June 1945, nobody at the time could have foreseen that the very development, possession and production of such weapons could be seen as a 'threat of force'. Nevertheless, this was the conviction that prompted the conclusion of the Nuclear Non-Proliferation Treaty: a prohibition of use was not seen as sufficient – the very development and possession should be prevented. However, no forceful mechanism was created to enjoin unwilling non-nuclear weapon states – like India, Israel and Pakistan – to adhere to the NPT or to tackle the problem of states ignoring its obligations and moving to make nuclear weapons.

In 1981, Israel took the step of destroying the Iraqi research reactor Osirak that, it was argued, could, when it had become operational, contribute to producing plutonium for a nuclear bomb. Israel claimed at the Security Council that the action was in self-defence, but the action was condemned by the Council. Much later, the Israeli argument received some understanding,

---

[22] See quotation from report of the UN Secretary-General, above, Chapter 16, p. 250.
[23] See above, Chapter 16, p. 246.

when the US National Security Strategy of 2002 asserted a right – at least for the US – of anticipatory self-defence to act against adversaries' armed with weapons of mass destruction. The so-called 'Begin doctrine' received further understanding when in 2003 the United States and its allies invaded Iraq claiming that an important reason was to stop alleged renewed Iraqi efforts to make weapons of mass destruction. In 2007, again asserting a right of self-defence, Israel attacked and destroyed what it alleged was a Syrian nuclear research reactor at Al Kibar.[24] That case was not considered by the Security Council.

Considering that Art. 51 of the Charter allows self-defence if '*an armed attack occurs*', the US and Israeli claimed justifications do not look plausible. They look like claims that an exception to Art. 2:4 should allow the use of force in anticipated self-defence to destroy or impede a nascent capacity to develop nuclear or other weapons of mass destruction that could pose future threats.

While, as noted above, there is support for reading Art. 51 as allowing self-defence against 'imminent' attacks – including nuclear – there is no support for a reading that would allow individual states to use force in 'anticipatory self-defence' at times of their discretion.[25] There would be overwhelming support instead for the approach that led in the case of Iran's nuclear program to a negotiation involving the great powers – notably the P5 – and a settlement endorsed by the Security Council.

However, on several occasions, the US Trump administration made it clear that it would 'not allow' Iran to acquire nuclear weapons. This suggested that – like Israel – the US (at least under President Trump) could have been ready to use force to eliminate not just imminent dangers but remote ones. However, Israel's actions at Osirak and Al Kibar and a number of assassinations of nuclear scientists – all widely believed to have been led by Israel – make it realistic to think that Israel does not exclude further go-it-alone actions at times unrelated to the imminence of a threat. A Security Council resolution condoning such actions as acts of anticipatory self-defence would certainly be rejected.

ADJUSTMENT OF RULES NOT CONSIDERED: INDIVIDUAL STATES' USE OF FORCE TO PUNISH ANOTHER STATE FOR WAR CRIMES WAS NEITHER CONDEMNED NOR ACCEPTED BY UN SECURITY COUNCIL

The case of the air strikes that were launched against Syria on 14 April 2018 by the United States joined by the United Kingdom and France has been

---

[24] See above, Chapter 15, p. 237.
[25] See above, Chapter 15, p. 230 ff.

described in some detail above.[26] They were neither acts of self-defence nor acts to retaliate. International public opinion seems to have felt the punishment was deserved and many governments expressed understanding but avoided voicing any view on the legality. The United Kingdom sought to justify the action as a 'humanitarian intervention'. A few governments and several experts on international law objected to the action as illegal. A resolution that condemned it was tabled by Russia in the Security Council but did not attain majority support. How are we to assess the events?

At a time when there exists an international criminal court for the trial of war crimes, it would be peculiar if it were accepted as a precedent that major outside powers can bomb to punish war crimes in a war in which they do not participate. It is submitted that the Security Council's unwillingness to condemn the action cannot be read as an acceptance of such actions as permissible exceptions from the Charter prohibition of the use of interstate force. It is probable that governments read the events for what they were – responses to public opinion understandably angry with a brutal Syrian government and a breach of a taboo.

In addition, a sizeable part of the US foreign policy elite that seemed unconcerned about the legality of the operation felt US credibility required that earlier warnings by President Obama against the use of chemical weapons must be followed by kinetic action. President Obama's reluctance to go along with the elite pressure and public feeling was politically courageous. He was clearly aware that bombing required authorization by the Security Council and, while he would have been ready to give an order ignoring the rule of the Charter, the diplomatic solution jointly worked out with Russia solved his dilemma. That President Trump later would show no hesitation to have the US act as self-appointed international sheriff ignoring the UN Charter surprises nobody. The willingness of the United Kingdom and French governments to join him does surprise, however, and suggests that they took their cooperation with the United States more seriously than their attachment to the UN Charter rule in Art. 2:4.

SOME READINGS OF CHARTER ARTICLES ON THE USE OF FORCE AND SELF-DEFENCE ADJUSTED DUE TO DEVELOPMENTS THAT PUT THEM UNDER STRAIN

Some developments that were not foreseen at the time of the adoption of the UN Charter were discussed in Chapter 15 as having put respect for the rules

---

[26]   See above, Chapter 16, p. 251 ff and see Gray, p. 57.

adopted on the use of force and self-defence under strain and having resulted in many breaches of the rules but also some new readings of them.[27]

First, the emancipation of peoples who had been under colonial rule was generally welcomed, but when the issue arose of how 'wars of national liberation' were to be judged under the Charter's prohibition of the use of force the way out was often diplomatic doubletalk.[28] With decolonization accomplished, the issue has disappeared, but we should note that modern movements that seek secession of territory in the name of self-determination meet no automatic sympathy in the contemporary community of states.[29]

A second development that put respect for the adopted UN Charter rules in jeopardy, but also led to some new readings of them, was the Cold War. The struggle was pursued by a variety of means from aid, trade and propaganda to subversion by the sending of weapons and money, use of proxies and the engineering of armed insurgency. Through fresh readings of the relevant Charter rules some of the means now used – often termed 'indirect aggression' – were placed on par with the traditional upfront interstate uses of force, provided they included elements of force.[30] On the other hand, efforts to bring about regime change by means such as propaganda and economic pressure were not deemed prohibited. International law was thus deemed to protect states against various uses of force and intrusions equivalent to force, but it did not protect any particular ideological brand of government.

With the collapse of the Soviet Union, the Cold War struggles and interventions came to an end, but in the post détente world other struggles for global or regional dominance have surfaced – with revivals of subversion in some places. In other places – Georgia (2008) and Ukraine (2014 and 2022) – Russia has stood for an insertion of armed forces in full awareness that it was in breach of the rules on the use of force or the rule of proportionality. However, the costs have been high. In the case of the interventions in Ukraine in 2014, where Russia occupied Crimea and used subversive means, the General Assembly, in censuring Russia, affirmed the territorial integrity of Ukraine.[31] The EU and the US inflicted extensive economic sanctions and nothing was left of the détente with Europe and the United States. The full-scale armed Russian invasion of Ukraine in 2022 has triggered the most

---

[27] See Chapter 15, p. 212 ff.

[28] See above, Chapter 15, p. 258 India's marching into Portuguese Goa (1961) prompted sharply divided views at the UN but was not censured. See Franck, pp. 114–117 and see Gray, p. 68 ff.

[29] See Goertz (2016), p. 123 ff.

[30] In the Friendly Relations Declaration and in the Judgment by the International Court of Justice in the Nicaragua case. See above, Chapter 15, p. 213 ff.

[31] See above, Chapter 15, p. 219 ff.

draconian economic and financial sanctions by a large number of market economy countries and the General Assembly has categorically censured the action and demanded Russian withdrawal.[32]

It might be added in this context that subversive means of struggle and interventions in civil wars both by states and movements have long been common in the Middle East. Indeed, perhaps they have become so endemic that no state in the region has bothered to ask for condemnations from the United Nations. Many states have injected armed personnel, mercenaries, weapons or money into the civil wars, not only in Syria but also in Yemen, Iraq and Iran, and used political, economic and cyber power to exert influence and maintain or attain influence.[33] The ignoring of the rules against the interstate use of force and intervention by so many state actors in the Middle East and Libya and the lack of international reactions mean a severe erosion of the rules in these areas. Only Turkey's military seizure of a sliver of Syrian land has been generally branded as a violation of the rules and been seen as other than business as usual for the region. The cost of all the interventions and the poor returns obtained – and the misery and horror achieved – should lead to some second thoughts in many capitals of the bitter consequences of wrecking the non-intervention principle.

A third development was the state-based (Libya under Gaddafi) and non-state-based (mostly Al-Qaeda) terrorism that used force internationally triggering counter-measures that placed the relevant Charter rules under strain and modified the reading of some of them. The terrorism that culminated in the 9/11 events caused acceptance by the Security Council of several adjustments in the reading of the UN Charter articles on the use of force and self-defence.[34] The understanding developed that terrorist actions scattered in time and place, varying in gravity and performed by state or non-state actors could qualify as 'armed attacks' and trigger the right of armed self-defence of the victim state. Moreover, the acts of self-defence did not need to be an immediate countering of an ongoing attack but could be taken separately from and subsequently to the terrorist action(s). Actually, what came to be seen as compatible with Art. 51 was not so much 'defence' as retaliation, and this even on the territory of states that while hosting the terrorist actors were not co-authors of their attacks.

---

[32] UN General Assembly, 'Aggression against Ukraine', A/RES/ES-11/1 (2 March 2022). A full text and vote tally appears at www.aljazeera.com/news/2022/3/3/un-general-assembly-demands-russia-withdraw-troops-from-ukraine, 3 March 2022.

[33] See Chapter 2, pp. 15, 18 ff and above, Chapter 12, pp. 193 ff.

[34] See above, Chapter 15, p. 224 ff.

Given that, in the last decades, the lethal actions of various terrorist groups have been scattered both in time and place and that practically all states condemn terrorism, it was inevitable that a more permissive reading of the UN Charter rules on the use of force and self-defence would emerge. There is a risk, however, that the utter brutality of terrorist groups and their disregard for restraint may lead the United States and other states engaged in antiterrorist fighting to go beyond even the greater latitudes that have come to be read in the rules. This could occur under the sweeping claim in the US National Security Strategy of 2002 to a right to take armed action in (anticipatory) self-defence against threats to its national security – even before such threats appear to be imminent.[35]

Allowing – indeed mandating – police and other national armed units to guard against terrorist acts and to use means given to them, including armed force, to prevent and investigate acts that are 'imminent' is one thing. To order such units to consider international terrorist actions as constantly imminent, and to take action at any time within areas or on objects under the jurisdiction of other states, is quite another matter. To do so without the cooperation or consent of the states in question is unlikely to get an international stamp of approval except within very narrow confines, such as cases of complicity between the states and the terrorists. The US bombing of a chemical factory in Sudan that proved unrelated to the prior terrorist attacks on US embassies in Kenya and Tanzania,[36] and the US killing of the Iranian military leader Soleimani at Baghdad airport in US-allied state Iraq[37] would appear to have been actions that went beyond the adjusted readings of rules.

EFFECTIVENESS OF THE NORM PROHIBITING THE INTERSTATE USE OF FORCE

The preceding sections have shed light on how the terse Charter rules prohibiting the interstate use of force have evolved through practice and interpretation to become clearer and – on a few points – less categorical. Have they had an impact on states' behaviour? The survey of cases in this chapter has recorded many instances when states have acted in breach of or questionable conformity with the rules, and in not so few of these cases it seems obvious that force was used in full awareness that existing rules were ignored. The attitude seems to have been: 'Our security requires the action. Go ahead! Then

---

[35] See above, Chapter 15, p. 230 ff.
[36] See above, Chapter 15, p. 227.
[37] See above, Chapter 15, p. 234.

choose whatever justification you wish!' This attitude appears in cases where
states have perceived that 'vital interests' have been at stake, for instance in
cases where the US or the Soviet Union/Russia were determined to defend
their heavy influence in particular spheres.

During the Cold War, these cases included: US interventions in the
Dominican Republic and Grenada, and Soviet interventions in Hungary and
Czechoslovakia; and after the Cold War, Russia's large-scale intervention in
Georgia and invasions of Ukraine. In some actions, different participants show
different attitudes to the question of legality. To invade Iraq in 2003 clearly did
not cause the US administration any legal headaches, but it led to prolonged
agony in London. Bombing to punish Syria for the use of chemical weapons
raised legal problems in President Obama's mind, while President Trump,
appeared to have felt only pride at his own ability to act with determination.
Again, before President Obama decided on the action that led to the killing
of Osama bin Laden in Pakistan, he had legal memoranda worked out[38] while
under the Trump administration the drone attack and killing in Baghdad of
the leader of the Iranian Quds forces, Soleimani, was given a perfunctory
and barely credible justification.[39] Israel seems ready often to ignore the UN
Charter rules – bombing targets (in Syria) and apparently letting its intelligence organs ensure the killing of persons seen as potential or future dangers
to its security, notably objects and persons linked to possible future nuclear
weapons capacity in Iraq, Syria or Iran.[40]

The common use of subversive operations is obviously often explained by
the ambition to operate without being detected and stopped, but the hiding
of actions may also suggest an awareness that the actions are in breach of law.
The use of mercenaries instead of regular national units – as in Ukraine in
2014 and Libya in 2020 – may also be to enable the sender to deny responsibility for a use of force known to be prohibited.[41]

How often did governments actually refrain from a contemplated interstate
use of force? Was it done for military, political, economic or legal reasons?
Perhaps diplomatic memoirs can provide examples. One rare and famous
case was, of course, the Cuban Missile Crisis in 1962 in which US President
Kennedy's awareness of the risk of nuclear war, rather than legal conscience,
prevented the use of force. Another case was President Obama's way of shap-
ing a US reaction to the use of chemical weapons in Syria in 2013. It showed

[38] See above Chapter 15, p. 232.
[39] See above, Chapter 15, p. 234.
[40] See Bergman (2018).
[41] See below, Chapter 18, p. 287 ff.

his awareness of the legal barrier against a US punitive strike without Security Council authorization and a reluctance to ignore it.

We have seen that interstate force has come to be rarely used for some purposes, like the seizing of territory and no more for, say, the collection of contract debts,[42] but is this because of respect for a legal norm that has emerged or for other reasons, notably the pressure of the 'public mind'? It is true that law often seeks to shape new patterns of human behaviour and succeeds in doing so, but sometimes it just confirms and articulates pressures that are already exerted by the 'public mind'.

As we have seen, majorities in UN organs have through their handling of concrete cases adjusted the readings of the Charter's terse rules on the use of force on a few points. However, it is noteworthy that they have mostly stayed with rather orthodox readings – no doubt with a hope that states will come to adapt to the rules' command for restraint.

It may be appropriate to end this discussion about governments' respect for the general rule prohibiting the use of force with two quotes from former President Obama. In the presidential race in 2007, then Senator Obama expressed a view that did not crave greater freedom for the US to use force than was allowed under the dominant interpretation of Article 51 of the UN Charter. Without citing the article, he said he would 'not hesitate to use force, unilaterally if necessary, to protect the American people or our vital interests whenever we are attacked or imminently threatened'.[43]

When he accepted the Nobel Peace Prize in Oslo in 2009, he did not commit himself in terms so close to Article 51 and the dominant interpretation of it but instead recognized more broadly the importance of states respecting norms governing the use of force:

> '...I believe that all nations — strong and weak alike — must adhere to standards that govern the use of force'. He continued: 'I — like any head of state — reserve the right to act unilaterally if necessary to defend my nation. Nevertheless, I am convinced that adhering to standards strengthens those who do and isolates — and weakens — those who don't'.[44]

---

[42] See above, Chapter 12, p. 188.

[43] *Foreign Affairs*, July/Aug. 2007 'Renewing American Leadership'.

[44] President Barack Obama, Nobel Peace Lecture, Oslo, 10 December 2009, www.nobelprize .org/prizes/peace/2009/obama/lecture/.

18

States are Saying Farewell to Wars

STATES ARE SAYING FAREWELL TO WARS ABOUT LAND AND BORDERS. COMPETITION IS TAKING OTHER FORMS

In the preceding chapters, we have examined many kinds of incentives as well as disincentives and restraints to the interstate use of force. In this chapter, we shall draw on our observations and findings and try to reach some conclusions as to where the community of states may stand and be heading in its rejection of the use of force and at the same time not infrequently resorting to it.

Let us start with the incontrovertible tenet that humanity's DNA-anchored urge to defend and compete for scarce resources remains in place. The urge does not and has actually never automatically led to onslaughts with physical force. The fittest – who survived – were not those who wildly charged into walls. Rather, they must have wisely allowed themselves to be deflected not only by 'hard' obstacles, like the probability of defeat or revenge by powerful adversaries but also by risks of reactions and penalties by their own communities. This has enabled communities to discourage conduct deemed reprehensible – by reactions and norms aimed at setting some limits on the means used in the ever-ongoing competition between their human members. We mostly associate the term 'rules of competition' with commercial relations and regulation, but we could actually also see our laws – for instance on murder, theft, fraud and embezzlement – as ruling out some actions as impermissible kinds of competition between individuals.

In the state community, we see the most obvious evidence that means are used to influence human behaviour to be restrained or channelled. Here an organization has emerged whose governing leadership is – or should be – conscious that to thrive the community has an interest in steering its human members' competition to means and methods that do not hurt its own collective well-being – which excludes most uses of force. In line with Hobbes' tenets, it is generally believed that this steering requires a Leviathan[1] – a ruler/government that is powerful, notably through a monopoly on the possession and use of arms, that adopts and implements laws, that establishes courts to settle disputes and that metes out punishment, which together excludes and obviates the need for revenge.

THE HANDICAPPED LEVIATHAN OF THE INTERNATIONAL COMMUNITY

As it is clearly possible to steer the behaviour of members of state communities, there is no reason why it should be impossible to steer the behaviour of members of the global community of states. The first major attempt was made about a hundred years ago through the League of Nations. However, it is obvious that central parts of the organizational structure in place to steer the subjects of states – citizens – away from the use of physical force have been and remain missing in the community of states – and will do so for a long time. The members of the international community are armed but the community itself is not. Until a hundred years ago states even considered themselves unhindered by any common norm or institution to go to war for conquest or intervene for other aims.

Through the Covenant of the League of Nations, an important part of the community of states agreed on a common rule obliging its members to respect each other's territorial integrity and political independence. Yet, far from being able to constitute itself as a forceful global governing institution – a Leviathan – to uphold the rule, the League built on cooperation among great powers, on an ambition to disarm, and on fragile commitments by all members to 'collective security'. Several governments (Germany, Italy, Japan and the Soviet Union) ignored the agreed rules, gravely defied the organization and used force for territorial conquest. The first global community scheme of regulating the use of force among members failed.

The Charter of the United Nations is the second attempt of the community of states to organize itself as a peaceful order. It was a decisive step forward. Perhaps one could say it created a potential world ruler – a 'collective Leviathan' – by investing extensive power of action and enforcement in a Security Council dominated by the five great powers that were the victors of WW II. The power of the Council was made greater by rules committing all members to carry out its decisions, to abide by severe restrictions on the

---

[1]   See above, Chapter 17, p. 256.

interstate use of force, and to use arms in self-defence against armed attacks only until the Council could take action.

The ambition to create a peaceful order and the UN construction that was designed to prevent the use of force between states have been affected by many factors. Two stand out:

- The veto power of the five permanent members of the Security Council signals that the Council – the collective Leviathan – that is to maintain international peace and uphold agreed norms is handicapped and often unable to reach decisions on the action.
- Nuclear weapons and other modern arms systems have made the risk of nuclear war an existential threat, and at the same time, through the likeli-hood of devastating retaliation, created restraints against uses of force that could lead to the launching of nuclear weapons.

Some other factors impacting the effort to prevent the interstate use of force are:

- That the interest to acquire territory and to change borders has receded causing these incentives to the use of force to be rare.[2]
- That the 'public mind' in many states of the world has become increas-ingly active and supportive of bans against the use of force between states and of gross violations of human rights.[3]
- That the build-up and expansion of the European Union have made the use of force between states in this blood-soaked area almost unthinkable.
- That the interdependence and proximity of states has increased vastly (MED – mutual economic dependence, *globalization*), intensifying cooperation, facilitating non-force-based mutual influencing, and mak-ing ruptures more costly.[4]

Below, the focus will be first on the crucial effect of the veto power in the Security Council and on the equally crucial impact of nuclear weapons. Thereafter, the role of the three factors discussed in previous chapters as means of restraining the interstate use of force – military deterrence, diplo-macy and legal norms – will be reviewed and the tendencies to downplay the role of armed force and to turn to non-kinetic means of pressures and compe-tition will be discussed.

---

[2] See above, Chapter 6, p. 108 and Chapter 7, p. 117.
[3] See Chapter 6, p. 115.
[4] See Chapter 6, p. 113.

UN SECURITY COUNCIL UNABLE TO
ACT BECAUSE OF THE VETO

Instead of joining hands to lead the Security Council in its mission to prevent the use of force, the five great powers' permanent members showed as of the Cold War that they would rarely be able to agree in conflicts involving perceived important national interests.

Before the resulting paralysis is described, it needs to be noted that the veto has not stood in the way of innumerable measures like peacekeeping operations to monitor cease-fires, prevent illicit arms transfers and other post-conflict tasks. With peacekeeping, the UN under the leadership of Secretary-General Dag Hammarskjöld created one of its principal instruments of practical action – even though the term is not even mentioned in the Charter – and it is financed by voluntary contributions. In 2021, for instance, there were twelve peacekeeping operations underway and half of them were in Africa, with a combined peacekeeping budget for 2021–2022 of 6.4 billion dollars.

While Council agreement on peacekeeping operations has been of immense value, the lack of required consensus among the permanent members often left the Council passive and obliged member states to act alone or together with allies to tackle controversies and threats and uses of force. The issue of the veto remains intractable and a fundamental handicap. As has been noted,[5] while the veto might appear like a simple matter of procedure, it is rooted in the refusal of great powers to commit themselves to bow to unknown future majority decisions. It has blocked the Council from many actions and from performing its mandate to develop plans for disarmament and making use of its 'Military Staff Committee'. Frustration over the veto is understandable and justified but should perhaps be directed more at the inability of the P5 to agree on action than at the procedure that manifests their disagreement. This said it is clear that the veto has been used much more than to guard what P5 states regard as truly vital interests. The 'Lichtenstein' resolution that allows the General Assembly to examine vetoes cast may become a small pressure against unwarranted vetoes.[6] If a reform of the composition of the Council were to be agreed some limitation of the use of the veto might also be attained.[7]

---

[5]   See above, Chapter 11, p. 183 Chapter 13, p. 200.
[6]   See above, Chapter 13, p. 200.
[7]   In his address to the 77th Session of the UN General Assembly on 21 September 2022, President Biden proposed some reforms of the Security Council, including limits in the use of the veto 'except in rare, extraordinary situations' and an increase in both the permanent and non-permanent members of the Council. He also stated that 'I reject the use of violence

NUCLEAR WEAPONS AND THE RISK OF UNACCEPTABLE PAIN HAVE CREATED INCENTIVES FOR CAUTION AND RESTRAINT ON THE USE OF FORCE

The arrival and development of nuclear weapons and capacities to deliver them in matters of minutes on increasingly urbanized adversaries gave, as described above,[8] a drastically new potential dimension to the force that could be used in any conflicts between or touching the interests of NWS.

The threats posed by nuclear weapons have caused constant worldwide government concern and public engagement for their outlawing. The Nuclear Non-Proliferation Treaty (NPT) created an avenue for the NNWS to make legally binding renunciations of nuclear weapons and for NWS parties to assume equally binding obligations for good faith nuclear disarmament negotiations. While the International Court of Justice (ICJ) in an advisory opinion in 1996 concluded that most uses of nuclear weapons would be illegal, it stopped short of holding that this applied in extreme circumstances of national survival.[9] The 2017 Treaty on the Prohibition of Nuclear Weapons (TPNW), seeks to undermine the legitimacy of nuclear weapons, but cannot and does not create obligations for non-party states to refrain from possessing or using the weapons.[10]

Nuclear-weapon states, for their part, invariably declare that the principal function of their arsenals is to deter possible nuclear attacks. Nevertheless, national nuclear posture statements seem to retain much freedom of action, an ambition that is apparent also in the development of low-yield, nuclear weapons for battlefield use. The horrors of Hiroshima and Nagasaki must nevertheless constantly remind the nuclear-weapon states of the concept of 'unacceptable pain', the clinically sounding term meaning that some actions will bring such unbearable (unacceptable) pain that they must be reliably prevented.[11] As the NPT parties have twice noted by consensus (in 2000 and 2010) that only the physical elimination and continued absence of all nuclear weapons could give such a guarantee, this conclusion is often cited by defenders of 'global zero' as a goal.

Such a course did not seem excluded in the first decade of this century, for instance, at the Obama–Medvedev meeting in London in 2010, but has not been within reach in the armament climate that has prevailed since then.

---

and war to conquer nations or expand borders through bloodshed.' Full text is available at: www.whitehouse.gov/briefing-room/speeches-remarks/2022/09/21/remarks-by-president-biden-before-the-77th-hsession-of-the-united-nations-general-assembly/.

[8] Chapter 8, p. 131 ff.
[9] See above, Chapter 8, p. 135, note 27.
[10] See above, Chapter 8, p. 137.
[11] See above, Chapter 8, p. 139.

A minimum measure of confidence and cooperation would be required and such confidence could grow with concrete progress in disarmament. Confidence and disarmament are mutually promoting.

To be sure, there is a good deal that the nuclear-weapon states could do and should be doing after the end of the war in Ukraine when the world is beginning to look for détente. The discussion could again be devoted to the idea of 'a no first use commitment'.[12] Such commitments – not to be the first to use a nuclear weapon in a conflict – would be valuable but not by themselves lead any state to do away with a capacity for a second strike, even less do away with research and development. Further ratifications to the Comprehensive Nuclear-Test-Ban treaty are long overdue and there should be room for further reductions in nuclear arsenals.

However, the continued possession of an arsenal of nuclear weapons with the capacity to launch an effective retaliatory second strike is how the nuclear-weapon states believe they are achieving their ultimate protection against a possible nuclear attack. No reliable shields against second strikes have materialized nor are any expected to do so – despite decades of efforts and trillions of dollars spent.

So far, various restraints have reduced the credibility and probability of a first nuclear strike. These include the existence in a potential victim state of a retaliatory second nuclear strike capability and the risks of a head-on nuclear war between the United States, Russia and China, or the consequences of a war between any one of these states and a state promised or otherwise expected protection by them against nuclear attack. These restraints are strengthened by the recent addition of several new means to bring 'unacceptable' pain – cyber techniques, space weapons and perhaps the use of automated systems or capabilities.[13]

The effectiveness of all restraints is of course subject to caveats, notably recognition of the risks of misunderstandings or technical errors and the assumption that governments act rationally.

Throughout the post-World War II era, similar restraints have also served to prevent head-on wars with conventional weapons between the US, Russia, or China and between any one of them with a state-promised protection, due to the risk that any conflict in which NWS meet each other with conventional weapons may escalate to a nuclear conflict.

Logic would suggest that the possession of nuclear weapons by the United States, Russia and China should not influence conflicts between NNWS, such as between Iran and Iraq in the 1980s. Nor, subject to the caveats above, should

---

[12] See above, Chapter 8, p. 134.
[13] See the discussion above, Chapter 8, p. 129 ff.

a NWS necessarily be concerned about a conflict between a NNWS with which it is not allied and another NWS. Consider, for example, Russia vs. Georgia or Ukraine with the United States as a bystander; or United States vs. Iran with Russia as a bystander. Historically, the three major nuclear-armed states have shared a common recognition of the risk of drifting into clashes between themselves, which has led them to caution against being drawn into conflicts where this risk may arise. In the civil war in Syria (2011–2021), for example, both Russia and the US have intervened – on different sides – but reached agreements on measures to avoid ('deconflict') direct confrontations in the air and on the ground.[14] In the case of Ukraine, it has been clear that the US, although supplying Ukraine with weapons, has not wished to intervene on the ground against Russia's armed actions for fear of a direct confrontation – and risk of escalation – with Russia.

It is hard to avoid the conclusion that while the existence of nuclear weapons is the source of justified anguish it has also – so far – been a general factor for some caution and restraint on the use of armed force. While this is part of what has been termed the 'nuclear taboo' there are, of course, no guarantees that such restraints will always prevail.[15]

What risks are posed to the peace by nuclear weapons in the hands of others than the major nuclear weapon states? Proliferation complicates the geopolitical situation and increases risks not only for the major powers but for all. However, while the risk of war between the nuclear-armed states India and Pakistan (both with vulnerable megacities) is not excluded, it is reduced by the awareness of the two states that any armed engagement between them raises risk of escalation. North Korea might threaten, but would be highly unlikely to launch a nuclear first strike on the US or a US ally and the US is unlikely to launch an armed attack on North Korea as long as it is feared that the country could manage a second strike – especially one reaching the American continent. Israel is likely to use its nuclear weapons only if it judged its existence threatened.

It seems natural at the end of this discussion to consider the words of Alfred Nobel, the founder of the Nobel Peace Prize and also the inventor of dynamite and owner of war material industries. In an oft-quoted letter to his friend, the peace activist Bertha von Suttner, he wrote that he thought a likely path to peace would be to make weapons so terrible that they made war unthinkable: 'Perhaps my factories will put an end to war sooner than your congresses: on the day that two army corps can mutually annihilate each other in a second, all civilised nations will surely recoil with horror and disband their troops'.[16]

---

[14]   BBC (2015), 'US and Russia Sign Deal to Avoid Syria Air Incidents', 20 October 2015.
[15]   On the future prospects for the nuclear taboo, see Tannenwald (2007), p. 383 ff.
[16]   Tägil (1998).

While nuclear weapons may have created incentives for restraint in the use of force, their existence has not led their possessors to 'dismiss their troops' and made the world reach the point that Alfred Nobel thought would be decisive. He also limited his prediction of restraint to 'civilized states'. Perhaps today he would have said 'a world with sane rulers'. He also did not take into account the risks of mistakes and misunderstandings, chillingly described by former US Secretary of Defence, William J. Perry.[17] Nevertheless, Nobel's prediction still remains a farsighted reflexion on the role of weapons of mass destruction and the elimination of wars.

NON-NUCLEAR RELATED RESTRAINTS TO THE INTERSTATE USE OF FORCE

It is concluded above that while the UN Security Council is no functioning international Leviathan, the presence of nuclear (and newer) weapons, unwelcome as it is, has caused restraints in the use of force not only directly between the nuclear weapon states but much more broadly. What importance do traditional non-nuclear-related factors have to create restraints on the interstate use of force?

In Chapter 6 we pointed to factors such as the cost of lives and resources, and domestic and international public opinion that may act as restraints. We noted that in most parts of the modern world of close relations between states, a happy absence of incentives to use force rather than restraints seems to explain peaceful regional relations. Civil wars stand for much of the use of force in the world and interventions (sometimes in civil wars) make up many of the cases where restraints have not been enough to prevent the interstate use of force after WWII. Beyond interventions, there have been some but not many cases of interstate uses of force, such as between Algeria-Morocco, India-Pakistan, Armenia-Azerbaijan, Ethiopia-Eritrea, Iraq-Iran /Kuwait, Israel and neighbours, Russia and Ukraine. Tensions between, say, Greece and Turkey, Argentina and Chile and Ecuador and Peru have played out without any use of force.

NON-NUCLEAR RELATED MILITARY DETERRENCE

In Chapter 6, we concurred with the general view that military deterrence may, indeed, create significant restraints in the resort to the use of force in today's world. This is evidently in line with the convictions of the many

---

[17] For further discussion of these risks, see Perry (2015), Chapter 8, 'Nuclear Alerts, Arms Control, and Missed Opportunities in Nonproliferation'.

governments and parliaments that vote billions of dollars each year for defence budgets.

Yet, this conclusion deserves both some questions and some comments. Most states live in peace most of the time, with small or big military forces available for defence (or the maintenance of internal order). Is the external peace mainly, or even partly, due to the deterrence of their military force and possible military alliances? Or are potential incentives to use force against other states mostly restrained by other factors than loaded weapons on the other side? Do we really know that it would make any difference for their peace if, say Austria or Switzerland were to dismantle their military forces? Would Russia or the US rush in to occupy the countries to fill the military vacuum? Or: did the Soviet Union refrain from expanding through force in Europe during the Cold War because it was deterred by the military force of the 'policy of containment'?

An answer might be that there are good reasons to think that the military defence was, indeed, an effective deterrent – but one that might have been superfluous. It was like a very expensive insurance policy against a very low probability risk of a catastrophic accident.

Another question to ask is whether buying an over-insurance – aiming at unquestionable military superiority – is rational.[18] Assuming that there is no wish to start and win an armed contest, would it not suffice – and give more stability and less cost – to abstain from defence capacity in excess of the need to deter an adversary? Indeed, it seems this was the philosophy of Art. 26 of the UN Charter that urges the promotion of peace and security '*with the least diversion for armaments of the world's human and economic resources*'. Art. 8 of the Covenant of the League of Nations expressed the thought even more explicitly:

> The Members of the League recognize that the maintenance of peace requires the reduction of national armaments to the lowest point consistent with national safety and the enforcement by common action of international obligations.[19]

It is understandable that the military sphere in any country may find it difficult to determine what the level of parity is and may prefer capacities that are more than reassuring as a deterrent against any attack. However, such capacities are likely to trigger arms races. The current fierce arms race has

---

[18]   See above, Chapter 7, p. 118 about On the US declared intention to have 'full spectrum dominance', see p. 121.

[19]   The emphasis on arms for enforcement action is remarkable testimony to the wish of the authors of the Covenant to replace national defence with collective security.

brought the world to spend around 2 trillion dollars annually on the military sphere.[20] Will awareness of the urgent need for huge programmes of change and resources to defend the living conditions for all humans on the planet rally support for a *redirection* of the torrent of funds that the world now spends on the military sector?

DIPLOMACY TO OBVIATE THE USE OF FORCE

The role of diplomacy to defuse conflicts and prevent possible interstate uses of force was discussed above in Chapters 7 and 10 and examples of successes and failures were given. One modern development facilitating diplomacy at the highest level is the growing opportunity for government leaders to communicate. As noted in Chapter 10, modern communications enable leaders to talk to each other instantly directly or in circles of allies or groups like the G7. While these groups are – reasonably – like-minded and serve to forge common positions, bilateral summit meetings are from time to time nearly obligatory for leaders of great powers with uneasy relations and present opportunities for high-level diplomacy. Nevertheless, the UN Security Council – and the very frequent informal meetings of the New York representatives of its five permanent members – remains a place where today's three main powers (plus France and the UK) remain in constant communication.

Will states – notably the great military powers – in the brave new world of instantly available destruction and instantly available opportunities for communication continue in an incessant race for more and innovative arms and for deterrent or deterrent plus?[21] Or, will they recognize that they have by now attained such a capability of mutual mega-destruction that they find any weapons use too risky and conclude that they must use diplomacy to edge away from positions that may trigger confrontations between themselves and think of longer-term security? Even at the time when China did not yet have nuclear weapons, US presidents on several occasions considered and refused to approve nuclear attacks proposed to them and during the Cuban Missile Crisis in 1962, the United States and the Soviet Union were held back by awareness of a risk of nuclear war. With many times stronger, destructive capacity at their disposal including cyber and space weapons and artificial

---

[20] Summary, *SIPRI Yearbook 2021*, p. 12, www.sipri.org/sites/default/files/2021-06/sipri_yb21_summary_en_v2_0.pdf.

[21] There is of course no guarantee that the information transmitted through these 'instantly available' communications will be reliable. For a discussion focusing on reports about Iran's nuclear activities, see Porter (2014).

intelligence and no ability to foresee the consequences of the use of any of it, will the leadership of today's major powers – once Russia's war in Ukraine is over and reconstruction is underway – turn to diplomacy?

THE NORMS OF THE INTERNATIONAL COMMUNITY SET LIMITS FOR STATE BEHAVIOUR. HOW EFFECTIVE ARE THEY?

In Chapter 12, it was suggested that UN Charter norms on the use of force might be seen as fundamental agreed limitations on the ways in which states may compete. While governments, including the most powerful ones, routinely proclaim their acceptance of these norms, we have seen in Chapters 15 and 16 how in many cases they have knowingly ignored or sought to circumvent the rules. A few glimpses will be noted below of the reasonings within the United States and the United Kingdom governments of how relevant the restrictions on the use of force appeared to them in some specific cases.

GLIMPSES OF GOVERNMENT REASONINGS ABOUT NORMS OF RESTRAINT

We described above how, in the internal discussions in the United Kingdom during the early phase of the march-up to the attack on Iraq in 2003, the British Prime Minister was told by his legal advisers that a wish to change an abhorrent regime in a foreign state could not justify armed action.[22] While in his 1999 Chicago speech, Prime Minister Tony Blair voiced the thought that powerful (and decent) governments might have a mission unilaterally to topple odious dictators, but that thought was not tried in the Security Council. Rather, as long as it was politically possible in 2003, the UK sought to mobilize support for a Security Council resolution that would give green light to the use of force against Saddam Hussein. When these efforts failed, the UK felt politically constrained to join the US in the attack without any such authorization. The legal justification presented was strained and left no doubt that the political pressure had prevailed over respect for the relevant and well-understood norms.[23]

In another instance cited above, memoranda from within the US Obama administration show a discussion of justifications contemplated prior to the 2011 military operation to catch or kill the Al-Qaeda leader Osama Bin Laden in Pakistan. Interestingly, officials in the administration thought President

---

[22] See above, Chapter 16, p. 241.
[23] See above, p. 246 ff.

Obama might be more concerned about US constitutional and legal restraints than about those in international law.[24]

More direct Insight into President Obama's thinking is gained in an interview in *the Atlantic* about a possible armed attack on Syria in 2013 as punishment for the use of chemical weapons. Obama is cited as being conscious of and bothered by the absence of Security Council authorization for military action (apart from pressures from Congress to take such action). In the end, he found together with Russia a diplomatic solution under which Syria was persuaded to join the Chemical Weapons Convention and surrender its chemical weapons.[25]

On two other occasions cited above, President Obama showed that he was aware of the value of the existing legal norms governing the use of force, the need to respect them and the extent of the right to self-defence.[26] As a trained lawyer, President Obama understood the value of legal norms both in the national and the international community and his answers should not be read as perfunctory rhetoric. He had vigorously criticized the United States for launching the 2003 Iraq war and he showed himself reticent to let the United States take a leading role in the later – UN authorized – action in Libya in 2011. While he allowed the United States to continue the war in Afghanistan and low-intensity but lethal and widely dispersed belligerent engagements against terrorism in the Middle East and Africa, his attitude perhaps reflected both legal qualms and a growing US skepsis about 'endless wars'.

HOW EFFECTIVE HAS THE UN CHARTER'S RULE PROHIBITING THE INTERSTATE USE OF FORCE BEEN TO PREVENT INTERVENTIONS?

We have noted that the 'classic' interstate use of force and acquisition of territory have become rare,[27] but said it would be rash to conclude that the changed behaviour had been a result of the adoption of rules in the UN Charter (Art. 2:4). Perhaps the public mind and a lesser interest in the acquisition of land had helped to bring state conduct in line with a norm that had ripened and been agreed. When we find[28] that not a few cases have occurred

---

[24] Charlie Savage, 'How 4 Federal Lawyers Paved the Way to Kill Osama bin Laden'. *New York Times*. October 28, 2015; see also Chapter 15, p. 232
[25] See above, Chapter 16, p. 251. Subsequently suspicions have arisen that some weapons had been retained.
[26] See above, Chapter 17, p. 264.
[27] Chapter 12, p. 187.
[28] Chapter 17, p. 258.

in which governments have ignored the broader reach of the Charter rule covering the uses of force without the seizing of territory – mostly interventions – we submit that it would be rash conversely to conclude that the Charter rule and the 'public mind' underpinning it have been without effects.

For one thing, resolutions by the Security Council and the General Assembly demonstrate that the majority of states support the rule and condemn conduct they have deemed to disregard the rule. Further, we discern a post-World War II trend among states to deny their use of force or to downplay it by hiding or blurring it. States appear also to turn to means of exerting pressure and influence without direct – or any – use of armed force.[29] The trends show at least awareness of the rule. Had the states perceived the use of force as lawful there would – as in past times – have been little reason for denying, downplaying, or hiding it.

Let us recall that armed interventions – like armed conquests – were commonplace in past centuries.[30] With increased respect for territorial integrity and the principle of equality of states attitudes to armed interventions have changed over time. Views expressed to President T. Roosevelt in 1903 and by Secretary of State Dulles in 1958 were cited above to illustrate the mental mileage that was made in some 50 years.[31]

POST WWII CASES OF INTERVENTIONS USING ARMED FORCE

Despite the changes in attitudes, interventions by force have not ceased. It is striking, however, that in the many cases of intervention that have come before the UN, these have met a rather orthodox reading of the Charter's broad prohibition of the use of force. On many occasions, states have invoked 'self-defence' almost as a 'default' justification for interventions using force. However, under Art. 51 of the Charter, the use of force in 'self-defence' is justified only 'if an armed attack occurs', and in the absence of concrete such attacks most of the pleas have been deemed irrelevant. Only armed interventions in response to 'imminent' attacks or as part of 'war against terrorism' have been accepted as 'self-defence'.[32]

---

[29] See above, Chapter 17, p. 265 and Chapter 8, p. 142.
[30] See Chapter 6, p. 114; Chapter 12, p. 189: Chapter 17, p. 257.
[31] See above, Chapter 6, p. 112.
[32] For the case of US bombings in Afghanistan and Sudan following the Al Qaeda terrorist acts against US embassies in Nairobi and Dar-es-Salaam, see above, Chapter 15, p. 227. For the Security Council's prompt explicit prior approval – directly after Al Qaeda's 9/11 attacks – of actions in self-defence in areas from which terrorist acts were launched, see Chapter 15, p. 227.

The firmness with which UN organs have applied the rule against the inter-state use of force – including interventions – was striking, when Israel's claim of self-defence was not accepted as a justification for the armed intervention to rescue hostages at Entebbe in Uganda in 1976.[33] It was also striking when the General Assembly showed no understanding but, on the contrary, implicitly criticized the armed intervention through which Vietnam in 1978 intervened in Kampuchea and ousted the blood-stained genocidal government of Pol Pot.[34]

A conclusion from the foregoing is that while UN organs – for lack of enforcement readiness – have been unable to undo interventions assessed by them to have been unlawful, they have been remarkably firm in asserting the rules prohibiting interventions using force.[35]

The other observation that emerged from the examination of many post-World War II cases of intervention surveyed was that governments often show awareness of the legal rules by choosing modes of action or postures in ways designed to minimize their visibility and their own responsibility for elements of force used – or at least maximize the deniability of this role. There were, moreover, signs that governments increasingly resort to interventions in which economic and political measures and cyber actions rather than physical force were used as means of pressure. These new tendencies will now be discussed.

INTERVENTION WITH THE USE OF FORCE SIMPLY DENIED

Like individuals who have committed violent crimes, States using force unlawfully may seek to reject responsibility by claiming that they had played an innocent role or by flatly denying having had anything to do with the violence that has taken place. An example is the posture taken by the Soviet Union after its suppression of the uprising in Hungary (1956) and the Prague Spring (1968). In the wake of WWII, the two states had been made satellites of the Soviet Union and parts of the Socialist camp. This was used as an argument for the claim that the armed suppression was no occupation by force of the Soviet Union and no interstate use of force, but internal acts and friendly defence against foreign interference in the common camp (Warsaw Pact or Socialist 'Commonwealth'). The world had no difficulty seeing that the actions constituted interstate interventions and denounced them.[36]

---

[33] See above, Chapter 16, p. 244.
[34] The position of the Assembly is criticized in Franck, p. 150. See also above, Chapter 16, p. 243.
[35] Cf. above, p. 281, and see Chapter 17, p. 258.
[36] See Chapter 15, p. 218 ff. and see Chapter 12, p. 193.

Another example is offered by the Sunni Arab states that opposed the Assad regime throughout the Syrian civil war (2011–) and that avoided open-armed participation but reportedly were behind extensive unlawful armed intervention whose authorship they did not acknowledge. Similarly, Israel intervened frequently in Syria by unacknowledged aerial incursions to bomb regime-controlled Iranian-linked targets in Syria.[37]

The Russian seizure by force of Crimea in 2014 provided an instance of naked denial of the reality and of the responsibility for the 'little green men' and armed forces of Russia that helped take control of the peninsula. It was a thin and unblushing way to deny the Russian engineering of and responsibility for the armed occupation. By a strong majority vote, the UN General Assembly ignored the charade.[38]

In the initial phase of the Russian invasion of Ukraine in early 2022, the *théâtre russe* again performed the act of denying Russian aggression: the use of the terms 'war' and 'intervention' to describe the Russian actions was penalized in Russia and the invasion was explained as a 'special military operation' to defend against alleged Ukrainian attacks on Russian speaking people. The target audience this time may have been the large Russian public exposed mainly to national news channels to avoid its possible opposition to the armed action. The world audience had no difficulty, however, in seeing the reality of naked aggression and condemning it. Huge military assistance was provided by Western states, notably the United States and, although not decided by the Security Council and not adopted by all countries, far-reaching economic sanctions were imposed on Russia.[39] The reaction of the world was very different from the failed effort of the League of Nations in 1935–36 to impose sanctions on Italy for its war against Ethiopia.[40]

Assassinations and Sabotage – With No Acknowledgement of Authorship

Assassinations and sabotage engineered by states abroad constitute interventions violating the prohibition of the use of force and encroachment on the territory. Awareness of the illegality of the actions leads states responsible simply to deny or refuse acknowledgment of the actions. Most noted modern cases are the several failed attempts on the life of President Fidel Castro.

---

[37] See Chapter 12, p. 194 ff. As has been developed, armed assistance is deemed legal if given at the request of recognized governments in civil war, while providing armed assistance to rebels constitutes illegal intervention.
[38] See above, Chapter 15, p. 221 ff.
[39] Discussed further in Chapter 3, p. 46 ff.
[40] See Walters (1965), pp. 627–691.

As noted above, the US involvement in these attempts and other cases were examined by an official American Commission in 1976 and led to bans on the US practice.[41]

Nevertheless, from time to time it is reported that some assassination or sabotage has occurred and that some foreign government is the likely perpetrator. Sometimes the actions are part of persecutions by regimes of their own adversaries abroad but sometimes they are directed against another state. The list of reported cases is long. Examples include the assassination in France in 1980 of a nuclear expert working for Iraq. It was preceded in 1979 by sabotage in France of nuclear equipment ready for shipment to Iraq. In 2020 and a number of years earlier several Iranian nuclear scientists were assassinated.[42] The attempted poisoning of a former Russian spy (Skripal) in the United Kingdom in 2018, though not directed against the UK, also constituted an unlawful intervention.

The same can be said about the killing of an Iranian regime opponent in France in 2011, the killing in Kuala Lumpur of a half-brother of the North Korean leader in 2017 and the killing and dismembering of the Saudi journalist, Jamal Khashoggi at the Saudi Consulate in Istanbul in 2016. A common feature is that states denounced as responsible simply flatly deny having had any hand in the events. Acts like those mentioned demonstrate – apart from all else – a cold defiance of rules of jurisdiction that are crystal clear and officially recognized by all. Authorizing kills by poison or kidnapping abroad is engaging in international gangsterism.

SUBVERSION

Seeking to influence who is in power in other states is neither a new nor necessarily a forbidden government activity. While foreign funding may today politically discredit political parties, and violate national constitutional or other national law, it is not per se forbidden by any international legal rules. However, as noted, the prohibition of the use of 'force' between states is deemed to outlaw *'the organizing, instigating. assisting or participating in acts of civil strife…'* when the acts *'involve a threat or use of force'*.[43] In its judgment in the Nicaragua case, the International Court of Justice (ICJ) considered it

---

[41] See above, Chapter 16, p. 241 and see National Security Archives, Washington D.C. 16 April 2021. The killing of Osama bin Laden by a US operation in Pakistan in 2011 is discussed above in Chapter 15, p. 232. It may not have constituted an unlawful intervention as the incursion appears to have been accepted by Pakistan government.

[42] See Chapter 4, p. 73.

[43] From the 1970 Friendly Relations Declaration, above Chapter 12, p. 185

unlawful for states to influence other states' choice of government or foreign or other policies through *'support for subversive or terrorist armed activities'* using methods of coercion.[44]

'Subversive' action of various gravity, including the fomenting of civil strife to undermine or topple foreign governments, has remained a part of the international political landscape.[45] Through various acts of subversion, governments seek to destabilize or attain changes in foreign regimes or their policies without using armed force openly and without provoking others to use force. One senses a wish to pursue actions that may escape discovery and counteraction but also to allow denial of authorship and responsibility for acts recognized to be breaches of international norms.

The declaration made by US President Truman in 1947, and occasioned by efforts in Greece by foreign-supported Communist groups to take over the country, marked the readiness of the United States to give help to governments defending themselves against subversion.[46] The United States has also, however, devoted itself extensively to subversion. In 1953, after the nationalization of the Anglo-Iranian Oil Company (AIOC), the CIA conspired with Iranian military groups to engineer the quick internal coup that in 1953 ousted Iran's first democratically elected leader, Mossadegh.[47] Another case occurred in Chile in 1973 when the CIA covertly assisted a group of Chilean militaries to topple President, Salvador Allende. Washington had feared he would lead Chile to Socialist policies including nationalizations – in the same direction as Cuba. The Nixon government while presumably pleased with the Pinochet government taking over, denied any involvement in the coup.[48]

INTERVENTIONS WITH RESPONSIBILITY
FOR THE USE OF FORCE BLURRED

While the practice of subversion shows not only a wish to hide that a state may be using force or coercion equivalent to force that may violate legal norms, some means of state conduct have the aim of reducing the public footprint and responsibility for various open armed operations. They are designed to blur authorship for activities that might constitute an unlawful use of force or might, if not blurred, be likely to provoke counteractions.

---

[44] Cited above, Chapter 15, p. 213 ff.
[45] Cf. Chapter 17, p. 266.
[46] See Chapter 3, p. 34.
[47] Allen-Ebrahimian (2017).
[48] Peter Kornbluh (ed), 'Extreme Option: Overthrow Allende', National Security Archive, 15 September 2020.

One category of such means is terming troops volunteers. It was done by China in Korea in 1950 and could have reduced the impression of a war between the state of China and its army, the People's Liberation Army (PLA) and the United States that led the United Nations operations against North Korea.[49] Another case was Russian claims that troops sent into the insurgency in East Ukraine after 2014 were volunteers.[50] Like the use of 'little green men' rather than regular Russian soldiers in the occupation of Crimea, the use of 'volunteers' in Donbas could be invoked to deny that the state of Russia was responsible for waging both an armed attack and an illegal intervention in Ukraine. It should be added that none of the measures to disclaim responsibility stopped international condemnation, economic sanctions by the European Union and the United States, and recommendations by the UN General Assembly.

In the Bay of Pigs operations (1961), the participants were exiled Cubans recruited by the CIA giving the US a – flimsy – ground to deny authorship and responsibility for the illegal intervention.[51]

A second type of action showing awareness of legal rules of restraint can be seen in the US actions in the Syrian civil war. The United States has actively assisted anti-government groups with funds and weapons but has chosen to refrain from sending fighting cadres and to blur direct armed participation by sending 'advisers'.[52] Apart from domestic legal and political concerns, the US undoubtedly has had in mind avoiding a charge of unlawful armed intervention – and also preventing any direct armed confrontation with Russian-controlled units invited by the Syrian government.

A third type of means to blur or deny engagement in armed actions may be using mercenaries. States' use of mercenaries may be quite open, as the use by Saudi Arabia and Abu Dhabi of mercenaries from Sudan and Latin America for the war against the Houthi rebels in Yemen.[53] The United States' well-known and extensive use of armed personnel from large commercial security organizations (earlier 'Blackwater') is not for combat but for the protection of military sites and activities.[54] However, units named Wagner coming from Russia have been in active armed service in several conflicts – Ukraine, Syria, Libya and Sahelian countries – apparently deployed by Russia for armed actions but not acknowledged as participation by the Russian government. Thus, reliance on mercenaries may be simply to reduce the number of regular

---

[49] See above, Chapter 3, p. 34.
[50] See Chapter 15, p. 221.
[51] See Chapter 4, p. 67.
[52] See Chapter 12, p. 194.
[53] See Chapter 6, p. 110 note 9.
[54] Scahill (2007); and Marten (2019), pp. 181–204. And see above, Chapter 6, p. 110 note 9.

troops that a state may otherwise need to deploy (Saudi Arabia, Abu Dhabi). However, reliance on mercenaries may also be used to blur a state's participation in an intervention understood to be unlawful or of questionable legality, as in the Russian reliance on Wagner units in East Ukraine and Libya.[55]

THE USE OF FORCE REPLACED BY OTHER MEANS OF PRESSURE: THREATS OF FORCE, ECONOMIC PRESSURES, CYBER ACTIONS

As we discern the ambitions of states to reduce the element – or at least the footprint – of force in interventions because of legal and other concerns, we can see efforts to replace the actual use of force with other means of exerting pressures. While the 'threat' of force' and actions 'equivalent' to force remain outlawed under Art 2:4 of the Charter, and some other kinds of pressures may be violating the rule of non-intervention, yet other pressures are permissible.[56]

A specific problem is that little guidance is available on what constitutes unlawful 'threats' of force. As noted in Chapter 12 the Helsinki Declaration (1975) commits states to refrain from *'manifestations of force'* that bring other states *'to renounce the full exercise of their sovereign rights'*.[57] However, as also noted, no threats of force seem to have been brought before and condemned by the Security Council or General Assembly. Must we draw the conclusion that menacing oral postures, military movements or manoeuvres near each other's borders and 'prodding' not combined with explicit demands, may be regarded as tolerable 'warnings' or 'reminders of force' rather than 'threats of force'? Are governments and the military around the world granting each other the freedom to flex their military muscles in front of each other – even at the risk of increased tension and unintended clashes?[58] Query whether it would not be time for some states to come to the Security Council or – perhaps better – the General Assembly of the UN to submit that some action of the kinds described in Chapter 12 constitutes 'threats' prohibited under Art. 2:4?

If naval demonstrations may be chosen as means of pressure to avoid an actual use of force, the same may be true of economic blockades. They have a long history. The 'continental blockade' during the Napoleonic wars stands out as a

---

[55] France24, 'EU imposes sanctions on Russian mercenary group Wagner over human rights abuses', 13 December 2021.

[56] See above, Chapter 12, p. 189.

[57] See above, Chapter 12, p. 185 This language – a promise to refrain from 'economic coercion designed to subordinate…' – was used in the so-called Budapest memorandum of 5 December 1994 upon the acceptance by Ukraine of the commitment to eliminate all nuclear weapons from its territory.

[58] See above, Chapter 7, p. 121 and Chapter 12, p. 191.

'classic' example.[59] In modern times, collective international economic sanctions have been tools used with mixed success, both by the League of Nations and the United Nations. With accelerating interdependence economic pressures have become tools of influence and constraint used by individual states or groups of states.[60] The Arab oil embargo in 1973–74, following the Yom Kippur War sought to exert pressure on a number of states, including the US.[61]

In the past decades, especially the US government has made extensive use of economic sanctions as a means of pressure on – or a sign of displeasure with – a variety of foreign governments. In 2018, the US unilaterally breached the Security Council resolution that lifted sanctions and economic measures against Iran. It imposed extensive US economic and financial sanctions that it urged other states to join.[62] In recent years the US has also adopted far-reaching restrictive economic measures (2020) as a part of wider economic warfare and as reactions to China's policies against the Uighur population and increased control over Hong Kong.

The European Union adopted economic sanctions against Russia after the annexation of Crimea in 2014 and the interventions in East Ukraine – and Russia responded with economic sanctions against European Union countries.[63] In 2022, after Russia's invasion of Ukraine, the United States, NATO and the EU made it clear that while they would not intervene with arms in Ukraine they would support Ukraine by supplying arms. At the same time, they adopted more far-reaching economic and financial sanctions than ever on Russia. A general question is how effective economic sanctions are. EU and US economic sanctions in 2014 did not make Russia return Crimea to Ukraine. We also know that draconian US-led economic and financial sanctions gravely hurt Iran (2018), even though they may not have had much influence on Iranian policies that the United States opposed. However, when in February 2022 Russia proceeded to the armed invasion of Ukraine – while terming its action 'special military operation' – unprecedently severe economic and financial sanctions have been inflicted on Russia and are expected to hit hard. As noted in Chapter 1 US President Biden thought that these sanctions could inflict damage *rivalling* military might.

Economic sanctions might sometimes be launched in response to domestic opinions reacting and demanding some action – other than by arms – against a foreign state for some conduct deemed reprehensible. They are, as we have

---

[59] Aaslestad and Joor (2014).
[60] Cf. Chapter 6, p. 113.
[61] US Department of State, Office of the Historian, 'Oil Embargo, 1973–1974' (2021).
[62] See above, Chapter 6, p. 113.
[63] For EU, see European Council, 'EU restrictive measures in response to the crisis in Ukraine' (2021); for Russia, see Gray (2021).

noted, pressures of uneven effects. Nevertheless, a continued modern shift from the use of physical force to the use of economic sanctions and financial pressures may suggest that governments are increasingly pursuing interests by methods that do not involve direct use of arms and violate international norms. The reliance on economic pressures has been conspicuous in the response to Russia's 2022 invasion of Ukraine.[64] While the kinetic war on the ground has been dramatic and decisive, economic warfare has been of great importance. Inflicting pain on itself. Western Europe has drastically cut its imports from Russia to deprive Russia of export income. Russia, on its part has cut, reduced or impeded the export of volumes of gas that European states needed to import. This evidently hurt its own export income but it did, as intended, lead to a painful shortage of gas in parts of Europe. Mutually Economic Dependence (MED) leads to partial Mutual Economic Destruction (MED).

Cyber techniques, despite their transformative positive uses, are also used by individuals and states to do harm. There is a discussion about the risk even of cyber war[65] and previews of injuries that may be inflicted have been given, for instance when Iranian centrifuges for the enrichment of uranium were damaged by the *Stuxnet* malware in 2010.[66] However, to the misgivings about the grave dangers that cyber techniques may pose one should perhaps add that – like economic pressures – they offer a means for states to exert influence and pressure on one another while foregoing the use of physical force.

COMPETITION THROUGH 'CULTURAL WARS' OR 'BEAUTY CONTESTS'

States have long sought to promote goodwill for themselves around the world through cultural programs and propaganda. Much of this is enriching and far from pressures of any kind. Yet, we find signs of sensitivity to foreign cultural and ideological presence. Some activities may be suspected to aim at or at least result in pressures for political or ideological change. Public or private programs or publications that are foreign-run or financed covering, say, human rights, freedom of speech and press, or equal treatment of all people including racial or ethnic minorities may in some states be seen – not quite as unlawful foreign subversion but – as 'destabilizing' interference.

---

[64] 'Fact Sheet: United States and Allies and Partners Impose Additional Costs on Russia' (Washington, D.C.: The White House, 24 March 2022), www.whitehouse.gov/briefing-room/statements-releases/2022/03/24/fact-sheet-united-states-and-allies-and-partners-impose-additional-costs-on-russia/. And see above, Chapter 1.

[65] See above, Chapter 8, p. 129.

[66] See above, Chapter 4, p. 73 and Chapter 15, p. 237.

A modern phenomenon of a similar kind is the 'beauty contests' in which states seek to attract other states and peoples to their side in the ongoing global competition about status and domination. We are treated to frequent reports about which state and political order stood for the origin of the Covid 19 pandemic and which was first with a vaccine, which state system will be first on Mars or in various technological feats. Self-praise or adversary smearing may be tempting as means to convey strength and as image-building but there is a serious underlying motivation of competition about domination – or at least influence – by 'smart power'. One would hope that this 'beauty contest' serves to substitute rather than supplement the competition by the threat or use of force.

THE NON-FORCE RELATED ROLE OF THE UN SYSTEM TO PREVENT THE USE OF FORCE

After many chapters focusing on the prevention of the use of interstate force through three widely recognized factors – military deterrence, diplomacy and legal norms with institutions for enforcement – both wider barriers and some significant specific measures provided by the UN system to prevent the use of interstate force need to be noted.

First, in national communities, the wider barrier to force – criminal law, courts, police and prisons – are vital elements, but peace and order are built above all on social and economic cooperation, norms, pressures and common institutions. Something similar applies in the community of states that cooperate with relative ease. A private sector with innumerable international networks and the UN and its family of intergovernmental organizations help manage joint interests – in trade, communications, health etc. – and help eliminate or reduce friction, and conflict.

Second, not least due to the Security Council's frequent inability to take decisions on forceful measures, the UN has often come to rely on softer measures in the efforts to maintain international peace. It has been a necessity, but one that has fit well with the Charter's emphasis on the peaceful means of settling disputes (Art. 33). Mediation, fact-finding and the quiet diplomacy of the Secretary-General have been described above. Among other specific means UN peacekeeping operations have been and remain a major remarkable UN tool to help forestall armed confrontations between states.[67]

---

[67] See above, p. 273. There is an extensive literature on UN peacekeeping operations. An excellent source is 'Report of the Panel on United Nations Peace Operations [Brahimi Report]', United Nations, 2000.

Non-Recognition

A policy espoused both by the UN and the League of Nations has been to deny giving legal recognition to actions or conditions based on the illegal use of force. The 'Friendly Relations' Declaration of the UN General Assembly stipulates that: 'no territorial acquisition resulting from the threat or use of force shall be recognized as legal'[68] and Art. 52 of the Vienna Convention on the Law of Treaties stipulates that *'a treaty is void if its conclusion has been procured by the threat or use of force...'* The aim of the pursuit of this policy and doctrine is more practical than the abstract concept may suggest: it is to exert pressure by denying – or reducing – possible benefits from violations of international norms, notably seizure of land by the illegal use of force. Thus, non-recognizing states are not closing their eyes to the illegality of occupation or annexation of a territory. On the contrary, they focus on it and seek to make the occupation or annexation more problematic, for instance, by refusing to act upon (recognize) documents – such as passports – issued by the occupying or annexing power.

The policy of non-recognition was used by the League of Nations, for instance on Japan's illegal occupation of Chinese territory and the creation of the state of Manchukuo. The US espoused the policy in the *Stimson doctrine*.[69] The UN General Assembly has urged members to pursue non-recognition in relation to Israel's occupation of the Golan Heights and the West Bank of the Jordan River and against Russia's annexation of Crimea.[70] It would be hard to show that the risk of non-recognition has in fact helped to deter any state from an illegal use of force or contributed to undoing results of such use. Nevertheless, it signals illegality for all to see and possible negative consequences for the lawbreaker.

CRIMINALIZATION OF CONDUCT

The international criminalization of aggression, genocide, crimes against humanity and war crimes began in serious with the statute and judgment of the Nuremberg tribunal. Several war crime tribunals and the International

---

[68] A/Res/25/2625 of 24 October 1970. The Assembly's definition of aggression (A/Res/29/3314 of 14 December 1974) has a similar provision.

[69] For an official history of this occupation, see United States Department of State (1943). In 1932, the US announced the 'Stimson Doctrine' on the non-recognition of territory acquired by force. (Discussed further in McNair, 1933).

[70] For a discussion of the General Assembly's resolutions on the Israeli issue in 2019, see 'General Assembly Adopts 5 Resolutions on Middle East, including Text Urging States Not to Recognize Changes on Status of Jerusalem, Pre-1967 Borders' United Nations, 2019; the General Assembly's 2014 resolution on Crimea is discussed in 'General Assembly Adopts Resolution Calling upon States Not to Recognize Changes in Status of Crimea Region' 2014.

Criminal Court (ICC) have since been created and in many cases passed judgments imposing prison sentences. The Rome statute of 1998 (in force in 2002) accepted by 123 states may now be seen as the penal code of the international community.[71] With time and the continued use of sentencing, meting out penalties and imprisonment may help to make political and military leaders aware of and – hopefully – more respectful of rules requiring restraints in the use of force.

The demand by non-governmental groups for the public examination of the responsibility of Western leaders for the Viet Nam war and for the 2003 Iraq war and of Russian leaders for the 2022 war against Ukraine is testimony to a public opinion that calls for the evenhanded application of international criminal law. An absence of judicial reactions to violations of that law – whether by victors or losers – inevitably contributes to a feeling that the international community often protests the initiation and use of force by states and insurgent groups but does not care to look for personal responsibility for claimed illegal actions by leaders of victorious parties.

Former US President Donald Trump's decision to boycott the International Criminal Court and the agreements concluded by the US with over one hundred states to ensure the immunity of US soldiers from local and ICC jurisdiction gives rise to a perception that states are not equal before international criminal law.

SUMMING UP

The material examined in this book is vast and heterogenous. Yet, several facts and trends stand out that together point to some conclusions and questions

- .The major military powers' possession of nuclear weapons and ability to launch first and second strikes raise risks of catastrophic events and developments – *in extremis* mutual assured destruction (MAD) and civilizational suicide – triggered by mistake, technical error or leadership insanity. At the same time, these risks have served as a restraint in their direct relations and more generally in the world through their global relations, alliances and leverages.
- For more than 75 years since the end of World War II, there have been only a few major armed interstate conflicts. None of them has taken place between great powers and no nuclear weapons have been used in armed conflict since Hiroshima and Nagasaki.[72] The acquisition of

---

[71] International Criminal Court, 'The states parties to the Rome Statute', 2021.
[72] The fighting during the Korean war in 1950–51 between a big army of 'volunteers' sent by China and US led UN troops moving toward the Yalu border river (described in Chapter 3)

territory has only rarely been an aim. These developments leave interventions as the predominant actions that still involve the active interstate use of force. Indeed, even in interventions, a trend is discerned away from the use of force – or visible force. The Russian aggression and attempted land grabbing in Ukraine stand like erratic actions and hardly vitiate this conclusion.

- The evolution in transport, communication, trade and finance has resulted in greater interdependence and the need for cooperation and common action. Relations and competition between most states are free of any use of force and the opportunities have increased for exerting influence and pressures without the use of force. Modern means of communication offer the possibility for instantaneous information and diplomacy. The European Union ensures cooperation and precludes the use of force in a large region that historically was plagued by innumerable wars.

- International norms have evolved backed by a 'public mind' and crystallized in the UN Charter as the 'rule-based international order', restricting the interstate use of armed force. The Security Council and General Assembly, while mostly unable to prevent or reverse breaches of the order, have offered the world's governments fora for exposure and judgment of claimed violations and often provided firm assertions of the norms.

The circumstances mentioned above, especially the feared consequences of any nuclear conflict and growing awareness of norms, have together with remaining traditional military deterrence combined to strengthen restraints against the use of force between states and to turn states to a further increased use of methods of competition and pressures that exclude, downplay, or hide the use of armed force. The response of the world to the Russian armed invasion of Ukraine in 2022 shows that while the rule-based international order of the UN Charter did not prevent the action, the UN offered the central world arena for exposure and judgment. Resistance on the ground to the Russian action was provided by Ukrainian armed self-defence supported by a massive supply of arms – but no foreign troops – from the outside. The concerns for a nuclear escalation and expansion of the conflict have created restraints against the direct active participation of more states.

might be argued to have been an exception. However, it is striking that in that situation the United States and others on the UN side agreed that they would not risk a war with China and opted for negotiations about a cease-fire. See a very detailed account in Sjöberg, Tommie., *From Korea and Suez to Iraq (Lund, 2006)*, pp. 145 ff.

A FAREWELL TO WARS

The net result of the many factors discussed is a reduction of the risk for inter-state uses of force. It seems justified to conclude that – rare cases excepted – the states of the international community have said *farewell* to direct interstate wars and are in the process of taking farewell to the use of force in interventions. In their continued competition they are turning to other means of exerting pressure and influence.

WHAT ABOUT THE FUTURE?

Given the importance of the existing nuclear capacities for the conclusion drawn above, one is bound to ask whether such capacities will be needed also to uphold peace in the future. Here, one can only speculate. Even at a time when China had not carried out a nuclear test and the Soviet program had not yet gathered potency US presidents on several concrete occasions considered and refused to approve nuclear attacks proposed to them and during the Cuban Missile Crisis in 1962 the US and Soviet Union were held back by an awareness of a risk of nuclear war.

At the present time, the arms race between the US, China and Russia suggests a continued determination to maintain effective second-strike capacities at all costs. Military strategists and engineers continue to develop ever more advanced means of defeating an enemy on Earth or in space. Will these powers continue in an incessant race for more and innovative arms and for deterrent – or deterrent plus – or will they recognize that they have long attained such a capability of mutual mega-destruction that in a concrete conflict they would find any weapons use too risky and conclude that they must turn to de-escalation and diplomacy?

A turn to diplomacy would require the prior political conclusions in the three states that further military development is meaningless – and wasteful. It would require a genuine acceptance of the declaration announced by Reagan and Gorbachev at their 1985 Geneva summit and jointly reaffirmed by the five nuclear-weapon states on 3 January 2022 and by the G20 group in 2022 that 'a nuclear war cannot be won and must never be fought'. That declaration once initiated détente and significant disarmament. One would hope that a shock like the Cuban Missile Crisis in 1962 would not be needed and that the sight of death and destruction following Russia's invasion of Ukraine in 2022 and reflection on it will suffice to take the major actors out of their present arms race and lead them to renew détente and disarmament. A drastic shift is needed and it will take time.

To gradually restore mutual confidence, renewed dialogue, more mutual inspection and generally increased transparency will, of course, be needed. Even so, the states will certainly long retain residuary destructive capacity, preserve abilities to restore capacity, and probably continue research. Confidence would grow, however, not only from measures in the military sector but perhaps even more from policies of détente. Just as there may be spiralling in arms races there can be down-spiralling. For the time post the Ukrainian disaster, one might expect a reaffirmation of UN norms, greater use of multilateral machinery and some arms control measures that might help to initiate the more decisive turn that is required for a world climate of peace.

Another speculation is whether today the ever more frequent natural disasters and recognition of the existential threat of climate change and loss of biodiversity can trigger the conclusion that a path to détente and disarmament must now be chosen. A shift of a major part of the some 2 trillion dollars that are currently globally devoted to the military sector would be of decisive importance to help defend global living conditions and preserve human civilization! Which defence need has the highest priority?

ROLE OF THE PUBLIC MIND TO STRENGTHEN THE RESTRAINTS ON THE INTERSTATE USE OF FORCE?

This study has sought to establish what is the role and what are the trends of interstate use of force in today's world – not to look for ways of increasing restraints through reforms of the UN or otherwise, a subject on which there is a vast amount of knowledgeable analysis and proposals.

Nevertheless, after the speculations about the future action of governments, it needs to be said that the public mind will continue to be of the greatest importance for what forms of competition between states will be accepted and practiced by the international community. It has been behind the positive changes in state conduct for nearly two hundred years. It helped to abolish the slave trade, and it waged successful public campaigns against particularly cruel and indiscriminate weapons and in favour of arbitration and other peaceful means of settling disputes. It was the force that after WWI stood behind President Wilson's introduction in the League Covenant of the first legal ban on the use of force between states. That public mind, globally better connected than ever before, can and should now assert itself to demand diplomacy, disarmament and détente and the use of released resources to help defend and preserve an environment and develop an order that will sustain human civilization.

Bibliography

Aaslestad, K. B. and Joor, J. (eds.). *Revisiting Napoleon's Continental System: Local, Regional and European Experiences*. London: Palgrave Macmillan, 2014.

Ahlström, C. *Demilitarised and Neutralised Territories in Europe*. Mariehamn, Finland: Åland Islands Peace Institute, 2004.

Allen-Ebrahimian, B. '64 Years Later, CIA Finally Releases Details of Iranian Coup', *Foreign Policy*. 20 June 2017. https://foreignpolicy.com/2017/06/20/64-years-later-cia-finally-releases-details-of-iranian-coup-iran-tehran-oil/.

Angell, N. *The Great Illusion*. New York: G. P. Putnam's Sons, 1910.

Anthony, I., Klimenko, E. and Su, F. *A Strategic Triangle in the Arctic? Implications of China–Russia–United States Power Dynamics for Regional Security*. SIPRI Insights on Peace and Security 2021/3. Stockholm: Stockholm International Peace Research Institute, March 2021. www.sipri.org/publications/2021/sipri- insights-peace-and-security/strategic-triangle-arctic-implications-china-russia-united-states-power-dynamics- regional-security.

Arechaga, E. J. 'International Law in the Past Third of a Century' in *Recueil des Cours*, vol. I (1978).

Arechaga, E. J. *Voting and the Handling of Disputes in the Security Council*. New York: Carnegie Endowment for International Peace, 1950.

Arms Control Association (2022). Press Release. 'NPT Review Outcome Highlights Deficit in Disarmament, Diplomacy, Divisions between Nuclear Rivals'. Washington, DC: Arms Control Association, 26 August 2022. www.armscontrol.org/aca-press-releases/2022-08/npt-review-outcome-highlights-deficit-disarmament-diplomacy

Bailey, S. *Prohibitions and Restraints in War*. Oxford: Oxford University Press, 1972.

Bascomb, N. *The Winter Fortress: The Epic Mission to Sabotage Hitler's Atomic Bomb*. New York: Houghton Mifflin, 2016.

Beckman, O. *Armed Intervention*. Lund: Lund University, 2005.

Bercovitch, J. and Rubin, J. Z. (eds). *Mediation in International Relations*. New York: St Martin's Press, 1992.

Bergman, R. *Rise and Kill First: The Secret History of Israeli Targeted Assassinations*. New York: Random House, 2018.

Berner, Ö. *Krig eller Fred*. Stockholm: Carlssons, 2020.

Bildt, C. *Den nya oredans tid*. Stockholm: Bonniers, 2019.

Bildt, C. *Mina Krig*. Stockholm: Bonniers, 2022.

Blair, T. *A Journey*. New York: Random House, 2010.

Blix, H. *Treaty-Making Power*. New York: Praeger, 1960.

Blix, H. 'The Helsinki Declaration on Principles Guiding Relations between States in Europe'. *Egyptian Journal of International Law*, vol. 31 (1975).

Blix, H. 'Area Bombardment: Rules and Reasons'. *British Yearbook of International Law*, vol. 49, no. 1. Oxford: Oxford University Press, 1978, pp. 31–69.

Blix, H. 'Iraq 2003: What the Leaders Say, and What They Leave Out'. *Inside Story*. 21 March 2011. https://insidestory.org.au/iraq-2003-what-the-leaders-say-and-what-they-leave-out/.

Blockmans, W. and Hoppenbrouwers, P. *Introduction to Medieval Europe 300–1550*. New York: Routledge, 2018.

Bowett, D. *The Law of International Institutions*. London: Stevens, 1963.

Braut-Hegghammer, M. 'Revisiting Osirak'. *International Security*, vol. 36 (2011), pp. 101–132.

Bridge, F. R. and Bullen, R. *The Great Powers and the European States System 1814–1914*. 2nd ed. London: Routledge, 2014.

Brierly, J. L. *The Outlook for International Law*. Oxford: Oxford University Press, 1944.

Bring, O. *Nedrustningens Folkrätt*. Stockholm: Norstedts, 1987.

Bring, O. *FN-stadgans folkrätt*. Stockholm: Norstedts, 1992.

Bring, O. 'The Westphalia Peace Tradition in International Law'. *International Law Studies*, vol. 75 (2000), pp. 57–80. https://digital-commons.usnwc.edu/cgi/viewcontent.cgi?articl e=1435&context=ils

Bring, O. *Neutralitetens uppgång och fall*. Stockholm: Atlantis, 2008.

Britannica (2021). 'The Continental System and the blockade, 1807–11'. www.britannica .com/event/Napoleonic-Wars/The-Continental-System-and-the-blockade-1807-11. Accessed: 31 December 2021.

Brownlie, I. *International Law and the Use of Force by States*. New York: Oxford University Press, 1963.

Bunde, T. and Franke, B. (eds.). *The Art of Diplomacy: 75+ Views Behind the Scenes of World Politics*. Berlin: Econ, 2022, ISBN: 9783430210775.

Bush, G. W. 'US National Security Strategy'. Washington, DC: The White House, 1 June 2002. https://2001-2009.state.gov/r/pa/ei/wh/15425.htm.

Carlsson, S. and Rosén, J. *Svensk Historia*. Stockholm: Svenska Bokförlaget, 1961.

Carpenter, T. G. 'Why Russia Likes to Play Aerial "Chicken" with America'. *The National Interest*. 8 August 2020. https://nationalinterest.org/feature/why-russia-likes-play-aerial-'chicken'-america-166450. Accessed: 31 December 2021.

Cassese, A. (ed), *The Current Legal Regulation of the Use of Force*. Boston: Nijhoff Publishers, 1986.

Chapman, T. *The Congress of Vienna*. London: Routledge, 1998.

Ciment, J. (ed.). *Encyclopedia of Conflicts since World War II*. 2nd ed. London: Routledge, 2007.

Cohen, D. and Totani, Y. *The Tokyo War Crimes Tribunal: Law, History and Jurisprudence*. 1st ed. Cambridge: Cambridge University Press, 2018.

Crisis Group. 'Turkey-Greece: From Maritime Brinksmanship to Dialogue'. Crisis Group. 31 May 2021. www.crisisgroup.org/europe-central-asia/western-europemedit erranean/263-turkey-greece-maritime-brinkmanship-dialogue. Accessed: 4 January 2022.

Dalay, G. 'Turkey, Europe, and the Eastern Mediterranean: Charting a way out of the current deadlock'. *Brookings Institution Report*. 28 January 2021. www.brookings.edu/research/turkey-europe-and-the-eastern-mediterranean-charting-a-way-out-of-the-current-deadlock/.

Damrosch, L. F. 'Use of Force and Constitutionalism'. *Columbia Journal of Transnational Law*, vol. 36 (1997), pp. 449–472.

Davis, I (ed.). 'Armed Conflict and Peace Processes in South Asia'. *SIPRI Yearbook 2021: Armaments, Disarmament and International Security*. Oxford: Oxford University Press, 2021a, pp. 95–109.

Davis, I (ed.). 'The Interstate Armed Conflict Between Armenia and Azerbaijan'. *SIPRI Yearbook 2021: Armaments, Disarmament and International Security*. Oxford: Oxford University Press, 2021b, pp. 127–132.

Deller, N. Makhijani, A. and Burroughs, J. *Rule of Power or Rule of Law*. New York: The Apex Press, 2003.

Detter, I. *The Laws of War*. Cambridge: Cambridge University Press, 1987.

Devere, H., Mark, S. and Verbitsky, J. 'A History of the Language of Friendship in International Treaties'. *International Politics*, vol. 48, no. 1 (January 2011), pp. 46–70.

Dhanapala, J. *Multilateral Diplomacy and the NPT: An Insider's Account*. Geneva: UNIDIR, 2005.

Dobson, H. *The Group of 7/8*. London: Routledge, 2007.

Donner, R. 'Public International Law and King Magnus Eriksson's Law of the Realm'. *Journal of the History of International Law*, vol. 4 (2002), pp. 114–134.

Dower, J. W. *The Violent American Century. War on Terror since World War II*. Chicago: Haymarket, 2017.

Duarte, S. 'Moral Leadership and Nuclear Weapons'. Lecture at Yale Divinity School on 19 September 2008. New York: United Nations Office for Disarmament Affairs (2008). https://unoda-web.s3-accelerate.amazonaws.com/wp-content/uploads/assets/HomePage/HR/docs/2008/2008Sept19_Yale_Divinity.pdf

Duelfer, C. 'Comprehensive Report of the Special Advisor to the DCI on Iraq's WMD, with Addendums' (Duelfer Report), Revised Edition, 25 April 2005, www.govinfo.gov/app/details/GPO-DUELFERREPORT.

ElBaradei, M. *The Age of Deception*. New York: Metropolitan Books, 2011.

Ellsberg, D. *The Doomsday Machine*. London: Bloomsbury, 2019.

Engdahl, O. and Wrange, P. (ed.) *Law at War: The Law as it Was and the Law as it Should Be*. Leiden: Nijhoff Publishers, 2008.

Erästö, T. 'Implementation of the Joint Comprehensive Plan of Action on Iran's Nuclear Programme'. In Ian Davis (ed.). *SIPRI Yearbook 2021: Armaments, Disarmament and International Security*. Oxford: Oxford University Press, 2021, pp. 426–433.

Ertman, T. *Birth of the Leviathan: Building States and Regimes in Medieval and Early Modern Europe*. Cambridge, MA: Harvard University Press, 1997.

European Council. 'EU restrictive measures in response to the crisis in Ukraine'. www.consilium.europa.eu/en/policies/sanctions/ukraine-crisis/. Accessed: 31 December 2021.

Evans, G. *The Responsibility to Protect: Ending Mass Atrocity Crimes Once and for All*. Washington, DC: Brookings, 2008.

Evans, G. and Kawaguchi, T. (co-chairs) Eliminating Nuclear Threats, Report of the International Commission on Nuclear Non-Proliferation and Disarmament (2009)

Falk, R. 'Viet Nam and international law'. *Yale Law Journal*, vol. 75 (1966).

Finnemore, M. *The Purpose of Intervention*. Ithaca, NY: Cornell University Press, 2003.

Franck, T. M. *Recourse to Force*. Cambridge: Cambridge University Press, 2002.

Franck, T. M. 'The Power of Legitimacy and the Legitimacy of Power: International Law in an Age of Disequilibrium'. *American Journal of International Law*, vol. 100 (2006), pp. 88–106.

Freedman, L. 'The Chicago Speech and Criteria for the Use of Force'. *International Relations*, vol. 31 no. 2 (2017), pp. 107–124.

Fukuyama, F. 'Soviet Threats to Intervene in the Middle East 1956–1973', RAND Report N-1577-FF. June 1980. www.rand.org/content/dam/rand/pubs/notes/2005/N1577.pdf. Accessed: 1 January 2022.

Fukuyama, F. *The End of History and the Last Man*. New York: Free Press, 1992.

Fulbright, J. W. *The Arrogance of Power* [originally published 1966]. Fayetteville, AR: University of Arkansas Press, 2018.

Gat, A. *War in Human Civilization*. 2006. New York: Oxford University Press, 2006.

Gbadanosi, N. 'What's in Store for Africa in 2022', *Foreign Policy*. 29 December 2021. https://foreignpolicy.com/2021/12/29/africa-2022-conflict-ethiopia-sudan-somalia/. Accessed: 1 January 2022.

Gihl, T. *Om freden och säkerheten – nationalism och internationalism*. Stockholm: Norstedt, 1962.

Goertz, G., Diehl, Paul F. and Balas. A. *The Puzzle of Peace: The Evolution of Peace in the International System*. New York: Oxford University Press, 2016.

Goldblat, J. *Arms Control: The New Guide to Negotiations and Agreements*. Revised and updated second edition. London: Sage, 2002 [earlier edition, 1994].

Goldstein, J. S. *Winning the War on War. The Decline of Armed Conflict Worldwide*. New York: Penguin, 2011.

Goodrich, L. M. and Hambro, E. *Charter of the United Nations: Commentary and Documents*. Boston: World Peace Foundation, 1947.

Gómez, J. M. et al. 'The Phylogenetic Roots of Human Lethal Violence'. *Nature*, vol. 538 (13 October 2016), pp. 233–237.

Gottemoeller, R. 'What's Eating Putin?'. *Bulletin of the Atomic Scientists*. 3 March 2022. https://thebulletin.org/2022/03/whats-eating-putin/.

Gray, A. 'Russia bans top EU officials in retaliation for sanctions'. *Politico*. 30 April 2021. www.politico.eu/article/russia-bans-top-eu-officials-in-retaliation-for-sanctions/. Accessed: 31 December 2021.

Gray, C. *International Law and the Use of Force*. Oxford: Oxford University Press, 4th ed., 2018.

Green, J. A., Henderson, C. and Ruys, T. 'Russia's attack on Ukraine and the *jus ad bellum*'. *Journal on the Use of Force and International Law*. DOI:10. 1080/20531702.2022 2056803.

Hafkin, G. 'The Russo-Georgian war of 2008. Developing the Law of Unauthorized Humanitarian Intervention after Kosovo'. *Boston University International Law Journal*, vol. 28. (2010), p. 219. www.bu.edu/law/journals-archive/international/volume28n1/documents/219-240.pdf.

Harari, Y. N. *Sapiens: A Brief History of Humankind*. New York: Harper, 2015.

Harrer, G. *Dismantling the Iraqi Nuclear Programme: The Inspections of the International Atomic Energy Agency. 1991–1998*. London: Routledge, 2014.

Hart, H. L. A. *The Concept of Law*. Oxford: Oxford University Press, 1961.

Hedges, C. *War Is a Force That Gives Us Meaning*. New York: Public Affairs, 2002.

Henderson, C. *The Use of Force and International Law*. Cambridge: Cambridge University Press, 2018.

Henkin, L. *How Nations Behave*. New York: Praeger, 1968.

Hinsley, F. H. *Power and the Pursuit of Peace*. Cambridge: Cambridge University Press, 1962.

Hobbes, T. *Leviathan*. Baltimore: Penguin Books (English Edition), 1968.

Hoffmann, S. 'Rousseau on War and Peace'. New York: Cambridge University Press. *American Political Science Review*, vol. 57 no. 2 (1963–06), pp. 317–333.

Huntington, S. P. *The Clash of Civilizations and the Remaking of World Order*. New York: Simon and Schuster, 1996.

Imsen, S., *Senmedeltiden. Europas historia 1300–1550*. Stockholm: Dialogos, 2011.

International Court of Justice. 'Legality of the Threat or Use of Nuclear Weapons'. Advisory Opinion of 8 July 1996. *I.C.J. Reports 1996*, 2006. p. 226. www.icj-cij.org/public/files/case-related/95/095-19960708-ADV-01-00-EN.pdf

International Criminal Court. 'The states parties to the Rome Statute'. 2021. https://asp.icc-cpi.int/en_menus/asp/states%20parties/pages/the%20states%20parties%20to%20the%20rome%20statute.aspx. Accessed: 31 December 2021.

International Criminal Court. 'List of All Cases-' International Court of Justice. 2022. www.icj-cij.org/en/list-of-all-cases. Accessed: 4 January 2022.

Intoccia, G. F. 'American Bombing of Libya: An International Legal Analysis'. *Case Western Reserve Journal*, vol. 19, no. 2 (1987), pp. 177–213.

Jackson, J. H. *Sovereignty, the WTO, and Change Fundamentals of International Law*. Cambridge: Cambridge University Press, 2006. www.ibiblio.org/hyperwar/Dip/PaW/index.html#foreword. Accessed: 16 May 2023.

Joyner, D. H. 'The Proliferation Security Initiative: Nonproliferation, Counterproliferation, and International Law'. *Yale Journal of International Law*, vol. 30 (2005), p. 507 ff.

Joyner, D. H. *International Law and the Proliferation of Weapons of Mass Destruction*. New York: Oxford University Press, 2009.

Joyner, D. H. 'United Nations Counter-Proliferation Sanctions and International Law'. *Working Paper*. Alabama Law Scholarly Commons. Tuscaloosa, AL: University of Alabama. 22 March 2016. https://scholarship.law.ua.edu/cgi/viewcontent.cgi?article=1554&context=fac_working_papers.

Kaldor, M. 'From Just War to Just Peace'. In den Boer, Monica and Wilde, Jaap de (eds.) *The Viability of Human Security*. Amsterdam: Amsterdam University Press, 2008, pp. 21–46.

Kane, A. *The New Zealand Lectures on Disarmament*. Occasional Paper Number 26. New York: United Nations Office for Disarmament Affairs, June 2014, pp. 11–16. https://disarmament.unoda.org/publications/occasionalpapers/no-26/

Kennedy, R. F. *Thirteen Days*. New York: W. W. Norton & Company, 1969.

Killelea, S. *Peace in the Age of Chaos*. Melbourne: Hardic Grant Books, 2020.

Kissinger, H. *Diplomacy*. New York: Simon and Schuster, 1994.

Kissinger, H. *World Order*. London: Penguin, 2016.

Klare, M. 'Cyber Battles, Nuclear Outcomes?' *Arms Control Today*, November 2019. www.armscontrol.org/act/2019-11/features/cyber-battles-nuclear-outcomes-dangerous-new-pathways-escalation.

Kornbluh, P. (ed.) '*Extreme Option: Overthrow Allende*'. Washington, DC: National Security Archive, 15 September 2020. https://nsarchive.gwu.edu/briefing-book/chile/2020-09-15/extreme-option-overthrow-allende.

Krepong, M. *Winning and Losing the Nuclear Peace, The Rise, Demise, and Revival of Arms Control*. Oxford: Oxford University Press, 2021.

Kress, B. *The Crime of Aggression: A Commentary*. Cambridge: Cambridge University Press, 2016.

Kress, C. *The Ukraine War and the Prohibition of the Use of Force in International Law*. Brussels: Torkel Opsahl Academic EPublisher, 2022.

Lacina, B. and Gleditsch, N. P. 'Monitoring Trends in Global Combat: A New Dataset of Battle Deaths'. *European Journal of Population / Revue Européenne de Démographie*, vol. 21, no. 2–3 (June 2005), pp. 145–166.

LeGrande, W. and Kornblum, P. *Back Channel to Cuba*. Chapel Hill, NC: University of North Carolina Press, 2015.

Lehmköster, J. et al. 'The Arctic and Antarctic – Extreme, Climatically Crucial and in Crisis'. *World Ocean Review*, no. 6. (2019), Hamburg: Maribus. https://worldoceanreview.com/en/wor-6/.

Leitenberg, M. *Deaths in War*. Ithaca, NY: Cornell University Peace studies program, Occasional paper. July 2003. https://ecommons.cornell.edu/bitstream/handle/1813/69395/29-Leitenberg-Deaths-in-Wars-3ed.pdf.

Leitenberg, M. *The Hazards of Operations Involving Nuclear Weapons during the Cold War*. Cambridge, MA: MIT Press, 2018.

Lesaffer, R. 'Peace through Law: The Hague Peace Conferences and the Rise of the Ius Contra Bellum'. In Maartje Abbenhuis, Christopher Ernest Barber, and Annalise R. Higgins (eds.) *War, Peace and International Order? The Legacies of the Hague Conferences of 1899 and 1907*, 1st ed. London: Routledge, 2017, pp. 31–51.

Mack, R. E. *The Code of Hammurabi*. Baghdad: Ministry of Culture and Information, 1979.

Mahmoudi, S. 'Self-Defense and "Unwilling or Unable States" in *Recueil des Cours* of the Hague Academy of International Law, vol. 422 (2021).

Malkasian, C. *The American War in Afghanistan: A History*. New York: Oxford University Press, 2021.

Mandel, R. 'Sources of International River Disputes', *Conflict Quarterly*, Fall 1992. https://journals.lib.unb.ca/index.php/JCS/article/download/15069/16138/0.

Marten, K. 'Russia's Use of the Semi-State Security Forces: The Case of the Wagner Group'. *Post-Soviet Affairs*, vol. 35, no. 3 (2019), pp. 181–204, DOI: 10.1080/1060586X.2019.1591142. Accessed: 31 December 2021.

Mazower, M. *Governing the World*. New York: Penguin Books, 2012.

McNair, A. D. 'The Stimson Doctrine of Non-Recognition'. *British Yearbook of International Law*, vol. 14 (1933), p. 65.

Menon, R. *The Conceit of Humanitarian Intervention*. New York: Oxford University Press, 2016.

Moberg, E. *Towards a Science of States: Their Evolution and Properties*. Lövestad: Moberg Publications, 2014.

Morgenthau, H. *Politics among Nations*. 8th ed. Boston: McGraw Hill, 2006.

Morris, I. *War! What Is It Good For?* New York: Farrar, Straus and Giroux, 2014.

Müller, H. and Wunderlich, C. *Norm Dynamics in Multilateral Arms Control*. Athens and London: The University of Georgia Press, 2013.

Myrdal, A. *The Game of Disarmament: How the United States and Russia Run the Arms Race*. New York: Pantheon, 1982.

Neff, S. *War and the Law of Nations: A General History*. 1st ed. Cambridge: Cambridge University Press, 2005.

Neff, S. *Justice among Nations: A History of International Law*. 1st ed. Cambridge, MA: Harvard University Press, 2014.

Neumann, T. 'Norway and Russia Agree on Maritime Boundary in the Barents Sea and the Arctic Ocean'. American Society of International Law. *Insights*. 10 December 2010. www.asil.org/insights/volume/14/issue/34/norway-and-russia-agree-maritime-boundary-barents-sea-and-arctic-ocean. Accessed: 4 January 2022.

Nichol, J. 'Russia-Georgia Conflict in August 2008: Context and Implications for US Interests'. US Congressional Research Service, Report RL34618, 3 March 2009. https://sgp.fas.org/crs/row/RL34618.pdf.

Nussbaum, A. *A Concise History of the Law of Nations*. Revised edition. New York: MacMillan, 1954.

Obama, B. Remarks at the Hiroshima Peace Memorial, 27 May 2016. https://obamawhitehouse.archives.gov/the-press-office/2016/05/27/remarks-president-obama-and-prime-minister-abe-japan-hiroshima-peace. Accessed: 3 January 2022.

O'Driscoll, C. 'Rewriting the Just War Tradition: Just War in Classical Greek Political Thought and Practice'. *International Studies Quarterly*, vol. 59, no. 1 (March 2015), pp. 1–10.

Office of the Historian. 'Oil Embargo, 1973–1974'. US Department of State. 2021. https://history.state.gov/milestones/1969-1976/oil-embargo. Accessed: 31 December 2021.

Ohlsson, E. *Armbrytning med Ondskan. Staffan de Mistura: Ett Liv med Krig och Konfliktlösning*. Stockholm: Ordfront, 2022.

Oppenheim, L. *The Future of International Law*. Oxford: Clarendon Press, 1921, p. 1.

Oppenheim, L. *International Law*. 7th ed. by H. Lauterpacht. London: Longmans, Green, 1948.

Osiander, A. 'Sovereignty, International Relations, and the Westphalian Myth'. *International Organization*, vol. 55 no 2 (Spring, 2001), pp. 251–287.

Ouimet, M. *The Rise and Fall of the Brezhnev Doctrine in Soviet Foreign Policy*. Chapel Hill, NC: University of North Carolina Press, 2003.

Paulus, A. 'Treaties of Friendship, Commerce and Navigation'. *Max Planck Encyclopedia of Public International Law* (2011). https://opil.ouplaw.com/display/10.1093/law:epil/9780199231690/law-9780199231690-e1482.

Perry, W. *My Journey at the Nuclear Brink*. Stanford: Stanford University Press, 2015.

Pettersson, T. et al. 'Organized Violence 1989–2020, with a Special Emphasis on Syria'. *Journal of Peace Research*, vol. 58, no. 4 (July 2021), pp. 593–610.

Pinker, S. *The Better Angels of our Nature*. New York: Viking, 2011.

Pirrone, P. 'The Use of Force in the Framework of the O.A.S'. In Cassese, A (ed.). *The Current Legal Regulation of the Use of Force'*. Dordrecht: Netherlands, 1986, pp. 223–240.

Porter, G. *Perils of Dominance: Imbalance of Power and the Road to War in Vietnam*. Berkeley: University of California Press, 2006.

Porter, G. *Manufactured Crisis: The Untold Story of the Iran Nuclear Scare*. New York: Just World Books, 2014.

Rifkind, G. and Picco, G. *The Fog of Peace, The Human Face of Conflict Resolution.* London: I.B. Tauris, 2014.

Roehrlich. E. *Inspectors for Peace.* A History of the International Atomic Energy Agency. Baltimore: Johns Hopkins University Press, 2022.

Rostow, N. 'Law and the Use of Force by States: The Brezhnev Doctrine'. *Yale Journal of International Law,* vol. 7 no. 2, (1981), pp. 209–243. https://openyls.law.yale .edu/bitstream/handle/20.500.13051/6783/14_7YaleJWorldPubOrd209_1980_1981_ .pdf?sequence=2&isAllowed=y.

Rousseau, J. J. *The Social Contract* [originally published 1762]. London: Penguin, 1968.

Rousseau, J. J. *The Plan for Perpetual Peace, on the Government of Poland, and Other Writings on History and Politics* [originally published 1756]. Hanover, NH: Dartmouth College Press, 2011.

Rudd, K. 'Why the QUAD alarms China' in *Foreign Affairs.* 6 August 2021.

Rydell, R. 'Disarmament without Agreements?' *International Negotiations,* vol. 10 (2005), pp. 363–380.

Sands, P. *Lawless World.* London: Penguin, 2006.

Savage, C. 'How 4 Federal Lawyers Paved the Way to Kill Osama bin Laden'. *The New York Times.* 28 October 2015. www.nytimes.com/2015/10/29/us/politics/obama-legal-authorization-osama-bin-laden-raid.html. Accessed: 31 December 2021.

Scahill, J. *Blackwater: The Rise of the World's Most Powerful Mercenary Army.* New York: Nation Books, 2007.

Schachter, O. 'Dag Hammarskjöld and the Relation of Law to Politics'. *American Journal of International Law,* vol. 56, no. 1 (Jan. 1962), pp. 1–8.

Schindler, D. and Toman, J. *The Laws of Armed Conflicts.* 2nd ed. Geneva: Henry Dunant Institute, 1981.

Schulte, C. *Compliance with Decisions of the International Court of Justice.* New York: Oxford University Press, 2004.

Schwebel, S. M. 'Aggression, Intervention and Self-Defence in Modern International Law' in *Recueil des Cours* 1972, vol. II, p. 451.

Schwebel, S. M. 'International Law: Being the Collected Papers of Hersch Lauterpacht. Vol. 5: Disputes, War and Neutrality: Parts IX-XIV by Elihu Lauterpacht'. *American Journal of International Law,* vol. 99, no. 3 (July 2005), pp. 726–729.

Simma, B. et al. *The Charter of the United Nations.* Oxford: Oxford University Press, 2013.

Simpson, G. 'The War in Iraq and International Law'. *Melbourne Journal of International Law,* vol. 6, (2005), pp. 167–188. https://law.unimelb.edu.au/__data/assets/ pdf_file/0003/1681149/Simpson.pdf.

SIPRI. *SIPRI Yearbook 2021.* https://sipri.org/yearbook/2021/08. Accessed: 31 December 2021.

Sjöberg, T. *From Korea and Suez to Iraq.* Lund: Sekel, 2006.

Solingen, E. *Nuclear Logics.* Princeton, NJ: Princeton University Press, 2007.

Spiers, E. M. *Agents of War: A History of Chemical and Biological Weapons, Second Expanded Edition.* Chicago: University of Chicago Press, 2021.

Stone, J. *Legal Controls of International Conflict.* New York: Reinhart, 1954.

Stürchler, N. *The Threat of Force in International Law.* Cambridge: Cambridge University Press, 2007.

Tägli, S. 'Alfred Nobel's Thoughts about War and Peace'. Nobel Prize Outreach AB. www.nobelprize.org/alfred-nobel/alfred-nobels-thoughts-about-war-and-peace/. 20 November 1998. Accessed: 31 December 2021.

Tannenwald, N. *The Nuclear Taboo*. New York: Cambridge University Press, 2007.

Taylor, Emily. 'A Breakthrough for UN Governance of Cyberspace'. *World Politics Review*. 16 March 2021, www.worldpoliticsreview.com/articles/29496/a-breakthrough-for-global-cyber-governance.

Thakur, R. 'Review Article: The Responsibility to Protect at 15'. *International Affairs*, vol. 92, no. 2 (2016). www.chathamhouse.org/sites/default/files/publications/ia/inta92-2-10-thakur_o.pdf.

Thurer, D. *International Humanitarian Law*. Leiden: Nijhoff Publishers, 2011.

Tilly, C. *Coercion, Capital and European States. AD 990–1992*. Cambridge, MA: Blackwell, 1992.

Tolstrup, J. *Russia vs. The EU: The Competition for Influence in Post-Soviet States*. Boulder, CO: Lynne Rienner, 2013.

Trachtenberg, M. 'The United States and the NATO Non-extension Assurances of 1990: New Light on an Old Problem?' *International Security*, Winter 2020/2021, pp. 162–203.

'Treaty of Tordesillas'. 7 June 1494. Indigenous Values Initiative, *Doctrine of Discovery Project*, 23 July 2018. https://doctrineofdiscovery.org/treaty-of-tordesillas/.

Tuerk, H. '20 years of the International Tribunal for the Law of the Sea (ITLOS): An Overview'. *Revue Belge de Droit International* 49 (2), (2016), pp. 449–486.

United Kingdom Ministry of Defense. *Global Strategic Trends: The Future Starts Today* (2018).

United States Department of State. 'Japanese Conquest of Manchuria 1931–1932'. In U.S., Department of State, Publication 1983, *Peace and War: United States Foreign Policy, 1931–1941*. Washington, DC: U.S., Government Printing Office, 1943, pp. 3–8. www.ibiblio.org/hyperwar/Dip/PaW/index.html#foreword. Accessed: 16 May 2023.

UN. 'Antarctic Treaty'. United Nations Office for Disarmament Affairs. 1959. https://treaties.unoda.org/t/antarctic. Accessed: 4 January 2022.

UN. General Assembly, 'Declaration on Principles of International Law concerning Friendly Relations and Co-operation among States in accordance with the Charter of the United Nations'. A/RES/25/2625. 24 October 1970. 1970. http://un-documents.net/a25r2625.htm. Accessed: 3 January 2022.

UN. 'Declaration on the Inadmissibility of Intervention and Interference in the Internal Affairs of States'. Resolution Adopted by the General Assembly. A/Res/36/103, 9 December 1981. 1981. www.un-documents.net/a36r103.htm#:~:text=A%2FRES%2F36%2F103%20-%20Declaration%20on%20the%20Inadmissibility%20of%20Intervention,and%20non-violence%20for%20the%20children%20of%20the%20world. Accessed: 3 January 2022.

UN. *'Report of the Panel on United Nations Peace Operations [Brahimi Report]'*. New York: United Nations, 2000. www.un.org/ruleoflaw/files/brahimi%20report%20peacekeeping.pdf. Accessed: 31 December 2021.

UN. *A More Secure World: Our Shared Responsibility*. New York: United Nations, 2004. www.un.org/peacebuilding/sites/www.un.org.peacebuilding/files/documents/hlp_more_secure_world.pdf.

UN. 'General Assembly Adopts Resolution Calling upon States Not to Recognize Changes in Status of Crimea Region'. GA/11493 (press release on A/RES/68/262). 27 March 2014. www.un.org/press/en/2014/ga11493.doc.htm. Accessed: 31 December 2021.

UN. Security Council, S/RES/2231, 20 July 2015, on Iran Nuclear Issue. 2015. www.un.org/securitycouncil/content/2231/background. Accessed: 1 January 2022.

UN. United Nations Treaty Series. 'Agreement between the Government of the Russian Federation, the Government of the Kingdom of Sweden and the Government of the Republic of Lithuania regarding the junction point of the boundaries of the Exclusive Economic Zones and continental shelf in the Baltic sea'. 30 November 2005. 2016. www.un.org/depts/los/LEGISLATIONANDTREATIES/PDFFILES/TREATIES/Sweden-Lithuania-Russia%20treaty.pdf. Accessed: 7 June 2022.

UN. 'General Assembly Adopts 5 Resolutions on Middle East, including Text Urging States Not to Recognize Changes on Status of Jerusalem, Pre-1967 Borders'. 2019. www.un.org/press/en/2019/ga12220.doc.htm. Accessed: 31 December 2021.

Uppsala Conflict Data. 2014. http://ucdp.uu.se. Accessed: 1 January 2022.

Vargo, M. E. *The Mossad Intelligence 1960–1990*. Jefferson, NC: McFarland, 2015.

Vervey, W. D. 'Humanitarian Intervention' in Cassese. *The Current Legal Regulation of the Use of Force*, 1986.

Walsh, D. and Dahir, A. L. 'Why Is Ethiopia at War with Itself?'. *New York Times*. 14 December 2021. www.nytimes.com/article/ethiopia-tigray-conflict-explained.html.

Walters, F. P. A *History of the League of Nations*. New York: Oxford University Press, 1965.

Waslekar, S. A *World Without War*. New Delhi: HarperCollins Publishers India, 2022.

Watkins, N. J. 'Disputed Sovereignty in the Falkland Islands: The Argentina-Great Britain Conflict of 1982'. *Florida State University Law Review*, Fall 1983. https://ir.law.fsu.edu/cgi/viewcontent.cgi?article=2142&context=lr. Accessed: 4 January 2022.

Weapons of Mass Destruction Commission. *Weapons of Terror: Freeing the World of Nuclear, Biological and Chemical Arms (Report)*. Stockholm: WMD Commission, 2006. https://ycsg.yale.edu/sites/default/files/files/weapons_of_terror.pdf.

Williams, P. and Wallace, D. *Unit 731*. London: Hodder & Stoughton, 1989.

Wolf, A. T. 'Shared Waters: Conflict and Cooperation'. *Annual Review of Environment and Resources*, vol. 32, no. 1 (1 November 2007), pp. 241–269. https://doi.org/10.1146/annurev.energy.32.041006.101434.

Woolf, A. F. *'Russia's Nuclear Weapons: Doctrine, Forces, and Modernization'*, report R45861. Washington, DC: Congressional Research Service, 21 April 2022. https://crsreports.congress.gov/product/pdf/R/R45861/15.

Wright, T. *All measures Short of War: The Contest for the 21st Century & The Future of American Power*. Washington, DC: Brookings, 2017.

Index

Milton Keynes UK
Ingram Content Group UK Ltd.
UKHW020620201223
434696UK00019B/85